Microfinance, Financial Innovation, and Sustainable Entrepreneurship in Economics

Yahaya Alhassan
University of Sunderland in London, UK

Lawrence C. Bellamy
University of Sunderland in London, UK

Uzoechi Nwagbara
University of Sunderland in London, UK

John Kwaku Mensah Mawutor
University of Professional Studies, Accra, Ghana

IGI Global
Scientific Publishing
Publishing Tomorrow's Research Today

Published in the United States of America by
IGI Global Scientific Publishing
701 East Chocolate Avenue
Hershey, PA, 17033, USA
Tel: 717-533-8845
Fax: 717-533-8661
Website: https://www.igi-global.com E-mail: cust@igi-global.com

Library of Congress Cataloging-in-Publication Data

Names: Alhassan, Yahaya, 1971- editor. | Bellamy, Lawrence, 1967- editor. | Nwagbara, Uzoechi, editor. | Mawutor, John, 1977- editor.
Title: Microfinance, financial innovation, and sustainable entrepreneurship in economics / edited by Yahaya Alhassan, Lawrence Bellamy, Uzoechi Nwagbara, John Mawutor.
Description: Hershey, PA : IGI Global Scientific Publishing, [2025] | Includes bibliographical references and index. | Summary: "This book aims to examine and bring on board the various views and perspectives on the role of financial innovation and microfinance in the development of sustainable entrepreneurship through industry experts, experienced researchers, and policymakers"-- Provided by publisher.
Identifiers: LCCN 2024057015 (print) | LCCN 2024057016 (ebook) | ISBN 9798369366226 (hardcover) | ISBN 9798369366233 (paperback) | ISBN 9798369366240 (ebook)
Subjects: LCSH: Sustainable development. | Entrepreneurship. | Microfinance.
Classification: LCC HC79.E5 M4625 2025 (print) | LCC HC79.E5 (ebook) | DDC 338.9/27--dc23/eng/20250131
LC record available at https://lccn.loc.gov/2024057015
LC ebook record available at https://lccn.loc.gov/2024057016

British Cataloguing in Publication Data
A Cataloguing in Publication record for this book is available from the British Library.

Table of Contents

Detailed Table of Contents

This chapter explores the evolution of microfinance by reviewing existing literature. The chapter reviews the development of microfinance to understand how the concept emerged and the extent to which it has evolved. It specifically explores the history of microfinance and how it evolved in some countries before and after the emergence of Muhammad Yunus's microfinance era. The chapter concludes that the evolution of microfinance is a testament to its adaptability and resilience which started as a tool for poverty alleviation and has since transformed into a multifaceted industry that empowers marginalised individuals and communities while contributing to economic development. However, there are variations in opinions regarding the origins of microfinance as some researchers argue that it started in the 15th century, while others claim it was in the 17th or the 19th century. This analysis provides insights into how microcredit evolved into modern microfinance.

Microfinance institutions are considered a miracle to reduce poverty, promote empowerment, reducing gender inequality by providing microcredit and other financial services to strata of people outside the ambit of the formal financial system. Such micro-credit and other services lead to promoting entrepreneurship ventures among women leading to financial freedom and economic development of the country. This chapter studied the status of microfinance institutions across all continents and their pace of evolution with respective objectives. India-specific mission objectives and business models of microfinance institutions were dealt

This study investigates the impact of microcredit on income distribution in India from 1993 to 2022. Using secondary data from the National Bank for Agriculture and Rural Development (NABARD), Reserve Bank of India, the World Bank, and the Global Data Lab, an OLS regression model analyzes the relationship between microcredit and the Gini Index. Findings indicate a significant negative relationship between microcredit loans and income inequality, suggesting that increased microfinance access reduces income disparities. Other significant determinants include GDP growth, educational expenditure, gross capital formation, unemployment, and patrilocality. The study highlights the need to expand microfinance programs and implement policies for equitable economic benefit distribution. Limitations include reliance on secondary data and lack of regional disparity consideration. Despite these, the research enriches existing literature by offering insights specific to India and underscores microfinance's role in fostering inclusive economic growth.

Innovations in clean technology provide a dual advantage by reducing environmental impact and improving the quality of life for users. These technologies empower micro-entrepreneurs by cutting operational costs, boosting productivity, and expanding their market opportunities. Through inclusive financing mechanisms and capacity-building initiatives, microfinance institutions cultivate a culture of sustainability among entrepreneurs, driving the adoption of environmentally conscious practices and products. The Grounded Theory approach and secondary research analysis was employed here. Stakeholders can create inclusive ecosystems that empower individuals and communities to participate in the formal economy while preserving natural resources. This study advocates collaborative efforts among governments, financial institutions, technology providers, and social enterprises to scale innovative solutions that promote both economic growth and environmental protection globally. Thus, a Policy Framework for Microfinance is hereby proposed.

This chapter investigates the impact of FinTech integration on the accessibility and sustainability of microfinance institutions (MFIs) using a case study approach and secondary data. The chapter examines how the use of FinTech solutions by MFIs have enhanced the accessibility of microfinance services by the poor and financially excluded individuals and groups. The chapter also evaluates the potential impact of FinTech integration on the financial sustainability and operational efficiency of MFIs. The chapter identifies key challenges of microfinance-FinTech integration such as high initial investment costs, cybersecurity risks, regulatory complexities, and the potential for over-indebtedness. This investigation provides insights into the opportunities and challenges that MFIs face in adopting FinTech solutions to achieve their aim of enhancing financial inclusion and long-term sustainability in the evolving digital landscape.

The COVID-19 pandemic has accelerated the adoption of digital payments worldwide, fundamentally altering consumer behavior patterns. This study investigates the impact of digital payment trends on consumer behavior, comparing pre- and post-pandemic scenarios. It delves into the factors which drove the shift towards digital payments, exploring the changing preferences and perceptions of consumers. The study examines the influence of demographics, socio-economic factors, and technological advancements on consumer adoption of digital payment methods. It also analyzes the effect of the pandemic on e-commerce, online shopping, and mobile payments, highlighting the emergence of new trends and preferences. The findings provide valuable insights into the evolving landscape of digital payments and consumer behavior, offering implications for businesses, policymakers, and researchers

Preface

The nexus between microfinance, financial innovation, and sustainable entrepreneurship presents a compelling narrative of socio-economic transformation in the developing world. This book, *Microfinance, Financial Innovation, and Sustainable Entrepreneurship in Economics*, offers an interdisciplinary exploration of how these elements interact to drive growth, reduce poverty, and empower marginalized communities. As editors, we are thrilled to present this timely contribution, drawing on the expertise of scholars, practitioners, and policymakers from diverse regions and disciplines.

Microfinance has long been heralded as a powerful tool for improving socio-economic well-being, particularly in developing countries. Numerous studies (Trokic et al., 2020; Hassan and Saleem, 2017) have documented its role in reducing poverty and empowering women, while recent research (Samineni and Ramesh, 2023; Alhassan et al., 2022) underscores its transformative potential. Similarly, financial innovation—the development of new financial instruments, services, and technologies—has emerged as a critical enabler for extending the reach and impact of microfinance institutions. Despite these advances, the question of how microfinance and financial innovation can be harnessed to foster sustainable entrepreneurship remains underexplored.

This book seeks to address this critical gap by investigating the interplay between microfinance, financial innovation, and sustainable entrepreneurship across different contexts. How are microfinance institutions leveraging financial innovation to help the poor start and sustain businesses? How are these innovations fostering sustainable entrepreneurship and empowering women? In what ways are they contributing to poverty reduction and economic growth? These are some of the key questions that guide the chapters in this book.

Each chapter provides unique insights into these questions through a thematic lens, offering both theoretical and empirical analyses. The geographic scope of the book spans Asia, Africa, the Middle East, Eastern Europe, and South America—regions where microfinance institutions have seen significant activity and innovation. By examining diverse contexts, this book presents a holistic understanding of the challenges and opportunities at the intersection of microfinance, financial innovation, and sustainable entrepreneurship.

Entrepreneurship, as defined by Cole (1959), is "purposeful activity to initiate and develop a profit-oriented business." Dollinger (2008) adds that it involves the control and deployment of resources to create innovative economic organizations under conditions of risk and uncertainty. Sustainable entrepreneurship, as defined by Katsikis and Kyrgidou (2007), goes a step further, aiming at sustainable development through economic, social, and environmental value creation. This book argues that financial innovation and microfinance can act as catalysts for such entrepreneurship, addressing pressing global challenges such as poverty, inequality, and environmental sustainability.

The contributions to this volume examine a range of critical issues. For example, how do microfinance institutions innovate to minimize transaction costs and manage risks? What role does financial innovation play in expanding access to credit and training for marginalized groups, particularly women? How can these innovations contribute to building resilient, sustainable businesses in developing economies? By addressing these questions, the book offers actionable insights for academics, practitioners, and policymakers alike.

The theoretical and empirical insights presented in this book will serve as a valuable resource for a wide audience. Researchers and students in economics, finance, entrepreneurship, and development studies will find new perspectives on the synergies between microfinance, financial innovation, and sustainable entrepreneurship. Policymakers and development practitioners will gain evidence-based guidance on designing and implementing programs to maximize the socio-economic impact of microfinance. Financial institutions, particularly those operating in developing regions, will discover innovative strategies for expanding their reach and product offerings. Moreover, professionals in technology and innovation management will benefit from understanding how financial technologies can be leveraged to address development challenges.

This edited volume provides a comprehensive exploration of microfinance, financial inclusion, and their transformative impacts on poverty alleviation, entrepreneurship, and economic development. Each chapter offers a unique perspective on the evolution, challenges, and opportunities within the realm of microfinance and financial inclusion, showcasing diverse methodologies and global contexts.

CHAPTER OVERVIEW

Chapter 1 begins by tracing the historical evolution of microfinance, highlighting its adaptability and resilience as a tool for poverty alleviation and economic development. The chapter examines the origins of microfinance, from its early roots to the transformative influence of Muhammad Yunus, offering a nuanced understanding of how microcredit has evolved into a multifaceted industry that empowers marginalized communities.

Chapter 2 delves into the global landscape of microfinance institutions (MFIs), emphasizing their role in reducing poverty, promoting women's empowerment, and fostering entrepreneurship. The chapter employs a systematic review of literature, with a focus on India-specific models and missions, underscoring the critical role of microfinance in achieving financial freedom and economic development, particularly for women entrepreneurs.

Chapter 3 investigates the pivotal role of MFIs in advancing financial inclusion in India, emphasizing their innovative approaches, technological integration, and partnerships. By extending financial services to the unbanked, MFIs stimulate local markets, create employment opportunities, and contribute to poverty reduction, while addressing challenges such as sustainability and scalability.

Chapter 4 explores the transformative impact of microfinance on sustainable entrepreneurship and women's empowerment in India. This chapter highlights the effectiveness of microfinance initiatives in enhancing economic independence, decision-making, and social status for women, while also identifying key challenges that must be addressed to sustain and expand these benefits.

Chapter 5 examines the relationship between microcredit and income inequality in India over a nearly three-decade period. Through a rigorous time series analysis, the chapter demonstrates how increased access to microfinance reduces income disparities, offering policy recommendations to expand microfinance programs for equitable economic development.

Chapter 6 focuses on the intersection of microfinance and clean technology, showcasing how innovations in environmentally sustainable practices empower micro-entrepreneurs. The chapter advocates for collaborative efforts among stakeholders to scale sustainable solutions that drive economic growth while preserving natural resources, culminating in a proposed policy framework for inclusive microfinance ecosystems.

Chapter 7 investigates the integration of FinTech solutions into microfinance, highlighting their role in enhancing accessibility and operational efficiency. The chapter addresses challenges such as regulatory complexities and cybersecurity risks, providing insights into how FinTech can help MFIs achieve financial inclusion and long-term sustainability in an evolving digital landscape.

Chapter 8 explores the impact of digital payment adoption on consumer behavior, with a comparative analysis of pre- and post-COVID-19 scenarios. The chapter examines how demographic and technological factors influence consumer preferences, providing valuable insights for businesses and policymakers in navigating the rapidly changing digital payments landscape.

Chapter 9 introduces a financial literacy theory of financial inclusion, emphasizing the critical role of education in maximizing the benefits of formal financial systems. The chapter underscores the importance of financial literacy programs in reducing financial exclusion and fostering meaningful engagement with formal financial services.

Chapter 10 examines the integration of Islamic finance principles into sustainable business practices, revealing their potential to address complex economic and environmental challenges ethically and inclusively. The chapter offers actionable insights for business practitioners and policymakers to develop strategies that align with both sustainability and Islamic financial principles.

Chapter 11 provides a quantitative analysis of the relationship between exports and exchange rates in India, leveraging advanced econometric models to uncover both short-term and long-term dynamics. The chapter highlights the implications of these findings for economic policies and global trade strategies.

Chapter 12 concludes the volume by envisioning a world of full financial inclusion, examining the philosophical and practical implications of achieving this goal. The chapter offers policymakers and scholars thought-provoking insights into the actions and considerations necessary to sustain progress in financial inclusion.

The idea for this book emerged from the recognition that while significant progress has been made in leveraging microfinance and financial innovation for poverty reduction, much remains to be done to ensure their contributions to sustainable entrepreneurship. By bringing together diverse perspectives and case studies, we hope to advance the discourse on this critical topic and inspire further research and practice.

We extend our gratitude to the contributors whose work has enriched this volume, and to the reviewers whose insights have enhanced its quality. Special thanks go to our respective institutions—the University of Sunderland in London, the University of Sunderland, and the University of Professional Studies, Accra—for their support in bringing this project to fruition. We also acknowledge the invaluable role of microfinance practitioners and beneficiaries, whose experiences and innovations are at the heart of this book.

We invite you to engage with the ideas and insights presented in this book, and to join us in exploring the transformative potential of microfinance and financial innovation for sustainable entrepreneurship. It is our hope that this work will contribute to meaningful progress in addressing some of the most pressing challenges facing our global community.

Yahaya Alhassan
University of Sunderland in London, UK

Lawrence C. Bellamy
University of Sunderland in London, UK

Uzoechi Nwagbara
University of Sunderland in London, UK

John Kwaku Mensah Mawutor
University of Professional Studies, Accra, Ghana

Acknowledgements

We wish to offer this rider: without the various effort made by all and sundry, this book would not have been possible, although, Dr Yahaya Alhassan, Professor Lawrence Bellamy, Dr Uzoechi Nwagbara and Professor John Mawutor ''fathered'' the concept of the volume! Having said that, we wish to heartily thank and congratulate those who have been instrumental to the writing and production of this book.

First, without God the writing of this book would not have been possible. We thank Him for giving us the strength, knowledge and sound mind to execute this book project!

Second, we would also like to thank the members of the editorial and acquisition team of IGI for their professionalism, dedication, prop, and hard work during the production of this book. We want to say a big 'thank-you' to them, for the opportunity to co-edit this book. Particularly, we are indebted to Elizabeth Barrantes, Managing Editor (Book Development); Jan Travers, Director of Intellectual Property & Contracts IGI Global; and Melissa Wagner; Vice President of Editorial, IGI Global.

Third, we are sincerely grateful to all the contributors – Joy Meme, Dr. Yahaya Alhassan, Professor Lawrence Bellamy, Dr. Mayank Kumar, Dr. Pankaj Dhaundiyal, Dr. Sunil Kumar, Dr. Vijay Kumar, Mr. Pranjit Kr Paul, Mr. Subrata Halder, Dr. Maybel Fernandez-Vallado, Dr. Uzoechi Nwagbara, Ms. Ananya Chaturvedi, Prof. Shruti Ranjan, Dr. Peterson K. Ozili, Dr. Early Ridho Kismawadi, Dr. Mohammad Irfan, Ms. Umang Bhutani and Ms. Shefali Saini – for the spirit and sense of commitment shown.

Finally, our profound gratitude goes to our families for the time granted us to write this book!

Yahaya, Lawrence, Uzoechi and John, January 2025

Introduction

The use of microfinance as a strategy for improving the socio-economic wellbeing of beneficiaries in developing countries has been extensively reported (Trokic, et al, 2020; Hassan and Saleem, 2017). The provision of microfinance has also been shown to be a viable strategy for women empowerment in most parts of the developing and emerging world (Samineni and Ramesh, 2023; Alhassan, et al., 2022). In this regard, various books on the role of microfinance in reducing poverty and facilitating women empowerment in developing and emerging world have been written to aid our understanding (Alhassan and Nwagbara, 2023; Adjei, et al, 2009, Christabell, 2009).

Evidence of financial innovation by microfinance institutions has also been reported (Mia, 2023; Omwanza and Jagongo, 2019; Elle, 2018). However, how microfinance institutions have used financial innovation to promote sustainable entrepreneurship is not well understood. So, this book asks, what is the influence of microfinance and financial innovation on sustainable entrepreneurship?

Responding to the above question, this book is driven by the argument that microfinance institutions have used financial innovation to increase their distribution channels to reach more poor people in rural and urban communities, but it remains unclear how microfinance institutions are using financial innovation to help the poor sustain their businesses. In this spirit, this book investigates:

(a) How are microfinance institutions through financial innovation helping the poor to start and sustain their businesses?
(b) How are microfinance institutions using financial innovation to foster sustainable entrepreneurship and empowering women?
(c) In what manner are microfinance institutions using financial innovation to promote sustainable entrepreneurship and reducing poverty?
(d) In what way are microfinance institutions promoting sustainable entrepreneurship and economic growth through financial innovation?

Each chapter of the book approaches these questions by analysing the influence of microfinance and financial innovation on sustainable entrepreneurship through a different thematic lens. The result is a diverse reading of the content, contexts, and the nexus between microfinance, financial innovation and sustainable entrepreneurial activities in Asia, Africa and South America which have witnessed growing activities of microfinance institutions.

The role that financial innovation and microfinance institutions have played in sustainable entrepreneurship is therefore the focus of this book. Entrepreneurship is defined by Cole (1959) as "purposeful activity to initiate and develop a profit-oriented business". According to Dollinger (2008) entrepreneurship is the control and deployment of resources to create an innovative economic organization (or network of organizations) for the purpose of gain or growth under conditions of risk and uncertainty.

Sustainable entrepreneurship has been defined by Katsikis and Kyrgidou (2007) as "the teleological process aimed at the achievement of sustainable development, by discovering, evaluating and exploiting opportunities and creating value that produces economic prosperity, social cohesion and environmental protection".

Financial innovation, on the other hand, refers to the process of creating new financial or investment products, services, or processes. De Haan et al. (2020) defines financial innovation as "the act of creating and then popularising new financial instruments, as well as new financial technologies, institutions, and markets". However, the question is "how can sustainable entrepreneurship be enhanced using microfinance and financial innovation in the developing world?"

Various studies (Abebe and Kegne 2023; Agarwal and Pokhriyal, 2022; Nair and Njolomole, 2020) provide evidence of a positive relationship between provision of microfinance and entrepreneurship. The work of Agarwal and Pokhriyal (2022) for example, suggests that access to microfinance contributed positively to business expansion in India. Similarly, Abebe and Kegne (2023) found a positive and significant association between saving practice, access to credit, skill development training provided by microfinance institutions, and the development of women entrepreneurs in Ethiopia. Babajide, et al. (2022) have also shown that microfinance had a positive and significant influence on female entrepreneurial success in Nigeria. Evidence from Omwanza and Jagongo (2019) suggest that microfinance institutions have used financial innovation to increase their distribution channels to reach more people in rural and urban communities.

Some microfinance institutions innovate to minimize transaction costs (Mia, 2023). Duho, et al. (2023) have also shown that microfinance institutions employ financial innovation to manage risks likely to affect their income and assets. However, it remains unclear how microfinance institutions are using financial innovation to foster sustainable entrepreneurship. To this end, this book examines the role of financial innovation and microfinance in the development of sustainable entrepreneurship.

This book aims to examine and bring on board the various views and perspectives on the role of financial innovation and microfinance in the development of sustainable entrepreneurship through industry experts, experienced researchers, and policymakers. The role of financial innovation and microfinance in fostering sustainable entrepreneurship will be explored by these experts and contributors from different perspectives with the view to forming an opinion on the problems, processes, and prospects of using microfinance as a catalyst for fostering sustainable entrepreneurship. This book will focus on the nexus between microfinance, financial innovation and sustainable entrepreneurial activities in Asia, Africa and South America which have witnessed growing activities of microfinance institutions.

Theoretical and empirical insight provided in this book will be a priceless resource to researchers, students, microfinance institutions, policymakers, state institutions, managers, and non-governmental organisations. This book will also benefit financial institutions that are seeking to use recent technological development to expand their product portfolio and outreach. Furthermore, the book will offer great insight into theoretical, policy-oriented, and practical ways to address some of the challenges of using financial innovation and microfinance as a catalyst for fostering sustainable entrepreneurial activities. Given the focus of this book on the nexus between financial innovation, microfinance and sustainable entrepreneurship, there will be a broadening of ideas on how the provision of microfinance can aid sustainable entrepreneurship.

Yahaya Alhassan
University of Sunderland in London, UK

Lawrence C. Bellamy
University of Sunderland in London, UK

Uzoechi Nwagbara
University of Sunderland in London, UK

John Kwaku Mensah Mawutor
University of Professional Studies, Accra, Ghana

REFERENCES

Abebe, A., & Kegne, M. (2023). The role of microfinance institutions on women's entrepreneurship development. *Journal of Innovation and Entrepreneurship*, 12(1), 1–24. DOI: 10.1186/s13731-023-00285-0 PMID: 36968150

Adjei, J. K., Arun, T., & Hossain, F. (2009). *The role of microfinance in asset-building and poverty reduction: The case of Sinapi Aba Trust of Ghana*. Brooks World Poverty Institute, University of Manchester.

Agarwal, R., & Pokhriyal, A. K. (2022). The moderating effect of attitude to risk on the role of microfinance in entrepreneurship development in Uttarakhand region, India. *Journal of Global Entrepreneurship Research*, 12(1), 107–117. DOI: 10.1007/s40497-022-00317-1

Alhassan, Y., Kuagbela, F., Nurokina, C. D., & Appiah, B. (2022). *The Role of Microfinance in Africa: A Review of Outcomes from Ghana and Nigeria*. Microfinance and Sustainable Development in Africa.

Alhassan, Y., & Nwagbara, U. (Eds.). (2023). *Empowering Women Through Microfinance in Developing Countries*. IGI Global. DOI: 10.4018/978-1-6684-8979-6

Babajide, A. A., Obembe, D., Solomon, H., & Woldesenbet, K. (2022). Microfinance and entrepreneurship: The enabling role of social capital amongst female entrepreneurs. *International Journal of Social Economics*, 49(8), 1152–1171. DOI: 10.1108/IJSE-11-2020-0745

Christabell, P. J. (2009). *Women empowerment through capacity building: The Role of Microfinance*. Concept Publishing Company.

Cole, A. (1959). *Business Enterprise in its Social Setting*. Harvard University Press.

De Haan, J., Schoenmaker, D., & Wierts, P. (2020). *Financial markets and institutions: A European perspective*. Cambridge University Press. DOI: 10.1017/9781108643849

Dollinger, M. J. 2008. *Entrepreneurship*. United States of America.

Duho, K. C. T., Duho, D. M., & Forson, J. A. (2023). Impact of income diversification strategy on credit risk and market risk among microfinance institutions. *Journal of Economic and Administrative Sciences*, 39(2), 523–546. DOI: 10.1108/JEAS-09-2020-0166

Elle, S. M. (2018). Financial and institutional innovations in microfinance institutions and commercial banks in Cameroon. *International Journal of Financial Innovation in Banking*, 2(2), 143–157. DOI: 10.1504/IJFIB.2018.097148

Hassan, A., & Saleem, S. (2017). An Islamic microfinance business model in Bangladesh: Its role in alleviation of poverty and socio-economic well-being of women. *Humanomics*, 33(1), 15–37. DOI: 10.1108/H-08-2016-0066

Katsikis, I. N., & Kyrgidou, L. P. 2007, August. The concept of sustainable entrepreneurship: a conceptual framework and empirical analysis. In *Academy of Management Proceedings* (Vol. 2007, No. 1, pp. 1-6). Briarcliff Manor, NY 10510: Academy of Management. DOI: 10.5465/ambpp.2007.26530537

Khalaf, L. S., & Saqfalhait, N. I. (2019). The effect of microfinance institutions activities on economic growth in Arab countries. *Academy of Accounting and Financial Studies Journal*, 23(1), 1–8.

Krahnen, J. P. (2022). *Development finance as institution building: A new approach to poverty-oriented banking*. Routledge.

Mia, M. A. (2023). Technological change and innovations in microfinance institutions: What matters? *Global Business Review*, 24(6), 1454–1467. DOI: 10.1177/0972150920927368

Nair, M., & Njolomole, M. (2020). Microfinance, entrepreneurship, and institutional quality. *Journal of Entrepreneurship and Public Policy*, 9(1), 137–148. DOI: 10.1108/JEPP-07-2019-0061

Omwanza, C. O., & Jagongo, A. (2019). Financial innovations and financial performance of microfinance institutions in Kenya: A theoretical review. *International Academic Journal of Economics and Finance*, 3(4), 32–46.

Samineni, S., & Ramesh, K. (2023). Measuring the impact of microfinance on economic enhancement of women: Analysis with special reference to India. *Global Business Review*, 24(5), 1076–1091. DOI: 10.1177/0972150920923108

Trokic, A., Barakovac, E., & Efendic, V. (2020). The Socio-Economic Benefits of Microfinance: Conventional Vs. Islamic. *Journal of Islamic Monetary Economics and Finance*, 6(1), 95–116. DOI: 10.21098/jimf.v6i1.1162

Chapter 1
The Evolution of Microfinance:

Joy Meme
https://orcid.org/0000-0001-6873-3743
University of Sunderland in London, UK

Yahaya Alhassan
https://orcid.org/0000-0001-6700-635X
University of Sunderland in London, UK

Lawrence Bellamy
University of Staffordshire, UK

ABSTRACT

This chapter explores the evolution of microfinance by reviewing existing literature. The chapter reviews the development of microfinance to understand how the concept emerged and the extent to which it has evolved. It specifically explores the history of microfinance and how it evolved in some countries before and after the emergence of Muhammad Yunus's microfinance era. The chapter concludes that the evolution of microfinance is a testament to its adaptability and resilience which started as a tool for poverty alleviation and has since transformed into a multifaceted industry that empowers marginalised individuals and communities while contributing to economic development. However, there are variations in opinions regarding the origins of microfinance as some researchers argue that it started in the 15th century, while others claim it was in the 17th or the 19th century. This analysis provides insights into how microcredit evolved into modern microfinance.

DOI: 10.4018/979-8-3693-6622-6.ch001

1. INTRODUCTION

Microfinance is described as the small amount of loans given to low-income earners and small business owners who are unable to meet the requirements needed to access credit facilities from traditional banks (Cai, et al., 2023; Mandrawal, 2022). The concept has evolved significantly over a period dating back from the 15th century, emerging as potent strategy for alleviating poverty and promoting financial inclusion in poor communities around the world. As stated above, microfinance was initially considered as a potent and often a compelling tool for providing small loans to small businesses, individuals and groups excluded from the formal financial system. However, the concept in recent years has expanded to includes a diverse range of financial services, including savings, insurance and capacity building. This development or evolution is a proof of the growing demand and popularity of microfinance services and the ability of microfinance institutions (MFIs) to adapt to diverse economic environments to foster financial inclusion.

In view of the increasing growth and adoption of microfinance by different stakeholders across the world, the academic literature on the concept has kept pace with this evolution, offering a wealth of insights into its impact on poverty reduction, economic development and women empowerment (see Fuentes, 2023; Illangakoon, et al., 2021 and Zulfiqar, 2013). However, less attention has been paid to the development of microfinance, implicitly, ignoring the evolution of the concept which is critical for understanding how microfinance has transitioned from microcredit. Against this backdrop, this chapter addresses a critical gap in the literature by examining the evolution and expansion of microfinance with the aim of understanding the history of microfinance and how it evolved from the 15th century to date. The chapter specifically seeks to explore the theoretical foundation of the concept of microfinance, key milestones and the future direction of microfinance industry. By examining these developments, the chapter aims to shed light on the evolution, current state of microfinance and its future trajectory in the global financial landscape.

The rest of the chapter proceeds as follows. The next section discusses the background to the chapter focusing on existing literature on the definition and role of microfinance. This is followed by a comprehensive review of existing literature on the evolution of microfinance in section 3. Appropriate solutions and recommendations for the evolution of microfinance are discussed in section 4, while section 5 presents the conclusions.

2. BACKGROUND

Multiple studies (Milana and Ashta, 2020; El-Nasharty, 2022) have shown that microfinance facilitates the provision of small loans, savings opportunities and other essential financial services to disadvantaged communities worldwide. Poverty around the world has become a continuous challenge resulting in limited access to finance for both individuals and business owners who are often excluded from the formal banking system. Thus, an increase in the growth and adoption of microfinance by different stakeholders. The expectation is that microfinance would provide accessible finance to groups and individuals with fewer resources who intend to start up or grow their businesses (Kaberia and Muathe, 2022).

Visconti (2016) defined microfinance as a means of delivering financial services to households and businesses that have been excluded from standard banks. These businesses vary from micro to small businesses. Kaberia and Muathe (2022) have demonstrated that the exclusion from accessing credit, which could be partial or total, differs between developed and developing countries. Similarly, Taiwo and Benson (2016) defined microfinance as a small amount of loans given to low-income business owners and individuals who are unable to meet the requirements needed to access credit facilities from traditional banks. A further definition of Microfinance is given by Gebrehiwot and Chawla (2016) who described microfinance as the process whereby financial services such as loans, insurance products and other financial products are made available to the poor with the aim of promoting micro and small business projects. Clearly, microfinance plays a significant role in providing credit to low-income earners and small businesses that fail to meet the strict requirements of traditional banks (Taiwo and Benson, 2016). This is aimed at poverty reduction, financial inclusion and social empowerment, often spearheaded by various microfinance institutions (MFIs). Microfinance institutions (MFIs) as described by Creedy and Hoang (2018) are community based financial institutions, sometimes NGOs or non-profit organisation that offer microfinance or microcredits to the poor. Over the years, large commercial banks have diversified into the provision of microfinance services and microfinance institutions (MFIs) have evolved from being credit driven to becoming an institution that attracts deposit savings, as it is believed that the poor may sometimes need to save much more than obtaining a loan (Lieberman, 2020).

Microfinance institutions can exist in different forms, this could be a microfinance bank or even a non-profit organisation (Mumi, et al., 2020). These institutions offer diverse facilities that go beyond profit seeking. This is evident in the study of Thalib et al. (2021) who defined microfinance institution (MFI) as a financial institution that acts as a liaison organisation whose main objectives and activities are not profit focused but for social and community development. This suggests that a large number of MFIs are non-governmental organisations (NGOs) whose focus is on social and economic development of deprived individuals and communities (see Biswas and Rao, 2014). The services offered by MFIs not only include credit facilities for the poor and business owners but also provide different support and training on the necessary skills required to start and grow a business successfully. The discussion above provides an overview of the concept of microfinance and the role of microfinance institutions.

3. THE EVOLUTION AND EXPANSION OF MICROFINANCE

Research into microfinance has a long history which dates as far back as the 15th century (Tripathi, 2015). According to Geleta et.al. (2019) the idea behind the concept of microfinance is not new as governments and non-governmental organisations (NGOs) regularly set up developmental projects that help in fostering economic development while also trying to reduce the level of poverty particularly in developing countries. Mago (2013) has shown that microfinance is rather a phenomenon that evolved from microcredit which has its origin in informal lending practices that have been in existence for centuries in many parts of the world. Reppey (2007) on the other hand opines that microfinance has been present in West, East and North Africa for centuries and has gained popularity in several continents. This is consistent with the thoughts of Zainuddin and Yasin (2020), Ashta, et al. (2014) and Avallone and Strangio (2024) who have also demonstrated that microfinance has been present for centuries but started off as microcredit. Mia (2022) agrees with the opinion of previous researchers on the transition to microfinance but went further to suggest that microcredit which has been replaced by microfinance provides a small amount of loans to the poor while microfinance goes beyond that by offering a wider variety of financial services to the poor. These financial services include savings, insurance and training schemes (Jalil, et al., 2022; Audu, et al., 2021 and Mutuma 2020).

Evidence from existing literature suggests that some studies have explored the history of microfinance and how it evolved in some countries. For instance, Seibel (2005) have demonstrated that the movement of microfinance has existed as far back as 200 years ago, when different informal sources of finance were offered to people within some communities before the "formal" arrival of microfinance. Besides, Seibel (2013) provides evidence that the informal sources of finance vary across countries and are called different names. For example, in China this type of finance was called "Hui". The Indians called it "Chit Funds", while the Indonesians called theirs "Paluwagan". Ojera (2018) supported this by highlighting that the South Africans called this source of funds "Stokvel" while some parts of West Africa like Nigeria and Ghana called it "Esusu or Susu". Addae-Korankye (2020) who investigated the "historic emergence of microfinance" concludes that the concept of microfinance which started off as pawnshops has transitioned from one historic stage to another and finally now most known as microfinance. Figure 1 below shows how microfinance, which started as pawnshops, has evolved from one stage to another over time and is currently at the stage where it is mostly referred to as microfinance. These different stages vary in different ways with diverse features and characteristics but have one commonality, which is providing financial services for the poor designed to alleviate poverty (Rahman, 2023; Chikwira, et al., 2022; Ashta et al., 2014).

Figure 1. Stages of the evolution of microfinance

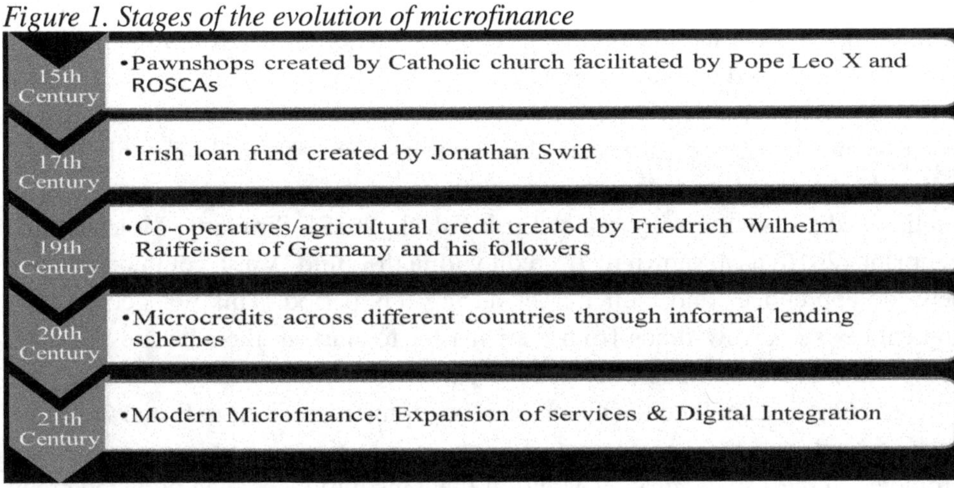

Source: Author (2024).

3.1 Microfinance in the 15th Century

Analysis of microfinance literature suggests that microloans originated from small communities, where friends and family formed money-sharing groups, known by different names worldwide (Addae-Korankye, 2020; Ojera, 2018 and Seibel, 2013). However, access to credit and other financial products was limited for low-income earners and the poor until the 15th century (Bernards, 2022). For example, "the institutions called monte di Pietà originated in 15th century in Italy, where these institutions gave poor people access to loans with reasonable interest rates (İstekli and Ustaoğlu, 2020)". Other early microcredit initiatives can be traced back to ancient financial inclusion schemes, including the rotating savings and credit associations (ROSCAs) in the 15th century (Hossein, 2020).

Certainly, during the 15th century, the provision of microcredit existed in different forms outside the regulations of central banks (Mia, 2022). These credit systems were essential for economic development and social integration, providing a protective institution that enabled the underserved and salary workers to augment their unstable and uncertain income (Bernards, 2022). The Rotating Savings and Credit Associations (ROSCAs) and Accumulating Savings and Credit Associations (ASCAs) were popular around the world in the 15th century as credit tools before the existence of microfinance, even though they may have been identified using different names in different cultures and countries. These systems allowed members to contribute a fixed amount of money regularly, which was then given as a lump sum to one member at a time in a rotating manner (Sadr, 2017). According to Briggs and Koyama (2012) formal financial institutions were absent during this period. However, the agrarian credit market made it possible for peasants to benefit from lending and borrowing with reduced risk (Black, 2017). Similarly, Molenaar and Lehmann (2016) have shown that "credit within the guild" was a common practice between apprentices and their master during this period. This practice enabled apprentices to borrow funds from their master to start up their businesses upon completing their training and service period.

Gatto (2018) examined the historical roots of microcredit in Italy and the Kingdom of Naples in the 15th century. The study investigates how microcredit was promoted in the 15th century by Monti di Pietà institutions, which provided credit to the underserved to eradicate usury and develop the local community. Usury is the practice of lending money at unreasonably high interest rates, which was a common problem during this period (Geisst, 2013). The Monti di Pieta institutions offered low-interest loans to combat the high interest rates credits that were offered at the time. Guillaume (2013) suggests that the Monti di Pietà was established in the Northern part of Italy during the 15th century and concludes that it was useful in fighting off usury while acting as an essential actor for financial inclusion through pawnbroking. Pawnbroking was a common practice during this period that allowed people to borrow money by providing collateral in the form of personal property (Carter and Skiba, 2012). This practice was used to provide low-income owners or the poor with access to credit and financial services.

ROSCAs, which are still prevalent in many countries, operate by pooling resources from a group of individuals who take turns to receive a lump sum of money (Zainuddin and Yasin, 2020). The Monti di Pietà in Italy on the other hand was one of the earliest microcredit institutions established to curb the widespread practice of usury and provided consumption loans to the underserved to address liquidity crises, in exchange for emotionally valued assets (Gatto, 2018). Skambraks (2024) have shown that these institutions were governed by donations and ethical principles, serving local beneficiaries, and engaging in activities to generate political, social, religious, and cultural impact in their territories. This is consistent with Svoboda (2015) opinion that the existence of microfinance can be dated as far back as the 15th century when the Catholic church invented the pawnshop as an alternative source of finance. The aim was to create an affordable source of finance that would replace the existing informal savings and credit groups that were offering loans with high interest rates. This was achieved when Pope Leo X lifted the ban and gave permission to pawnshops in 1515 to charge interest on loans being offered at an affordable rate (Rahman, 2023; Addae-Korankye, 2020). It is therefore plausible to say that the 15th century is an important period in the development of financial inclusion schemes, due to the emergence of various credit tools and institutions enabling access to credit for the underserved and salary workers, fostering economic development and social integration.

3.2 Microfinance in the 17th Century

The small loan practices in the 17th century differ from those of today. The key characteristics of these lending practices, their impact and implications for modern-day microfinance are examined in this section. The modern-day microfinance movement is based on the innovative practices that started during the 17th century and continued to evolve. This is evident in Abdulhakim (2020) who has demonstrated that one of the earliest known microcredit organisations was the Irish Loan Fund system, established in the early 1700s, to provide small loans to the rural poor without requiring collateral, thus becoming a foundation of modern microcredit. In this regard, it is plausible to hypothesise that the historical roots of microcredit demonstrate the enduring need for small loans in the form of informal credits that have existed for centuries across different nations to empower the poor and promote financial inclusion.

According to Hollis and Sweetman (1996) the Irish loan funds are a notable example of microfinance evolution based on the significant role it played in providing capital to the "industrious poor" inspired by Jonathan Swift's donation of £500 for loans under £10 to impoverished Dublin artisans, which later inspired the Dublin Musical Society to establish a similar lending model that proved highly successful. Within a few years, the society's loan program had provided relief to "several thousand families". Overall, the funds empowered individuals to start or expand their businesses, contributing to the overall prosperity of the nation. This is consistent with Roodman (2012) who suggests that the Irish fund was offered credit without collaterals to the "industrious tradesmen" in the 1720s. In his view, the funds were offered to develop the Irish countryside. However, those who received the funds were required to pay back every week (Hollis and Sweetman, 1996; Rahman, 2010).

The Irish fund gained popularity over a period of time, but this wasn't without difficulties due to some challenges encountered along the way. This is evident in Hollis and Sweetman (1998) who argues that the Irish Loan fund had a slow growth due to management know-how and intense competition from the commercial banks. However, McLaughlin (2009) found that the Irish Loan Fund improved its operations, such that by the 1840s it was fairly developed with 300 micro-lending financial institutions providing non-collateral small loans to over 20% of the Irish population. This is consistent with Ashta, et al. (2014) who have shown that the total loan granted by the Irish Loan Fund was "an average per capita income of the poor" which makes up two-third of the entire Irish population. However, Seibel (2005) opines that the Irish Loan Fund experienced an incremental decline in the second half of the 19th century before completely disappearing in the 1950s due loss of its competitive edge to mainstream banks. Thus, the Irish Loan Fund evolved in three phases namely early period of incremental growth, the period of swift expansion and the period of decline. Based on the argument that the Irish loan funds and pawnshops served as early examples of microfinance institutions that provided access to capital and played a crucial role in the economic development of their communities. It can be argued that the historical roots of microcredit in the 17th century demonstrate the enduring need for small loans to empower the poor and foster financial inclusion.

3.3 Microfinance in the 19th Century

Evidence from Hermes and Lensink, (2020) suggests that another phase of the evolution of microfinance was the idea of financial cooperatives in the 19th century which originated in Germany. After realising that rural farmers were relying on money lenders with high interest rates, Friedrich Wilhelm Raiffeisen of Germany and his followers sought ways to manage the situation by allowing farmers access credit to alienate poverty and create wealth. This led to the creation of the first rural credit union, also referred to as a financial cooperative (Hollis. and Sweetman, 1998; Rahman, 2010). This is consistent with Cozarenco and Szafarz (2019) who argues that there is a longstanding belief that microfinance in the 19th century originated in Germany with the launch of credit cooperatives by Hermann Schulze-Delitzsch and Friedrich Raiffeisen. However, the English Rochdale Society of Equitable Pioneers also initiated a cooperative movement during the same period (Walton, 2015).

According to Wilson, et al. (2013) the main reason for creating the cooperative in 1846, was to teach the poor farmers how to work together and support one another by means of saving and creating cooperatives where members of the union could borrow at an affordable rate. This view is supported by Van Leeuwen and van

Leeuwen (2016) who have shown that the inception of the first mutual insurance association in the Netherlands dates back to the 19th century. This association was established by a group of farmers who had encountered losses of their produce due to the occurrence of haystack or fire outbreak. In a bid to assist one another, they pooled their financial resources together to support each other. However, Seibel (2005) argues that Raiffeisen believed there is a relationship between poverty and dependency, thus, to create wealth, the poor farmers would have to embrace dependency. This led to the adoption of the three 'S' formula (self-help, self-governance and self-responsibility) in the development of the cooperative movement (Zimnoch, 2017). Friedrich Wilhelm Raiffeisen's financial cooperative movement that started in Germany grew swiftly in countries around Europe and other developing countries (Addae-Korankye, 2020). The cooperatives which started with 245 branches in 1885 increased to over 14,500 branches in 1910 with over 1.4million members.

Schmidt (2018) have also demonstrated that microfinance emerged with the establishment of German savings and cooperative banks pioneered to provide financial services to marginalised communities in the 19th century. However, Shone (2010) suggest the concept of microfinance in the 19th century emerged with Lysander Spooner advocating for small credits for entrepreneurs. This is consistent with Singh (2024) opinion that Lysander Spooner in the 1800s advocated for the benefits of offering support in the form of small credit to underserved entrepreneurs. Other studies such as Bulut and Korkut (2019) suggest that Cash waqfs in the Ottoman Empire in the 19th century functioned as an MFI that adapted their services to meet the needs of low-income earners by creating an inclusive financial system. It is therefore plausible to say that the emergence of MFIs during the 19th century brought about a profound change in the lives of the poor. By providing access to credit, savings, and other financial services, microfinance empowered individuals to establish enterprises, enhance their standard of living, and mitigate the risk of poverty. Thus, the progress of microfinance during this era constituted a bedrock for its sustained expansion and influence in the 20th and 21st centuries which is reviewed in the next section.

3.4 Microfinance in the 20th Century

Analysis of existing literature suggests that the early foundations of microfinance as we know it today commenced in the early part of the 20th century with the establishment of informal lending schemes such as the cooperatives, community lending groups and rotating savings and credit associations. Evidence of these cooperative movement in Europe was Raiffeisen movement in Germany, which was set up to provide credit and other services to farmers (Hilson, 2018). Evidence of the cooperative movement was also reported in India, with the creation of the agricultural banks to provide loans to rural and farming communities (Sahoo, et al., 2020). According to Appietu, et al. (2021) these schemes at that time were designed to provide small loans to low-income earners who have no access to traditional banks due to poor credit or lack of appropriate collateral assets, therefore laying the foundation for the concept of microfinance. Therefore, the concept of microfinance in its current form is said to have originated in the 20th century as various studies have shown that it laid the foundation for using microfinance as a poverty alleviation and financial inclusion strategy. For instance, evidence from Bernards (2022) suggests that the concept of microfinance can be traced to lending practices that have existed for centuries, but the formalisation of the lending practices started in the 20th century. Perhaps, it is in this context that Bateman and Chang (2012) argue that the recognition of microfinance as a formal financial product for alleviating poverty and fostering economic development in rural and poor communities emerged in the 20th century.

Prior studies have also shown that various models of microfinance in operation today started around the 1950s and 1960s. For instance, Meyerowitz (2021) have demonstrated that various schemes to provide small loans to the poor were piloted in various countries during this period. In Latin America for example, a scheme initiated by Accion International was established purposely to provide small loans to individuals and groups for entrepreneurial activities (Craan, 2018). Therefore, the role of microfinance in fostering entrepreneurship and economic development emerged in the 20th century. Another scheme that was piloted to provide credit to the poor is the Self-Employed Women's Association (SEWA) in India. This Association which was founded in 1972 was established to help women who were not able to get credit or open accounts with traditional banks to access financial services through their membership of the SEWA (Colovic and Mehrotra, 2020). Hence, the role of microfinance in empowering women may have started in the 20th century.

With regards to models of microfinance, evidence from Anandhi (2019) suggests that the Grameen model which was pioneered by Muhammad Yunus in the 1970s was one of the most innovative models of microcredit. Similar to the SEWA in India, the Grameen model focused on providing credit to women in poor rural communities in Bangladesh. Through the Grameen Bank, Muhammad Yunus gave small loans to women considered to be poor without any collateral requirements (Arifa, 2021). The Grameen model was based on trust where members supported each other in repaying loans instead of using collateral to ensure repayment (see Sinha, 2020). The Grameen model's success of helping women develop income-generating activities and achieving high repayment rates among borrowers became widely replicated across the world and laid the foundation for what became known as "microcredit." Consequently, the microcredit model of microfinance, which involves providing small loans to people with poor credit history without collateral, expanded quickly to other parts of the developing world, leading to the establishment of numerous microfinance institutions (MFIs) in the latter part of the 20th century.

The success and subsequent influence of the Grameen model on the microfinance sector influenced some researchers to conclude that microfinance started with Muhammad Yunus's Grameen model. For instance, Addae-Korankye (2020) suggests that microfinance started in the mid-1970s the establishment of the Grameen Bank in Bangladesh to support poor people who were excluded from commercial banks. However, Mago (2013) disagrees and rather opines that Muhammad Yunus is not the originator of microfinance and goes further to suggest that microcredit has been in existence for centuries, but only gained worldwide popularity due to the Grameen model developed by Muhammad Yunus. This is consistent with Lindsay (2010) who has shown that the popularity of microfinance can be associated with the Bangladeshi economist Muhammad Yunus in the 1970s.

Another aspect of the evolution of microfinance in the 20th century that has been reported in existing literature is the international recognition of the concept of microfinance as a poverty alleviation tool. In this regard, Mia (2022) has shown that various governments around the world and international organisations such as the World Bank and United Nations started to provide financial support to Microfinance Institutions in the 1980s and 1990s. Perhaps, it is in this context that Bernards (2022) argues that formalisation of the operations of microfinance institutions begun in the 20th century. Besides, Sengupta and Aubuchon (2008) have demonstrated that the expansion of microfinance services to large populations of people across the world started in the 20th century.

A Further development in the evolution of microfinance services in the 20th century is the creation of regulatory frameworks by various governments to support the operations of microfinance institutions, which helped microfinance institutions to further increase their outreach across the world. Perhaps, this account for the entry of the microfinance services sector by various commercial banks and other investors in the 1990s.

3.5 Microfinance in 21st Century

Analysis of Illangakoon, et al. (2021) suggests that microfinance known to contribute positively to poverty alleviation and women empowerment continued to grow significantly in the 21st century. One notable development of the concept of microfinance in the 21st century is its expansion to include services such as training, insurance and savings. Perhaps, it is in this context that Miller (2021) argues that the microfinance experiment in the 21st century is broader than envisaged by economists such as Mohammed Yunus.

The integration of digital financial technology in the provision of microfinance services is another major development in the microfinance sector in the 21st century. For instance, Chuc, et al. (2023) have shown that the adoption of FinTech solutions including mobile banking and digital payment platforms has positively impacted on the operations of microfinance institutions (MFIs). This is consistent with Aithal (2024) who has demonstrated that the integration of digital technologies such as mobile money and digital payment platforms have contributed positively to microfinance outreach across the world. Evidence from Thulani, et al. (2014) suggest that the use of mobile money applications for instance, has helped microfinance institutions to provide financial services to people in rural communities with limited access to formal banks. The integration of these mobile money platforms has particularly helped the poor in rural areas to access credit and make payments using their mobile phone devices. The integration of digital technology in the delivery of microfinance services has also been shown to have helped microfinance institutions reduce their delivery cost thereby enhancing their profitability and sustainability (Jalil, 2021). The technological integration reported in the microfinance sector in the 21st century has been shown to be more transformative in Africa, where mobile phone penetration is high, but traditional banking infrastructure is lacking (Siano, et al., 2020).

Another significant development in the evolution of microfinance in the 21st century has been its impact on women empowerment (see Illangakoon, et al., 2021). Various studies (Fuentes, 2023; Mostafa, 2020 and Maclean, 2017) have shown that microfinance institutions have often prioritise lending to women because the female have often been disproportionately excluded from the formal banking sector. Evidence from Zulfiqar (2013) suggest that the 21st century has seen a significant increase and focus on using microfinance as a gender empowerment tool. Perhaps it is in this context that Sindhav (2017) concludes that the positive contribution of women to economic activities in the 21st century can be attributed to the rise and popularity of microfinance as a gender empowerment tool.

Finally, the most recent development in the evolution of microfinance in the 21st century is the provision of small loans to support green business ventures and sustainable environmental projects aimed at combating the negative effects of climate change. Thus, one of the contributions of microfinance in the 21st century is its positive impact on climate change mitigating projects and sustainable development (Dowla, 2018). such as clean energy projects, climate-smart agriculture, and disaster preparedness. In this regard, the outcomes of Manko and Watkins (2022) suggest that microfinance institutions in Sub Saharan Africa and elsewhere provide credit to the poor for renewable energy solutions, such as the purchase of solar panels or clean cooking technologies, which improve living standards and contribute to environmental sustainability.

4. SOLUTIONS AND RECOMMENDATIONS

Various solutions and recommendations that have emerged from the review of existing literature on the evolution of microfinance are discussed next. First and foremost, microfinance institutions should further expand their services beyond loans to comprehensively address the needs of people excluded from the formal financial system. Providing a broader range of services has the potential of helping microfinance institutions to achieve a high growth rate, diversified product portfolio and increased revenue stream, which could improve MFIs sustainability.

Secondly, deeper integration of cutting-edge technologies such as blockchain, artificial intelligence and mobile phone applications has the potential to foster effective and efficient MFIs operations helping to extend their services to the unbanked in remote communities. Overall, innovative use of appropriate FinTech solutions by microfinance institutions could improve MFIs outreach and deepen financial inclusion in rural and poor communities. The integration of digital technologies such mobile phone applications has been shown to help microfinance beneficiaries to access credit and make payments remotely thereby helping to increase loan repayments significantly in the sector.

Although some microfinance institutions have broadened their services to include financial literacy, most MFIs still focus on providing microcredit. In this regard, it is recommended that microfinance institutions should provide financial literature training alongside the traditional small loans to help beneficiaries to make better financial decisions. The provision of financial literacy training also has the potential to deepen client knowledge and understanding of the risks and benefits associated with financial products offered by MFIs.

Evidence from the literature reviewed above suggests that the microfinance sector in most countries is not regulated, putting the unbanked population at risk of exploitation. It is therefore recommended that Governments and international financial institutions should develop a comprehensive framework to regulate the microfinance sectors to protect beneficiaries and foster transparency. The increasing use and integration of digital technology in the provision of microfinance services raises data protection issues which reinforces the need for robust regulatory framework to protect consumers.

A further initiative that could unlock new growth opportunities and expand MFI outreach is collaboration with FinTech companies and traditional commercial banks. Working with these institutions has the potential to help MFIs to overcome funding constraints, improve access to technology, and reach underserved communities more effectively.

By implementing these solutions, the microfinance sector can continue evolving as a key driver of financial inclusion while addressing existing challenges and improving its overall impact on poverty reduction and development.

5. CONCLUSION

The evolution of microfinance over the years is an indication of its critical role in deepening financial inclusion and alleviating poverty across the developing world and poor communities. Although microfinance was initially designed to provide small loans to the unbanked, it has developed into a diverse sector providing various financial services including savings, insurance, and digital payments. This development has helped microfinance institutions to increase their outreach and address a broader range of financial needs of the unbanked across the world.

One of the key successes of microfinance has been its ability to empower individuals, especially women, by giving them the financial tools to start or expand small businesses, manage household finances, and build economic resilience. It has also played a transformative role in encouraging entrepreneurship and facilitating community-level development. Despite these achievements, the sector has faced significant challenges that have shaped its evolution, including concerns about over-indebtedness, mission drift, and the limitations of microfinance in addressing structural poverty. These challenges highlight the need for a more nuanced understanding of microfinance as both a social and financial instrument.

As the microfinance sector continues to evolve, it has embraced new innovations, particularly in the areas of digital finance and fintech. The integration of mobile banking and digital platforms has made financial services more accessible and affordable, extending microfinance's reach to previously excluded populations. However, the rapid digitization of microfinance also presents new risks, including data privacy concerns, cybersecurity threats, and the potential for deepening the digital divide. As technology reshapes the landscape, MFIs must strike a careful balance between innovation and consumer protection.

Looking forward, the microfinance sector must continue to evolve by embracing new technologies, fostering innovative partnerships, and developing more inclusive financial models. Research will be key to guiding this evolution, helping practitioners and policymakers better understand the complex dynamics of financial inclusion and the role of microfinance in addressing multidimensional poverty. By incorporating lessons from the past and anticipating future needs, microfinance can continue to make significant contributions to global development, while addressing the structural barriers that limit financial access for millions of people worldwide.

Overall, while microfinance has made considerable progress in expanding financial inclusion, its journey is far from complete. The next phase of evolution must focus on refining its approach to client needs, leveraging technology responsibly, and ensuring that its social mission remains central to its operations. By doing so, microfinance can continue to evolve as a vital tool for economic empowerment and poverty reduction in an increasingly complex and interconnected world.

REFERENCES

Abdulhakim, N. (2020). Determinants of financial sustainability of microfinance institutions in Ethiopia. [HAJBE]. *Horn of African Journal of Business and Economics*, 3(2), 47–59.

Addae-Korankye, A., 2020. Historical emergence of microfinance and the microfinance sector in Ghana. *Business Management Dynamics, 10*(2).

Aithal, P. S. (2024). Influence of Digital Technology on Microfinance Sector: A Study in Kerala. [IJAEML]. *International Journal of Applied Engineering and Management Letters*, 8(2), 186–197.

Anandhi, A. K. (2019). Microfinance An Overview. *Think India Journal*, 22(14), 12465–12469.

Appietu, R. K., Dankwa, I. O., & Caesar, L. D. (2021). Exploring the nexus between microfinance activities and economic wellbeing at the grassroots: Evidence from an emerging market economy. *Global Social Welfare : Research, Policy & Practice*, 8(4), 337–349. DOI: 10.1007/s40609-020-00172-6

Arifa, L. N. (2021). Banker To the Poor and Its Urgency Based on Indonesian Context (Perceiving the Toughts and Experiences of Muhammad Yunus). *Risâlah. Jurnal Pendidikan Dan Studi Islam*, 7(2), 226–238. DOI: 10.31943/jurnal_risalah.v7i2.188

Ashta, A., Couchoro, M., & Musa, A. S. M. (2014). Dialectic evolution through the social innovation process: From microcredit to microfinance. *Journal of Innovation and Entrepreneurship*, 3(1), 1–23. DOI: 10.1186/2192-5372-3-4

Audu, I., Abubakar, A. M., & Baba, M. (2021). The Role of Microfinance Institutions' Services on the Performance of Small and Medium Entreprises in Gombe State, Nigeria. *Journal of Management Sciences*, 4(1), 500–517.

Avallone, P., & Strangio, D. (2024). Different Forms of Microcredit and Social Business—Microfinance in Global History from the Late Medieval to the Modern. In *Different Forms of Microcredit and Social Business: Microfinance in Global History from the Late Medieval to the Modern* (pp. 1–15). Springer Nature Switzerland. DOI: 10.1007/978-3-031-60942-8_1

Bateman, M., & Chang, H.J., 2012. Microfinance and the illusion of development: From hubris to nemesis in thirty years. *World Economic Review*, (1).

Bernards, N. (2022). *A critical history of poverty finance: Colonial roots and neoliberal failures*. Pluto Press. DOI: 10.2307/j.ctv2tjd6qs

Biswas, M. P., & Rao, M. R. M. (2014). Role of NGO in empowering women through microfinance: A conceptual study. *Journal of Small Business and Entrepreneurship Development*, 2(2), 141–150.

Black, A. H. (2017). *Capital, saving and credit in peasant societies*. Routledge. DOI: 10.4324/9781315081786

Briggs, C., & Koyama, M., 2012. Pledging and credit markets in medieval England.

Bulut, M., & Korkut, C. E. M. (2019). Ottoman cash waqfs. *Insight Turkey*, 21(3), 91–112.

Cai, J., Meki, M., Quinn, S., Field, E., Kinnan, C., Morduch, J., & Said, F. (2023). Microfinance. *VoxDevLit*, 3(2), 26.

Carter, S. P., & Skiba, P. M. (2012). Pawnshops, behavioral economics, and self-regulation. *Rev. Banking & Fin. L.*, 32, 193.

Chikwira, C., Vengesai, E., & Mandude, P. (2022). The impact of microfinance institutions on poverty alleviation. *Journal of Risk and Financial Management*, 15(9), 393. DOI: 10.3390/jrfm15090393

Chuc, A. A. M., Atayah, A. A., & Özer, S. Q. (2023). Impact of financial technology (fintech) on financial performance of micro finance institutions in Bahrain. *African Journal of Emerging Issues*, 5(17), 1–11.

Colovic, A., & Mehrotra, S. (2020). Lifelong activism and women's entrepreneurship: How a social movement organization improves conditions for self-employed women in India. *European Business Review*, 32(5), 937–958. DOI: 10.1108/EBR-09-2019-0215

Cozarenco, A., & Szafarz, A. 2019. Microfinance in the North: Where do we stand? In *A Research Agenda for Financial Inclusion and Microfinance* (pp. 125-137). Edward Elgar Publishing.

Craan, V. 2019. *Entrepreneurial Financing of Micro-Small-Medium Enterprises in Haiti: Barriers and Proposed Solutions* (Doctoral dissertation, Universidad ESAN).

Creedy, J., & Hoang, H. T. (2018). Types of microfinance organisation: A taxonomy. *Third Sector Review*, 24(2), 105–136.

El-Nasharty, H. (2022). The Role Of Microfinance In Poverty Reduction: Countries Experiences by Regions 2000-2018. *Innovation Journal of Social Sciences and Economic Review*, 4(1), 1–09. DOI: 10.36923/ijsser.v4i1.101

Fuentes, M.P., 2023. Unveiling the Constraints: Exploring Limiting Factors for Microfinance Institutions Effectiveness in Fostering Women's Empowerment in India.

Gatto, A. (2018). Historical roots of microcredit and usury: The role of Monti di Pietà in Italy and in the kingdom of Naples in XV–XX centuries. *Journal of International Development*, 30(5), 911–914. DOI: 10.1002/jid.3386

Gebrehiwot, G., & Chawla, A.S., 2016. Outreach and Sustainability of Microfinance Institutions of Ethiopia: A Case Study on Specialized Financial and Promotional Institution (sfpi). *Research Journal of Finance and Accounting, 7 (5), 87, 107*. DOI: 10.1002/jid.3386

Geisst, C. R. (2013). *Beggar thy neighbor: A history of usury and debt.* University of Pennsylvania Press. DOI: 10.9783/9780812207507

Geleta, T. E., Mengistu, A. A., & Gesese, S. A. (2019). Determinants of rural households' participation in microfinance services: The case of Cheliya District, West Shoa Zone, Oromia National Regional State, Ethiopia. *Journal of Development and Agricultural Economics*, 11(2), 24–32. DOI: 10.5897/JDAE2018.1008

Guirkinger, C., & Boucher, S. R. (2008). Credit constraints and productivity in Peruvian agriculture. *Agricultural Economics*, 39(3), 295–308. DOI: 10.1111/j.1574-0862.2008.00334.x

Hermes, N., & Lensink, R. (2020). Microfinance and development. In *Contemporary issues in development finance* (pp. 51–72). Routledge. DOI: 10.4324/9780429450952-3

Hilson, M. (2018). The International Co-operative Alliance and the consumer co-operative movement in northern Europe, c. 1860–1939. In *The International Co-operative Alliance and the consumer co-operative movement in northern* [Manchester University Press.]. *Europe*, c, 1860–1939.

Hollis, A., & Sweetman, A. 1996. THE EVOLUTION OF AMicrocredit INSTITUTION: THE IRISH LOAN FUNDS, 1720-1920. *Department of Economics University of Toronto Working Paper.*

Hollis, A., & Sweetman, A. (1998). Microcredit in prefamine Ireland. *Explorations in Economic History*, 35(4), 347–380. DOI: 10.1006/exeh.1998.0702

Illangakoon, A. G., Azam, S. M., Khatibi, A., & Sudasinghe, S. (2021). Women empowerment in microfinance: Poverty alleviation tool. *South Asian Journal of Social Studies and Economics*, 12(4), 159–172. DOI: 10.9734/sajsse/2021/v12i430324

İstekli, M., & Ustaoğlu, M. (2020). Monte di Pietà. In *The Evolution of Interest and Debt* (pp. 86–96). Routledge. DOI: 10.4324/9781003041245-9

Jalil, M. F. (2021). Microfinance towards micro-enterprises development in rural Malaysia through digital finance. *Discover Sustainability*, 2(1), 55. DOI: 10.1007/s43621-021-00066-3 PMID: 35425910

Jalil, M.F., Ali, A., & Ahmed, Z., 2022. Microfinance services and MSE growth in Pakistan: The mediating perspective of social and psychological capital. DOI: 10.1002/jid.3386

Lieberman, I. W. 2020. The growth and commercial evolution of microfinance. *The future of microfinance*, pp.9-35.

Maclean, K. 2017. Microfinance and the "woman" question. *Seduced and Betrayed: Exposing the Contemporary Microfinance Phenomenon; Bateman, M., Maclean, K., Galbraith, JK, Eds*, pp.251-264.

Mago, S. (2013). Microfinance in Zimbabwe: A historical overview. *Mediterranean Journal of Social Sciences*, 4(14), 599–608.

Mandrawal, M. S. (2022). A Theoretical Evaluation of the Microfinance and its impact on Living Standards and Poverty Reduction in India. *International Journal for Global Academic & Scientific Research*, 1(3), 11–19. DOI: 10.55938/ijgasr.v1i3.21

McLaughlin, E. J. 2009. *Microfinance institutions in nineteenth century Ireland* (Doctoral dissertation, National University of Ireland Maynooth).

Meyerowitz, J. (2021). *A War on Global Poverty: the lost promise of redistribution and the rise of microcredit*. Princeton University Press.

Mia, M. A. (2022). Microfinance and microfinance institutions: History, concept and purpose. In *Social Purpose, Commercialization, and Innovations in Microfinance: A Global Perspective* (pp. 17–45). Springer Singapore. DOI: 10.1007/978-981-19-0217-8_2

Milana, C., & Ashta, A. (2020). Microfinance and financial inclusion: Challenges and opportunities. *Strategic Change*, 29(3), 257–266. DOI: 10.1002/jsc.2339

Miller, M., 2021. The Microfinance Experiment: An Evaluation of Programs and Effectiveness in St. Louis. DOI: 10.1002/jsc.2339

Molenaar, K., & Lehmann, J. M. (2016). *Microfinance, what is it all about?* The Hague University of Applied Sciences. [online]

Mutuma, K. G. 2020. *Microfinance services and financial performance of Small and Medium Enterprises in Meru Town, Kenya* (Doctoral dissertation, KENYATTA UNIVERSITY).

Ojera, P. (2018). Indigenous financial management practices in Africa: A guide for educators and practitioners. In *Indigenous Management Practices in Africa: A Guide for Educators and Practitioners* (pp. 71–96). Emerald Publishing Limited. DOI: 10.1108/S1877-636120180000020005

Rahman, M. O. (2023). The Impact of Microfinance on Poverty Alleviation and Employment Creation. *International Research Journal of Management and Social Sciences*, 4(3), 509–527.

Rahman, W. A. A. (2010). An overview of microfinance: History and evolution, definition and practice. *The Ahfad Journal*, 27(2), 3–21.

Rippey, P. 2007. Princes, peasants and pretenders: the past and future of African microfinance. *What's wrong with microfinance*, pp.109-20.

Roodman, D. (2012). *Due diligence: An impertinent inquiry into microfinance*. CGD Books.

Sadr, S. K. (2017). The optimum size of rotating qar asan savings and credit associations. *ISRA International Journal of Islamic Finance*, 9(1), 15–26. DOI: 10.1108/IJIF-07-2017-003

Sahoo, A.K., Meher, S.K., Panda, T.C., Sahu, S., Begum, R., & Barik, N.C., 2020. Critical review on cooperative societies in agricultural development in India. *Current Journal of Applied science and technology, 39*(22), pp.114-121. DOI: 10.1002/jsc.2339

Schmidt, R. H. (2018). Microfinance–once and today. *Credit and Capital Markets–Kredit und Kapital*, 51(2), 183–203. DOI: 10.3790/ccm.51.2.183

Seibel, H. D. 2005. *Does history matter? The old and the new world of microfinance in Europe and Asia* (No. 2005, 10). Working paper.

Seibel, H. D. (2013). 3 Old and new worlds of microfinance in Europe and Asia. In *Southeast Asia's Credit Revolution* (pp. 40–57). Routledge.

Sengupta, R., & Aubuchon, C. P. (2008, January/February). The microfinance revolution: An overview. *Review - Federal Reserve Bank of St. Louis*, •••, 90.

Shone, S. J. (2010). *Lysander Spooner: American Anarchist*. Lexington Books.

Siano, A., Raimi, L., Palazzo, M., & Panait, M. C. (2020). Mobile banking: An innovative solution for increasing financial inclusion in Sub-Saharan African Countries: Evidence from Nigeria. *Sustainability (Basel)*, 12(23), 10130. DOI: 10.3390/su122310130

Sindhav, K. 2017. *Women Empowerment Through Microfinance (A Study of Need, Practices and Future Trends)* (Doctoral dissertation, Maharaja Sayajirao University of Baroda (India)).

Sinha, S. (2020). Study of the Functionally Effective Credit Lending Models of Microfinance. *International Journal of Business Insights & Transformation*, 13(2).

Skambraks, T. (2024). Two German Monti di Pietà—Microcredit in Early Modern Augsburg and Nuremberg. In *Different Forms of Microcredit and Social Business: Microfinance in Global History from the Late Medieval to the Modern* (pp. 167–191). Springer Nature Switzerland. DOI: 10.1007/978-3-031-60942-8_9

Svoboda, F. (2015). The other banking charitable loans in pre-modern era. *European Journal of Science and Theology*, 11(5), 9–22.

Taiwo, J.N., & Benson, K.N., 2016. The role of microfinance institutions in financing small businesses. *JIBC, 21*(1).

Thalib, P., Hajati, S., Kurniawan, F., & Aldiansyah, K. (2021). The urgence regulation of business activities on Islamic microfinance institution according law no. 1 year 2013 of microfinance institutions. *Arena Hukum*, 14(2), 207–221. DOI: 10.21776/ub.arenahukum.2021.01402.1

Thulani, M., Chitakunye, P., & Chummun, B. Z. (2014). Mobile money as a strategy for financial inclusion in rural communities. *Mediterranean Journal of Social Sciences*, 5(25), 216–224.

Van Leeuwen, M. H., & van Leeuwen, M. H. 2016. The Age of the Friendly Societies: Mutual Insurance in the Nineteenth Century. *Mutual Insurance 1550-2015: From Guild Welfare and Friendly Societies to Contemporary Micro-Insurers*, pp.83-165.

Visconti, R. M. (2016). Microfinance vs. traditional banking in developing countries. *International Journal of Financial Innovation in Banking*, 1(1-2), 43–61. DOI: 10.1504/IJFIB.2016.076613

Walton, J. K. (2015). Revisiting the Rochdale pioneers. *Labour History Review*, 80(3), 215–248. DOI: 10.3828/lhr.2015.10

Wilson, J. F., Webster, A., & Vorberg-Rugh, R. (2013). *Building co-operation: a business history of the co-operative group, 1863-2013*. Oxford University Press.

Zainuddin, M., & Yasin, I. M. (2020). Resurgence of an ancient idea? A study on the history of microfinance. *FIIB Business Review*, 9(2), 78–84. DOI: 10.1177/2319714520925933

Zimnoch, B. M. K. (2017). *The cooperative paradigm of development-towards values*. Central and Eastern Europe in the Changing Business Environment.

Zulfiqar, G. M. (2013). *Microfinance: A tool for financial access, poverty alleviation or gender empowerment?–Empirical findings from Pakistan*. University of Massachusetts Boston.

KEY TERMS AND DEFINITIONS

ASCAs: Accumulating Savings and Credit Associations.
FinTech: Financial technology.
MFIs: Microfinance institutions.
NGOs: Non-governmental organisations.
ROSCAs: Rotating Savings and Credit Associations.
SEWA: Self-Employed Women's Association.

Chapter 2

Micro-Finance Institutions and Women's Entrepreneurship in India

Mayank Kumar
https://orcid.org/0000-0002-9643-5871
Christ University, Bengaluru, India

Pankaj Dhaundiyal
Christ University, Bengaluru, India

ABSTRACT

Microfinance institutions are considered a miracle to reduce poverty, promote empowerment, reducing gender inequality by providing microcredit and other financial services to strata of people outside the ambit of the formal financial system. Such micro-credit and other services lead to promoting entrepreneurship ventures among women leading to financial freedom and economic development of the country. This chapter studied the status of microfinance institutions across all continents and their pace of evolution with respective objectives. India-specific mission objectives and business models of microfinance institutions were dealt with in detail. 200 literatures based on the keywords related to the theme of chapter titles were fetched from the Scopus database and were subjected to cooccurrence analysis using network visualization on VOS viewer software. Microfinance has been identified as one of the important tools for poverty reduction and women's empowerment by promoting women entrepreneurship.

DOI: 10.4018/979-8-3693-6622-6.ch002

1. INTRODUCTION

1.1 Global Perspective

The word microfinance is an amalgamation of two words, micro and finance, Micro means small while finance means credit or loan. Together, both make the term microfinance mean small loans or credit. So conceptually microfinance means a small loan to unbanked customers generally poor strata of people not having access to the banking system. Over some time, the horizon of microfinance has grown many folds. It has grown from providing credit to providing savings opportunities, insurance needs and many more. The organisations providing such products are known as Microfinance Institutions or MFIs.

MFIs have tried to supplement or replace century-old practices of unorganised lending to poor strata of people with very high rates of interest. Across the globe, MFI operates on the principle of either for-profit or non-profit organisations governed by local land laws or Islamic Shariya laws. If we talk about microfinance then one would not forget Md Yunus a Noble Laureate of Bangladesh known as the Godfather of microfinance who started Grameen Bank in the early 70's for the social upliftment of the underprivileged class in Bangladesh, especially women.

Globally Microfinance has developed as a tool for reducing poverty and economic upliftment. In the last few decades, MFISs have grown and spread their wings across the globe to cater for the needs of under-banked populations. Microfinance Institutions work on the belief that providing access to financial services to the poor will empower them which in turn leads to the development of entrepreneurship and economic self-sufficiency.

Although Microfinance has its roots in the 1970's of Md Yunus's initiative of Grameen Bank, since then it has evolved and expanded its reach across continents. It has grown as per the regional needs and operates in diverse environments like urban areas to remote villages in the Asian and African subcontinent.

Globally the microfinance sector is dominated by NGO's, Credit Unions, Non-Banking Financial Institutions or even a commercial bank. Each of these organisations has different working styles that vary from traditional group lending to more innovative products like tech-enabled solutions. Still irrespective of their nature they operate to provide financial inclusion to a stratum of people currently outside the ambit of a functional financial system.

Over the period landscape of microfinance has transformed due to technological advancements. With the advent of fintech clubbed with digital payment, mobile banking has increased the reach of MFI and now they are catering to a larger set of people with lower cost and higher efficiency. MFI business has become more scalable. Clients' creditworthiness can be better tracked with the help of these technologies and can further track repayment behaviour, reducing risks for lenders (Cull & Morduch, 2018).

Microfinance has demonstrated considerable success in improving the livelihoods of its clients. Research has indicated that having access to microfinance services can result in higher household incomes, better educational and health results, and more stability in the economy (Banerjee et al., 2015). Women, who constitute a significant proportion of microfinance beneficiaries, have reported enhanced empowerment and decision-making capabilities as a result of financial independence (Chliova et al., 2015)

However, the sector is not without challenges. Issues such as high interest rates, over-indebtedness, and the sustainability of MFIs remain pressing concerns. Regulatory frameworks vary significantly across countries, impacting the operational efficiency and outreach of microfinance institutions. Furthermore, maintaining customers' financial literacy is essential to the long-term viability of microfinance programs so they can make wise borrowing and investing decisions (Rosenberg, 2010).

In the real world, there are various issues related to microfinance institutions, which are debatable. One such issue is that in reality MFI supported social upliftment in the long run or has a limited impact. This issue puts a question mark on the existence of MFI. On the other hand, there is another issue related to micro-financial institutions. Whether MFI should be a non-profit organisation catering with the sole aim of social upliftment or a profit organisation with a self-sustainable business model for long-term sustainability.

Whether a non-profit or for a profit micro financial institution operates with the objective of providing micro-credit to the underprivileged group. Such groups do not have access to formal banking systems for their day-to-day operational need, small business capital or for their micro-entrepreneurship ventures. It has been observed by some of the literature that the status of women in developing countries is even poorer than the status of male in underdeveloped countries. On the other side, women enjoy a better credit history and repayment rate than men across the globe. Such factors influenced the modus operandi of micro-financial institutions and the majority of them started focusing on women borrowers (Babajide et al., 2022). Mostly such lending is done in a rural part of the country having a large size of underprivileged populations. In this parlance concept of self-help groups is very popular and most of the MFI's are operating with this mode.

Now the question arises whether by providing small credit to women in rural areas really works as a miracle as intended by MFI's. Does such small credit really generate micro-entrepreneurship opportunities for rural women and lead to their social and financial upliftment (Nair & Njolomole, 2020)? On the other side if such upliftment has occurred, in that case, is it uniform across geographies or has a concentrated effect in a particular zone (Samineni & Ramesh, 2020)?

This book chapter intends to address the following concerns, namely whether the growth of microfinance institutions is at the same pace across the geographies. Do the microfinance institutions operate with the same philosophies across the globe? Does microfinance help in poverty reduction and empowerment of the underprivileged especially women? Does credit provided by microfinance institutions promote entrepreneurship among women? Status of microfinance institutions in India with their mission and objective along with business models. Have microfinance institutions in India helped promote women's entrepreneurship leading to poverty reduction, empowering women, and reducing gender inequality?

Over the period Micro Finance Institutions have grown at different paces and objectives across the globe. Priorities are different in various geographies. The following part covers the evolution of microfinance in different continents.

1.1.1. Status of Microfinance Institutions in African Continent

Microfinance is crucial in the African setting because of the distinct socioeconomic issues that the continent faces, such as high rates of poverty, unemployment, and financial marginalization. Microfinance has changed since it was first introduced in the 1970s, moving from a limited concentration on micro business loans to a more all-encompassing strategy that includes a gamut of micro-financial products including insurance, savings accounts, and other financial services. Their most important contribution is closing the gap between formal financial systems and underprivileged groups, especially women and rural communities.

African microfinance, which was first fashioned after the innovative microfinance initiatives in Bangladesh and Latin America, has adapted to local circumstances, reflecting the different cultural, political, and economic landscapes of the continent. Kenya, Nigeria, and Uganda are now well-known instances of how microfinance may be included in national development plans. For instance, by allowing low-income people to access credit and savings using mobile technology, Kenya's mobile money platform, M-Pesa, has revolutionized access to financial services and changed the microfinance environment (Jack et al, 2016).

The industry has had considerable expansion, but it has also encountered difficulties, such as finance constraints, operational inefficiencies, and regulatory obstacles. The digitalization of financial services, the fusion of microfinance and social enterprises, and the encouragement of financial literacy among micro-entrepreneurs have been the main focuses of more recent trends. The African Development Bank (AfDB) asserts that Africa's microfinance sector needs to keep changing to satisfy the needs of a more digital economy and to adjust to the impacts of worldwide events like the COVID-19 pandemic and climate change (AfDB, 2022).

1.1.2. Status of Microfinance Institutions in South American Continent

South American countries have evolved a more diverse approach to financial services, combining savings, insurance, and non-financial services like financial education and business training. This is in contrast to other regions where microfinance is primarily focused on small loans (microcredit). The emergence of organizations such as Bolivia's BancoSol, one of the first authorized microfinance banks, shows that the industry can grow while adhering to its social objective. Bolivia continues to be a pioneer in the development of microfinance, serving as a model for other nations on the continent with its creative strategy of converting non-governmental organizations into regulated financial institutions (Morduch & Armendáriz, 2010).

Microfinance has also merged seamlessly with rural and agricultural economies in nations like Ecuador and Peru. Organizations like Mibanco in Peru are playing a vital role in enhancing the productivity and revenue creation of small businesses and farmers by offering microloans. Brazil and Argentina have come to understand the value of microfinance in advancing financial inclusion in recent years, especially for women-owned enterprises and underprivileged metropolitan regions.

Nonetheless, the industry has encountered noteworthy obstacles such as excessive debt, legislative limitations, and market saturation in certain nations. As a result of the 2008 global financial crisis and the ensuing economic downturns risk management procedures were reevaluated by microfinance institutions (MFIs) throughout South America. Mobile banking and digitalization are starting to influence the future of microfinance in South America. Digital financial platforms present new chances to reach underprivileged areas with microfinance services as more individuals acquire smartphones and internet access.

1.1.3. Status of Microfinance Institutions in North American Continent

North America's distinctive path in the development of microfinance has been molded by the region's sophisticated financial institutions, regulatory framework, and socioeconomic heterogeneity. In contrast to developing nations, where the primary goal of microfinance is to serve underprivileged and low-income populations, in North America, the field has developed to fill gaps in the formal banking system and support marginalized groups such as women, immigrants, and small businesses. Microfinance institutions (MFIs) in North America strive to stimulate entrepreneurship and financial inclusion by delivering small loans, savings, and other financial products to people excluded from regular banking services.

Credit unions and community-based lending initiatives, which were started to assist low-income and rural communities, are credited with helping to develop microfinance in North America. Organizations like Grameen America and ACCION USA, which tailored the global microfinance movement's tenets to local circumstances, were instrumental in the microfinance sector's growth in the United States during the 1980s and 1990s. The objective of these establishments was to furnish modest loans to enterprising people who did not have access to conventional financial services, especially in impoverished urban regions (Schreiner & Morduch, 2002).

The objective of microfinance in North America is unique and different and it boasts small business development and entrepreneurship rather than just reducing poverty. To assist clients in effectively expanding their businesses, microfinance institutions (MFIs) in the United States and Canada regularly provide mentorship, financial literacy initiatives, and business training in addition to microloans. This all-inclusive support structure has shown to be successful in addressing inequities in capital access, especially for minority- and women-owned firms.

However, this industry has had its share of difficulties in North America. In a divergence from developing nations where formal banking infrastructure is lacking and there is a high demand for microfinance, MFIs in North America frequently operate in a crowded financial market, where they share the space with fintech firms and traditional banks that are increasingly using digital platforms to target underserved populations. In North America, the growth of microfinance has also been hampered by financial shortages, regulatory obstacles, and very low demand for extremely small loans when compared to underdeveloped nations.

To expedite loan disbursement, repayment, and financial education, North American MFIs have been using technology more and more in recent years, marking a trend towards digital financial services. Microfinance now offers more options thanks to the growth of fintech in the US and Canada, especially in reaching underprivileged areas through peer-to-peer lending platforms and mobile banking.

1.1.4. Status of Microfinance Institutions in Southeast Asia

Poverty reduction and promoting financial inclusion for low-income rural populations have been central themes for the development of microfinance institutions in Southeast Asia. Since the 1980s, microfinance has emerged as a key development strategy across the region, with countries like Bangladesh, Indonesia, the Philippines, and Cambodia becoming global examples of successful microfinance models. Rooted in the principles of community-based financial services, Southeast Asian microfinance industry has grown to include a gamut of financial products and services aimed at empowering underserved populations, especially women and small-scale entrepreneurs.

One of the most significant and pioneering microfinance initiatives in Southeast Asia was started by Professor Muhammad Yunus in 1976 with the establishment of the Grameen Bank in Bangladesh. Grameen Bank model has been extensively replicated throughout Southeast Asia and beyond. Its main objective is to support micro-entrepreneurial activities by offering small, collateral-free loans to groups of borrowers, primarily women. The Grameen model's success demonstrated the potential of microfinance as a tool for social change and poverty alleviation, earning Yunus the Nobel Peace Prize in 2006.

Bank Rakyat Indonesia (BRI), which grew from a state-owned rural bank to one of the largest and most successful microfinance institutions in the world, has performed similar functions in Indonesia. The microfinance section of BRI provides a range of services to millions of Indonesians., It was founded in the 1980s and offers microloans, savings accounts, and insurance products. The financial sustainability of the BRI model, which combines social impact with commercial profitability, has made it noteworthy (Robinson, 2001).

In countries like Vietnam, the Philippines, and Cambodia, the microfinance sector has grown dramatically. For instance, economic liberalization in the 1990s led to the development of a robust microfinance sector in Cambodia in the country's financial system, ACLEDA Bank and other microfinance institutions (MFIs) play a significant role by providing essential services to rural communities and promoting the reduction of poverty. In a similar vein, the Philippines has included microfinance in its larger plans to reduce poverty, with official directives promoting the growth of rural banks and MFIs to assist small companies and boost agricultural output (Llanto, 2007).

Although microfinance has been fairly successful, the industry is still facing several obstacles in Southeast Asia. In response, some governments and MFIs have started implementing more responsible lending practices and concentrating on client protection initiatives to reduce the risks associated with over-lending. In countries like Cambodia and Vietnam, where microcredit services have expanded quickly, borrowers have accumulated unmanageable levels of debt (Emokpae, 2021).

The digital revolution is also influencing microfinance in Southeast Asia going forward. The rising integration of fintech solutions, mobile banking, and digital payment platforms into the microfinance industry allows for greater accessibility to financial services, particularly for those who live in remote areas. In nations like Indonesia and Myanmar, mobile-based microfinance services have been growing quickly, reaching unbanked populations and contributing to the reduction of the financial inclusion gap.

1.1.5. Status of Microfinance Institutions in Indian Subcontinent

Microfinance has grown significantly in Sri Lanka, Pakistan, and Nepal during the last few decades. In Pakistan, institutions such as the Pakistan Poverty Alleviation Fund and the Kashf Foundation have led the way in offering microloans to women and small enterprises, thereby enhancing their standard of living and promoting financial stability. Likewise, in Nepal, where organizations such as Nirdhan Utthan Bank and Sana Kisan Bikas Bank spearhead initiatives to reach marginalized populations, microfinance is intimately associated with rural development. With a focus on women's entrepreneurship and empowerment, the microfinance sector has grown in Sri Lanka as part of post-conflict reconstruction efforts and efforts to combat poverty.

1.2 Status of Microfinance Institutions in Indian Perspective

India is one of the biggest and most significant markets for microfinance, reflecting both the sector's potential and challenges on a large scale. The Indian microfinance landscape is diverse, comprising a mix of microfinance institutions, self-help groups (SHGs) and traditional banks offering microfinance products.

In the early 90's the National Bank for Agriculture and Rural Development (NABARD) initiated the SHG-Bank Linkage Program (SBLP), which is one of the largest microfinance programs globally. This initiative aims to link self-help groups of women with formal banking institutions, promoting savings and providing credit facilities. Tens of millions of women nationwide benefited from the recent bank connections that have been made possible by millions of SHGs (NABARD, 2023).

The growth of microfinance institutions (MFIs) in India is substantial, with notable entities like SKS Microfinance, Bandhan Bank, and Bharat Financial Inclusion Limited leading the way. These institutions cater to millions of low-income clients, predominantly women, providing them with micro-loans for entrepreneurial activities, agriculture, and consumption needs.

The Indian microfinance sector has got their challenges, which include regulatory hurdles, issues of over-indebtedness, and crises of confidence due to high-profile repayment defaults. The Andhra Pradesh microfinance crisis of 2010 is a notable example, where aggressive lending and coercive recovery practices led to widespread distress among borrowers and stricter regulatory oversight (Sane & Thomas, 2020)

In response to these challenges, the regulator of micro microfinance industry, the Reserve Bank of India (RBI) and other regulatory bodies have introduced measures to strengthen the sector. These include setting caps on interest rates, promoting transparency in lending practices, and encouraging the adoption of technology to improve efficiency and customer service (RBI, 2022).

Microfinance has appeared as a strong instrument for financial inclusion and poverty alleviation, predominantly in developing countries like India. By providing access to financial services to low-income individuals who are typically deprived of access to traditional banking systems, microfinance organizations (MFOs) play a vital role in fostering economic empowerment and sustainable development.

India's microfinance sector is one of the largest and most dynamic in the world. The landscape comprises a variety of institutions, including non-governmental organizations (NGOs), non-bank financial companies (NBFCs), cooperatives, and self-help groups (SHGs). These entities collectively aim to provide financial services to the underserved and unbanked populations, promoting inclusive economic growth.

1.2.1 Business Models of Microfinance Institutions in India

The business models of microfinance organizations in India vary widely, reflecting the diverse needs and contexts of their target populations. The primary models include:

1. **Self-Help Group (SHG) Model:** This model involves forming groups of 10-20 individuals, predominantly women, who pool their savings and lend to each other. The SHG-Bank Linkage Program (SBLP), initiated by NABARD, links these groups with formal banking institutions, enabling access to larger credit facilities. This model emphasizes community involvement and mutual support.
2. **Joint Liability Group (JLG) Model:** In this model, small groups of individuals (usually 4-10) guarantee each other's loans. The mutual guarantee reduces the risk for the lender and ensures high repayment rates. Institutions like Bandhan Bank and Bharat Financial Inclusion Limited (formerly SKS Microfinance) primarily operate using this model.
3. **Grameen Model:** Inspired by the Grameen Bank in Bangladesh, this model involves lending to small groups of individuals who are jointly liable for repayment. The focus is on providing small, short-term loans without collateral to foster entrepreneurial activities among the poor.
4. **Individual Banking Model:** This model targets individual borrowers rather than groups, offering tailored financial products based on the specific needs of each client. This approach requires more robust risk assessment and monitoring mechanisms. Ujjivan Small Finance Bank and Janalakshmi Financial Services are notable examples of institutions using this model.

1.2.2 Missions and Visions of Microfinance Institutions in India

In India, microfinance institutions (MFIs) are essential for meeting the financial needs of marginalized populations and low-income people, particularly in rural areas. By giving those without access to conventional banking services to have financial services like micro-credit, savings, and micro-insurance, these organizations hop in to fill the void created by more established financial institutions. The objectives of MFIs are to promote women's empowerment, inclusive growth, and poverty alleviation. As a strategic tool for financial inclusion, the Reserve Bank of India (RBI) has encouraged the expansion of the microfinance industry in coordination with government programs.

The key missions and objectives of various microfinance institutions in India can be summarized as follows:

1. Poverty Alleviation and Financial Inclusion
    - **Mission**: Reduction of poverty is the primary goal of MFIs' and they achieve it by providing small-scale financial services to people not having access to traditional banking services. This mission is in sync with the nation's financial inclusion goals to have universal access to fundamental financial services and products.
    - **Objective**: To give people access to reasonably priced financial services, especially microcredit, so they can work on projects that generate money and get out of poverty. For instance, groups like SKS Microfinance and Bandhan Bank work to provide microloans and other financial products that empower the economically underprivileged especially those living in rural areas.
2. Women's Empowerment
    - **Mission**: In India, a large proportion of MFIs prioritize women's empowerment as a key component of their work. MFIs aim to address the economic dependence of women, especially in marginalized and rural communities, by directly providing them with financial resources.
    - **Objective**: To improve women's social and economic empowerment through microloans, savings incentives, and financial literacy initiatives. Ujjivan Small Finance Bank, for example, focuses only on helping female clients and hopes to provide them with more financial freedom enabling them to make bigger decisions for their households and communities.
3. Promoting Self-Help Groups (SHGs)
    - **Mission**: Self-Help Groups (SHGs) are being promoted by many Indian MFIs as a means of fostering group financial responsibility and growth.

Self-Help Groups (SHGs) are seen as a viable model for promoting community-based lending and saving practices, as well as financial inclusion.

- **Objective**: Establishing, bolstering, and connecting Self-Help Groups (SHGs) with the official banking system so they can obtain loans at reduced interest rates. One of the biggest microfinance programs in the world, NABARD's SHG-Bank Linkage Programme connects SHGs with official banking institutions to enable rural women to save and obtain credit on advantageous conditions.

4. Sustainable Livelihood Creation
    - **Mission**: Sustainable livelihoods are frequently the focus of MFIs in India as part of their long-term goals. Through financial inclusion, they hope to encourage self-employment and entrepreneurship, especially in small-scale and agricultural enterprises.
    - **Objective**: The aim is to enable the establishment of small enterprises and opportunities for self-employment by offering financial services and capital through microloans. To support sustainable income generation and community development, Equitas Small Finance Bank, for instance, encourages its clients to engage in small-scale entrepreneurial endeavours, especially in the retail, services, and agricultural sectors.
5. Responsible Lending and Financial Literacy
    - **Mission**: Responsible lending procedures are given top priority by many MFIs, and they also stress the value of financial literacy. Their goal is to make the customers aware of the terms and conditions of financial products and are not overly indebted.
    - **Objective**: To instruct debtors on prudent credit usage, savings, and money management. Financial literacy initiatives are carried out by MFIs such as Janalakshmi Financial Services to make sure that their clients handle credit wisely, lowering the chance of loan default and promoting long-term financial stability.
6. Social Impact and Community Development
    - **Mission**: In addition to financial services, some MFIs in India strive to provide comprehensive community development. The aim is to enhance the general welfare of societies using health, education, and social development programs, frequently combined with their banking services.
    - **Objective**: To aid in the implementation of social welfare, health, and education initiatives that enhance financial inclusion. To guarantee that financial inclusion promotes greater community well-being, ESAFL Microfinance and Investments Pvt. Ltd., for instance, combines health insurance and health awareness initiatives with its loan services.

7. Reducing Regional Disparities
   - **Mission**: For many MFIs, addressing the geographical differences in financial services availability is a top priority. Formal financial institutions have historically provided inadequate services to some parts of India, especially those in the north and northeast.
   - **Objective**: To provide specialized microfinance solutions that can meet the unique needs of communities in underserved and distant areas. For example, North East Small Finance Bank concentrates on offering financial services to underprivileged communities in India's northeastern states, where financial penetration is typically low.

The larger aims of inclusive growth and economic development are closely related to the missions and purposes of microfinance institutions (MFIs) in India. These organizations provide a substantial contribution to the nation's efforts to reduce poverty, empower women, and establish sustainable livelihoods by offering microfinance services to the underprivileged. MFIs assist in bridging the gap between formal banking and financially excluded people through creative models like Self-Help Groups (SHGs) and a focus on financial literacy; these goals are closely aligned with those of national financial inclusion programs.

If we look at various leading micro finance institutions in India, either they have converted themselves into a small finance bank to cater larger set of people or still operating as micro finance institutions. Their mission and vision are summarized as follows:

1. Bandhan Bank:

   Mission: To provide our customers with affordable and holistic financial solutions.

   Vision: To be a bank of choice for the aspiring and the underserved, promoting financial inclusion and contributing to economic growth.
2. Bharat Financial Inclusion Limited:

   Mission: To provide financial services to the poor in a sustainable manner, leveraging technology and innovation.

   Vision: To be a leading financial services provider to the underserved, empowering them to achieve economic self-sufficiency.
3. Ujjivan Small Finance Bank:

   Mission: To provide a full range of financial services to the unbanked and underbanked, promoting financial inclusion and community development.

   Vision: To build a sustainable and scalable institution that addresses the diverse financial needs of our customers.
4. Janalakshmi Financial Services:

Mission: To provide financial services to the urban underserved with a focus on improving their quality of life.
Vision: To be the most trusted financial partner of the urban underserved, fostering economic empowerment and inclusion.

While microfinance has significantly impacted financial inclusion in India, the sector faces several challenges. These include regulatory hurdles, high-interest rates, over-indebtedness among borrowers, and the sustainability of MFIs. The Andhra Pradesh crisis in 2010, where aggressive lending practices led to widespread distress among borrowers, highlighted the need for balanced regulation and responsible lending practices (Sane & Thomas, 2020)

2. LITERATURE REVIEW

Inclusive growth is an essential element for social and economic justice. The Government and Reserve Bank of India have taken several measures to address financial exclusion, including Service Area approaches, priority sector lending, differential rates of interest, Lead Bank Schemes, and credit card issues. Promoting Self Help Groups (SHGs) and their linkages with the Bank are also being taken into consideration to strengthen the poor, particularly women. (HR U. & KN, R., 2013). India's recent growth and development, with 1.2 billion people and the world's fourth-largest economy, are significant achievements. States are implementing innovative initiatives for inclusive growth, demonstrating the potential for poorer states to learn from prosperous ones. (Tripathi & Tripathi, 2014).

A good number of literatures can be found on the central theme of the article. These literatures can be further sub categorised in following sub parts.

2.1. Micro Finance Institutions and Its Reason for Existence

Microfinance provides loans and financial services to the poor, promoting self-employment and poverty alleviation.

Minai et al. (2021) explores the challenges faced by Microfinance Institutions (MFIs) in maintaining their social mission while generating profits, a phenomenon known as mission drift. Their study explored the role of institutional investors in preventing this drift, benefiting MFIs, investors, borrowers, NGOs, and governments.

Zeb et al. (2021) argued that the microfinance industry's reliance on traditional funding sources contributes to financial instability. The sector is also hampered by a variety of external and internal environmental factors.

India has developed its model of microfinance organizations, such as Self-Help Groups (SHGs), managed by women, leading to women's empowerment and social change. Most microfinance institutions offer savings and insurance services. (Poddar, 2015)

Indian microfinance institutions' (MFIs) performance is crucial for providing financial services to the underprivileged. The improvement of technology is essential for expanding microfinance services and ensuring fair returns. Muneer (2016) in his paper analyses technological trends in 34 MFIs from 2005-2011 using a technological index and data envelopment analysis. Results show that technological change in MFIs is positively influenced by GDP growth rate and economy size.

International microlenders are expanding small business loans to the world's poor, but understanding this domain is limited. Bruton et al. (2011) in their study at Guatemala and the Dominican Republic reveal high performance and business failure causes for microloan recipients, laying the groundwork for future research on microlending.

2.2. Micro Finance Institutions and Poverty Reduction

Kabeer (2005) in his paper examined how microfinance has impacted poverty reduction and women's empowerment. It discloses that financial services do contribute to economic productivity and social well-being, but do not inevitably empower women. Other interventions such as education and political quotas also play a role in achieving such social transformation, but their success depends on context, commitment, and capacity.

Microfinance is a crucial institution for credit delivery, particularly for the poor and deprived in developing countries like India. Dhar (2016) in their study shows its success in alleviating poverty, promoting holistic development, and fostering entrepreneurship, especially for women. However, formal financial institutions have been non-responsive in rural development and rural credit. In India, a concentration of Self-Help Groups (SHGs) and Microfinance Institutions (MFIs) are mainly found in the southern part of India and are not thoroughly present across the country.

Khandker & Samad (2013) in their study argues that microcredit participants in Bangladesh are not trapped in poverty and debt, despite numerous years of participation. The analysis of data from a 20-year panel survey shows that microcredit benefits include income generation, consumption, asset accumulation, investment in education, and poverty reduction. Both participants and non-participants have progressed as the economy grows, with higher poverty reduction rates for participants. The study also shows significant welfare gains, especially for women, and a decline in poverty and debt-asset ratio.

Addae (2012) in their study examines the impact of microfinance banks (MFBs) on poverty reduction in Nigeria from 1992 to 2012. The results show a long-term relationship between poverty rate and MFBs activities, with loans-to-deposit ratio and liquidity ratio causing long-term poverty reduction. However, short-term estimates show MFBs struggle to achieve poverty reduction within a short period.

Banerjee et al. (2021) found that only for existing entrepreneurs or low wealth talented entrepreneurs, short-term access to credit can indeed facilitate escape from a poverty trap but no effect was found on average household.

Nukpezah & Blankson (2017) studied the microfinance intervention in rural poverty reduction in Ghana and found that the success of the microfinance program can be attributed to the farmers' close-knit communities and robust social networks. The study concludes that social and human development elements of microfinance policies should be prioritized in developing nation poverty reduction initiatives.

Field et al. (2013) studied the repayment requirements of classic micro finance contract inhibit investment in high-return but illiquid business opportunities among the poor. The results, thus, indicate that debt contracts that require early repayment discourage illiquid risky investment and thereby limit the potential impact of microfinance on microenterprise growth and household poverty.

2.3. Women Empowerment

Empowerment refers to women's power and agency in economic domains and market interactions. However, measuring empowerment has been limited. Fox & Romero (2017) suggests measuring empowerment in eight facets: attitudes and behaviours, social interactions, political and civic participation, and psychology. This approach is more accurate and correlates with other economic and social outcomes, as it considers attitudes, behaviours, social interactions, and psychological aspects.

Alemu et al. (2018) in their study examines the impact of self-help groups (SHGs) on women's empowerment in Southern Ethiopia's Chencha district. Results show positive community-level empowerment, as SHGs provide a platform for women to share information and raise awareness about their rights. However, attitudinal differences suggest conflict between spouses, possibly due to a fight for control over household resources, potentially leading to a "backlash effect."

Swain & Wallentin (2009) in their article highlights that true women empowerment occurs when women challenge norms and culture to improve their well-being. It differentiates between community-driven development and activities truly empowering women. Focus Group Discussions and interviews show that while only a fraction of Self-Help Groups are truly empowering, preliminary results suggest they could be contributing to women's empowerment.

2.4. Micro Finance Institution and Women Empowerment

Microfinance programs aim to improve economic opportunities for women, promoting empowerment. Across countries, microfinance outreach varies, with higher outreach in India correlated with higher women empowerment. An all-inclusive microfinance system could enhance financial inclusion and promote women's empowerment. (Laha & Kuri, 2014)

Gender discrimination affects women globally, necessitating empowerment to improve their status. The role of microfinance in empowering women and alleviating poverty was studied by (Rehman et al. 2020). The qualitative approach and case study method were used to analyse Akhuwat, an interest-free microfinance organization. Factors such as age, education, marital status, and family type influence women's empowerment. By nature, being an altruistic woman tends to spend the majority of their income on their family.

Sarumathi & Mohan (2011) studied how microfinance empowers women, measurement was done through three factors namely psychological, social and economical, and they found that microfinance gradually has a positive impact on all three factors among rural women. By participating in microfinance through the SHG programme, improvement in psychological well-being and social empowerment among rural women was evident.

Haile et al. (2012) found conflicting evidence suggesting that empowerment may or may not happen in small doses. By comparing the outcomes of two microfinance providers in Ethiopia, their study investigated whether differences in the socio-cultural, economic, and microfinance organizational environments are evident and explained the different effectiveness of such programs. They revealed that either microfinance programs can help women increase their income and asset base, or may reinforce gender-based labour divisions leading to inequality.

Nilakantan et al. (2013) studied the role of microfinance on women's empowerment and they discovered that larger access to microfinance is linked to either no empowerment effects or negative empowerment effects on the economic dimensions of empowerment, such as enterprise management, credit-related decisions, and expenditure-related decisions. However, this greater access to microfinance can lead to empowerment in terms of decisions about children, by gender-based rebalancing of influence within a family.

Sinha et al. (2023) their study revalidated the findings of Nilakantan et al. (2013) and they also found that greater access to credit through microfinance hurts women's empowerment as they struggle with credit and expenditure-related issues.

Kato & Kratzer (2013) in their study found that non-members of microfinance institutions especially women are less empowered than those who are members. As members, they enjoy higher control over income generation and savings leading to higher self-efficacy and esteem. They play a bigger role in decision-making and enjoy freedom from home leading to increased outside activities.

2.5. Entrepreneurship

Kuzilwa (2005) in their study based on cases and surveys of Tanzanian government-sourced businesses, explored the impact of credit on entrepreneurial activities. Results showed increased output and better performance in enterprises with business training and extension advice. They also identified that issues faced by entrepreneurs are not capital-related but macroeconomic and institutional.

Vossenberg (2013) in their paper explores the persistent gender gap in entrepreneurship, arguing that current policies benefit individual women, but if the gender bias remains intact, efforts may be in vain without significant macroeconomic or social impact, despite the growing number of women-led businesses.

2.6. Woman Entrepreneurship

Nawaz (2018) in their study explores the challenges faced by female entrepreneurs in Pakistan, focusing on societal and cultural aspects. With a 49.6% female population, the research aims to understand the societal and cultural influences on these women entrepreneurs.

Abdullah & Quayes (2016) examined whether female borrowers have better repayment rates than male borrowers and found that targeting women has a significant positive impact on their financial performance.

Henrekson & Johansson (1999) in their study reaffirm the finding of previous pieces of literature that female entrepreneurs underperform in aggregate compared to their male counterparts. However, they also found that structural differences between male and female entrepreneurs. Female underperformance disappears for three out of four performance variables except sales. The evidence of female underperformance is weaker in larger firms and non-existent in firms with only one employee. The study provides no support for female underperformance due to differences in preferences

Entrepreneurship is crucial for wealth creation, reducing unemployment, and poverty reduction. However, many micro-enterprises in Nigeria have low survival rates, and some entrepreneurs access micro-credits for non-business issues. Ekpe (2011) found that women entrepreneurs in Nigeria possess all the necessary characteristics for entrepreneurial success, as most failed enterprises belong to men.

Women-owned businesses are rapidly growing, contributing significantly to innovation, employment, and wealth creation in all economies. There is a higher probability of starting businesses in developed economies due to opportunity motivation, while those in less developed ones are motivated by necessity. In comparison to Europe and the United States, Latin America and Asia have higher rates of entrepreneurial activity for women. However, Brush & Cooper (2012) found that women entrepreneurs are yet to be studied in detail and their counting is less than 10% of all research.

2.7. Micro Finance and Entrepreneurship

Sustainable development can be achieved through entrepreneurial initiatives among underprivileged socio-economic groups. Microfinance, which involves small loans, can help lift the poor above poverty levels by providing increased self-employment opportunities and making them credit-worthy. The Self-Help Groups (SHG)-Bank linkage program is the largest micro-credit program globally, linking SHGs to banks gradually through savings and loan products. (Thakur, 2016)

Ferdousi (2015) in their study examines the effectiveness of microenterprise loans in increasing entrepreneurs' incomes and innovation. Results suggest larger loans increase income, but less innovative business practices may threaten it. The study recommends careful screening and monitoring of loans associated with proper business skills, information, and technologies by microfinance institutions.

Academic discussions on microentrepreneurs are more focused on credit constraints, but the self-employed poor often lack formal business training. This led microfinance organizations to start working on building the human capital of microentrepreneurs to improve their livelihoods and poverty alleviation mission. Karlan & Valdivia (2011) in a controlled trial found that adding business training to a Peruvian group lending program improved business knowledge and client retention rates, but it didn't change the key outcomes significantly.

Ranabahu and Tanima (2022) found in their study that microfinance services encourage women to start their businesses, but they can make exclusion and discrimination worse. Women's ability to obtain and use loans and engage in entrepreneurial activities are shaped by institutions at the individual, home, institutional, and community levels; this leads to economic empowerment in the end.

2.8. Micro Finance and Women Entrepreneurship

Akanmu et al. (2018) in their study evaluates the impact of cooperative microfinance on women's entrepreneurship in Kwara State, Nigeria, identifying entrepreneurial activities, contributions, and constraints faced by co-operators.

Microfinance institutions (MFIs) are crucial for low-income individuals and businesses, particularly women, who often face financial challenges. Shkodra et al. (2021) in their study c with 200 women entrepreneurs in Kosovo to understand the impact of MFI loans on the success of these businesses revealed a positive effect.

Thaher et al. (2021) in their study examines the impact of microfinance institutions' financial and non-financial services on women's entrepreneurship and empowerment in Jordan. Results showed that financial services, such as reducing interest and extending grace periods, are crucial for women entrepreneurs. Non-financial services include specialized courses, counselling, incentives, marketing support, and monitoring. These factors contribute to uplifting women entrepreneurs and eliminating gender inequality.

Tariq & Sangmi (2019) in their study investigated the role played by microfinance in promoting women's micro-entrepreneurship in Kashmir Valley. They found a positive impact of microfinance on women's micro-entrepreneurship. They also found age as a negative determinant of women's entrepreneurship. This highlights the need for further research on this topic.

Yousfani et al. (2019) examined the tendency of low growth of entrepreneurship in women who take a small loan from microfinance institutions and found that lower credit limits and lack of entrepreneurial training hamper the growth of women's entrepreneurship.

Abebe and Kenge (2023) found that the microfinance institutions' financial and non-financial services offered were unable to significantly empower disadvantaged and poor women by improving their livelihood and the development of their businesses. They also found that saving and the credit or loan services of the microfinance institution have the most decisive influence on women's entrepreneurship development.

The literature review highlights the crucial role of inclusive growth in ensuring social and economic justice, particularly in India. Various initiatives by the Indian government, such as Self-Help Groups (SHGs) and microfinance programs, have been instrumental in addressing financial exclusion and promoting development, especially among women. Further existing literature can be summarised as follows.

- **Existence of MFIs**: Microfinance institutions (MFIs) help the underprivileged by offering financial services that promote self-employment and reduce poverty. Research emphasizes the difficulties MFIs encounter, including mission drift (Minai et al., 2021) and the volatility brought on by depending too heavily on traditional finance (Zeb et al., 2021). The global influence of MFIs is demonstrated by technological improvements (Muneer, 2016) and multinational viewpoints (Bruton et al., 2011).

- **Impact on Poverty**: Studies conducted on microfinance institutions (MFIs) show to have a good impact on reducing poverty, especially for women. Studies conducted, for instance, in Nigeria (Addae, 2012) and Bangladesh (Khandker & Samad, 2013) demonstrate the long-term decline in poverty brought about by microfinance. However, there is variability in the short-term effects; in certain circumstances, Banerjee et al. (2021) report limited influence. Aspects of personal and social development are also very important (Nukpezah & Blankson, 2017).
- **Definition and Measurement**: Although economic power is frequently used to define empowerment, Fox & Romero (2017) propose more comprehensive metrics including social and psychological factors for consideration. Though disputes may occur within families, studies such as Alemu et al. (2018) emphasize the significance of SHGs in empowering women at the community level.
- **Empowerment through SHGs**: Mixed results are visible on the impact of SHGs truly empowering women (Swain & Wallentin, 2009).
- **Economic Opportunities**: There is a strong correlation between microfinance and increased economic prospects for women. While some studies—like Rehman et al. (2020)—examine the variables influencing microfinance-based empowerment, others (Nilakantan et al., 2013) show contradictory findings. According to Kato & Kratzer (2013), microfinance has influenced the participating members in contrast to non-participants.
- **Role of Credit**: Studies like Kuzilwa (2005) highlight the positive role of credit in improving entrepreneurial outcomes. However, gender gaps in entrepreneurship remain persistent (Vossenberg, 2013).
- **Challenges and Impacts**: A series of studies found that female entrepreneurs encounter distinct obstacles, especially in communities that uphold patriarchy. Studies by Nawaz (2018) and Abdullah & Quayes (2016) highlight the significance of socioeconomic and cultural factors, however, if such differences are to be considered, there is no apparent difference in the performance of male and female entrepreneurs (Henrekson & Johansson, 1999).
- **Support for Entrepreneurs**: An important factor in encouraging business is microfinance, especially for the underprivileged. (Ferdousi, 2015; Thakur, 2016) in their research demonstrates how microfinance can increase innovative ideas and entrepreneurial earnings. However, proper training and assistance are necessary for entrepreneurs to achieve such goals (Karlan & Valdivia, 2011).

- **Empowerment through Microfinance:** Research such as Akanmu et al. (2018) and Shkodra et al. (2021) demonstrate the beneficial effects of microfinance for women entrepreneurs, especially in developing nations. But there are still issues, especially with regard to resolving gender inequality and marginalization (Ranabahu & Tanima, 2022).

3. RESEARCH METHODOLOGY

Scopus database was used to fetch the data useful for the article. The search was done on September 26, 2024. Documents were searched with the following keywords namely a) microfinance institutions b) poverty reduction c) woman empowerment d) entrepreneurship e) woman entrepreneurship. Articles to date were considered. Finally, 200 documents were obtained. These documents were exported in CSV files.

Bibliometrics is a quantitative analysis method. VOS viewer is a bibliometric software, that introduces sample pieces of literature data into it and draws a knowledge map. It can present the overall external characteristics of subject areas and the software has a unique advantage, especially in clustering analysis.

3.1 Output of Publication

The number of publications related to keywords retrieved from the Scopus database was counted. As shown in Table 1, a total of 5 types of documents were found.

Table 1. Compiled by researcher

Rank	Type of Document	No of Documents	Percentage
1	Article	163	81.5
2	Book Chapter	16	8
3	Conference Paper	12	6
4	Review	8	4
5	Editorial	1	0.5
	Total	200	100

3.2 Co-Occurrence Analysis

To identify frequently occurring terms together in a given text corpus, a quantitative technique known as co-occurrence analysis was employed. This method is particularly helpful for understanding the relationships and connections among concepts within a certain topic. Based on the authors' chosen keywords related to the chapter, the bibliometric data of 200 articles were obtained from the Scopus database and cooccurrence analysis was performed using network visualization.

Minimum number of occurrences of keywords were set to 5. Out of 585 keywords, 25 keywords met the threshold. Out of these 25 keywords, a further 16 keywords were identified by the author matching to theme and subtheme of the paper. Based on these 16 keywords network visualization was applied in VOS Viewer. Based on the three components of the chapter title network visualization image was created as

3.2.1 Keyword: Micro Finance Network Visualization

Figure 1. Created by Author

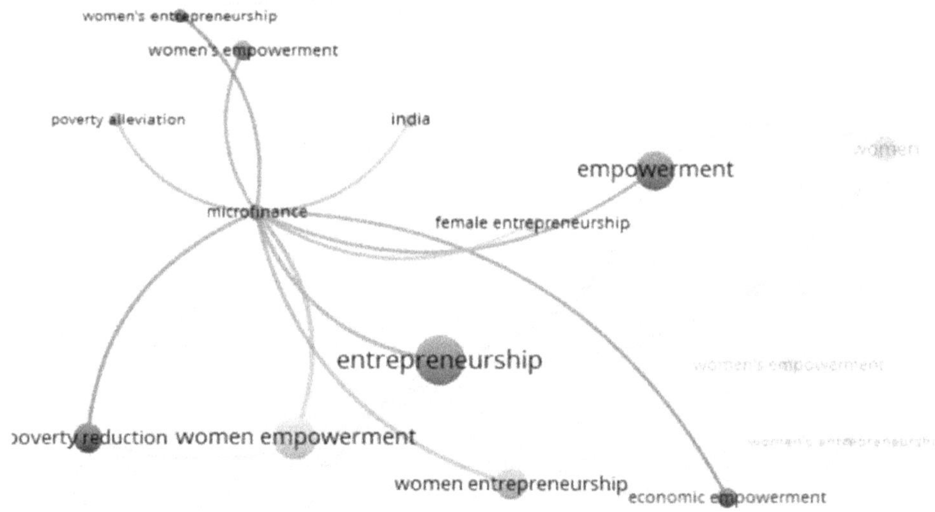

3.2.2 Keyword: Women Entrepreneurship Network Visualization

Figure 2. Created by Author

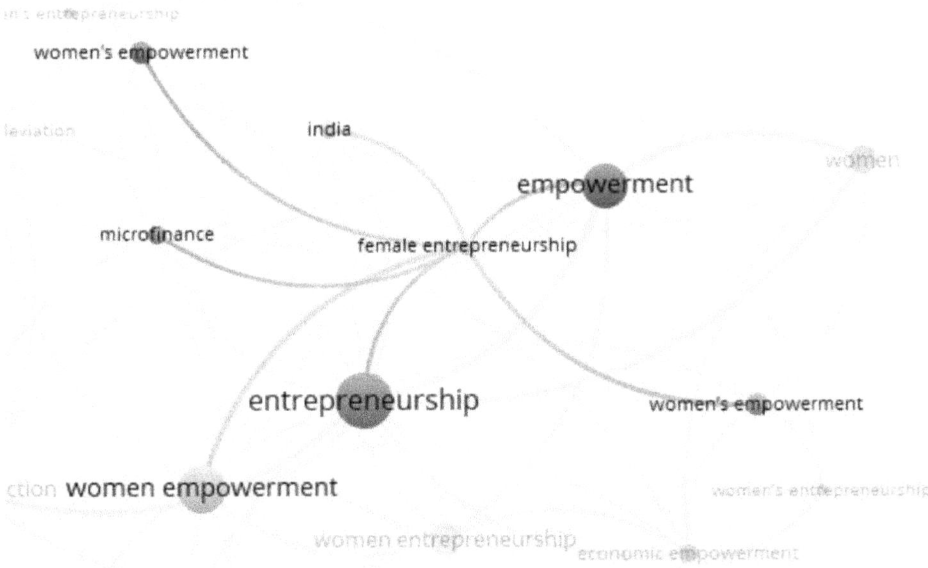

3.2.3 Keyword: India Network Visualization

Figure 3. Created by Author

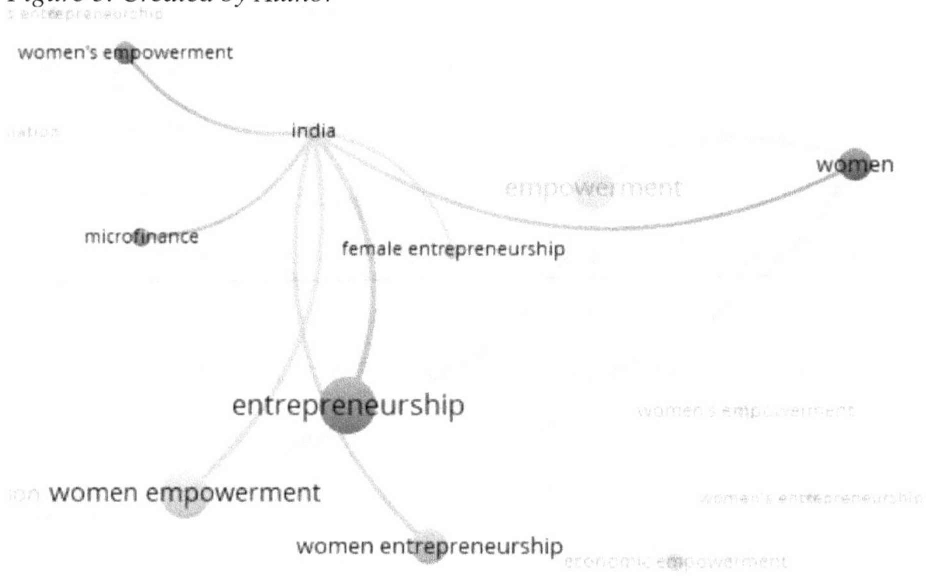

4. ANALYSIS, INTERPRETATION AND CONCLUSIONS

4.1 Analysis

4.1.1 Network Visualization Analysis of Keyword: Microfinance

1. **Central Position:** The network's central focus point of microfinance suggests that it is highly correlated with other keywords. This implies that it is an important theme in the research literature.
2. **Relationships to Women's Empowerment:** Microfinance is closely related to women's entrepreneurship, poverty alleviation, and women's empowerment. These links demonstrate how microfinance helps reduce poverty and empower women.
3. **Connection to India:** Given its association with India, microfinance is likely to be important for women's entrepreneurship and empowerment in this particular setting.

4. **Cluster Membership:** There is a strong correlation between the notions of poverty alleviation and female entrepreneurship, and microfinance looks to be a component of the same cluster.

4.1.2 Network Visualization Analysis of Keyword: Women Entrepreneurship

1. **Central Position:** The network's central focus point of female entrepreneurship suggests a strong correlation between it and other keywords. This makes women's entrepreneurship as an important theme in works of literature.
2. **Relationships to Women's Empowerment:** Links are visible between female entrepreneurship, economic empowerment, and women's empowerment. These linkages emphasize how female entrepreneurship empowers women and advances economic growth.
3. **Relation to India:** There is a direct connection between female entrepreneurship and India, indicating that the former is important for the latter's entrepreneurship and women's empowerment in this particular setting.
4. **Cluster Membership:** Microfinance and women's empowerment are closely associated and female entrepreneurship seems to be a part of the same cluster.

4.1.3 Network Visualization Analysis of Keyword: India

1. **Central Position:** The position of the keyword India in the network indicates that it has a high correlation with other keywords. This implies that it is an important theme in the research literature.
2. **Relationships to Women's Empowerment:** India is directly related to female entrepreneurship, poverty alleviation, and women's empowerment. These connections demonstrate India's significance for women's economic progress and empowerment.
3. **Cluster Membership:** Microfinance and women's empowerment appear to be closely related concepts in the Indian context.

4.2 Interpretation

4.2.1 Interpretation of Network Visualization Analysis of Keyword Microfinance

- **Empowerment Tool:** In underdeveloped nations like India, microfinance is a particularly effective instrument for empowering women. Microfinance gives women the access to small loans they need to launch their own companies, achieve financial independence, and enhance their standard of living.

- **Poverty Reduction:** Microfinance provides initial capital to poor women to start their small businesses, which in turn makes them financially stable by providing them a stable source of income leading to freedom from poverty by ending the cycle of poverty.
- **Women's Entrepreneurship:** Since microfinance gives women the financial resources they need to launch and expand their enterprises, the two are closely related. Development and economic prosperity may result from this.

4.2.2 Interpretation of Network Visualization Analysis of Keyword Women Entrepreneurship

- **Empowerment Weapon:** Women entrepreneurship is a potent weapon for empowering women by giving women the chance to become financially independent and enhance their standard of living.
- **Economic Development:** Entrepreneurship ventures, help generate revenue, jobs, and innovation, thus female entrepreneurship can have a major positive impact on the economy.
- **Social Change:** By challenging gender inequality and prejudices, female entrepreneurship can promote more gender equality and social changes.
- **Microfinance:** By providing access to financial resources and technical skills, microfinance plays a crucial role in promoting women's entrepreneurship.

4.2.3 Interpretation of Network Visualization Analysis of Keyword India

- **Contextual Framework:** India has distinct cultural, social, and economic elements that influence the experiences and difficulties that women in this nation encounter. This makes the researching women's entrepreneurship and empowerment particularly relevant in the context of India.
- **Implementation of Policies and Programs:** India has put in place several policies and initiatives to support women's entrepreneurship and empowerment. It's critical to comprehend the Indian environment to assess these projects' efficacy.
- **Opportunities and Problems:** In the context of women's entrepreneurship and empowerment, India has its own set of opportunities as well as problems. Addressing particular problems and capitalising on current advantages can make things go going.

4.3 Conclusion

Based on the analysis and interpretation of cooccurrence analysis using network visualization of the author's defined keyword related to the chapter title like microfinance institutions, women entrepreneurship and India highlights the interconnection of these keywords in the Indian context. Microfinance has been identified as one of the important tools for poverty reduction and women's empowerment. It facilitates the financial means required for initiating or expanding the business. This facilitation helps in fostering women's entrepreneurship ventures. Such initiatives lead to the reduction of gender inequality, increasing financial freedom and generating higher employment contributing towards economic development of the economy. The Indian example emphasizes how crucial it is to consider the social, cultural, and economic contexts that influence the chances and obstacles facing women's empowerment. India shows its dedication to supporting women's entrepreneurship and empowerment by putting policies and initiatives that focus on these areas into place, but there are still issues that need to be resolved. The interplay of these ideas' points to a dynamic framework where empowerment, entrepreneurship, and microfinance not only intersect but also support one another. This framework will pave the way for social change and sustainable development, especially for women in developing countries like India.

4.4 Research Trends and Gaps

- **Microfinance and Women's Empowerment:** The network diagram makes a strong case for the relationship between microfinance and women's entrepreneurship and emphasizes how crucial financial access is to the empowerment of women. This is probably a major area of study interest.
- **Using India as an Example:** India is one of the fastest growing economies in the world and its large population living below the poverty line makes it an ideal place for microfinance operations. The government-initiated Jan Dhan Yojana the largest initiative of financial inclusion and other women empowerment initiatives for women entrepreneurship has attracted researchers for India-specific studies and it has led to a large number of studies in the Indian context.
- **Possible Vulnerabilities:** Although several important subjects are covered, including microfinance, women's empowerment, and particular national settings like India, the relative lack of words about technology or innovation raises the possibility that these fields are not sufficiently studied about female entrepreneurship.

4.5 Implications for Future Research

- **Literature:** Since most of the literatures are centred on economic empowerment, social and political empowerment are yet to be explored in detail. These aspects required further studies to find the connection with entrepreneurship.
- **Comparative Analysis of Regions:** India's prominence indicates a major emphasis on this region. Future research could examine the similarities and variations in worldwide trends of female entrepreneurship by comparing various regional contexts.
- **Integration of Technology with Female Entrepreneurship:** In the era of digitization and fintech evolution, the technological aspect of microfinance and its impact on women entrepreneurship requires further study.

REFERENCES

Abdullah, S., & Quayes, S. (2016). Do women borrowers augment financial performance of MFIs? *Applied Economics*, 48(57), 5593–5604. DOI: 10.1080/00036846.2016.1181831

Abebe, A., & Kegne, M. (2023). The role of microfinance institutions on women's entrepreneurship development. *Journal of Innovation and Entrepreneurship*, 12(1), 17. DOI: 10.1186/s13731-023-00285-0 PMID: 36968150

About Bharat financial inclusion limited. (n.d.). Bharat Financial Inclusion Limited I. https://www.bfil.co.in/about-us.php

Addae-Korankye, A. (2012). Microfinance: A tool for poverty reduction in developing countries. *The Journal of Business and Retail Management Research*, 7(1), 138–149.

Administrator. (n.d.). *Our vision & mission*. https://joomlakave.com. https://www.janabank.com/about-us/who-we-are/our-vision-mission//

Akanmu, P. M., Clement, J. O., & Samaila, M. (2018). Impact of cooperative Microfinance on the performance of women entrepreneurship in Kwara state Nigeria. *Financial Markets. Institutions and Risks*, 2(4), 20–28. DOI: 10.21272/fmir.2(4).20-28.2018

Alemu, S. H., Van Kempen, L., & Ruben, R. (2018). Women empowerment through self-help groups: The bittersweet fruits of collective Apple cultivation in Highland Ethiopia. *Journal of Human Development and Capabilities*, 19(3), 308–330. DOI: 10.1080/19452829.2018.1454407

Aram Mkhitaryan, A. M. (2022). Mission drift between the balance of social mission vs. financial performance of microfinance institutions. *Issue 3, 33*(3), 211-231. https://doi.org/DOI: 10.1080/19452829.2018.1454407

Armendáriz, B. (2010). *The economics of microfinance*. MIT press.

Banerjee, A., Breza, E., Duflo, E., & Kinnan, C. (2019). Can microfinance unlock a poverty trap for some entrepreneurs? (No. w26346). National Bureau of Economic Research. DOI: 10.3386/w26346

Banerjee, A., Karlan, D., & Zinman, J. (2015). Six randomized evaluations of Microcredit: Introduction and further steps. *American Economic Journal. Applied Economics*, 7(1), 1–21. DOI: 10.1257/app.20140287

Brush, C. G., & Cooper, S. Y. (2012). Female entrepreneurship and economic development: An international perspective. *Entrepreneurship and Regional Development*, 24(1-2), 1–6. DOI: 10.1080/08985626.2012.637340

Bruton, G. D., Khavul, S., & Chavez, H. (2011). Microlending in emerging economies: Building a new line of inquiry from the ground up. *Journal of International Business Studies*, 42(5), 718–739. DOI: 10.1057/jibs.2010.58

Building a better life - About us | Ujjivan small finance bank. (n.d.). Ujjivan Small Finance Bank. https://www.ujjivansfb.in/about-us

Chliova, M., Brinckmann, J., & Rosenbusch, N. (2015). Is microcredit a blessing for the poor? A meta-analysis examining development outcomes and contextual considerations. *Journal of Business Venturing*, 30(3), 467–487. DOI: 10.1016/j.jbusvent.2014.10.003

Citaristi, I. (2022). African Development Bank—AfDB. In *The Europa Directory of International*

Cull, R., & Morduch, J. (2018). Microfinance and economic development. *Handbook of Finance and Development*, 550-572. https://doi.org/DOI: 10.4337/9781785360510.00030

Dhar, P. (2016). Microfinance penetration in India: A state wise analysis. *International Journal of Interdisciplinary Research in science society and culture, 2*(2), 86-96. DOI: 10.1257/app.5.1.163

Dupas, P., & Robinson, J. (2013). Savings constraints and Microenterprise development: Evidence from a Field experiment in Kenya. *American Economic Journal. Applied Economics*, 5(1), 163–192. DOI: 10.1257/app.5.1.163

Ekpe, I. (2011). Women entrepreneurs and economic development in Nigeria: Characteristics for success. *International Journal of Business and Social Science*, 2(1).

Emokpae, P. O. (2021). An Exploratory Study of How and Why Some Micro-Finance Banks Overcome Adversity and Why Others Do Not. DOI: 10.1257/app.5.1.163

Ferdousi, F. (2015). Impact of microfinance on sustainable entrepreneurship development. *Development Studies Research*, 2(1), 51–63. DOI: 10.1080/21665095.2015.1058718

Field, E., Pande, R., Papp, J., & Rigol, N. (2013). Does the classic microfinance model discourage entrepreneurship among the poor? Experimental evidence from India. *The American Economic Review*, 103(6), 2196–2226. DOI: 10.1257/aer.103.6.2196

Fox, L., & Romero, C. (2017). In the mind, the household, or the market? Concepts and measurement of women's economic empowerment. *Policy Research Working Papers*. https://doi.org/DOI: 10.1596/1813-9450-8079

Haile, H. B., Bock, B., & Folmer, H. (2012, July). Microfinance and female empowerment: Do institutions matter? [). Pergamon.]. *Women's Studies International Forum*, 35(4), 256–265. DOI: 10.1016/j.wsif.2012.04.001

Henrekson, M., & Johansson, D. (1999)... *Small Business Economics*, 12(1), 11–23. DOI: 10.1023/A:1008002330051

Hermes, N., & Lensink, R. (2008). Does financial liberalization influence saving, investment and economic growth? Evidence from 25 emerging market economies, 1973–96. *Financial Development, Institutions, Growth and Poverty Reduction*, 164-189. https://doi.org/DOI: 10.1023/A:1008002330051

HR. U., & KN, R. (2013). The role of SHGS in financial inclusion. A case study. *International Journal of Scientific and Research Publications, 3*(6).

Jack, W., Kremer, M., De Laat, J., & Suri, T. (2016). *Borrowing requirements, credit access, and adverse selection: Evidence from kenya* (No. w22686). National Bureau of Economic Research.

Kabeer, N. (2005). Is microfinance a'magic bullet' for women's empowerment? Analysis of findings from South Asia. *Economic and Political Weekly*, •••, 4709–4718.

Karlan, D., & Valdivia, M. (2011). Teaching entrepreneurship: Impact of business training on Microfinance clients and institutions. *The Review of Economics and Statistics*, 93(2), 510–527. DOI: 10.1162/REST_a_00074

Kato, M. P., & Kratzer, J. (2013). Empowering women through microfinance: Evidence from TanzaniaDOI: 10.1023/A:1008002330051

Khandker, S. R., & Samad, H. A. (2013). Are Microcredit participants in Bangladesh trapped in poverty and debt? *Policy Research Working Papers*. https://doi.org/DOI: 10.1596/1813-9450-6404

Kuzilwa, J. A. (2005). The role of credit for small business success. *The Journal of Entrepreneurship*, 14(2), 131–161. DOI: 10.1177/097135570501400204

Laha, A., & Kuri, P. K. (2014). Measuring the impact of Microfinance on women empowerment: A cross country analysis with special reference to India. *International Journal of Public Administration*, 37(7), 397–408. DOI: 10.1080/01900692.2013.858354

Ledgerwood, J., & Gibson, A. (2013). The evolving financial landscape. *The New Microfinance Handbook*, 15-48. https://doi.org/DOI: 10.1023/A:1008002330051

Llanto, G. M. (2007). Overcoming obstacles to agricultural microfinance: Looking at broader issues. *Asian Journal of Agriculture and Development*, 4(2), 23–40. DOI: 10.37801/ajad2007.4.2.2

Microfinance in the United States, 19. DOI: 10.37801/ajad2007.4.2.2

Morduch, J. (2002). MARK SCHREINER AND JONATHAN MORDUCH. *Replicating*DOI: 10.37801/ajad2007.4.2.2

Muneer Babu, M.Muneer Babu M. (2016). Macroeconomic determinants of technological change in Indian Microfinance institutions. *Global Business Review*, 17(5), 1179–1195. DOI: 10.1177/0972150916656685

NABARD. (2023). *Status of Microfinance in India 2022-23*. National Bank for Agriculture and Rural Development.

Nandera, S. (2016). Building women's economic empowerment. *International Trade Forum*, 2016(1), 20–21. DOI: 10.18356/ce9df046-en

Nawaz, A. (2018). Challenges faced by women entrepreneurs in Pakistan: A qualitative study. *Management and Organizational Studies*, 5(2), 13. DOI: 10.5430/mos.v5n2p13

Nilakantan, R. A. H. U. L., Datta, S. C., Sinha, P., & Datta, S. K. (2013). The impact of microfinance on women empowerment: Evidence from Eastern India. *International Journal of Development and Conflict*, 3(1), 27–40.

Nukpezah, J. A., & Blankson, C. (2017). Microfinance intervention in poverty reduction: A study of women farmer-entrepreneurs in rural Ghana. *Journal of African Business*, 18(4), 457–475. DOI: 10.1080/15228916.2017.1336915

Organizations. (2022). (pp. 417–423). Routledge.

Our philosophy | Bandhan bank. (n.d.). Bandhan Bank |. https://bandhanbank.com/our-philosophy

Poddar, K. K. (2015). Microfinance and self help groups. *Anusandhanika*, 7(1), 174.

Ranabahu, N., & Tanima, F. A. (2022). Empowering vulnerable microfinance women through entrepreneurship: Opportunities, challenges and the way forward. *International Journal of Gender and Entrepreneurship*, 14(2), 145–166. DOI: 10.1108/IJGE-01-2021-0020

RBI. (2022). *Report on Trends and Progress of Banking in India 2021-22*. Reserve Bank of India.

Rehman, H., Moazzam, D. A., & Ansari, N. (2020). Role of microfinance institutions in women empowerment: A case study of Akhuwat, Pakistan. *South Asian Studies*, 30(1).

Robinson, M. S. (2001). *The microfinance revolution: Lessons from Indonesia* (Vol. 2). World Bank Publications. DOI: 10.1596/0-8213-4524-9

Rosenberg, R. (2010). *Does microcredit really help poor people*. DOI: 10.37801/ajad2007.4.2.2

Sane, R., & Thomas, S. (2020). The Way Forward for Microfinance Institutions in India. *Economic and Political Weekly*, 55(36), 40–48.

Sarumathi, S., & Mohan, K. (2011). Role of Micro Finance in Women's Empowerment (An Empirical study in Pondicherry region rural SHG's). *Journal of Management and Science*, 1(1), 1–8.

Shkodra, J., Ymeri, P., & Ibishi, L. (2021). Role of microfinance institutions for developing women entrepreneurship – the case study of Kosovo. *Economics & Sociology (Ternopil)*, 14(1), 120–129. DOI: 10.14254/2071-789X.2021/14-1/8

Sinha, M., Mahapatra, S. S., Dutta, A., & Sengupta, P. P. (2023). Microfinance and women empowerment: An empirical analysis. In *Research anthology on microfinance services and roles in social progress* (pp. 1–13). IGI Global.

Swain, R. B., & Wallentin, F. Y. (2009). Does microfinance empower women? Evidence from self-help groups in India. *International Review of Applied Economics*, 23(5), 541–556. DOI: 10.1080/02692170903007540

Tariq, S., & Sangmi, M. (2019). Impact of Microfinance on women entrepreneurship. *Oman Chapter of Arabian Journal of Business and Management Review*, 8(1), 7–16. DOI: 10.12816/0052847

Thaher, L. M., & Radieah, N. M., & WAN NORHANIZA, W. H. (2021). The effect of microfinance services on women entrepreneurship: A case study in Jordan. *The Journal of Asian Finance, Economics and Business*, 8(5), 807–815.

Thakur, S. (2016). Microfinance through self helps groups (SHGs): A key driver for sustainable growth in India. *IOSR Journal of Business and Management*, 18(2), 1–6.

Tripathi, V., & Tripathi, V. (2014). Recent development of Microfinance in India. SSRN *Electronic Journal*. https://doi.org/DOI: 10.2139/ssrn.2462251

Vossenberg, S. (2013). Women Entrepreneurship Promotion in Developing Countries: What explains the gender gap in entrepreneurship and how to close it. *Maastricht School of Management Working Paper Series, 8*(1), 1-27.

Yousfani, K., Aslam, Y., Mahar, Q., & Kazi, H. (2019). The impact of microfinance on growth of women entrepreneurship in Pakistan. *Journal of Entrepreneurship. Business Economics (Cleveland, Ohio)*, 7(1), 133–152.

Zeb, N., Jalal, R. N. U. D., Fayyaz, U. E., & Zaheer, M. A. (2021). Micro finance and economic development: The role of microfinance institutions outreach in Pakistan. *The Journal of Asian Finance, Economics and Business*, 8(5), 117–126.

Chapter 3
The Multifaceted Role of MFIs in Fostering Financial Inclusion in India

Sunil Kumar
https://orcid.org/0000-0002-2362-1972
Shoolini University, India

Vijay Kumar
https://orcid.org/0000-0002-6532-0430
Shoolini University, India

ABSTRACT

This chapter investigates the pivotal role of Microfinance Institutions (MFIs) in advancing financial inclusion in India, focusing on their impact on poverty alleviation, entrepreneurship, and social development. It highlights how MFIs extend beyond traditional banking through innovative approaches, technology, and partnerships, providing financial services to the unbanked and underserved. The study examines the challenges and opportunities faced by MFIs and underscores their significance in fostering economic empowerment and inclusive growth. By providing microloans, savings accounts, and financial literacy programs, MFIs help stimulate local markets, create employment, and contribute to poverty reduction, emphasizing the need for comprehensive strategies to enhance financial inclusion in developing economies.

DOI: 10.4018/979-8-3693-6622-6.ch003

INTRODUCTION

Microfinance Institutions (MFIs) are crucial for promoting financial inclusion and literacy in India, providing services to the unbanked and underserved. This research examines the diverse roles of MFIs in extending beyond traditional banking through innovative approaches, technology, and partnerships. It explores their impact on poverty alleviation, entrepreneurship, and social development, highlighting challenges and opportunities. The study aims to inform policymakers and stakeholders about the significance of comprehensive strategies in advancing financial inclusion in India.

The financial landscape of developing economies like India is characterized by a significant underbanked population. This segment, often comprising low-income households and microentrepreneurs, faces significant hurdles in accessing formal financial services. This lack of financial inclusion not only hinders individual economic empowerment but also acts as a roadblock to broader national development goals. In recent decades, Microfinance Institutions (MFIs) have emerged as a powerful tool to bridge this gap, offering financial products and services tailored to meet the specific needs of these underserved communities.

MFIs play a critical role in promoting financial inclusion by providing essential financial services such as microloans, savings accounts, and remittance facilities to those traditionally excluded from the formal financial system. These microloans empower individuals to launch or expand small businesses, invest in education and healthcare, and build resilience against financial shocks. The resulting economic activity stimulates local markets, creates employment opportunities, and contributes to poverty alleviation.

However, the impact of MFIs extends beyond mere financial inclusion. By fostering financial literacy and entrepreneurial skills development, MFIs empower individuals to take control of their financial destinies and contribute meaningfully to the socio-economic fabric of their communities. This transformative potential of MFIs underscores the need for a comprehensive understanding of their role in the Indian context. This research aspires to contribute to the ongoing dialogue on leveraging MFIs as a powerful tool for inclusive growth and poverty reduction in developing economies.

MICRO FINANCE

Microfinance stands out as a crucial tool in the global fight against urban poverty, as highlighted by Sharma et al. (2023). Their research underscores its evolution from recognizing the borrowing potential of the poor to becoming a pivotal force for inclusive economic growth. Despite ongoing debates over its commercialization, with some advocating profit-sharing models to benefit the impoverished, Nobel laureate Mohammad Yunus opposes profiting from microfinance, advocating instead for models prioritizing direct service to the poor (Banerjee et al., 2015). Singh and Yadav (2012) emphasize the essential role of microfinance institutions (MFIs) in advancing financial inclusion through services like microcredit, savings accounts, and microinsurance. They highlight how MFIs enhance financial literacy and leverage technology to effectively reach marginalized populations, empowering women (Kumar and Subedi, 2023), stimulating entrepreneurship, and contributing significantly to economic development.

In India, Chaturvedi (2022) discusses the critical contribution of Small Finance Banks (SFBs) to rural financial inclusion, despite challenges like slowing asset growth. SFBs play a pivotal role in meeting the credit needs of rural communities, thereby enhancing access to banking services and fostering socio-economic upliftment. Adnan and Kumar (2021) reinforce these benefits, highlighting how MFIs promote economic development and financial inclusion through tailored services and support for entrepreneurship, while advocating strongly for gender equality in policy and practice (Kabeer, 2001). Quinones and Remenyi (2014) examine the positive outcomes of robust microfinance sectors across Asia, linking them to improved socio-economic indicators and advocating for policies that support inclusive development in the region. Collectively, these studies underscore the transformative impact of microfinance and related institutions in empowering individuals, reducing poverty, and promoting inclusive economic growth globally and locally (Gomathy, 2015; Nagaraja & Kusugal, 2013; Lopez & Winkler, 2018; Rasel & Win, 2020).

Microfinance Institutions in India

Table 1. Market share of credit lenders for microfinance industry in India from December 2020 to September 2023, by lender type (in %age)

Year	Banks	Non-banking financial companies-Micro financial institutions (NBFC-MFIs)	Small finance banks (SFBs)	Non-banking financial companies (NBFCs)	Not for Profit MFIs
December 2020	42	32	17	8	1
September 2021	41	35	16	7	1
September 2022	36	38	17	8	1
September 2023	30	41	19	9	1

Source: Statista.com

As of September 2023, NBFC-microfinance institutions commanded a significant 41% market share in India's microfinance sector, exceeding banks which held 30%. This represents a shift since 2020, with NBFCs increasing their market dominance while banks have seen a decline in their share. The outstanding portfolio of microfinance loans in India rose to approximately 3.55 trillion in the fiscal year 2023, continuing its upward trajectory from previous years (CRIF High Mark, 2024).

By the end of the financial year 2023, investment and credit companies (ICCs) alongside infrastructure finance companies (IFCs) accounted for 96.1% of the total credit extended by NBFCs. There was a noticeable increase in the share held by IFCs and NBFC-MFIs, resulting in a decline in the ICCs' share, as reported by the Reserve Bank of India (2024). Delinquency rates in the microfinance sector as of March 31, 2023, indicated that bank loans had the highest rate of 1.47% for loans overdue by 90 days or more, while loans provided by NBFCs recorded the lowest delinquency rate at 0.44% (SIDBI, 2023).

Microfinance institutions (MFIs) in India are pivotal in addressing the financial inclusion challenges faced by women in rural areas, who often lack access to traditional banking services due to stringent eligibility criteria. MFIs, leveraging initiatives like the SHG-Bank Linkage Programme facilitated by NABARD, have successfully connected millions of households to formal banking, with a notable focus on women-led Self-Help Groups (SHGs). This targeted approach not only improves financial access but also empowers women economically by providing microloans tailored to their needs, which are predominantly used for enhancing household welfare and investing in small businesses and education. Such initiatives underscore MFIs' role in fostering economic stability and community development by promoting local infrastructure investment and stimulating economic activity at the grassroots level.

Furthermore, MFIs contribute significantly to financial system integration in India by expanding access to savings mechanisms, credit, and insurance products among marginalized populations. This integration is crucial for enhancing financial resilience and reducing poverty, as evidenced by higher repayment rates among female borrowers and increased adoption of micro-insurance products. Despite challenges like limited awareness and affordability, MFIs continue to innovate and expand their reach, aiming to improve financial security and promote inclusive growth. As they navigate these challenges, MFIs hold promise in further empowering women and integrating marginalized communities into India's evolving financial landscape.

Financial Inclusion: Meaning and Status

Financial inclusion aims to provide financial support to a significant number of people who are excluded from opportunities and services offered by institutional players (such as commercial banks, cooperative banks, and regional rural banks). According to the Planning Commission (2009), financial inclusion is defined as universal access to a broad range of financial services at a fair cost. This includes not only banking products but also other financial services such as insurance and equity products.

In a country like India, where the trend is towards globalization, liberalization, and a competitive market, according to Census 2011 up to 69.87 percent of the population still lives in rural areas. Our banking and financial markets have undergone significant modifications in recent decades due to this approach. Many reforms have been implemented to alleviate poverty, but our banking and financial sectors remain underdeveloped, making it challenging to provide financial services to rural people at a reasonable cost. It is not enough to simply open a bank account; it is also necessary to ensure that these vulnerable populations learn how to make the most of these financial services, which is only achievable if rural people are financially literate. According to the global forum AFI, almost 70% of the world's population is unbanked. Financial inclusion is defined as "the process of mainstream institutional entities providing relevant financial products and services to vulnerable groups such as weaker sections and low-income groups at an accessible cost in a fair and transparent manner" (Hannig & Jansen, 2010).

In the Indian context, the term "financial inclusion" was first used in April 2005 in the Annual Policy Statement presented by the then-Governor of the Reserve Bank of India. Later, this concept gained ground and came to be widely used in India and abroad. According to the Rangarajan Committee (2008) "financial inclusion may be defined as the process of ensuring access to financial services and timely and adequate credit where needed by vulnerable and disadvantaged groups such as weaker sections and low-income groups at an affordable cost."

It is the process of providing facilities and access to those segments of the population that are denied these facilities, enabling them to become part of the formal financial system, either as individuals or groups. The easiest way to ensure better financial inclusion is to open more branches of banks and financial institutions and remove various obstacles in accessing financial services from banks by very poor people (Karmakar, Banerjee, and Monapatra, 2011).

In India, in an attempt to improve access to financial services or financial inclusion, the Reserve Bank of India (RBI) promulgated a drive for financial inclusion, where banks take the lead in providing all 'unbanked' households in a district with savings accounts (Ramji, 2009). It is the process of ensuring access to appropriate financial products and services needed by all members of society, particularly vulnerable and disadvantaged groups, at an affordable cost in a fair and transparent manner by mainstream institutional players (Bora, 2020).

A strong regulatory mechanism, inherent strength in the economy, and progressive policy framework support, nurture, and help grow financial institutions. There has been significant growth in profits in our banking industry over the last two decades. The banking sector index has grown at a compounded annual rate of 51% since 2001 (Anjum and Rajeshwari, 2012). Therefore, financial inclusion is gaining importance among national policymakers, multilateral organizations, and others in the development field.

As inclusive growth is gaining trust globally as a sustainable growth and development strategy, financial inclusion is a topic of contemporary significance and relevance. Although the financial sector has made commendable progress in recent years, there are concerns that banks have not been able to include major segments of the population, especially underprivileged and vulnerable sections of society, in basic banking services. Therefore, in almost all developing countries, financial services are accessed by only a minority of the population. Such limited and minimal use of financial products and services in developing countries has become an international policy concern, leading to the adoption of the goal of building inclusive financial systems. The United Nations designated 2005 as the International Year of Microcredit, giving a required boost to financial inclusion and financial services on the global platform (Sarkar and Phatowali, 2012). However, many regions remain underbanked, and a sizable population is outside the reach of formal financial services. An important indicator of financial services and financial inclusion, the number of accounts held as a ratio to the adult population, was only 74.73% in India as of March 31, 2010, which is low compared to developed countries. For example, the same ratio is 202.10% in the USA, 292.32% in the UK, 106.53% in Brazil, and as high as 717.24% in Japan Consultative Group to Assist the Poor (CGAP), Financial Access 2009). As per the Reserve Bank of India (RBI), the central bank of the country, 66.9% of the country's population had bank accounts as of March 31, 2011.

The Average Annual Growth Rate (AAGR) of various financial inclusion indicators during the 21-year period between 1991-2011 shows that both per capita deposit and credit have grown at a very high rate against the marginal growth in the number of bank branches per million populations as well as the number of deposit and credit accounts per thousand populations. This again indicates the concentration of financial services among a few and in limited geographical areas (Sarkar and Phatowali, 2012). To increase the penetration of banking services in India and ensure that all households have at least one bank account, a National Mission on Financial Inclusion named Pradhan Mantri Jan Dhan Yojana was announced by the Prime Minister in his Independence Day speech on 15th August 2014, and the scheme was formally launched on 28th August 2014. Within a fortnight of its launch, the scheme entered the Guinness Book of Records for opening a record number of bank accounts. Significant progress was made by opening 29.48 crore accounts by mid-August 2017, out of which 17.61 crore accounts were in rural/semi-urban areas.

To further strengthen financial inclusion in the country, the government has advised banks to deploy Micro ATMs in rural areas. Consequently, 1,14,518 micro-ATMs have been deployed by December 2016. To explore innovative and participatory approaches to financial literacy, a block-level project was initiated in 2017 by the Reserve Bank across 80 blocks in 9 states. The project is being implemented by 6 NGOs in association with 10 sponsor banks.

Dimensions of Financial Inclusion

The level of financial inclusion is measured theoretically based on four basic elements of an inclusive financial system: banking services penetration/access, availability, usage, and quality (Amidžic, Massara, & Mialou, 2014; Sarma, 2016).

Banking Penetration: This is calculated as the number of bank branches per 100,000 people. It refers to the penetration of commercial bank branches and ATMs in rural areas to provide the most formal financial services possible. It shows the percentage of the population with a bank account. The number of bank accounts as a percentage of the adult population is a key indicator for this dimension (Sarma, 2010).

Availability of Banking Services: This dimension can be measured by counting the number of bank offices, bank branches, and ATMs (per 1,000 people), including their workers. In addition, internet/electronic mode services can be added to this dimension (Sarma, 2010; Sarma & Paris, 2011).

Usage of the Banking System: For an inclusive financial system, simply opening an account is insufficient; proper use of banking services must be ensured. This dimension encompasses two basic banking services: debit and credit cards. Credit and deposit penetration are distinct aspects.

1. **Credit Penetration:** This is evaluated based on the average of three characteristics: the number of loan accounts, the number of small borrowings by small borrowers in the form of loan accounts, and the number of agricultural advances, on a per 100,000 population.
2. **Deposit Penetration:** This is calculated as the number of savings deposit accounts per 100,000 people. These are important indicators for determining the extent to which the formal banking system is used (Amidzic, Massara & Mialou, 2014; Singh & Hietala, 2014).

Quality Dimension: This dimension assesses the scope of financial services available to meet consumer demands. The research found that the convenience and cost of transactions, as measured by the UNDP's methodology for computing the HDI in 2010, are crucial variables for a comprehensive view of financial inclusion. The ease of transactions refers to how simple or difficult it is for customers to obtain financial services, such as opening savings or checking accounts or taking out loans. The cost of transactions includes any monthly, quarterly, or annual fees or charges imposed on users for ATM cards or accounts, as well as any remittances or transfers (Gupte, Venkataramani & Gupta, 2012).

Objectives of Financial Inclusion

The primary goal of financial inclusion is to provide access to financial products and services to the unbanked masses and underbanked regions of a country without discrimination. For many years, only the higher and middle-income groups in society had access to formal credit, leaving the lower-income groups to rely on the informal and unorganized sectors to meet their credit demands. These poor individuals were often exploited by greedy moneylenders due to their lack of understanding of formal financial sources. In this context, financial inclusion enables disadvantaged members of society to develop saving and investing habits through the use of bank accounts and access to insurance, pension, and securities markets. This, in turn, helps them break the cycle of poverty.

Another significant facet of financial inclusion is the use of financial products and services. Individual financial inclusion causes a chain reaction that contributes to national prosperity. Thus, financial inclusion serves several aims, including meeting the needs of the nation's poor to unlock their growth potential, which eventually helps to exploit a nation's potential. The following are the primary goals of financial inclusion:

- **To Provide Financial Services at Economical Costs:** Financial inclusion aims to assist poor people in obtaining low-cost formal financial services and products such as deposits, cash transfer services, loans, insurance, and payment services.
- **To Create Financial Infrastructure:** Financial inclusion also aims to establish competent financial institutions to fulfill the financial demands of disadvantaged people. It intends to decentralize financial infrastructure to economically backward and unbanked communities.
- **To Contribute to Financial Sustainability:** Building and maintaining financial sustainability at the individual and societal levels is one of the goals of

financial inclusion. This will make it easier for the underprivileged to access finances and meet their demands on time.

- **To Promote Competition in the Financial Sector:** Financial inclusion aims to establish a network of financial institutions that provide financial aid to the masses at a fair cost. This will increase competition and provide customers with more options.
- **To Increase Financial Awareness:** Financial inclusion strives to impart information and awareness about various financial products and services, as well as to encourage sound financial management among the general public, to build formal and systematic credit opportunities for the poor.
- **To Promote Innovations in Financial Products and Services:** Financial inclusion also intends to develop innovative financial products and services tailored to the changing requirements of people, particularly the poor, for them to reap the greatest benefits.
- **To Provide Digital Financial Solutions:** Financial inclusion attempts to deliver digital financial solutions to the nation's economically disadvantaged population, particularly the younger generation, who rely heavily on smartphones and online portals.
- **To Promote Mobile Banking in Remote Locations:** Financial inclusion plans to introduce mobile banking services to reach the impoverished residing in exceedingly remote places. Mobile banking helps bring banking functions to people's fingertips.
- **To Provide Tailor-made Financial Solutions:** Another goal of financial inclusion is to provide people with tailored and customized financial solutions based on their circumstances, preferences, and financial needs.

A variety of government and non-government organizations are working in various ways to bring excluded people into the financial mainstream. These organizations primarily focus on providing disadvantaged people with access to various documents such as PAN cards, Aadhaar cards, election cards, and ration cards, which are required for accessing financial services. They are also running programs to encourage financial literacy by raising awareness and educating the public (Mani, 2016).

Financial Inclusion: Need and Importance

Globally, financial inclusion is regarded as a crucial indication of a society's development and well-being. It is a prerequisite for long-term equitable progress. In this context, financial inclusion is commonly seen in policy circles as a proactive strategy, and it is even regarded as a top priority by the majority of nations, including India.

Financial inclusion, as a crucial way of achieving long-term economic growth, ensures that every person of a country uses his or her income as a national financial resource for continued development in productive sectors of the country. Financial resources mobilized through these channels would aid in the development of industrial firms, hence accelerating the nation's economic advancement. This underlying theme has brought the concept of financial inclusion to the forefront and earned it a significant role in financial intermediation. Thus, financial inclusion attempts to liberate economically disadvantaged segments of society from numerous barriers that impede their access to financial services in order to make them financially independent without relying on charity or other non-sustainable sources of cash. This can be accomplished if all financial institutions, including banks, insurance firms, mutual fund companies, and others, adopt and execute inclusive financial practises. In this respect, the concept of financial inclusion is more essential from a rural standpoint, as there is a strong presence of financial institutions in many nations' metropolitan districts. Thus, financial inclusion is primarily regarded from a rural standpoint, as well as from the standpoint of socially and economically oppressed and excluded masses. In this context, financial inclusion refers to the availability of basic banking services such as deposit receipt, cash payment, balance inquiry, account statement, and other similar services to excluded populations on demand and without discrimination. Financial inclusion provides numerous benefits to the public as shown below:

- **Self-Employment:** The easy availability of transparent loans from the official banking sector enables rural people to launch their own businesses or engage in productive activities. This will contribute to the growth and development of rural communities (Akingunola et al., 2013).
- **Direct Transfer:** The direct transfer of money to a bank account will facilitate receipt and payment. This will also reduce the circulation of cash in the economy while increasing the use of bank money for transactions (Badran, 2009).
- **Savings Habit:** Financial inclusion may aid in the promotion of saving habits among the poor (Ouma et al., 2017). This may enable individuals to obtain various financial services such as insurance, loan facilities, online money transfers, and so on.
- **Step Towards Cashless Economy:** The expansion of the banking network and the instillation of banking habits among the rural population will encourage a cashless economy and the free flow of money in the financial ecosys-

tem and even demonetization promoted the same idea of cashless economy (Memdani, 2020).

- **Promotion of the Use of Savings Products:** Financial inclusion has a spread effect, which encourages the usage of various savings products such as recurring deposits fixed deposits, insurance plans and so on.
- **Reduction in Cost of Capital:** An inclusive financial system promotes the efficient deployment of financial and productive resources, potentially lowering the cost of capital (Jacobs and Mazzucato, 2016).
- **Payment of Utilities:** Access to relevant financial services can greatly enhance day-to-day financial management, such as payment of utility bills such as water bills, electricity bills, telephone bills, and so on.
- **Transfer of Money:** The extension of the financial inclusion spectrum allows for the easy and secure transfer of money from one location to another by cheque, demand draft cheque, internet, and mobile banking.
- **Passport to Other Financial Services:** A bank account also serves as a gateway to a variety of other financial products and services, such as short-term credit, overdraft facilities, and credit cards.
- **Access to Social Security Measures:** Furthermore, access to a bank account is required for a number of social security measures, such as insurance and pension products.
- **Helps to Reduce Poverty:** To combat poverty, it is vital to connect each individual to formal banking services in order to provide loans to micro and small entrepreneurs in order to assist them start their own businesses and eliminate poverty.
- **Increase in National Income:** By providing loans to micro and small businesses, business opportunities are generated, which may contribute to the GDP and raise national income.
- **Simplicity of Transactions:** Inclusive finance will aid in the simplification and facilitation of banking transactions, allowing people to use banking services without hesitation, and access to formal banking services will improve.

Role of Various Stakeholders in Financial Inclusion

The Indian government has taken a multi-level approach to financial inclusion, with a variety of agencies working at various levels to achieve financial inclusion goals. The table 2 below summarises the major stakeholders involved in financial inclusion and their respective roles.

Table 2. Stakeholders and their role in MFI.

S. No.	Stakeholder	Role
1.	Department of Financial Services	• Acting as a central advisory board to guide other stakeholders. • Planning and proposing the various schemes of financial inclusion.
2.	Reserve Bank of India (RBI)	• Acting as a nodal agency for financial inclusion. • Providing support to banks and financial institutions in promoting financial literacy. • Aligning operational course of banks for financial inclusion with the mission mode.
3.	NABARD	• Allocating funds to SHGs/joint liability groups for promoting financial literacy. • Monitoring the progress of financial inclusion programmes by stakeholders.
4.	Banks	• Providing easy access to banking facilities to the beneficiaries. • Setting up credit counselling and financial • literacy centers.
5.	NPCI	• Providing technological support for making USSD based mobile banking a reality. • Support to the banks for providing proper operations of RuPay cards.
6.	State Government	• Monitoring Financial Literacy Campaigns in Committee and all stakeholders within the state.
7.	Local bodies	• Assisting in implementing financial inclusion by organizing camps for opening bank accounts, driving financial literacy campaigns and educating the accountholders.

Source: Compiled by Author(s)

Factors Affecting Access to Financial Services

Poor people's access to financial services is a prerequisite for eliminating poverty and achieving a nation's long-term economic development. The level of financial inclusion in a country is determined by a number of factors. For example, socioeconomic factors such as population composition, income level and distribution, and general level of literacy influence the process of financial inclusion, whereas banking variables such as branch expansion, credit and deposit penetration, transaction costs, and time taken to deliver these services influence the pace of financial inclusion (Chithra and Selvam, 2013). Let's take a closer look at a few of these variables:

- **Geographical Locations:** Private sector commercial banks, mostly, established their branches in cities and semi-urban locations where they can earn a substantial profit from their activities. The absence of brick-and-mortar bank branches in rural and remote locations prevents rural people from having access to a variety of banking products and services.

- **Growth of Urbanisation:** The process of urbanisation promotes the expansion of numerous infrastructural amenities in that location, which aids in the facilitation of entrepreneurship and industrial growth. A higher rate of urbanisation encourages greater growth in the financial sector, resulting in a higher rate of financial inclusion in that region.
- **Legal Identities and Gender Biasness:** Lack of legal identities, such as original birth certificates, Voters Id cards, Aadhar cards, Ration cards, passports, and so on, also impedes access to financial services, particularly among minorities, economic and political migrants, women, refugee workers, illiterate populations, rural masses, and so on.
- **Financial Literacy:** The lack of financial literacy on the part of illiterate and underprivileged sections of society regarding the availability of various banking products and services makes them vulnerable to having access to various financial services in terms of having a bank account, availing insurance services, investment services, loan requirements, and so on.
- **Structural Procedural Formalities:** Furthermore, the complications involved in completing different procedural formalities for opening an account, obtaining a loan, obtaining insurance services, maintaining savings and investments, and so on make the underprivileged segments remain excluded from gaining the advantage of financial products and services.
- **Level of Income and Bank Charges:** A person is considered to remain poor because he is poor. A person with limited resources has limited access to financial resources for carrying out economic activity. As a result, he tends to be excluded from the financial fabric of the economy. Furthermore, varied fees for financial services may deter poor individuals from using them.
- **Nature of Economic Activity:** Every bank and financial institution has its own set of rules for delivering financial services that primarily benefit large depositors and borrowers. As a result, new and small entrepreneurs, as well as people working in the informal sector, remain outside the financial fold of the economy's banking sector.

In his lecture at the Seventeenth C.D. Deshmukh Memorial Lecture on April 25, 2019, titled "Central Banking and Innovation: Partners in the Quest for Financial Inclusion," Agustín Carstens, General Manager of the Bank for International Settlements (BIS), identified key hurdles to financial inclusion in India (Carstens, 2019).

- **Lack of Trust:** A history of bank failures and financial illiteracy contribute to people's distrust in the financial system.
- **High Cost of Services:** Financial services are either unaffordable for users or considered unprofitable by providers.

- **Lack of Documentation:** Essential documents are required to open bank accounts, limiting access to financial services.

Carstens emphasized the importance of government and financial innovations in overcoming these obstacles.

Initiatives Taken for Financial Inclusion

Several initiatives have been made over time to ensure that formal financial services reach the last-mile clients. Continuous efforts have been undertaken to provide basic formal financial services to daily wage workers, monthly wage workers, seasonal workers, and self-employed individuals. Several policies have been initiated at the international, national, and state levels, as detailed below.

International Perspectives: Globally, financial sector reforms are regarded as a critical component of the international development agenda for policymakers and financial institutions seeking to increase financial inclusion. The United Nations declared 2005 "the year of microfinance." Muhammad Yunus, a Nobel laureate, was awarded the Nobel Peace Prize in 2006 for establishing microfinance and Grameen Bank. The International Monetary Fund (IMF) is likewise concerned about this issue. Along with the IMF, the International Finance Corporation (IFC) and the World Bank collaborated with the Consultative Group to Assist the Poor (CGAP) and the Alliance for Financial Inclusion (AFI) to host a G-20 conversation on financial inclusion for SMEs and households (Ardic, Heimann & Mylenko, 2011). The IMF's Financial Access Survey and the World Bank Global Findex Database 2014 denote supply-side and demand-side worldwide data, demonstrating that countries such as Brazil, Malaysia, and Mexico are heavily investing in financial inclusion indicators that must be collected, examined, and analyzed to improve financial inclusion. It is believed that over two billion people worldwide currently lack access to safe financial services. Access to finance is regarded as a vital tool for poverty alleviation. The credibility of the financial system has been strengthened in European countries to make it more accessible. New European financial institutions have been set up with this purpose in mind, working collaboratively with member states and possessing broad capabilities in the event of a crisis, including the participation of supervisory authorities, the European Banking Authority (EBA), and other agencies. The European Commission is enhancing the internal market to make it easier for families and businesses to access lower-cost financial services (Claessens, 2003).

At an early point, the Bank of Indonesia initiated financial inclusion programmes with the primary goal of educating individuals. The major goal is to improve people's financial habits and attitudes about banks. Through these programmes, the Indonesian central bank will be able to observe household financial behaviour. Banks can then develop lending programmes for the benefit of the poor based on these action plans (Gitaharie et al., 2014).

Indian Scenario: Throughout history, numerous initiatives have been made to expand the scope of financial services to unbanked areas. After independence, a strong emphasis has been placed on creating a formal financial system, particularly the formal banking industry. Since 1951-52, the Reserve Bank of India (RBI) has established the All-India Rural Survey Committee to expand formal financial services to the underprivileged and weaker sections of society, which has been supported by institutional credit to the rural economy through cooperatives and commercial banks. (Biswas and Saha, 2013). The term "financial inclusion" has gained popularity in India since the Reserve Bank of India addressed it in its Annual Policy Statement for 2005-06. The government of India and the Central Bank of India have been concerned about the lack of access to the formal banking system by the underprivileged and weaker sections of society. As a result, several attempts have been launched to extend financial services to rural areas, including the following measures such as:

- The Agricultural Refinance Corporation was established by an Act of Parliament in 1963 and began operations in July of that year. The fundamental purpose of the ARDC refinancing agency is to give financial help to promote agricultural development in India, as well as to reach out to backward and undeveloped areas in order to improve regional imbalances.
- According to the ordinance, 14 major commercial banks with deposits of Rs. 50 crore or more were nationalized in 1969. In 1980, the Government of India added six new banks with deposits of Rs. 200 crores or more (Agarwal, 2012).
- The National Credit Council held a conference in July 1968, at which it urged commercial banks to increase lending to priority sectors such as agriculture, small and marginal farmers, and micro businesses.
- Loaning to the underprivileged section of society at a reduced interest rate.
- The Lead Bank Scheme was established in 1969 to address the credit needs of the economy, particularly the poor, in each district and state of the country.
- It was felt in the early mid-1970s that commercial banks were not adapting to the rural environment in the form of rural banking since it involves significant costs and some cultural hurdles to dealing with rural people. So, at the same time cooperative institutions with origins in rural areas were mourning for sufficient resources to meet loan demand. Therefore, it was thought that no single design of financial entities could handle the diversity of physical, social, geographical, and economic characteristics for credit distribution. Thus, in order to improve the rural economy, RRBs (Regional Rural Banks) was es-

tablished in 1975 under the RRB Act 1976, with the goal of increasing credit to rural people.

- Formation of NABARD, development of a developmental inclusion policy to serve the poorest of the poor through advocacy through District Level Review Committee (DLRC)/District Consultative Committee (DCC) or State Level Review Committee conventions to extend the facility of opening savings bank accounts under financial inclusion to have the benefit of an overdraft facility.
- The SHG-Bank Linkage Programme began in 1989 as an Action Research Project sponsored by NABARD to provide financial assistance to the Mysore Resettlement and Development Agency (MYRADA) for the testing of Credit Management Groups. Based on the early efforts of this Programme, the RBI led the approval of a pilot project in 1992, which was created as a partnership model between three institutions, namely banks, NGOs, and SHGs. The SHGs are concerned with two major dimensions. The first is to reduce poverty, and the second is to empower the poor and women (Suneetha and Ramanamma, 2018).
- In 2005, the Reserve Bank of India (RBI) introduced basic banking services such as "no-frill accounts" with very low or no balance requirements to create an account with no banking costs to the great majority of the underprivileged population.
- In December 2015, the Reserve Bank of India formed a group led by RBI Executive Director Deepak Mohanty with the purpose of developing a medium-term financial inclusion monitoring strategy. The group was tasked with reviewing all previous initiatives for financial inclusion and a supportive payment system. Prior to this, in August 2014, the government of India started the Pradhan Mantri Jan Dhan Yojana with the assistance of banks to expand financial inclusion. Approximately 167.3 million accounts were opened under this Scheme with a total balance of Rs. 20,000 crores as of July 8, with 51.1 percent of these accounts having a zero balance. According to Department of Financial Services, Ministry of Finance, Government of India (2024, July 24), As of 24th July 2024, it has benefited 52.90 Crore people, with Public Sector Banks leading at 41.23 Crore beneficiaries, followed by Regional Rural Banks at 9.85 Crore, Private Sector Banks at 1.63 Crore, and Rural Cooperative Banks at 0.19 Crore. The scheme has accumulated deposits totaling 228940.78 Crore and issued 35.89 Crore Rupay debit cards, reflecting its widespread impact and success in enhancing financial access for the Indian population.
- Apart from the aforementioned initiatives, the government of India has implemented a variety of financial inclusion programmes, such as the estab-

lishment of customer care centers, credit counselling centers, the Aadhar Scheme, and the Mahatma Gandhi Rural Employment Guarantee Scheme. With these increased efforts, a broader scope has been covered in order to comprehend and assess the current demands of the rural population (Kumar, 2022).

Table 3. Government of India schemes

Scheme	Key Highlights
National Rural Livelihoods Mission (NRLM)	The National Rural Livelihoods Mission (NRLM) has made significant strides, covering 34 states/UTs and mobilizing over 102 million households into Self-Help Groups (SHGs). Progress includes the promotion of 9.15 million SHGs and substantial financial support, with 7,660 million disbursed as revolving funds. The mission has also responded effectively to COVID-19, producing over 168 million masks and operating 122,682 community kitchens. Additionally, it has enhanced agricultural livelihoods for over 3 million women farmers through various interventions.
Pradhan Mantri Mudra Yojana (PMMY)	Since its inception, the Pradhan Mantri Mudra Yojana (PMMY) has sanctioned over 34.88 million loans in the first year (2015-2016) for 1,37,449.27 crore, with a steady increase each year. By 2023-2024, the scheme had sanctioned 66.78 million loans amounting to 5,41,012.86 crore. As of 2024-2025, approximately 22.46 million loans have been sanctioned for 2,15,407.99 crore. This remarkable growth underscores PMMY's vital role in promoting financial inclusion and supporting small businesses across India.
Credit Guarantee Fund for Micro and Small Enterprises (CGFMSE)	The Ministry of Micro, Small, and Medium Enterprises' Credit Guarantee Fund Trust extended 544,938 credit guarantees totaling 45,921.57 crore in 2022-23, down from 709,883 guarantees for 55,217.74 crore in 2021-22. In 2020-21, the trust provided 619,687 guarantees worth 31,349.39 crore, and in 2019-20, it extended 838,947 guarantees totaling 45,215.35 crore. This trend highlights the varying levels of support for MSMEs through credit guarantees over recent years.
Stand-Up India Scheme	The Stand-Up India Scheme has significantly supported Scheduled Castes (SC), Scheduled Tribes (ST), and women beneficiaries from 2019-20 up to November 23, 2021. A total of 5,398 accounts for SC beneficiaries received 1,174.80 crore, while 2,227 accounts for ST beneficiaries were sanctioned 481.33 crore. Women accounted for 28,299 accounts totaling 6,859.80 crore. By March 21, 2022, the cumulative figures included 19,310 SC borrowers with 3,976.84 crore, 6,435 ST borrowers receiving 1,373.71 crore, and 108,250 women borrowers benefiting from 24,809.89 crore, bringing the total to 133,995 accounts sanctioned for 30,160.45 crore.
NABARD Initiatives	NABARD's Micro Credit Innovations Department has facilitated access to microfinance for 16.19 crore households, primarily through the Self-Help Group-Bank Linkage Programme (SHG-BLP), which has grown to become the world's largest microfinance initiative. In the fiscal year 2023-24, NABARD provided 10,099.55 crore in refinance to banks, supporting 53,994 SHGs and JLGs. Additionally, NABARD has trained 50.20 lakh participants under various skill development programs, fostering sustainable livelihoods among rural populations.

Source: Compiled by authors(s).

MFI Key Functions in Financial Inclusion

Microfinance institutions (MFIs) are instrumental in advancing financial inclusion, particularly in underserved and economically disadvantaged communities. Financial inclusion denotes the accessibility and utilization of financial services by individuals and businesses, irrespective of their income levels or social standing. MFIs play a pivotal role in this endeavor by offering a spectrum of financial services customized to suit the needs of low-income individuals who lack access to traditional banking services. Here are the key functions performed by MFIs to facilitate financial inclusion:

Provision of Microcredit: MFIs are renowned for extending microcredit or small loans to entrepreneurs, small business owners, and individuals with limited collateral or credit history. These loans aid in initiating or expanding businesses, generating income, and enhancing living standards. By providing accessible credit options, MFIs empower individuals to attain financial self-sufficiency and contribute to local economic progress.

Encouragement of Savings Habits: MFIs foster savings habits among low-income individuals by offering secure and convenient savings accounts. These accounts serve as a reliable avenue to deposit money, accrue interest, and cultivate financial resilience. By promoting savings, MFIs facilitate the accumulation of funds for emergencies, future investments, or long-term aspirations, thereby promoting economic stability.

Facilitation of Microinsurance: Collaboration with insurance providers enables MFIs to offer microinsurance products to their clientele. Microinsurance provides coverage against risks such as illness, accidents, crop failures, and natural disasters. Access to affordable insurance options enables low-income individuals to safeguard themselves and their assets from unforeseen events, mitigating vulnerability and expediting recovery from setbacks.

Promotion of Financial Literacy: Many MFIs prioritize financial literacy and education programs alongside their financial services. They conduct training sessions and workshops to equip clients with fundamental financial concepts, money management skills, and the ability to make informed financial decisions. By enhancing financial literacy, MFIs empower individuals to effectively utilize financial services, evade exploitative practices, and plan for their future.

Integration of Social and Environmental Objectives: Beyond financial inclusion, MFIs often espouse broader social missions aimed at addressing development goals. They may lend support to initiatives concerning women's empowerment, rural development, healthcare, education, and environmental sustainability. By amalgamating social and environmental objectives into their operations, MFIs contribute to inclusive growth and the welfare of the communities they serve.

The microfinance sector in India has witnessed substantial growth, with a total loan portfolio outstanding of approximately INR 2.48 trillion (USD 33.9 billion) as of September 2021. This growth underscores the sector's significance in reaching millions of borrowers, predominantly comprising low-income individuals, women, and small businesses. Overall, MFIs serve as catalysts for expanding financial services to marginalized populations, fostering their economic empowerment, and breaking the cycle of poverty. Through their inclusive and customized approach, MFIs make significant contributions to achieving financial inclusion and nurturing sustainable development.

Best Practices, Innovative Solutions, and Policy Recommendations

To improve the effectiveness and sustainability of Micro Finance Institutions (MFIs) in India, it is essential to adopt a multifaceted approach that includes best practices, innovative solutions, and well-defined policy recommendations. One of the core best practices involves embracing a client-centric model that prioritizes understanding the unique financial challenges faced by different demographics (Ali, 2024). Conducting thorough needs assessments can guide MFIs in developing tailored financial products specifically designed for target groups, such as women and rural entrepreneurs (Tafotie, 2020). Transparent communication is crucial; MFIs should ensure that all loan terms and associated fees are clearly articulated, fostering a relationship of trust with borrowers (Henegar et al., 2024). Additionally, implementing comprehensive financial literacy programs will empower clients to make informed decisions about managing their finances effectively. To mitigate risk, MFIs must maintain a diversified loan portfolio and employ robust credit assessment methodologies to evaluate borrowers' creditworthiness accurately (Ssekiziyivu et al., 2017). Leveraging technology through digital lending platforms and mobile banking solutions can streamline the loan application process, enhance service delivery, and increase accessibility, particularly for clients in remote areas (Pazarbasioglu et al., 2020). Continuous monitoring and evaluation of the social and economic impact of microfinance services will enable MFIs to adapt their strategies and offerings, while establishing feedback mechanisms will ensure ongoing improvements in service quality.

To bolster MFI operations further, implementing innovative solutions is vital. Collaborations with fintech companies can harness advanced technology for improved data analytics, risk assessment, and customer outreach, ultimately enhancing operational efficiency. Group lending models can also be effective; they foster peer support among borrowers, promoting accountability and reducing default rates. Additionally, MFIs should explore crowdfunding platforms as alternative funding sources, facilitating the expansion of services and outreach to a broader client base (Luo et al., 2022). Introducing green microfinance products that fund sustainable initiatives can contribute to environmental stewardship while promoting economic development (Allet, 2014). Furthermore, offering micro-insurance products will help safeguard clients against unexpected risks, thereby enhancing their financial resilience.

To create an enabling environment for MFIs, policy recommendations should focus on several key areas. A robust regulatory framework that promotes innovation while ensuring consumer protection is crucial. This could involve revisiting interest rate caps and simplifying compliance requirements for smaller MFIs to ease their operational burdens (Quirk, 2023). Investing in capacity-building programs for MFI staff is equally important; improving their skills in areas such as client engagement, risk management, and technology utilization can enhance overall service delivery. Facilitating access to affordable capital through government-backed funding schemes, grants, or low-interest loans for MFIs serving underserved communities will also be beneficial (Surmanidze et al., 2023). Furthermore, promoting financial literacy initiatives through national campaigns can help educate potential borrowers about responsible financial practices. Encouraging MFIs to integrate their services with government programs focused on poverty alleviation, skill development, and entrepreneurship will provide a comprehensive approach to community development (Egharevba et al., 2016). Finally, establishing a solid framework for monitoring and evaluating the performance and impact of MFIs will ensure accountability and foster continuous improvement in their service offerings.

By embracing these best practices, innovative solutions, and strategic policy recommendations, MFIs in India can significantly enhance their role in promoting financial inclusion and empowering marginalized communities.

THEORETICAL IMPLICATIONS

Microfinance Institutions (MFIs) have been widely recognized for their critical role in promoting financial inclusion and financial literacy, particularly in developing economies like India. Theoretically, the research supports the notion that MFIs serve as catalysts for economic development by offering financial services to those excluded from traditional banking systems. MFIs provide microloans, savings accounts, and remittance facilities, which empower individuals to start or expand small businesses, invest in education and healthcare, and build resilience against financial shocks (Sharma et al., 2023). This aligns with the theoretical framework that posits financial inclusion as a means to achieve broader national development goals by fostering economic empowerment and reducing poverty (Banerjee et al., 2015).

Moreover, MFIs contribute to the development of financial literacy and entrepreneurial skills among the underserved populations, enabling them to make informed financial decisions and contribute meaningfully to their communities' socio-economic fabric (Singh & Yadav, 2012). This highlights the transformative potential of MFIs in driving inclusive growth and poverty reduction, which is a key theoretical underpinning of financial inclusion strategies (Kabeer, 2001).

PRACTICAL IMPLICATIONS

Practically, the findings of this research underscore the effectiveness of MFIs in enhancing financial inclusion through innovative approaches and partnerships. For instance, the use of technology and the implementation of initiatives like the SHG-Bank Linkage Programme facilitated by NABARD have significantly improved access to financial services for rural and marginalized populations, especially women (Chaturvedi, 2022). The increasing market share of NBFC-MFIs, as highlighted by the research, indicates a shift towards more specialized financial services tailored to the needs of the underserved (Statista.com, 2023).

Additionally, the research points to the importance of continuous innovation and adaptation in the microfinance sector to address challenges such as limited awareness and affordability of financial products. This practical insight emphasizes the need for MFIs to leverage technology and develop tailored financial solutions that cater to the specific needs of different segments of the population.

MANAGERIAL IMPLICATIONS

From a managerial perspective, the research provides valuable insights for policymakers and stakeholders in the microfinance sector. The significant role of MFIs in fostering economic stability and community development through tailored financial services and support for entrepreneurship calls for comprehensive strategies that prioritize financial inclusion (Nagaraja & Kusugal, 2013). Managers and policymakers should focus on creating an enabling environment for MFIs to thrive, which includes supportive regulatory frameworks, capacity-building initiatives, and fostering partnerships with other financial institutions.

Moreover, addressing gender disparities in financial access and promoting gender equality in policy and practice are crucial managerial considerations (Adnan and Kumar, 2021). Ensuring that financial inclusion efforts are inclusive and equitable will enhance the overall impact of MFIs on economic development and poverty alleviation.

CONCLUSION

In conclusion, the research highlights the multifaceted role of Microfinance Institutions in promoting financial inclusion and financial literacy in India. The theoretical, practical, and managerial implications derived from the study underscore the transformative potential of MFIs in fostering economic empowerment, reducing poverty, and driving inclusive growth. Policymakers, stakeholders, and managers must focus on creating a supportive environment for MFIs to innovate and expand their reach, ensuring that financial services are accessible to all segments of the population, particularly the underserved and marginalized communities. By doing so, MFIs can significantly contribute to the socio-economic development of India, bridging the gap between the formal financial system and the unbanked population.

REFERENCES

Adnan, S. A., & Kumar, P. (2021). Role of microfinance in economic development. *Adhyayan: A Journal of Management Sciences, 11*(2), 22-30.

Agarwal, A. (2012). A Guide to RBI's Weekly Statistical Supplement – II, STDI-Primary Dealer Ltd; 2012 Jan 27. Available from: http://www.stcipd.com/UserFiles/File/A%20Guide%20to%20RBI's%20Weekly% 20Statistical%20Supplement.pdf

Akingunola, R. O., Adekunle, O. A., Adegbesan, K. J., & Aninkan, O. O. (2013). Microfinance banks and entrepreneurship development in Nigeria: A case of Ogun State. *European Journal of Business and Management*, 5(28), 100–110.

Ali, H. (2024). *Islamic Microfinance: Landscape, Models and Future Prospects.* Walter de Gruyter GmbH & Co KG.

Allet, M. (2014). Why do microfinance institutions go green? An exploratory study. *Journal of Business Ethics*, 122(3), 405–424. DOI: 10.1007/s10551-013-1767-2

Amidžic, G., Massara, M. A., & Mialou, A. (2014). *Assessing countries' financial inclusion standing-A new composite index.* International Monetary Fund.

Anjum, B., & Tiwari, R. (2012). Role of private sector banks for financial inclusion. *Zenith International Journal of Multidisciplinary Research*, 2(1), 270–280.

Ardic, O. P., Heimann, M., & Mylenko, N. (2011). Access to financial services and the financial inclusion agenda around the world: A cross-country analysis with a new data set. *World Bank Policy Research Working Paper*, •••, 5537. DOI: 10.1596/1813-9450-5537

Badran, M. A. (2009). *Money Transfer Services* (Doctoral dissertation, Eastern Mediterranean University (EMU)).

Banerjee, A., Duflo, E., Glennerster, R., & Kinnan, C. (2015). The miracle of microfinance? Evidence from a randomized evaluation. *American Economic Journal. Applied Economics*, 7(1), 22–53. DOI: 10.1257/app.20130533

Biswas, S., & Saha, A. K. (2013). Structural transformation of rural finance in India: a critical review. *Microfinance, Risk-Taking Behaviour and Rural Livelihood*, 1-13. DOI: 10.1257/app.20130533

Bora, N. M. (2020). Financial inclusion in India: A case study of the north-eastern states. *International Journal of Scientific and Technology Research*, 9(2), 1319–1323.

Carstens, A. (2019). *Central banking and innovation: partners in the quest for financial inclusion. speech at the Reserve Bank of India.* CD Deshmukh Memorial Lecture.

Chaturvedi, P. (2022). The role of small finance banks in promoting financial inclusion in India. *International Journal of Multidisciplinary*, 7(5), 8–15. DOI: 10.31305/rrijm.2022.v07.i05.002

Chithra, N., & Selvam, M. (2013). Determinants of financial inclusion: An empirical study on the inter-state variations in India. *Available atSSRN* 2296096. DOI: 10.2139/ssrn.2296096

Claessens, S. (2003). Benefits and costs on integrated financial services provision in developing countries. *Brookings-Wharton papers on financial services, 2003*(1), 85-139. DOI: 10.1257/app.20130533

Current policy issues, *ADBI Working Paper*, No. 259, Asian Development Bank Institute (ADBI), Tokyo

Department of Financial Services, Ministry of Finance, Government of India. (2024, July 24). *Pradhan Mantri Jan - Dhan Yojana*. Pradhan Mantri Jan Dhan Yojana. Retrieved August 2, 2024, from https://www.pmjdy.gov.in/account

Egharevba, M. E., Eguavoen, A., Azuh, D., Iruonagbe, T. C., & Chiazor, I. A. (2016). Microfinance and poverty reduction strategy for promoting national development: The challenge of social/financial inclusion. *Social Sciences*, 11(22), 5373–5386.

Gitaharie, B. Y., Soelistianingsih, L., Djutaharta, T., Nursamsu, S., Hastiadi, F. F., Panennungi, M. A., & Listya, R. (2014). *Financial inclusion: Household access to credit in Indonesia (No. 201401)*. Faculty of Economics, University of Indonesia.

Gomathy, M. (2015). An overview of financial inclusion and rural development in India. *IOSR Journal of Business and Management (IOSRJBM), 17*(8), 06-11. DOI: 10.1016/j.sbspro.2012.03.281

Gupte, R., Venkataramani, B., & Gupta, D. (2012). Computation of financial inclusion index for India. *Procedia: Social and Behavioral Sciences*, 37, 133–149. DOI: 10.1016/j.sbspro.2012.03.281

Hannig, A., & Jansen, S. (2010). Financial inclusion and financial stability: Henegar, D., Ilie , G. L., Mure an, I. C., Poru iu, A. R., Arion, I. D., & Arion, F. H. (2024). Customers' perception of microfinance services as a tool for rural development: a Romanian case study. *Agriculture*, 14(7), 1087.

High Mark, C. R. I. F. (January 25, 2024). Portfolio outstanding of microfinance industry in India from financial year 2020 to 2023 (in trillion Indian rupees) [Graph]. In Statista. Retrieved June 21, 2024, from https://www.statista.com/statistics/1344112/india-microfinance-industry-portfolio-outstanding/

Jacobs, M., & Mazzucato, M. (Eds.). (2016). *Rethinking capitalism: Economics and policy for sustainable and inclusive growth*. John Wiley & Sons.

Kabeer, N. (2001). Conflicts over credit: Re-evaluating the empowerment potential of loans to women in rural Bangladesh. *World Development*, 29(1), 63–84. DOI: 10.1016/S0305-750X(00)00081-4

Karmakar, G. K., Banerjee, D. G., & Monapatra, P. N. (2011). *Towards financial inclusion in India* (1st ed.). Sage Publication.

Kumar, P. (2022). An Analysis of Some Poverty Alleviation and Employment Generation Programmes in India. *Ideal Research Review, 72*(1). DOI: 10.1080/00036846.2017.1368990

Kumar, S., & Subedi, S. (2023). Microfinance Schemes for Women Entrepreneurship in India: A Case Study of Sikkim State. In Alhassan, Y., & Nwagbara, U. (Eds.), *Empowering Women Through Microfinance in Developing Countries* (pp. 124–140). IGI Global., DOI: 10.4018/978-1-6684-8979-6.ch007

Lopez, T., & Winkler, A. (2018). The challenge of rural financial inclusion–evidence from microfinance. *Applied Economics*, 50(14), 1555–1577. DOI: 10.1080/00036846.2017.1368990

Luo, X., Ge, L., & Wang, C. A. (2022). Crowdfunding for microfinance institutions: The new hope? *Management Information Systems Quarterly*, 46(1), 373–400. DOI: 10.25300/MISQ/2022/15406

Mani, M. (2016). Financial inclusion in South Asia—Relative standing, challenges and initiatives. *South Asian Survey*, 23(2), 158–179. DOI: 10.1177/0971523118783353

Memdani, L. (2020). Demonetisation: A move towards cashless economy in India. *International Journal of Electronic Banking*, 2(3), 205–211. DOI: 10.1504/IJEBANK.2020.111428

Nagaraja, S., & Pallavi, K. S. (2013). Financial inclusion and rural development. *Global research analysis, 2*(7), 188-189. DOI: 10.1080/00036846.2017.1368990

Ouma, S. A., Odongo, T. M., & Were, M. (2017). Mobile financial services and financial inclusion: Is it a boon for savings mobilization?. *Review of development finance, 7*(1), 29-35. DOI: 10.1080/00036846.2017.1368990

Pazarbasioglu, C., Mora, A. G., Uttamchandani, M., Natarajan, H., Feyen, E., & Saal, M. (2020). Digital financial services. *World Bank, 54*, 1-54.

Planning Commission. (2009). *Annual Report*. Government of India.

Quinones, B., & Remenyi, J. (2014). *Microfinance and poverty alleviation: Case studies from Asia and the Pacific*. Routledge. DOI: 10.4324/9781315800455

Quirk, T. (2023). Interest Rate Caps, Segmented Markets, and Microfinance: A Cautionary Tale from Zambia. *Segmented Markets, and Microfinance: A Cautionary Tale from Zambia (April 15, 2023)*. DOI: 10.1108/JES-03-2019-0109

Ramji, M. (2009). Financial inclusion in Gulbarga: Finding usage in access. *Center for micro finance working paper, 26*.

Rangarajan, C. (2008). Report of the committee on financial inclusion. *Ministry of Finance, Government of India*, 155-167.

Rasel, M. A., & Win, S. (2020). Microfinance governance: A systematic review and future research directions. *Journal of Economic Studies (Glasgow, Scotland)*, 47(7), 1811–1847. DOI: 10.1108/JES-03-2019-0109

Reserve Bank of India. (July 27, 2022). Number of microfinance non-banking financial companies (NBFC-MFI) in India as of January 2022, by city [Graph]. In Statista. Retrieved June 21, 2024, from https://www.statista.com/statistics/1244619/india-number-of-microfinance-institutions-by-city/

Sarkar, S. S., & Phatowali, A. (2012). Urban Financial Inclusion: An Analysis Of Bankers' Perception-An Empirical Study In Assam. *SS International Journal of Business and Management Research*, 2(5), 91–104.

Sarma, M. (2010). *Index of financial inclusion* (CITD Discussion Paper No. 10-05). New Delhi: CITD, JNU.

Sarma, M. (2016). Measuring financial inclusion for Asian economies. *Financial inclusion in Asia: Issues and policy concerns*, 3-34. DOI: 10.1108/JES-03-2019-0109

Sarma, M., & Pais, J. (2011). Financial inclusion and development. *Journal of International Development*, 23(5), 613–628. DOI: 10.1002/jid.1698

Sharma, A., Sharma, M., Awasthi, M. G., & Poojari, M. L. (2023). Role of microfinance institutions in financial inclusion in India. *Journal of Contemporary Issues in Business and Government*, 29(1), 662–669.

Sharma, A., Sharma, M., Awasthi, M. G., & Poojari, M. L. (2023). Role of microfinance institutions in financial inclusion in India. *Journal of Contemporary Issues in Business and Government*, 29(1), 662–669.

SIDBI. (March 22, 2024). Market share of credit lenders for microfinance industry in India from December 2020 to September 2023, by lender type [Graph]. In *Statista*. Retrieved June 21, 2024, from https://www.statista.com/statistics/1243029/india-market-share-of-lenders-for-msme/

Singh, J., & Yadav, P. (2012). Micro finance as a tool for financial inclusion & reduction of poverty. *Journal of Business Management & Social Sciences Research (JBM&SSR), 1*(1), 1-12. DOI: 10.1080/23311975.2017.1374921

Singh, R. B., & Hietala, R. (2014). Livelihood security in northwestern Himalaya. *Springer Tokyo Heidelberg New York Dordrecht London, doi, 10*, 978-4. DOI: 10.1080/23311975.2017.1374921

Ssekiziyivu, B., Mwesigwa, R., Joseph, M., & Nkote Nabeta, I. (2017). Credit allocation, risk management and loan portfolio performance of MFIs—A case of Ugandan firms. *Cogent Business & Management*, 4(1), 1374921. DOI: 10.1080/23311975.2017.1374921

Suneetha, V., & Ramanamma, M. V. (2018). A study on the Role of Self Help Groups in Economic Empowerment of Women. *International Journal of Research in Social Sciences*, 8(9), 270–283.

Surmanidze, N., Beridze, M., Amashukeli, M., & Tskhadadze, K. (2023). Empowering small businesses in Georgia: Access to finance, economic resilience, and sustainable growth. *Agora International Journal of Economical Sciences*, 17(2), 158–169. DOI: 10.15837/aijes.v17i2.6453

Tafotie, R. (2020). Fostering Digital Financial Services in Africa: a case of embracing innovation for business and inclusion. *University of Luxembourg Law Working Paper*, (2020-005).

Chapter 4
Microfinance, Sustainable Entrepreneurship, and Women's Empowerment in the Indian Economy: Pathways to Prosperity

Pranjit Kr Paul
https://orcid.org/0000-0003-2799-4247
Vidyasagar University, India

ABSTRACT

India's microfinance programs have considerably advanced financial inclusion, economic growth, and social empowerment. Microfinance in India is poised to make a significant contribution to the nation's development. This study highlights the microfinance initiatives in India, focusing their outreach, effectiveness, and sustainability. Investigates the impact of sustainable entrepreneurship focusing on the employment generation on local economy. Deals with key challenges and opportunities faced by microfinance institutions (MFIs) in promoting sustainable entrepreneurship and women empowerment. In addition, the study focuses on the effectiveness of microfinance in enhancing women's economic independence, decision-making and social status. In summary, microfinance has revolutionized women's empowerment and sustainable entrepreneurship in the Indian economy. The current obstacles must be overcome in order to maintain and increase the benefits. This would guarantee that microfinance's advantages reach a larger number of people, helping to create inclusive economic environment in India.

DOI: 10.4018/979-8-3693-6622-6.ch004

1. INTRODUCTION

When India gained its independence, it was among the world's poorest nations. Thus, concerted efforts to reduce poverty commenced after independence. For the purpose of improving the general social, political, and economic status of the Indian populace, the government carried out a number of planning and program initiatives, including the Jawahar Gram Samridhi Yojana (JGSY), National Family Benefit Scheme (NFBS), Integrated Rural Development Program (IRDP), Self-Employment Programme for the Urban Poor (SEPUP), Nehru Rozgar Yojna (NRY), Pradhan Mantri Gramin Awaas Yojana, National Rural Employment Guarantee Act (NREGA), and many more. Mergers and Acquisitions (M&A) activity in India reached US$ 129 billion by the end of 2018, demonstrating the country's outstanding economic progress in recent years (Allirajan, 2019). India is now placed 77th out of 190 nations in the Doing Business Report (2019), up 23 ranks from its 2017 ranking, for having continuously well-designed business regulations and extensive reform over time. In the week ending November 22, 2019, India's foreign exchange reserves were valued at US$ 448.59 billion, as per the RBI Report on Management of Foreign Exchange Reserves, 2020. In addition to guaranteeing men and women equal rights, our constitution and preamble give the state the authority to enact laws that support women. In order to empower women and reduce poverty, the Indian government has implemented a number of initiatives in recent times, including the Swarnajayanti Gram Swarojgar Yojana (SGSY), the promotion of microfinance institutions (MFI), the Self-Help Group-Bank Linkage Program (SHGBLP), and the promotion of Women Self Help Groups (WSHGs). The world took the initiative in this direction when it adopted the eight Millennium Development Goals during the September 2000 United Nations Millennium Summit general assembly. As the UN Millennium Declaration was signed at the start of a new millennium, the nations pledged to work toward improving humankind everywhere by releasing all people from the wretched and dehumanizing grip of extreme poverty. The 2003 United Nations Development Group (UNDG) principles served as the basis for the Millennium Development Goals framework, which was adopted by 189 countries, including the government of India. The eight Millennium Development Goals (MDGs) prioritized progress in order to raise the average person's level of living. The assessment for our nation shows that, by the end of 2015, there was inconsistent improvement despite multiple efforts (MoSPI, 2015). India's failure to meet the MDG targets can be attributed primarily to multifaceted poverty. There is a domino effect. Since poverty is the root source of all problems, one problem invites more difficulties. In order to maintain the development momentum created by the MDGs, the 2030 agenda for sustainable development was unveiled at the United Nations Conference near the end of 2015. The government of India is among the 193 UN countries who have unanimously endorsed the 2030 Agenda for Sustainable Development. Therefore, India's poverty poses a threat to the world's Sustainable Development Goals in addition to having a negative impact on the country's economy. Thus, India's ability to reduce poverty will largely determine whether it meets the targets of the Sustainable Development Goals (SDGs) by 2030.

2. REVIEW OF THE LITERATURE

Microfinance is one of the most effective tools available for improving the socioeconomic situation of women among the many options. Access to microfinance has given women especially those in developing nations new opportunities for social advancement, entrepreneurship, and financial independence. A significant amount of research has examined the complex effects of microfinance on women's lives during the last few decades. These studies demonstrate how microfinance strengthens women's sense of agency, gives them more authority to make decisions in their homes, and enhances their general well-being in addition to giving them the funds they need to launch and grow small companies. Through an examination of several microfinance initiatives and their results, scholars have emphasized the revolutionary capacity of these financial services. This collection of works also discusses the drawbacks and objections to microfinance. The next review presents information from various geographic and socioeconomic situations and summarizes important findings from previous studies on women's empowerment through microfinance. It seeks to give a thorough picture of the advantages, difficulties, and potential paths for using microfinance as a tool for women's empowerment. The following are a few of the literatures that address these present issues:

Kabeer (2005) explored how microfinance programs have empowered women by enhancing their economic status, social networks, and decision-making power within households. The author emphasizes the role of microfinance in providing women with financial resources, which in turn helps them gain self-esteem and a sense of agency. Mayoux (2001) highlighted the impact of microfinance on women's empowerment, noting that while financial services can lead to increased income and self-reliance, the benefits are maximized when accompanied by gender awareness training and support networks. Cheston & Kuhn (2002) synthesized various case studies and reports to conclude that microfinance contributes significantly to women's empowerment. It points out that beyond financial gains, women experience improved social standing and greater participation in community activities. Pitt & Khandker (1998) provided empirical evidence from Bangladesh demonstrating that access to microfinance leads to higher household expenditure on education and health, reflecting women's increased influence over family decisions and improved quality of life. Hunt & Kasynathan (2002) investigated the non-economic benefits of microfinance for women, such as increased self-confidence, social capital, and community involvement. The findings suggest that these aspects are crucial for long-term empowerment. Aghion & Morduch (2000) discussed the dual role of microfinance in poverty alleviation and women's empowerment. It emphasizes that while financial independence is a significant outcome, the transformative potential of microfinance lies in its ability to alter gender dynamics and power relations. Swain & Wallentin (2009) explored using a sample of Indian women has shown that microfinance participation enhances women's autonomy and self-efficacy. The authors argue that these psychological changes are essential components of empowerment. Hashemi et al. (1996) identified key empowerment indicators, such as mobility, economic security, and freedom from violence, and links them to women's involvement in microfinance programs in rural Bangladesh. Armendáriz & Morduch (2010) presented a comprehensive overview of the microfinance sector and its impact on women, highlighting both successes and limitations. They argue that sustainable empowerment requires integrating microfinance with broader development initiatives. Khandker (2005) provided longitudinal data from Bangladesh, showing that microfinance not only improves women's income but also their bargaining power within households. The author emphasizes the importance of sustained access to financial services for lasting empowerment. Garikipati (2008) gave attention on the nuanced impacts of microfinance on women, noting that while economic benefits are clear, social empowerment is more complex and depends on various contextual factors, including cultural norms and family dynamics. Morduch (1999) explored the broader social implications of microfinance, suggesting that access to credit can help women escape cycles of poverty and marginalization. The author highlights successful case studies from various countries. Sanyal (2009) examined how microfinance groups foster collective action among women, leading to increased political participation and advocacy for women's rights. The study underscores the role of solidarity and peer support in empowerment. Rahman (1999) did ethnographic study from Bangladesh and provides an in-depth look at the lived experiences of women participating in microfinance programs. It highlights both the challenges and successes, emphasizing the importance of cultural sensitivity in program design. Goetz & Gupta (1996) analyzed the effectiveness of microfinance in achieving gender equality, pointing out that while financial access is crucial, addressing structural inequalities is equally important for genuine empowerment. Ledgerwood (1999) gave a comprehensive review of microfinance institutions (MFIs) discusses how different models impact women's empowerment. The research has conclude that client-centric approaches, which consider women's specific needs and constraints, are most effective. Rhyne (2001) explored the operational challenges faced by MFIs and their implications for women's empowerment. The study suggests that financial sustainability and outreach must be balanced to ensure long-term benefits for women. Karlan & Zinman (2011) presented experimental evidence on the impact of microfinance on women, showing that access to credit improves not only economic outcomes but also psychological well-being and social capital. Cull et al. (2009) analyzed global data on microfinance, highlighting best practices and key factors that contribute to successful empowerment outcomes for women. They emphasize the importance of context-specific approaches. Parveen (2009) examined the role of microfinance in empowering rural women in Pakistan. It finds that while financial access is a significant enabler, true empowerment also requires educational and social interventions to break down existing barriers. Though the many aspects have focusses by the researchers but they are scattered in nature. There are still needs for a comprehensive study to deep understand about the concern issues.

3. OBJECTIVES AND METHODOLOGY

3.1 Objectives

The main objectives of this study are:

- To analyze the existing state of microfinance initiatives in India, focusing on their outreach, effectiveness, and sustainability.
- To identify the key challenges and opportunities faced by microfinance institutions (MFIs) in promoting sustainable entrepreneurship and women empowerment.
- To assess the impact of sustainable entrepreneurship on local economies, employment generation, and environmental sustainability.
- To evaluate the effectiveness of microfinance programs in enhancing women's economic independence, decision-making power, and social status.

3.2 Methodology

The theoretical analysis of women empowerment through microfinance involves a systematic examination of existing theories, models, and frameworks that explain how microfinance initiatives contribute to the empowerment of women. The methodological approach encompasses several key steps:

Conduct a thorough search of academic databases, journals, and relevant publications to gather existing literature on microfinance and women empowerment. This includes peer-reviewed articles, books, case studies, and reports from reputable organizations. Select studies are considered which specifically focus on the impact of microfinance on women, considering various dimensions of empowerment such as economic, social aspects etc. Examine theories related to microfinance which helps in understand how microfinance mechanisms can lead to empowerment. Critically assess the challenges and limitations identified in the studies, including issues related to high-interest rates, debt sustainability, cultural barriers etc. Synthesize the findings from the theoretical analysis to provide a comprehensive understanding of how microfinance contributes to women's empowerment. Highlight common themes, patterns, and divergences in the literature. Discuss the practical and policy implications of the theoretical insights. Provide recommendations for designing and implementing microfinance programs that effectively empower women.

4. MICROFINANCE INITIATIVES IN INDIA, FOCUSING ON THEIR OUTREACH, EFFECTIVENESS, AND SUSTAINABILITY

4.1 Outreach

Microfinance, the provision of financial services to low-income populations traditionally excluded from formal banking, has been a significant tool for poverty alleviation and economic development in India. Microfinance initiatives encompass a range of financial products, including microloans, savings, insurance, and remittances. In India, the microfinance sector has evolved considerably over the past few decades, with various models and approaches being implemented to enhance financial inclusion.

The roots of microfinance in India can be traced back to the early 20th century, with the establishment of cooperative societies and self-help groups (SHGs). However, the sector gained significant momentum in the 1990s with the formation of institutions specifically aimed at providing microfinance services. Key milestones include the establishment of the Self-Help Group-Bank Linkage Programme (SHG-BLP) by NABARD in 1992 and the emergence of microfinance institutions (MFIs) in the early 2000s.

Microfinance initiatives have reached various parts of India, with a strong presence in states like Andhra Pradesh, Tamil Nadu, Karnataka, Odisha, and West Bengal. However, the penetration is uneven, with some regions, particularly in the North and Northeast, lagging behind in terms of outreach and access.

Microfinance services primarily target women, who constitute over 90% of the clientele. This focus on women is driven by the belief that they are more reliable borrowers and that empowering women has broader social and economic benefits. Microfinance clients typically include small farmers, artisans, petty traders, and micro-entrepreneurs.

Delivery Models

- **Self-Help Groups (SHGs)**: SHGs are small, informal groups of 10-20 members, primarily women, who come together to save regularly and access credit from formal financial institutions. The SHG-BLP, supported by NABARD, is the largest microfinance program in the world.
- **Joint Liability Groups (JLGs)**: JLGs are smaller groups of 4-10 individuals who guarantee each other's loans, thus mitigating the risk for lenders.
- **Microfinance Institutions (MFIs)**: MFIs are specialized financial institutions that provide microloans and other financial services. They operate either as Non-Banking Financial Companies (NBFCs), Non-Governmental Organizations (NGOs), or cooperatives.
- **Banks and Financial Institutions**: Commercial banks, regional rural banks (RRBs), and cooperative banks also participate in the microfinance sector, either directly or through linkage with SHGs and JLGs.

It has been acknowledged that microfinance is a powerful instrument for advancing financial inclusion and empowering underprivileged groups, especially women. Globally, a variety of microfinance models have been put into practice, each with unique strategies and effects. The most popular microfinance models and their unique contributions to women's empowerment are compared here:

Grameen Bank Model (Bangladesh Model) Structure

The Grameen model, pioneered by Nobel laureate Muhammad Yunus, involves creating small, self-formed groups of borrowers (usually five members). These members co-guarantee each other's loans, using peer pressure rather than collateral to ensure repayment.

Impact on Women's Empowerment:
Economic Empowerment: This model offers women access to credit, enabling them to start small businesses or expand existing ones, improving their income.
Social Empowerment: By participating in group meetings, women develop networking skills, confidence, and support systems, often leading to increased social standing. •
Limitations: The pressure from group-based liability can occasionally stress borrowers, particularly if one group member struggles to repay.

Self-Help Group (SHG) Model (India) Structure

SHGs consist of 10-20 women who pool their savings to create a shared fund, which members can borrow from at low interest rates. Over time, SHGs often receive loans from banks, which are guaranteed by the group's collective credit.

Impact on Women's Empowerment:
Financial Autonomy: SHGs allow women to make financial decisions and manage their pooled resources, fostering a sense of control over their finances.
Skill Development: The SHG model encourages training in financial literacy, bookkeeping, and business skills, which enhances women's capabilities.
Community Influence: As members often gain a voice in village development committees, SHGs can lead to increased political participation.
Limitations: SHGs are sometimes restricted by a lack of capital or weak institutional support, limiting the scale of empowerment.

Village Savings and Loan Associations (VSLA) Model (Africa) Structure

VSLAs are community-based groups where members save regularly and make small, member-driven loans. Loans are repaid with interest, building the capital within the group.

Impact on Women's Empowerment:
Access to Capital: VSLAs provide a platform for women to access loans for household needs and small businesses, helping them stabilize their income and savings.
Decision-Making Power: As VSLAs are self-managed, women play a significant role in group decisions, fostering leadership skills.
Social Capital: Group dynamics promote mutual trust and a collective approach to solving community issues, often leading to broader social inclusion.
Limitations: The VSLA model lacks external credit inflows, which may restrict members' access to larger loans.

Cooperative Model Structure

Microfinance cooperatives pool savings from community members and provide loans, typically at favorable interest rates. Cooperatives are owned and managed by the members themselves, who share the profits generated.

Impact on Women's Empowerment:

Enhanced Ownership: As cooperative members, women benefit from shared profits and influence over financial operations, which can be empowering.

Group Solidarity: Cooperatives encourage solidarity, mutual support, and collective growth, benefiting members socially and financially.

Skill Building: Participation often involves training in financial management, adding to women's capabilities and confidence.

Limitations: Cooperatives may face challenges with transparency and accountability, particularly in areas with weak governance structures.

Individual Lending Model: Structure

Unlike group-based models, individual lending focuses on providing loans to individuals, often based on their personal creditworthiness or small collateral.

Impact on Women's Empowerment:

Autonomy: Women have the flexibility to use funds according to their specific business or household needs, encouraging self-reliance.

Skill Development: Individual lending often includes training on business management and financial literacy, enhancing the borrower's skill set.

Limitations: Without group support, individual borrowers face the risk of over-indebtedness, and loan defaults may strain relationships with lenders.

4.2 Effectiveness of Microfinance Initiatives

4.2.1 Economic Impact

Microfinance has had a significant impact on economies, particularly in developing countries. Here are some key ways in which microfinance influences economic development:

Poverty Reduction: Microfinance provides financial services to the unbanked and underbanked populations, enabling them to start and expand small businesses. This leads to income generation and poverty alleviation as individuals and families increase their earnings and improve their standard of living.

Employment Generation: By providing the capital needed for small businesses to grow, microfinance helps create jobs. Entrepreneurs who receive microloans can hire more employees, contributing to lower unemployment rates in their communities.

Women Empowerment: Many microfinance institutions focus on lending to women, who often face greater barriers to accessing traditional financial services. Empowering women through microfinance has been shown to improve household welfare, children's education, and health outcomes.

Financial Inclusion: Microfinance promotes financial inclusion by providing access to credit, savings, insurance, and other financial services to those excluded from the formal banking sector. This inclusion helps individuals manage risks, invest in their futures, and build financial resilience.

Entrepreneurial Activity: Access to microfinance enables individuals to start new businesses or expand existing ones. This entrepreneurial activity can lead to innovation, diversification of the economy, and increased economic dynamism.

Social and Economic Stability: By improving livelihoods and providing financial stability to low-income households, microfinance contributes to social stability. It can reduce the incidence of economic shocks that might otherwise lead to social unrest or displacement.

Community Development: Microfinance can lead to the development of local communities by financing infrastructure projects, such as building schools, clinics, and sanitation facilities. These improvements enhance the overall quality of life and economic prospects of the community.

Access to Education and Healthcare: Microfinance clients often use loans to pay for education and healthcare expenses, leading to better educational outcomes and improved health, which are crucial for long-term economic development.

Improvement in Living Standards: Microfinance can lead to improvements in housing conditions, sanitation, and access to clean water, contributing to a higher standard of living for recipients and their families.

Growth of the Informal Economy: While often overlooked, the informal economy is a significant part of many developing economies. Microfinance supports the growth and formalization of this sector, helping integrate it into the broader economy.

4.2.2 Social Impact

Beyond economic benefits, microfinance has contributed to social empowerment, particularly of women. This impact helps in improving their education and health as well.

Women's Empowerment: Many microfinance institutions (MFIs) focus on providing loans to women, which can enhance their economic independence and social status within their communities.

Education: Increased household income can lead to higher investments in education for children, improving literacy rates and future economic prospects.
Healthcare: Improved financial stability can also lead to better access to healthcare services and better overall health outcomes.

4.2.3 Other Impact

In empowering women, microfinance has been shown to have a profound impact on their involvement in family and community decision-making, raise their social standing, and lessen their susceptibility to violence. Microfinance gives women access to loans, allowing them to become financially independent and actively participate in household and community issues including budgeting, healthcare, and education. This change challenges conventional gender roles and gives them a stronger voice. Women's social status is also raised by economic contributions made through microfinance, which enables them to be respected in their families and communities-particularly in areas where gender norms remain inflexible. Additionally, by reducing stress associated with dependency and encouraging female solidarity, which can offer emotional support and resilience, financial independence lessens women's susceptibility to domestic violence. There are still issues, though, as cultural rejection can lead to conflict and some women experience pressure from loan repayments. All things considered, microfinance is essential to women's empowerment since it helps them on their path to increased independence, dignity, and security while also aiding a larger social change movement.

4.2.4 Sustainability of Microfinance Initiatives

a. Financial Sustainability

The sustainability of microfinance initiatives hinges on their ability to achieve financial viability while serving the low-income segment. Key factors influencing financial sustainability include:

- **Cost Efficiency**: MFIs must manage operational costs efficiently to ensure that they can provide services at affordable rates. Technology adoption and process automation can enhance cost efficiency.
- **Portfolio Quality**: Maintaining a healthy loan portfolio with low default rates is crucial for sustainability. Effective risk assessment, client selection, and monitoring are essential to minimize credit risk.

- **Funding and Capital**: Access to adequate and affordable funding is vital for the growth and sustainability of MFIs. Diversified funding sources, including equity, debt, and grants, can strengthen financial stability.

b. Social and Environmental Sustainability

Microfinance initiatives must also focus on social and environmental sustainability to achieve long-term impact:

- **Client Protection**: Adhering to client protection principles, such as transparency, fair treatment, and grievance redressal, is essential to build trust and ensure client well-being.
- **Social Performance Management**: MFIs should integrate social performance indicators into their operations to measure and enhance their social impact. This includes tracking outcomes related to poverty alleviation, women's empowerment, and community development.
- **Environmental Responsibility**: Incorporating environmental considerations into microfinance operations, such as promoting green loans for eco-friendly businesses and adopting sustainable practices, can contribute to environmental sustainability.

c. Government and Policy Support

The Indian government and regulatory bodies have played a significant role in promoting and regulating the microfinance sector. Key initiatives and policies include:

- **Microfinance Institutions (Development and Regulation) Bill**: Proposed to provide a comprehensive regulatory framework for the microfinance sector, ensuring transparency, client protection, and sector stability.
- **Priority Sector Lending (PSL)**: Banks are mandated to allocate a certain percentage of their lending to priority sectors, including microfinance, to enhance financial inclusion.
- **MUDRA (Micro Units Development and Refinance Agency)**: Launched in 2015, MUDRA provides refinance support to MFIs and banks for extending loans to micro-enterprises, promoting entrepreneurship and job creation.
- **Financial Literacy and Inclusion Programs**: Various initiatives, such as the Pradhan Mantri Jan Dhan Yojana (PMJDY), aim to promote financial literacy and inclusion, creating an enabling environment for microfinance.

To ensure that microfinance programs last and can grow over time, we need a well-rounded approach. Sustainable business models are key, using cost-efficient operations, flexible products, and mixed financing to help them become financially independent. Focusing on social and environmental benefits can attract investors who care about positive impacts, while community-based models build customer loyalty and address various client needs. For managing risks, having a mix of loans, microinsurance, and regular monitoring through data analytics helps reduce losses and catch signs of default early.

Technology is also crucial: digital payments and mobile banking make it easier and more convenient for clients, while big data and AI provide reliable credit scoring for those without traditional financial histories. Blockchain brings transparency, boosting trust, and cloud platforms allow institutions to grow smoothly and securely. Altogether, these strategies help microfinance programs reach more people and become more resilient, promoting financial inclusion and economic empowerment in recent time.

5. IMPACT OF SUSTAINABLE ENTREPRENEURSHIP ON LOCAL ECONOMIES, EMPLOYMENT GENERATION, AND ENVIRONMENTAL SUSTAINABILITY IN INDIA

Globally, sustainable entrepreneurship is gaining traction. It entails starting and operating firms with an emphasis on social, economic, and environmental sustainability. This idea is growing more and more important in India because of the country's enormous population, varied ecosystems, and urgent socioeconomic and environmental issues. This essay examines how sustainable entrepreneurship affects Indian local economies, the creation of jobs, and environmental sustainability while emphasizing the potential for change.

5.1 Boosting Local Economies

Sustainable entrepreneurship plays a crucial role in revitalizing local economies in India. By prioritizing local resources, indigenous knowledge, and community engagement, sustainable businesses contribute to economic growth in several ways:

Promoting Local Production and Consumption: Sustainable entrepreneurs often emphasize locally sourced materials and products, which reduces dependency on imports and fosters local supply chains. This approach supports local farmers, artisans, and manufacturers, creating a ripple effect of economic benefits within the community.

Encouraging Small and Medium Enterprises (SMEs): Sustainable entrepreneurship often manifests in the form of SMEs, which are vital to India's economy. SMEs provide a significant share of employment and contribute to GDP growth. By adopting sustainable practices, these enterprises can become more competitive and resilient, ensuring long-term economic stability.

Enhancing Economic Diversification: Sustainable businesses often operate in sectors like renewable energy, organic farming, eco-tourism, and waste management, contributing to economic diversification. This reduces the reliance on traditional industries, such as agriculture and manufacturing, which are often subject to market fluctuations and environmental degradation.

Attracting Investment and Funding: Sustainable businesses are increasingly attracting investment from both domestic and international sources. Impact investors and venture capitalists are drawn to enterprises that prioritize social and environmental goals alongside profitability. This influx of capital can stimulate local economies, foster innovation, and create new market opportunities.

5.2 Employment Generation

Sustainable entrepreneurship has a significant impact on employment generation in India. By creating jobs that align with sustainable development goals, these businesses contribute to poverty reduction, skill development, and social inclusion:

Creating Green Jobs: Sustainable businesses often create green jobs that focus on environmental conservation, renewable energy, sustainable agriculture, and waste management. These jobs not only provide employment but also contribute to environmental sustainability, addressing critical issues such as climate change and resource depletion.

Empowering Marginalized Communities: Sustainable entrepreneurship can empower marginalized communities by providing them with employment opportunities and fostering social inclusion. For instance, initiatives like self-help groups, women-led cooperatives, and social enterprises enable disadvantaged groups to participate in economic activities, enhancing their livelihoods and social status.

Promoting Skill Development: Sustainable businesses often require specialized skills and knowledge, leading to the development of training programs and educational initiatives. These programs enhance the employability of the local workforce, equipping them with skills in areas such as renewable energy technology, organic farming techniques, and eco-friendly product design.

Fostering Entrepreneurship and Innovation: By promoting sustainable practices, these businesses inspire a culture of entrepreneurship and innovation. Aspiring entrepreneurs are encouraged to develop new solutions to environmental and social challenges, creating a vibrant ecosystem of startups and small businesses that contribute to employment generation and economic growth.

5.3 Environmental Sustainability

Sustainable entrepreneurship has a profound impact on environmental sustainability in India. By integrating eco-friendly practices and technologies, these businesses help mitigate environmental degradation and promote the conservation of natural resources:

Reducing Carbon Footprint: Sustainable businesses often focus on reducing their carbon footprint through energy-efficient practices, renewable energy adoption, and waste reduction strategies. This contributes to India's efforts to combat climate change and achieve its commitments under the Paris Agreement.
Promoting Resource Efficiency: Sustainable entrepreneurship encourages the efficient use of natural resources, such as water, energy, and raw materials. Practices like recycling, upcycling, and sustainable sourcing help minimize resource wastage and promote a circular economy, where materials are reused and repurposed rather than discarded.
Conserving Biodiversity: Many sustainable businesses operate in sectors like organic farming, eco-tourism, and wildlife conservation, which directly contribute to biodiversity conservation. By promoting sustainable land use practices and protecting natural habitats, these enterprises help preserve India's rich biodiversity and ecological balance.
Addressing Pollution and Waste Management: Sustainable entrepreneurs often develop innovative solutions to address pollution and waste management challenges. For example, businesses focused on recycling, composting, and waste-to-energy conversion help reduce the burden on landfills and mitigate environmental pollution.

To illustrate the impact of sustainable entrepreneurship in India, we can examine several case studies of successful enterprises that have made significant contributions to local economies, employment generation, and environmental sustainability:

SELCO India: SELCO India, a social enterprise focused on solar energy solutions, has transformed the lives of thousands of people in rural India. By providing affordable solar power systems to off-grid communities, SELCO has created numerous jobs in the renewable energy sector, empowered local entrepreneurs, and reduced reliance on fossil fuels, thereby promoting environmental sustainability.

Amul: Amul, a dairy cooperative, has played a pivotal role in the economic development of rural India. By organizing dairy farmers into cooperatives, Amul has provided them with stable incomes, improved access to markets, and better quality of life. The cooperative's emphasis on sustainable dairy farming practices has also contributed to environmental conservation.

Barefoot College: Barefoot College, a non-profit organization, has empowered women in rural India by training them as solar engineers. These women, known as "Solar Mamas," install and maintain solar power systems in their communities, creating employment opportunities, enhancing energy access, and promoting sustainable development.

6. EFFECTIVENESS OF MICROFINANCE PROGRAMS IN ENHANCING WOMEN'S ECONOMIC INDEPENDENCE, DECISION-MAKING POWER, AND SOCIAL STATUS

Microfinance programs, which provide small loans and financial services to low-income individuals, have been widely recognized as a tool for poverty alleviation and economic empowerment. These programs have a particular impact on women, who often face greater barriers to accessing financial resources. This document explores the effectiveness of microfinance programs in enhancing women's economic independence, decision-making power, and social status.

6.1 Economic Independence

Access to Capital

- o Microfinance provides women with access to capital, which is crucial for starting or expanding small businesses.
- o Loans help women invest in income-generating activities such as agriculture, handicrafts, retail, and services.

Income Generation

- o Increased access to financial resources enables women to generate their own income.
- o With stable income, women can support their families, pay for education, and improve their living standards.

Savings and Financial Literacy

- o Microfinance programs often include savings components, encouraging women to save part of their earnings.
- o Financial literacy training, frequently a part of microfinance programs, equips women with knowledge about managing finances, budgeting, and investment.

Asset Accumulation

- o Women who participate in microfinance programs can accumulate assets, such as property, livestock, or equipment, which further contributes to their economic stability and growth.

Diversification of Income Sources

- o Access to microfinance allows women to diversify their income sources, reducing vulnerability to economic shocks.
- o Women can engage in multiple economic activities, ensuring a more stable and secure financial base.

6.2 Decision-Making Power

Household Decision-Making

- o Economic empowerment through microfinance increases women's bargaining power within households.
- o Women who contribute financially to their households gain greater influence over household decisions, including spending, education, and healthcare.

Business Decisions

- o Women entrepreneurs make key decisions about their businesses, such as investment, production, and marketing strategies.
- o Financial independence boosts their confidence in making and implementing business-related decisions.

Community Participation

- o Economic independence enhances women's roles in community decision-making processes.
- o Women involved in microfinance programs often participate more actively in local governance and community development initiatives.

Negotiation Skills

- o Training provided by microfinance institutions includes skills in negotiation and leadership, empowering women to advocate for their interests more effectively.
- o Improved negotiation skills lead to better terms in business and personal dealings.

6.3 Social Status

Increased Respect and Recognition

- o Women who succeed in their entrepreneurial endeavors through microfinance gain respect and recognition in their communities.
- o Success stories inspire other women and contribute to changing societal perceptions of women's capabilities.

Reduction in Gender-Based Violence

- o Economic independence can lead to a reduction in gender-based violence, as women gain the financial means to leave abusive relationships and assert their rights.
- o Empowered women are better equipped to negotiate safer and more respectful relationships.

Education and Skill Development

- o Microfinance programs often provide education and skill development opportunities, enhancing women's knowledge and abilities.
- o Educated and skilled women are more likely to be valued and respected within their families and communities.

Improved Health and Well-being

- o With increased financial resources, women can afford better healthcare for themselves and their families.
- o Improved health and well-being contribute to higher social status and quality of life.

Networking and Social Capital

- o Participation in microfinance programs often involves group meetings and peer support, fostering networking and social capital among women.
- o Strong social networks provide emotional support, business advice, and collective bargaining power.

Despite being primarily aimed at women, microfinance initiatives have an indirect effect on households and males by transferring tasks, enhancing economic stability, and altering social dynamics. As women become financially independent, households have a wider range of income sources, which relieves financial pressure on males and encourages better savings, education, and health investments. This change has the potential to change conventional gender roles by promoting a cooperative approach to family decision-making and motivating males to take on additional household duties. Many men gradually adjust to these changes, even though some may first oppose them, particularly as they indirectly access the networks, resources, and training offered by microfinance programs. By encouraging men to understand the benefits of sharing domestic and financial duties, these initiatives can influence social norms surrounding masculinity and ultimately improve family harmony and the general well-being of the community.

7. CHALLENGES AND OPPORTUNITIES FACED BY MICROFINANCE INSTITUTIONS (MFIS) IN PROMOTING SUSTAINABLE ENTREPRENEURSHIP AND WOMEN EMPOWERMENT

Microfinance institutions (MFIs) play a crucial role in promoting sustainable entrepreneurship and women empowerment in India. They provide financial services to those who are traditionally excluded from the formal banking sector, particularly low-income individuals and women. By offering microloans, savings accounts, insurance, and other financial products, MFIs aim to foster economic development and social inclusion. However, the journey is fraught with challenges, and there are significant opportunities that MFIs can harness to enhance their impact.

7.1 Key Challenges Faced by MFIs

While sustainable entrepreneurship holds immense potential, it also faces several challenges in India. Addressing these challenges and leveraging opportunities is crucial for maximizing its impact:

Access to Capital and Funding: One of the primary challenges for MFIs is securing adequate funding to support their operations and expand their services. Many MFIs rely on a mix of grants, donations, and loans from domestic and international sources. However, the availability of these funds can be inconsistent, making it difficult for MFIs to plan long-term strategies. Additionally, high-interest rates on borrowed capital can increase the cost of lending, which may be passed on to the borrowers.

Regulatory Environment: The regulatory framework governing MFIs in India can be complex and evolving. Compliance with these regulations requires significant resources and expertise, which can be particularly challenging for smaller MFIs. Regulatory requirements often include capital adequacy norms, interest rate caps, and reporting standards, which can impact the operational efficiency and financial viability of MFIs.

High Operational Costs: MFIs often operate in rural and remote areas, which involves significant logistical challenges and higher operational costs. Reaching out to clients, conducting due diligence, and monitoring loan repayments in these regions require substantial resources. The lack of infrastructure, such as roads and communication networks, further exacerbates these costs.

Risk Management: The client base of MFIs typically includes low-income individuals with limited or no credit history, which increases the risk of default. Economic vulnerabilities, such as crop failures or health emergencies, can significantly impact borrowers' ability to repay loans. MFIs need to develop robust risk management strategies to mitigate these risks while ensuring the sustainability of their operations.

Financial Literacy: Many potential clients of MFIs have low levels of financial literacy, which can affect their ability to understand loan terms, manage their finances, and make informed decisions. This lack of understanding can lead to misuse of funds, over-indebtedness, and defaults. MFIs need to invest in financial education programs to enhance their clients' financial literacy and ensure responsible borrowing and repayment practices.

Technological Adoption: While technology has the potential to revolutionize microfinance, many MFIs face challenges in adopting and integrating technological solutions. Limited financial resources, lack of technical expertise, and resistance to change can hinder the implementation of digital tools that can improve efficiency, reduce costs, and enhance customer experience.

7.2 Key Opportunities for MFIs

Leveraging Technology: Technological advancements offer significant opportunities for MFIs to enhance their operations and reach. Mobile banking, digital wallets, and online platforms can facilitate easier access to financial services for clients in remote areas. The use of big data and artificial intelligence can help MFIs assess creditworthiness, monitor loan utilization, and manage risks more effectively. Additionally, technology can streamline operations, reduce costs, and improve customer service.

Diversifying Financial Products: To better serve their clients, MFIs can diversify their product offerings beyond traditional microloans. Providing insurance, savings accounts, remittance services, and financial education can help clients manage risks, save for the future, and improve their financial stability. By offering a comprehensive suite of financial services, MFIs can enhance their value proposition and build long-term relationships with their clients.

Partnerships and Collaborations: Collaborating with other organizations, such as non-profits, government agencies, and private sector companies, can help MFIs expand their reach and impact. Partnerships can provide access to additional resources, expertise, and networks, enabling MFIs to scale their operations and develop innovative solutions. For instance, partnerships with

technology companies can facilitate the adoption of digital tools, while collaborations with government programs can help MFIs tap into subsidies and grants.
Capacity Building and Training: Investing in capacity building and training for both staff and clients can enhance the effectiveness and sustainability of MFIs. Staff training can improve operational efficiency, customer service, and risk management, while client training can enhance financial literacy and entrepreneurship skills. Empowering clients with knowledge and skills can lead to better financial management, increased business success, and higher loan repayment rates.
Focus on Women Empowerment: MFIs have a unique opportunity to promote women empowerment by specifically targeting women entrepreneurs and providing them with tailored financial products and support services. Women often face additional barriers to accessing finance, such as cultural norms and lack of collateral. By offering collateral-free loans, group lending models, and business development support, MFIs can help women overcome these challenges and build successful enterprises. Empowering women not only contributes to gender equality but also has positive ripple effects on families and communities.
Impact Measurement and Reporting: Demonstrating the social and economic impact of their work can help MFIs attract more funding and support from donors, investors, and policymakers. By developing robust impact measurement and reporting frameworks, MFIs can track their progress, identify areas for improvement, and communicate their achievements to stakeholders. Transparent and credible impact reporting can enhance the reputation of MFIs and build trust with clients and partners.

7.3 Policies for Women Empowerment Through Microfinance in India

Interest Rate Regulation:

- **Cap on Interest Rates:** Implement a cap on interest rates charged by microfinance institutions (MFIs) to prevent exploitation and ensure loans are affordable for women borrowers.
- **Transparent Pricing:** Mandate MFIs to disclose all costs associated with loans, including interest rates, fees, and penalties, to ensure transparency and protect borrowers from hidden charges.

Financial Literacy Programs:

- **Comprehensive Training:** Develop and implement financial literacy programs tailored for women, covering topics such as budgeting, savings, credit management, and investment.

- **Community-Based Approach:** Utilize community-based organizations and self-help groups (SHGs) to deliver financial literacy training, leveraging existing social networks to enhance reach and effectiveness.

Capacity Building and Skill Development:

- **Entrepreneurship Training:** Provide training programs focused on entrepreneurship and business management skills to help women start and grow their own businesses.
- **Technical and Vocational Training:** Offer technical and vocational training in various fields to equip women with skills that are in demand in the local and global markets.

Enhanced Access to Microfinance Services:

- **Incentives for MFIs:** Provide incentives such as tax benefits or subsidies to MFIs that focus on lending to women entrepreneurs, especially in rural and underserved areas.
- **Digital Financial Services:** Promote the use of digital financial services and mobile banking to increase access to microfinance for women in remote and rural areas.

Supportive Legal and Regulatory Framework:

- **Strengthened Legal Rights:** Strengthen legal frameworks to protect women borrowers from harassment and coercive recovery practices by MFIs.
- **Grievance Redressal Mechanisms:** Establish robust grievance redressal mechanisms to address complaints and disputes between women borrowers and MFIs.

Social and Community Support Systems:

- **Self-Help Groups (SHGs):** Encourage the formation and strengthening of SHGs as a platform for collective savings, credit access, and peer support for women.
- **Mentorship Programs:** Develop mentorship programs that connect women entrepreneurs with experienced mentors who can provide guidance, advice, and networking opportunities.

Access to Markets and Networks:

- **Market Linkages:** Facilitate market linkages for women entrepreneurs to ensure they have access to local, national, and international markets for their products and services.
- **Trade Fairs and Exhibitions:** Organize trade fairs and exhibitions to showcase products made by women entrepreneurs, providing them with opportunities for exposure and sales.

Monitoring and Evaluation:

- **Impact Assessment:** Implement regular monitoring and evaluation of microfinance programs to assess their impact on women's empowerment and identify areas for improvement.
- **Data Collection and Analysis:** Collect and analyze gender-disaggregated data to understand the specific needs and challenges faced by women in accessing and benefiting from microfinance services.

Collaboration and Partnerships:

- **Public-Private Partnerships:** Promote public-private partnerships to leverage resources and expertise from both sectors to expand the reach and impact of microfinance programs.
- **NGO and Civil Society Engagement:** Engage NGOs and civil society organizations in the design, implementation, and monitoring of microfinance initiatives to ensure they are inclusive and responsive to women's needs.

Policy Integration:

- **Holistic Approach:** Integrate microfinance policies with broader gender equality and women's empowerment policies to ensure a comprehensive and cohesive approach.
- **Cross-Sectoral Collaboration:** Foster collaboration between various government departments, such as finance, women and child development, and rural development, to align policies and programs aimed at empowering women through microfinance.

These policies aim to create an enabling environment for women to access and benefit from microfinance services, ultimately leading to their economic and social empowerment.

8. CONCLUSION

In India, microfinance has become a potent instrument for empowering women and encouraging sustainable entrepreneurship. For low-income people, especially women, microfinance institutions (MFIs) have made it easier for them to obtain credit, savings accounts, and insurance by offering financial services to those who have historically been shut out of the conventional banking system. Many have been able to start and expand their own businesses as a result, which has helped to reduce poverty and promote economic growth. Microfinance has a significant influence on sustainable enterprise. Numerous small and medium-sized businesses (SMEs) have been established thanks to small loans and financial solutions designed to meet the needs of aspiring entrepreneurs. These businesses frequently concentrate on environmentally friendly methods, utilizing nearby resources and generating jobs for local residents. In addition to fostering economic growth, microfinance's promotion of sustainable entrepreneurship assures environmental sustainability by promoting environmentally responsible company practices. One important result of microfinance programs in India is the empowerment of women. Women now have more autonomy and decision-making authority in their homes and communities thanks to the availability of financial resources. Participation in economic activity and social status have increased as a result of this financial independence. Moreover, the participation of women in entrepreneurship has resulted in favourable side effects, such improved health outcomes for their families and increased educational possibilities for their offspring. Another way that microfinance has helped close gender gaps in the Indian economy is through lending. MFIs have contributed to closing the gender gap in financial inclusion by focusing on female borrowers, thereby advancing gender equality. Strong, independent women business owners serve as role models for other women, encouraging them to follow their own dreams and become more involved in the economy. But there are still difficulties. Even though microfinance has come a long way, problems including excessive debt, exorbitant interest rates, and the need for more comprehensive financial literacy programs still need to be addressed. Furthermore, stronger regulatory frameworks are required to guarantee MFIs' sustainability and moral behaviour. In conclusion, microfinance has transformed sustainable enterprise and women's empowerment inside the Indian economy. Its provision of financial resources to the disenfranchised, particularly women, has not only facilitated economic development but also social progress. To sustain and grow these advantages, the existing barriers must be removed, and creative methods of delivering microfinance services must be preserved. This would ensure that the benefits of microfinance are felt by a greater number of individuals, contributing to the development of an equitable and inclusive economic environment in India.

REFERENCES

Aghion, B. A., & Morduch, J. (2000). Microfinance beyond group lending. *Economics of Transition*, 8(2), 401–420. DOI: 10.1111/1468-0351.00049

Armendáriz, B., & Morduch, J. (2010). *The economics of microfinance*. MIT Press.

Cheston, S., & Kuhn, L. (2002). Empowering women through microfinance. In Daley-Harris, S. (Ed.), *Pathways out of poverty: Innovations in microfinance for the poorest families* (pp. 167–228). Kumarian Press.

Cull, R., Demirgüç-Kunt, A., & Morduch, J. (2009). Microfinance meets the market. *The Journal of Economic Perspectives*, 23(1), 167–192. DOI: 10.1257/jep.23.1.167

Garikipati, S. (2008). The impact of lending to women on household vulnerability and women's empowerment: Evidence from India. *World Development*, 36(12), 2620–2642. DOI: 10.1016/j.worlddev.2007.11.008

Goetz, A. M., & Gupta, R. S. (1996). Who takes the credit? Gender, power, and control over loan use in rural credit programs in Bangladesh. *World Development*, 24(1), 45–63. DOI: 10.1016/0305-750X(95)00124-U

Hashemi, S. M., Schuler, S. R., & Riley, A. P. (1996). Rural credit programs and women's empowerment in Bangladesh. *World Development*, 24(4), 635–653. DOI: 10.1016/0305-750X(95)00159-A

Hunt, J., & Kasynathan, N. (2002). Reflections on microfinance and women's empowerment. *Development Bulletin (Canberra)*, 57, 71–75.

Kabeer, N. (2005). Is microfinance a 'magic bullet' for women's empowerment? *Economic and Political Weekly*, 40(44/45), 4709–4718.

Karlan, D., & Zinman, J. (2011). Microcredit in theory and practice: Using randomized credit scoring for impact evaluation. *Science*, 332(6035), 1278–1284. DOI: 10.1126/science.1200138 PMID: 21659596

Khandker, S. R. (2005). Microfinance and poverty: Evidence using panel data from Bangladesh. *The World Bank Economic Review*, 19(2), 263–286. DOI: 10.1093/wber/lhi008

Ledgerwood, J. (1999). *Microfinance handbook: An institutional and financial perspective*. World Bank Publications.

Mayoux, L. (2001). Tackling the down side: Social capital, women's empowerment and micro-finance in Cameroon. *Development and Change*, 32(3), 435–464. DOI: 10.1111/1467-7660.00212

Morduch, J. (1999). The microfinance promise. *Journal of Economic Literature*, 37(4), 1569–1614. DOI: 10.1257/jel.37.4.1569

Parveen, S. (2009). An empirical analysis of the relationship between rural women's participation in microfinance and their empowerment: The case of rural Pakistan. *Pakistan Journal of Social Sciences*, 29(1), 189–204.

Pitt, M. M., & Khandker, S. R. (1998). The impact of group-based credit programs on poor households in Bangladesh: Does the gender of participants matter? *Journal of Political Economy*, 106(5), 958–996. DOI: 10.1086/250037

Rahman, A. (1999). Micro-credit initiatives for equitable and sustainable development: Who pays? *World Development*, 27(1), 67–82. DOI: 10.1016/S0305-750X(98)00105-3

Rhyne, E. (2001). *Mainstreaming microfinance: How lending to the poor began, grew, and came of age in Bolivia*. Kumarian Press.

Sanyal, P. (2009). From credit to collective action: The role of microfinance in promoting women's social capital and normative influence. *American Sociological Review*, 74(4), 529–550. DOI: 10.1177/000312240907400402

Swain, R. B., & Wallentin, F. Y. (2009). Does microfinance empower women? Evidence from self-help groups in India. *International Review of Applied Economics*, 23(5), 541–556. DOI: 10.1080/02692170903007540

Chapter 5
Microfinance Dynamics: Exploring the Interplay Between Microcredit and Income Distribution in India

Subrata Halder
https://orcid.org/0009-0002-4048-2756
Fakir Chand College, India

ABSTRACT

This study investigates the impact of microcredit on income distribution in India from 1993 to 2022. Using secondary data from the National Bank for Agriculture and Rural Development (NABARD), Reserve Bank of India, the World Bank, and the Global Data Lab, an OLS regression model analyzes the relationship between microcredit and the Gini Index. Findings indicate a significant negative relationship between microcredit loans and income inequality, suggesting that increased microfinance access reduces income disparities. Other significant determinants include GDP growth, educational expenditure, gross capital formation, unemployment, and patrilocality. The study highlights the need to expand microfinance programs and implement policies for equitable economic benefit distribution. Limitations include reliance on secondary data and lack of regional disparity consideration. Despite these, the research enriches existing literature by offering insights specific to India and underscores microfinance's role in fostering inclusive economic growth.

DOI: 10.4018/979-8-3693-6622-6.ch005

INTRODUCTION

Development economics, which began in the 1950s, initially focused more on economic growth than on inequality. For a long time, it was thought that rising inequality was a normal and unavoidable part of growth in poor countries, especially if poverty was decreasing. Efforts to reduce inequality were seen as potential obstacles to growth and poverty reduction. However, starting in the 1970s, the issue of high inequality alongside persistent poverty in developing countries began to draw attention. Despite this, the emphasis remained on growth throughout the 1980s and 1990s, with the belief that reducing poverty should come before addressing inequality. Since 2000, however, there has been a growing recognition that equity is crucial for sustainable development, challenging the notion that high inequality is acceptable (Ravallion, 2014).

The shortcomings of macro development policies recommended by developed nations opened the door for alternative development strategies, with microcredit emerging as a significant tool since the 1970s. Microcredit, as defined by the 1997 Microcredit Summit, refers to programs that offer credit, along with other financial and business services such as savings and technical support, to very poor individuals for self-employment. The term "microfinance" encompasses a range of small-scale financial services provided to people engaged in agriculture, fishing, small enterprises, wage work, and other local activities in both rural and urban areas of developing countries. While "microcredit" and "microfinance" are often used interchangeably, microfinance broadly includes both microcredit and micro-savings, with both typically involving small amounts. Microcredit helps create and support microenterprises, which are generally small, non-farm businesses focused on trading, small-scale processing, or manufacturing (Kaladhar, 1997). Although many microfinance institutions in developing countries primarily support non-farm enterprises, some extend their services to various types of microenterprises

Microfinance has captured considerable public interest by offering a means for the poor to escape poverty through profitable financial services. This model of "development" is closely linked with financialization, illustrated by slogans such as "finance for all" and Muhammad Yunus's claim that "credit is a human right." The microfinance sector provides essential services, including credit, savings, and insurance, to individuals at or near the poverty line in developing countries. Although there is increasing emphasis on broader "financial inclusion," credit remains the central focus of the industry. Originally driven by NGO efforts in the 1980s, microfinance has evolved into a lucrative global sector, with its loan portfolio now exceeding half of total aid (Mader, 2014).

The microfinance model aims to create an inclusive financial system that benefits the poor and underprivileged by offering better access to financial services. This model helps individuals save more effectively and invest in education or small businesses, which can significantly contribute to reducing poverty and income inequality. Access to formal financial systems also enhances asset ownership and empowers vulnerable groups, particularly women, fostering greater economic equality and diminishing income disparities (Sawadogo & Semedo, 2021). Numerous studies support the positive impact of financial inclusion on reducing income inequality [e.g. Kim (2016), Omar & Inaba (2020), Demir et al. (2022)].

This chapter delves into the intricate interplay between microcredit and income distribution in India, examining how microfinance initiatives influence economic disparities and contribute to broader socio-economic changes. By analyzing empirical data, this chapter aims to uncover the multifaceted impacts of microcredit on income inequality. In understanding the dynamics of microfinance in India, this article seeks to provide a nuanced perspective on the effectiveness of microcredit as a tool for economic development and social equity. Through this exploration, we hope to inform policy discussions, improve the design and implementation of microfinance programs, and contribute to the ongoing efforts to harness financial inclusion as a means of achieving sustainable and inclusive growth in India.

MICROCREDIT IN INDIA

While Muhammad Yunus's Landmark Loan to 42 villagers in Jobra, Bangladesh, in 1976, and the founding of Grameen Bank in 1982 are often seen as the start of the microcredit era, its origins go back to the colonial period in South Asia. To truly understand microfinance, it's important to look at local historical precedents rather than distant examples. During British colonial rule, cooperative credit was introduced in India, Bangladesh, Pakistan, and Burma to alleviate poverty and improve moral standards. This initiative aimed to reduce unrest and change rural economic dynamics, laying the foundation for modern microfinance nearly a century before Yunus's work. The British sought to replace rural moneylenders and promote virtuous behaviour among locals, driven by a strong moral agenda (Mader, 2015). By 1930, more than 100,000 cooperative credit societies operated throughout the provinces of British India, counting 4 million members (roughly 1 per cent of the population) (Mader, 2015, p.45).

After independence in 1947, India made significant institutional changes, yet the colonial credit system remained influential. While the early state-led industrialization process did not focus on rural credit, cooperative societies were encouraged, increasing their share of rural credit from less than 5% in 1954 to over 20% by 1971.

Despite governance issues and reliance on state governments, progress continued. In 1969, many major commercial banks were nationalized, unprofitable banks were consolidated, and a new focus on rural and agricultural credit emerged during the "Green Revolution." From 1970, new regulations led to a rapid increase in rural bank branches, boosting rural credit from 3% to 15%, enhancing non-agricultural output, and supporting small businesses. This shift significantly reduced the reliance on informal credit sources, and household debt to formal lenders rose from 15.8% to 31.7%, introducing many Indian households to formal credit for the first time (Mader, 2015).

In 1972, Ela Bhatt, a former labor union lawyer, founded the Self-Employed Women's Association (SEWA) in Ahmedabad. SEWA organized women into cooperatives and provided them with banking and social services. Instead of focusing on wage negotiations like traditional unions, SEWA aimed to create new job opportunities by helping women access credit, raw materials, and control over their earnings. Initial attempts to secure credit through nationalized banks failed due to a disconnect between the bankers and the largely illiterate clients. In response, SEWA set up its own bank in 1974 using contributions from its members. This bank prioritized savings and asset development, and has been profitable since its start, with ownership and management fully in the hands of the women involved (Mader, 2015).

To strengthen the financial system and promote inclusive growth, the National Bank of Agriculture and Rural Development (NABARD) launched the Self-Help Group (SHG)–Bank Linkage Programme (SBLP) in 1991–1992. The scheme was based on several key principles: starting with savings before extending credit, using savings as partial collateral, providing bank loans to SHGs for further lending to their members, and allowing SHGs to make credit decisions and set loan terms. Joint liability was used as an alternative to physical collateral, and the program began with small loans, clearly defining challenging credit cycles (Biswas & Sana, 2015).

SHGs are small, informal groups of 10–20 individuals who pool their savings and provide loans to members. Supported by banks or NGOs, these groups keep financial records, learn money management, and use their savings to access larger bank loans, which they distribute based on need. Recognized by the World Bank and the Reserve Bank of India (RBI), the program aims to alleviate poverty and improve rural living standards, particularly for women, by promoting financial discipline and breaking the cycle of debt. Initially slow, with only 32,995 groups linked by 1999, the program expanded significantly, reaching over 70 million poor households by March 2008 (Sinha et al., 2012). Between 2020-21 and 2022-23, the SHG-Bank Linkage Programme made significant strides. The total number of Self-Help Groups (SHGs) increased from 112.23 lakh to 134.03 lakh. The total savings with banks saw a notable rise from 37,477.61 crore to 58,892.68 crore. Women's SHGs have been particularly prominent, constituting 84-89% of the total

SHGs and showing consistent growth in both number and savings. The programme also experienced a substantial increase in loans disbursed, climbing from 58,070.68 crore to 1,45,200.23 crore. Women-led SHGs received a significant portion of these loans, underscoring the programme's focus on empowering women. Loans extended to NRLM/SGSY groups grew significantly, reflecting an emphasis on these groups within the programme, while loans to NULM/SJSRY groups also saw an increase. Outstanding loans against SHGs increased from 1,03,289.71 crore to 1,88,078.80 crore, with a notable share being linked to women's SHGs. Overall, the SHG-Bank Linkage Programme has demonstrated substantial progress in expanding financial inclusion, particularly for rural women, while adhering to its core principles of savings and sustainable credit management (NABARD, 2023).

In addition to the NABARD model, several other microcredit lending models have evolved over time. Self-Help Groups (SHGs), typically composed of 10-20 members, promote regular savings and mutual loans among members, using peer pressure in place of collateral to ensure responsible borrowing. Federated SHGs advance this approach by creating federations to enhance sustainability, broaden economic opportunities, and provide leadership and insurance services, with organizations like PRADAN pioneering these efforts. The Grameen Bank Model, developed in Bangladesh, involves group lending with joint liability and has been adopted by Indian MFIs such as SHARE Microfin Ltd. and CASHPOR Financial and Technical Services Ltd. The Cooperative Model, exemplified by the Cooperative Development Forum (CDF) in Hyderabad, relies on credit unions and a "savings first" philosophy. Joint Liability Groups (JLGs), made up of 4-10 members, guarantee each other's loans for collective activities, particularly in agriculture. Individual Lending is another approach where MFIs like SHARE Microfin offer direct loans, carefully assessing each borrower's capacity to repay. The ICICI Bank Model supports microfinance through wholesale linkage by buying MFI loan portfolios and providing mezzanine capital. Finally, the Business Correspondent Model, supported by the Reserve Bank of India (RBI), uses intermediaries to offer banking services such as small deposits, loans, and remittances in underserved areas (Biswas & Sana, 2015).

Despite NABARD's initiative and variety of microcredit approaches indicating the diversity and innovative business practices in the microcredit segment, in October 2010, the microfinance industry in Andhra Pradesh encountered a severe crisis, revealing significant flaws in its model. The crisis highlighted systemic issues. The suicides of borrowers overwhelmed by debt and aggressive collection tactics led the state government to suspend loan repayments, exposing the vulnerabilities of the microfinance sector. This crisis, fueled by the expansion of for-profit MFIs and the perception of them as exploitative moneylenders, prompted the Reserve Bank of India to introduce regulatory reforms. However, the problem was not only in the supply of credit but also in the deep-seated demand for unsustainable debt within rural communities. The microfinance model, while intended to alleviate poverty and provide financial access, instead often reinforced existing social and economic inequalities. The crisis underscored the complex interplay between microfinance, traditional debt practices, and entrenched socio-economic structures, showing that simply increasing credit access could exacerbate existing issues rather than solve them (Taylor, 2011).

In conclusion, the evolution of microcredit lending models—from colonial cooperative credit societies to contemporary initiatives like NABARD's SHG-Bank Linkage Programme and various innovative approaches—demonstrates a rich history of efforts to enhance financial inclusion and support rural livelihoods. Despite significant progress, the crisis in Andhra Pradesh in 2010 exposed critical vulnerabilities in the sector, revealing how systemic issues, aggressive lending practices, and deep-rooted socio-economic inequalities can undermine the goals of microfinance. The mixed outcomes underscore the need for ongoing reforms and a nuanced understanding of microfinance's role in rural development. Moving forward, balancing access to credit with rigorous regulation and sensitivity to local economic contexts will be essential for ensuring that microfinance continues to support, rather than exacerbate, the financial well-being of marginalized communities.

MICROCREDIT AND INCOME INEQUALITY

Microfinance, aimed at extending financial services to underserved populations, has been a central focus of debate regarding its effectiveness in reducing income inequality. The literature presents mixed outcomes, with some studies highlighting its potential for income redistribution, while others emphasize its limitations and unintended consequences.

Miled et al. (2022) provide compelling evidence that countries with a higher gross loan portfolio per capita from microfinance institutions experience reductions in income inequality. This suggests that broader access to microfinance can positively impact income distribution over time. Similarly, Lacalle-Calderon et al. (2019) found that expanding the scale of microcredit across 85 countries from 2001 to 2012 correlated with a decrease in income inequality, reinforcing the idea that increased microfinance outreach can contribute to a more equitable distribution of wealth. Chiazor et al. (2016) also emphasize that microfinance strategies, including microcredit, can effectively empower underserved populations and reduce income inequality in developing countries. These findings collectively suggest that microfinance, when scaled effectively, can have a meaningful impact on reducing income disparities.

However, other studies present a more nuanced view. Hermes (2014) argues that while higher levels of microfinance participation are associated with reduced inequality, the effect is relatively modest. This indicates that microfinance alone is insufficient to significantly alter income inequality without broader structural and economic reforms. Mahmoud Ali & Ghoneim (2019) further complicate the narrative by finding no significant impact of microfinance on the Gini index in a sample of 30 developing countries, suggesting that the effects of microfinance on income inequality may vary or be inconclusive. This underscores the idea that the macro-level impact of microfinance is contingent on context-specific factors.

Regional and local studies offer further insights into the varying effects of microfinance. Ahmed et al. (2019) found that Bangladesh's Grameen Bank microcredit program reduced income inequality in households with access to credit, underscoring the potential of microfinance to enhance income distribution within specific communities. Lassoued (2021) observed similar results in the MENA region, where microfinance contributed to reducing income inequality alongside improvements in governance, highlighting the interplay between financial access and institutional quality.

Oteng-Abayie et al. (2023) investigated Ghana and found that microfinance had a significant effect on reducing spatial inequality and poverty. Their findings revealed both direct and spillover effects of microfinance, suggesting that improved access to microfinance can reduce disparities within and between districts. The role of information and communication technology (ICT) in financial inclusion and poverty reduction has also been explored. Mushtaq & Bruneau, (2019) found that ICT diffusion positively affects financial inclusion and has a negative relationship with poverty and inequality. This indicates that integrating ICT with microfinance can further enhance its impact on reducing poverty and inequality.

However, the limitations and critiques of microfinance are equally significant. Copestake (2002) warns that while microcredit can provide short-term poverty alleviation, it may exacerbate income inequality during periods of economic stagnation. This highlights the complex relationship between microfinance and broader economic conditions, suggesting that microfinance alone cannot fully address inequality without stable macroeconomic environments. Similarly, Saïdou et al. (2013) note that while microcredit reduces income inequality in Burkina Faso, the success of such programs is dependent on credit institutions enhancing their social mission and accessibility to truly benefit the poorest segments of society.

Further critiques focus on the broader structural challenges of microfinance. Lucarelli (2005) cautions against the overemphasis on microcredit as a developmental solution, arguing that expanding microcredit programs without addressing broader social and economic inequalities could lead to limited long-term impacts. Subramaniam et al. (2021) also highlight that while microfinance can lower income inequality, its impact on poverty reduction is often limited for the most impoverished populations. They advocate for restructuring microfinance to better target the extreme poor, suggesting that more tailored approaches are necessary for microfinance to have a substantial impact on both poverty and inequality.

Critically, several studies raise concerns about microfinance exacerbating inequality rather than reducing it. Fritz & Lang (2012) argue that microcredits can increase income inequality, as wealthier individuals disproportionately benefit from improved access to finance, widening the income gap between rich and poor borrowers. Crépon et al. (2015) found that microcredit access did not significantly increase overall income or consumption, indicating a limited effect on reducing income inequality among participants. Hsu (2014) further complicates this view by suggesting that in rural China, microcredit often reinforces existing power dynamics, benefiting the already privileged while failing to support the disenfranchised.

Moreover, critiques focusing on gender and social dynamics raise additional concerns. Balasubramanian (2013) challenges the conventional wisdom surrounding microcredit's empowerment potential, arguing that without addressing underlying power dynamics and structural inequalities, microcredit may fail to truly empower women in South Asia. Similarly,

Microfinance in India has been a significant tool for addressing income inequality and promoting economic empowerment, particularly among underserved and marginalized populations. Datta & Sahu (2022) found that microcredit had a positive impact on livelihood transformation and economic empowerment among tribal communities in India, reducing income inequality by improving both their financial and mental well-being. Similarly, Chatterjee & Patil (2022) demonstrated that an increase in the number of microfinance borrowers in India significantly reduced income inequality, though they cautioned that larger loan sizes could exacerbate disparities, as wealthier individuals benefit more from higher loan amounts.

Maity (2024) emphasized the role of microcredit, particularly through Self-Help Groups (SHGs), in reducing inequality by promoting financial inclusion in India. However, the study noted that the effect on social cohesion has been limited, pointing to the need for more holistic approaches. Goel (2020) conducted research in Gujarat, India, and found that while microfinance had positive effects on participants' income, there remains a pressing need for targeted policies to address the extreme poor to ensure more equitable outcomes. Similarly, Maity & Sarania (2017), in their study of SHG programs in Assam, India, highlighted positive impacts on income, employment, and financial inclusion. However, the study also pointed out that while microfinance aids poverty reduction, its impact on income inequality has been less significant.

Mehta & Bhattacharya (2017) focused on financial sector development in India, finding that microcredit has a direct effect on reducing rural-urban consumption inequality, highlighting the broader role that microfinance can play in reducing income disparities. However, Mukhopadhyay (2016) found that while microcredit access can reduce long-term consumption inequality, it often exacerbates short-term disparities, particularly through non-food expenditures, revealing complex dynamics between consumption patterns and financial access.

Despite these positive impacts, the limitations of microfinance in India are notable. Subramaniam et al., (2021) argue that microfinance's effectiveness in reducing income inequality is limited because it often excludes the hardcore poor, who require more comprehensive support beyond financial services. Sanyal (2015) noted emergent inequality within microcredit groups in India, with Hindu groups benefiting more from collective action than Muslim groups, which has implications for income distribution and community benefits. Similarly, Singh & Lee (2020) found that microfinance interventions may inadvertently enhance income inequality, as access to social capital through SHGs is dominated by higher social categories, limiting the benefits for disadvantaged groups.

Earlier research by Guha & Gupta (2005) showed that microcredit programs, such as those implemented by Rosca, could help alleviate income inequality by providing the poor with access to credit, enabling them to engage in income-generating activities and improve loan repayment habits. Chowdhury (2000) also argued that microcredit enhances household income and assets, thereby improving the economic status of poorer borrowers and reducing income inequality. Finally, Al-Azzam (2023) emphasized that microfinance plays a critical role in lowering income inequality in developing countries, including India, with Gini coefficient analysis confirming its effectiveness in reducing income disparities.

The literature on microfinance and its impact on income inequality presents a complex and nuanced picture, especially within the Indian context. While microfinance has demonstrated significant potential in empowering underserved populations, enhancing financial inclusion, and reducing income disparities, the outcomes are often dependent on specific regional and socio-economic factors. Studies such as those by Datta & Sahu (2022) and Chatterjee & Patil (2022) highlight the positive impact of microcredit on reducing income inequality, particularly through livelihood transformation and the promotion of self-help groups (SHGs). These initiatives have proven effective in uplifting marginalized groups, especially tribal communities, and narrowing the rural-urban consumption inequality gap (Mehta & Bhattacharya, 2017).

However, the literature also reveals several limitations and unintended consequences of microfinance. Research by Mukhopadhyay (2016) and Subramaniam et al. (2021) suggests that while microcredit access can alleviate poverty, it may have a limited impact on income inequality and often excludes the extreme poor.

Additionally, concerns about exacerbating existing inequalities, as noted by Sanyal (2015) and Singh & Lee (2020), indicate that higher social categories tend to benefit more from microfinance interventions. The role of social capital and the exclusion of disadvantaged groups highlight the need for more targeted approaches to ensure that microfinance reaches the most vulnerable.

In summary, while microfinance has contributed to poverty reduction and income redistribution, its impact on income inequality in India remains uneven. This calls for a reevaluation of microfinance policies, emphasizing more inclusive financial services, tailored interventions for the extreme poor, and a stronger focus on addressing social and structural inequalities.

The present chapter is motivated by the need to address critical gaps and complexities highlighted in the existing literature on microfinance and income inequality. While a substantial body of research indicates that microfinance can potentially reduce income inequality, the evidence remains mixed and often context-dependent. A significant limitation in the current literature is the limited focus on the Indian context. While international studies provide valuable insights, there is a notable scarcity of research specifically addressing how microfinance affects income inequality within India. Thus, this chapter aims to address the existing gaps in the literature by focusing specifically on the Indian context, where there is limited research on the impact of microfinance on income inequality. By providing a comprehensive analysis that considers varying contexts, economic conditions, this study seeks to offer actionable insights for optimizing microfinance strategies and enhancing their effectiveness in reducing income inequality in India.

DATA AND METHODOLOGY

Income inequality is a complex and multi-faceted issue, influenced by various factors that contribute to disparities in income distribution. Generally, explanations for rising income inequality are categorized into two main groups: structural and institutional factors. Traditionally, economists focused on structural drivers such as globalization and technological advancements as key contributors to widening income gaps. However, more recent perspectives have shifted toward institutional and political explanations, highlighting the role of neoliberal policies implemented since the 1980s. These include privatization, deregulation, and reductions in taxes and welfare programs, which have played a significant role in exacerbating income inequality (Polacko, 2021).

Income inequality is shaped by a wide range of interrelated factors that influence the distribution of income within a society. Globalization, for instance, has integrated markets and increased competition, but it has also contributed to wage disparities, particularly between skilled and unskilled workers. Technological advancements, while boosting productivity, have often favoured higher-income individuals with access to education and specialized skills, further widening the income gap. Tax policies also play a crucial role, as regressive tax systems or tax cuts for the wealthy can exacerbate inequality. The decline of labour unions has weakened workers' bargaining power, leading to stagnating wages for lower- and middle-income groups (Polacko, 2021). Educational access and quality are equally important, as disparities in education often translate into differences in income-earning potential. Demographic changes, such as ageing populations or shifts in labour force participation, can also impact income distribution. Additionally, the supply and demand dynamics of capital and labour influence wages and returns on investment, often skewing income distribution in favour of capital owners (Nolan et al., 2019). Macroeconomic policies, including fiscal policies and government expenditure, shape the broader economic environment and determine how wealth and resources are distributed. Furthermore, wealth inequality, where assets are unevenly distributed, amplifies income inequality over time. Finally, labour market policies, such as minimum wage laws and employment protections, and fiscal policies, including social safety nets, also play a critical role in either mitigating or exacerbating income inequality (van der Hoeven, 2019).

The study is based on secondary data, spanning 30 years from 1993 to 2022, sourced from a variety of official platforms, including the National Bank for Agriculture and Rural Development (NABARD), the Reserve Bank of India (RBI), the World Bank (WB), and the Global Data Lab (GDL). These data sources provide a robust foundation for analyzing the relationship between microcredit and income distribution over this extended period.

This study employs a regression model to examine the impact of various macroeconomic and socio-economic variables on income inequality in India, as measured by the Gini Index. The model includes several independent variables that are rooted in relevant literature, highlighting their significance in shaping income distribution. The selection of variables—microcredit loan, GDP growth, foreign direct investment, unemployment, patrilocality index, educational expenditure, and gross capital formation—draws upon existing research to justify their inclusion in the analysis.

Dependent Variable

Gini Index (GI): The Gini Index is widely used in economic studies to measure income inequality within a population (e.g. Tabash et al., 2024; Walujadi et al., 2022; Heshmati, 2006). It captures the extent to which income distribution among individuals or households deviates from a perfectly equal distribution, and is a standard variable in studies examining the relationship between economic factors and inequality. In this study, the Gini Index is sourced from the Global Data Lab (GDL).

Independent Variable

Microcredit Loan: Microcredit loans have been central to reducing income inequality, particularly in developing countries where financial inclusion is limited. Microfinance institutions, particularly NABARD in India, have been instrumental in providing loans to Self Help Groups (SHGs), which facilitate economic empowerment for underserved populations. Several studies have found that microcredit positively affects income generation and reduces inequality by promoting self-employment and entrepreneurial activities (e.g. Miled et al., 2022; Chatterjee & Patil, 2022). This variable, sourced from NABARD and RBI data, captures the total microcredit loan provided to SHGs and is a critical factor in analyzing income redistribution in rural and semi-urban areas.

Control Variables

GDP Growth (GDP): Economic growth, as measured by annual GDP growth, has long been associated with changes in income distribution. The Kuznets curve hypothesis (Kuznets, 1955) posits that inequality first rises and then falls as a country's GDP increases. More recent studies argue that sustained economic growth can lead to a more equitable distribution of income, particularly when paired with inclusive policies (e.g. Naguib, 2015; Dollar & Kraay, 2002; Lechheb et al., 2019). Therefore, GDP growth is included as an independent variable to account for the overall economic health of the country and its potential role in moderating income inequality. Data for this variable is sourced from the World Bank and calculated using constant 2015 prices in USD.

Foreign Direct Investment (FDI): Foreign Direct Investment (FDI) plays a significant role in shaping economic development and income distribution. FDI has been linked to both positive and negative outcomes in terms of income inequality. While FDI can boost job creation and economic growth (e.g. Ucal et al., 2016; Chintrakarn et al., 2012; Kaulihowa & Adjasi, 2018)., some studies suggest that it can exacerbate inequality by disproportionately benefiting skilled labor and capital-intensive sectors (Huang et al., 2020). Therefore, FDI is included in this model to capture its potential effects on income inequality in India, with data sourced from the World Bank.

Unemployment: Unemployment has a direct impact on income inequality, as a higher unemployment rate typically leads to reduced household incomes, particularly among lower-income groups(Esquivias et al., 2021; Haini et al., 2023). Studies have shown that higher unemployment rates can worsen income distribution, as the unemployed are more likely to fall into poverty, which exacerbates the income gap between employed and unemployed populations (Cysne, 2009). The unemployment rate is sourced from the World Bank and included to account for the labor market's influence on inequality.

Patrilocality Index (PI): Cultural factors, particularly patrilocal practices, can significantly influence income distribution, especially in countries like India where traditional gender norms shape economic participation. The Patrilocality Index measures the prevalence of patrilocal practices, which refer to the cultural norm where women move to their husbands' households after marriage, limiting their access to economic resources (Rahman & Rao, 2004). This index is included as an independent variable to account for the socio-cultural barriers to economic equality, particularly for women, which could contribute to income inequality.

Educational Expenditure (EE): Investment in education is widely regarded as one of the most effective ways to reduce income inequality in the long term. By increasing access to quality education, governments can enable upward social mobility and enhance the earning potential of disadvantaged populations. Several studies have shown that higher public expenditure on education is linked to reduced income inequality (Artige & Cavenaile, 2023; Neuhuber & Schneider, 2024). Therefore, educational expenditure is included in the model to assess its role in moderating inequality, with data sourced from the World Bank.

Gross Capital Formation (GCF): Gross Capital Formation, which measures the outlays on additions to fixed assets and inventory levels, is included to capture the broader economic investments in infrastructure and production capacities. Research suggests that higher levels of capital formation can lead to economic growth and job creation, which in turn can reduce income inequality if the benefits of growth are equitably distributed (Purba et al., 2019). However, the relationship between capital formation and inequality can be complex, as increased capital investment may initially benefit capital owners more than labourers. This variable is sourced from the World Bank.

Regression Model

$$\text{Gini Index} = \beta_0 + \beta_1 \ln(\text{Microcredit Loan}) + \beta_2 \ln(\text{GDP Growth}) + \beta_3 \ln(\text{FDI}) + \beta_4 \ln(\text{Gross Capital Formation}) + \beta_5 \ln(\text{Educational expenditure}) + \beta_6 \text{Unemployment} + \beta_7 \text{Patrilocality Index} + \varepsilon$$

Where, ε stand for error term

RESULTS AND DISCUSSION

Table 1. Descriptive statistics

Variable	Obs	Mean	Std. Dev.	Min	Max
Gini Index	30	.351	.107	.14	.49
ln Microcredit Loan	30	7.282	3.926	-1.24	11.51
ln GDP Growth	30	2.502	.491	0	2.77
ln FDI	30	21.895	4.273	.03	23.85
ln Gross Capital Formation	30	3.456	.169	3.12	3.74
ln Educational expenditure	30	1.171	.103	1.06	1.46
Unemployment	30	7.713	.833	4.82	8.7
Patrilocality Index	30	2.631	.163	2.46	2.96

Table 2. Pairwise correlations

Variables	1	2	3	4	5	6	7	8
(1) Gini index	1							
(2) ln Microcredit Loan	-0.862**	1						
(3) ln GDP Growth	0.244	-0.137	1					
(4) ln FDI	-0.383**	0.455**	0.019	1				
(5) ln Gross Capital Formation	-0.316	0.664**	0.171	0.402**	1			
(6) ln Educational expenditure	0.399**	-0.282	0.032	0.031	-0.243	1		
(7) Unemployment	0.292	0.165	-0.025	0.106	0.538**	0.123	1	
(8) Patrilocality Index	-0.792**	0.703**	-0.138	0.315	0.405**	-0.447**	-0.154	1

*** p<0.01, ** p<0.05, * p<0.1

The correlation matrix provides insights into the relationships between the Gini index (a measure of income inequality) and the selected independent variables. There is a significant negative correlation between the Gini index and microcredit loans ($r = -0.862$, $p<0.05$), suggesting that an increase in microcredit loans is associated with a reduction in income inequality. Similarly, foreign direct investment (FDI) ($r = -0.383$, $p<0.05$) and gross capital formation ($r = -0.316$) are negatively correlated with the Gini index, though the correlation with gross capital formation is not statistically significant. This implies that higher FDI inflows and capital formation may contribute to reducing inequality, although the latter requires further investigation for significance. On the other hand, educational expenditure ($r = 0.399$, $p<0.05$)

is positively correlated with the Gini index, indicating that increased spending on education does not immediately reduce inequality and might be linked to existing disparities in access to quality education. Unemployment ($r = 0.292$) also shows a positive relationship with the Gini index, implying that higher unemployment is associated with greater income inequality, though this result is not statistically significant. The patrilocality index is significantly and negatively correlated with the Gini index ($r = -0.792, p<0.05$), suggesting that more prevalent patrilocal practices are linked to reduced income inequality, possibly reflecting stronger social safety nets or traditional support systems. Additionally, microcredit loans, FDI, and gross capital formation exhibit moderate positive correlations, indicating that these variables are interconnected and potentially influence income distribution collectively.

Table 3. OLS regression: Model summary

R	R Square	Adjusted R Square	Std. Error of the Estimate
.987	0.975	0.967	0.01945

Table 4. ANOVA

	Sum of Squares	df	Mean Square	F	Sig.
Regression	0.321	7	0.046	121.22	0.000
Residual	0.008	22	0.000		
Total	0.329	29			

Table 5. Coefficients

	Unstandardized Coefficients		Standardized Coefficients	t	Sig.
	B	Std. Error	Beta		
Constant	-0.112	0.159		-0.705	0.488
ln Microcredit Loan	-0.024	0.002	-0.887	-14.195	0.000
ln GDP Growth	0.017	0.008	0.08	2.076	0.050
ln FDI	-0.001	0.001	-0.053	-1.345	0.192
ln Gross Capital Formation	0.116	0.041	0.183	2.798	0.010
ln Educational expenditure	0.103	0.041	0.099	2.487	0.021
Unemployment	0.041	0.006	0.317	6.466	0.000
Patrilocality Index	-0.08	0.036	-0.122	-2.199	0.039

Dependent Variable: Gini Index

The multiple regression analysis reveals significant relationships between several independent variables and income inequality, measured by the Gini Index. **Microcredit Loan** was found to be a significant negative predictor of income inequality (β = -0.887, t = -14.195, p < .001), indicating that higher levels of microcredit lending are associated with a decrease in the Gini Index, suggesting reduced income inequality. **GDP Growth** also demonstrated a positive relationship with income inequality (β = 0.08, t = 2.076, p = .050), suggesting that as GDP grows, income inequality slightly increases. **Foreign Direct Investment (FDI)**, while negatively related to income inequality (β = -0.053), did not reach statistical significance (t = -1.345, p = .192), indicating that FDI may not have a strong direct impact on income inequality in this model. **Gross Capital Formation** was a significant positive predictor of income inequality (β = 0.183, t = 2.798, p = .010), suggesting that increases in capital investment are associated with higher income inequality. **Educational Expenditure** also significantly predicted income inequality, with a positive association (β = 0.099, t = 2.487, p = .021), implying that greater spending on education is linked to higher income inequality, possibly due to unequal access to educational opportunities. **Unemployment** showed a significant positive relationship with income inequality (β = 0.317, t = 6.466, p < .001), indicating that higher unemployment rates are associated with increased income inequality. Finally, **Patrilocality Index** was found to be a significant negative predictor of income inequality (β = -0.122, t = -2.199, p = .039), suggesting that more prevalent patrilocal practices are associated with a reduction in the Gini Index and lower income inequality. The model's R-squared value is 0.975, indicating that approximately 97.5% of the variance in the Gini Index is explained by the model, and the F-test result is highly significant (p-value = 0.000), confirming the overall model's statistical significance. Overall, these findings underscore the complex interplay of economic and social factors in shaping income inequality.

Table 6. Variance inflation factor (VIF)

	VIF	1/VIF
ln Gross Capital Formation	3.72	0.269
ln Microcredit Loan	3.4	0.294
Patrilocality Index	2.66	0.376
Unemployment	2.1	0.476
ln Educational expenditure	1.38	0.725
ln FDI	1.37	0.730
ln GDP Growth	1.29	0.775
Mean VIF	2.27	

The VIF values suggest that the predictors in the model are not excessively correlated with each other. This indicates that the estimates of the regression coefficients are stable and reliable. Since multicollinearity is not a severe problem, the interpretations of the coefficients are valid. The relationships identified between the predictors and the Gini index can be considered trustworthy.

Breusch-Pagan / Cook-Weisberg test for heteroskedasticity

Ho: Constant variance

Variables: fitted values of giniindex

chi2(1) = 0.75

Prob > chi2 = 0.3866

The Breusch-Pagan / Cook-Weisberg test for heteroskedasticity assesses whether the variance of the errors in a regression model is constant (homoskedasticity) or not (heteroskedasticity). In this case, the test results show a chi-squared value of 0.75 with a p-value of 0.3866. Since the p-value is greater than the common significance levels (0.05), we fail to reject the null hypothesis of constant variance. This indicates that there is no significant evidence of heteroskedasticity in the model. Therefore, we can assume that the residuals are homoskedastic, suggesting that the standard errors of the coefficient estimates are reliable and the model's assumptions are not violated.

Table 7. Breusch-Godfrey LM test for autocorrelation

chi2	df	Prob>Chi2
0.037	1	0.8481

H0: no serial correlation

The Breusch-Godfrey LM test for autocorrelation checks for the presence of serial correlation in the residuals of a regression model. The test results show a chi-squared value of 0.037 with 1 degree of freedom and a p-value of 0.8481. Since the p-value is significantly higher than common significance levels (0.05), we fail to reject the null hypothesis of no serial correlation. This indicates that there is no significant evidence of autocorrelation in the residuals, suggesting that the model's error terms are not correlated over time and the assumption of no serial correlation holds true.

Table 8. Shapiro-Wilk W test for normal data

Variable	Obs	W	V	z	Prob>z
r	30	0.961	1.248	0.459	0.323

The Shapiro-Wilk W test for normality assesses whether the residuals (denoted as “r”) from the model are normally distributed. The test results show a W value of 0.961, a V value of 1.248, a z value of 0.459, and a p-value of 0.323. Since the p-value is greater than common significance levels (0.05), we fail to reject the null hypothesis that the residuals are normally distributed. This suggests that there is no significant evidence against the normality assumption of the residuals in the model, indicating that the residuals are approximately normally distributed.

The findings from the regression analysis, complemented by the model diagnostics, offer significant insights into the determinants of income inequality in India over a 30-year period. The results indicate a multifaceted relationship between income inequality and various economic, social, and financial factors. The results are largely consistent with existing literature but also reveal some contrasts, contributing to a deeper understanding of income inequality's complex dynamics.

The regression analysis reveals a highly significant negative relationship between microcredit loans and the Gini Index, with a coefficient of -0.024. This finding underscores the effectiveness of microfinance in reducing income inequality, affirming that microcredit provided by institutions like NABARD to Self Help Groups (SHGs) has been instrumental in enabling underserved populations to engage in economic activities, thereby improving their income levels and reducing disparities. The findings supports the argument that microfinance can be an effective tool for reducing income disparities by enhancing financial inclusion (Miled et al., 2022; Chatterjee & Patil, 2022). This finding aligns with existing research demonstrating that microcredit helps empower low-income individuals, especially in rural areas, by enabling self-employment and entrepreneurship. However, this result contrasts with other studies, such as Fritz & Lang (2012), which found that microcredit might exacerbate inequality by disproportionately benefiting wealthier or more connected borrowers. This discrepancy highlights the importance of implementation, as well-designed microcredit programs like SHGs in India can have a more equitable impact on income distribution.

The study's finding that GDP growth is positively associated with income inequality supports the Kuznets curve hypothesis (Kuznets, 1955), which suggests that inequality tends to rise in the early stages of economic growth before stabilizing or declining as economies mature. This finding contrasts with Dollar & Kraay (2002), who argue that sustained growth can promote a more equal income distribution if paired with inclusive policies. In India, the unequal access to growth opportunities, particularly in rural regions, may explain why economic growth has not yet translated into reduced inequality. In the context of India, economic growth has often been uneven, benefiting urban and more developed regions disproportionately, which may explain why GDP growth is positively linked to rising inequality in this model.

The analysis shows an insignificant relationship between foreign direct investment (FDI) and income inequality, with a coefficient of -0.001. This suggests that FDI, in the context of India, does not significantly influence income distribution. This could be due to the concentration of FDI in specific sectors or regions, which may not directly impact the wider population.

Gross capital formation and educational expenditure both exhibit positive and significant relationships with income inequality, with coefficients of 0.116 and 0.103, respectively. These findings suggest that investments in capital and education, while crucial for overall development, may disproportionately benefit individuals or groups already in better positions to capitalize on these investments, thus potentially widening income gaps. This points to the necessity of ensuring that such investments are inclusive and accessible to all societal segments.

Unemployment has a significant positive effect on income inequality, with a coefficient of 0.041. High unemployment rates exacerbate income disparities, as the unemployed population typically has little to no income, increasing the gap between them and those who are employed.

The Patrilocality Index, with a negative and significant coefficient of -0.08, suggests that regions with higher levels of patrilocality (where married couples live with or near the husband's family) tend to have lower income inequality. This might be because such social structures promote resource sharing within families and communities, thereby reducing disparities.

The diagnostic tests further validate the robustness of the model. The robustness of the model is supported by several key factors. First, the inclusion of a diverse set of independent variables—ranging from microeconomic factors such as microcredit loans to macroeconomic variables like GDP growth and unemployment—ensures a comprehensive analysis of the determinants of income inequality. The model's use of 30 years of data (1993–2022) from reliable sources like NABARD, RBI, and the World Bank further strengthens its empirical foundation. Overall, the diagnostic tests indicate that the model is robust and well-specified. There are no significant issues related to multicollinearity, heteroscedasticity, autocorrelation, or model specification. The assumptions of OLS regression are adequately met, and the residuals exhibit normality, linearity, and independence. These diagnostic results confirm that the estimated coefficients and their significance levels are reliable, allowing for meaningful interpretation of the model's findings regarding the impact of microcredit, GDP growth, FDI, and other factors on income inequality in India.

In short, the study provides strong evidence that microfinance plays a critical role in reducing income inequality in India. However, addressing income inequality requires a comprehensive approach that includes fostering inclusive economic growth, ensuring equitable educational opportunities, and implementing comprehensive social policies. Policymakers must consider the broader implications of economic and social policies to ensure they contribute to a more equitable income distribution. The diagnostic tests reinforce the reliability and validity of the findings, underscoring the robustness of the regression model used in this study.

CONCLUSION

In conclusion, this study provides robust evidence supporting the role of microfinance in mitigating income inequality, while also highlighting areas for further scrutiny and improvement. The analysis demonstrates that microfinance loans can effectively reduce income inequality by enhancing the financial status of poorer households. This finding aligns with the results from previous studies that emphasize the positive impact of microfinance on poverty alleviation and income distribution.

This study contributes significantly to the existing literature by providing a comprehensive analysis of the impact of microfinance on income inequality in the Indian context, an area with limited prior research. The findings reinforce the role of microfinance as a vital tool for reducing income disparities, adding to the body of evidence supporting its implementation in development policies. Moreover, the study offers new insights into the relationships between GDP growth, educational expenditure, gross capital formation, unemployment, and income inequality, enhancing our understanding of the multifaceted nature of income distribution.

The significant negative impact of microcredit loans on income inequality underscores the importance of expanding microfinance programs. Policymakers should focus on enhancing the accessibility and reach of microfinance to marginalized communities, ensuring that these programs are inclusive and effective in uplifting the economically disadvantaged. Moreover, the positive relationship between GDP growth and income inequality indicates that economic growth alone is insufficient for reducing disparities. There is a need for policies that promote equitable distribution of economic benefits, such as progressive taxation, social safety nets, and targeted investment in education and health. The positive impacts of gross capital formation and educational expenditure on income inequality also call for more inclusive strategies that ensure these investments benefit a broader segment of the population.

While the study provides valuable insights, it has several limitations. The reliance on secondary data may introduce biases or inaccuracies inherent in the data sources. Additionally, the study does not account for potential lag effects of the independent variables on income inequality. Future research could benefit from incorporating more granular data and exploring the temporal dynamics of these relationships. Furthermore, the study focuses on a macro-level analysis, which may overlook regional disparities and local variations in income inequality and microfinance effectiveness.

In summary, while microfinance proves to be a valuable tool in reducing income inequality, it should be integrated into a broader economic strategy that includes policies for education, employment, and cultural transformation. Future research should explore the contextual nuances and long-term effects of microfinance, particularly in diverse settings like India, to develop more targeted and effective interventions.

REFERENCES

Ahmed, F., Begum, R. A., Siwar, C., Mia, M. S., & Wiboonpongse, A. (2019). Impact of microcredit on income inequality among rural women: The case of Panchagarh district in Bangladesh. *Pertanika Journal of Social Science & Humanities*, 27(4), 2367–2382.

Al-Azzam, M. (2023). For narrower income inequality: Traditional finance or microfinance? *Applied Economics*, •••, 1–18.

Artige, L., & Cavenaile, L. (2023). Public education expenditures, growth and income inequality. *Journal of Economic Theory*, 209, 105622. DOI: 10.1016/j.jet.2023.105622

Balasubramanian, S. (2013). Why micro-credit may leave women worse off: Non-cooperative bargaining and the marriage game in South Asia. *The Journal of Development Studies*, 49(5), 609–623. DOI: 10.1080/00220388.2012.709618

Biswas, B., & Sana, A. K. (2015).. . *MICROCREDIT DELIVERY.*, (July), 26–29.

Chatterjee, A., & Patil, K. (2022). Assessing the Impact of Microfinance on Inequality: A Study of Major SAARC Nations Using Panel Causality Analysis. In *Microfinance to Combat Global Recession and Social Exclusion: An Empirical Investigation* (pp. 195–208). Springer. DOI: 10.1007/978-981-16-4329-3_14

Chiazor, I. A., Egharevba, M. E., & Ozoya, M. I. (2016). Widening inequality and poverty in the developing world-micro-financing as a viable solution. In *The Social Sciences* (Vol. 11, Issue 13, pp. 3286–3293). https://doi.org/DOI: 10.3923/sscience.2016.3286.3293

Chintrakarn, P. HERZER, D., & NUNNENKAMP, P. (2012). FDI AND INCOME INEQUALITY: EVIDENCE FROM A PANEL OF U.S. STATES. *Economic Inquiry, 50*(3), 788–801. https://doi.org/https://doi.org/10.1111/j.1465-7295.2011.00384.x

Chowdhury, M. J. A. (2000). *Microcredit, enhancement of entitlement and alleviation of poverty: an investigation into the Grameen Bank's role in Bangladesh.*

Copestake, J. (2002). Inequality and the polarizing impact of microcredit: Evidence from Zambia's copperbelt. *Journal of International Development*, 14(6), 743–755. https://doi.org/https://doi.org/10.1002/jid.921. DOI: 10.1002/jid.921

Crépon, B., Devoto, F., Duflo, E., & Parienté, W. (2015). Estimating the impact of microcredit on those who take it up: Evidence from a randomized experiment in Morocco. *American Economic Journal. Applied Economics*, 7(1), 123–150. DOI: 10.1257/app.20130535

Cysne, R. P. (2009). On the positive correlation between income inequality and unemployment. *The Review of Economics and Statistics*, 91(1), 218–226. DOI: 10.1162/rest.91.1.218

Datta, S., & Sahu, T. N. (2022). Livelihood transformation through microfinance: An empirical investigation on tribal entrepreneurs in India. *International Journal of Business Innovation and Research*, 29(1), 127–140. DOI: 10.1504/IJBIR.2022.125671

Demir, A., Pesqué-Cela, V., Altunbas, Y., & Murinde, V. (2022). Fintech, financial inclusion and income inequality: A quantile regression approach. *European Journal of Finance*, 28(1), 86–107. DOI: 10.1080/1351847X.2020.1772335

Dollar, D., & Kraay, A. (2002). Institutions, trade, and growth. *Journal of Monetary Economics*, 50(1), 133–162. DOI: 10.1016/S0304-3932(02)00206-4

Esquivias, M. A., Sethi, N., & Iswanti, H. (2021). Dynamics of income inequality, investment, and unemployment in Indonesia. [JPSS]. *Journal of Population and Social Studies*, 29, 660–678. DOI: 10.25133/JPSSv292021.040

Fritz, H., & Lang, G. (2012). *Microcredit, Human Capital, and Personal Income Distribution: Empirical Evidence from Greater Cairo.*

Goel, D. V. (2020). Microfinance and Experiences in Measuring Income and Inequality : Evidence From an Indian State. *International Journal of Management*, 11(10), 1651–1664. DOI: 10.34218/IJM.11.10.2020.150

Guha, S., & Gupta, G. (2005). Microcredit for income generation: The role of RoSCA. *Economic and Political Weekly*, •••, 1470–1473.

Haini, H., Musa, S. F. P. D., Wei Loon, P., & Basir, K. H. (2023). Does unemployment affect the relationship between income inequality and food security? *The International Journal of Sociology and Social Policy*, 43(1/2), 48–66. DOI: 10.1108/IJSSP-12-2021-0303

Hermes, N. (2014). Does microfinance affect income inequality? *Applied Economics*, 46(9), 1021–1034. DOI: 10.1080/00036846.2013.864039

Heshmati, A. (2006). The world distribution of income and income inequality: A review of the economics literature. *Journal of World-systems Research*, •••, 61–107. DOI: 10.5195/jwsr.2006.372

Hsu, B. Y. (2014). Alleviating poverty or reinforcing inequality? Interpreting micro-finance in practice, with illustrations from rural C hina. *The British Journal of Sociology*, 65(2), 245–265. DOI: 10.1111/1468-4446.12076 PMID: 24784017

Huang, K., Sim, N., & Zhao, H. (2020). DOES FDI ACTUALLY AFFECT INCOME INEQUALITY? INSIGHTS FROM 25 YEARS OF RESEARCH. *Journal of Economic Surveys*, 34(3), 630–659. https://doi.org/https://doi.org/10.1111/joes.12373. DOI: 10.1111/joes.12373

Kaladhar, K. (1997). Microfinance in India: Design, Structure and Governance. *Economic and Political Weekly*, 32(42), 2687–2706. https://www.jstor.org/stable/4405979

Kaulihowa, T., & Adjasi, C. (2018). FDI and income inequality in Africa. *Oxford Development Studies*, 46(2), 250–265. DOI: 10.1080/13600818.2017.1381233

Kim, J.-H. (2016). A Study on the Effect of Financial Inclusion on the Relationship Between Income Inequality and Economic Growth. *Emerging Markets Finance & Trade*, 52(2), 498–512. DOI: 10.1080/1540496X.2016.1110467

Lacalle-Calderon, M., Larrú, J. M., Garrido, S. R., & Perez-Trujillo, M. (2019). Microfinance and income inequality: New macrolevel evidence. *Review of Development Economics*, 23(2), 860–876. https://doi.org/https://doi.org/10.1111/rode.12573. DOI: 10.1111/rode.12573

Lassoued, M. (2021). Control of corruption, microfinance, and income inequality in MENA countries: Evidence from panel data. *SN Business & Economics*, 1(7), 96. DOI: 10.1007/s43546-021-00099-w

Lechheb, H., Ouakil, H., & Jouilil, Y. (2019). Economic Growth, Poverty, and Income Inequality. *Journal of Private Equity*, 23(1), 137–145. DOI: 10.3905/jpe.2019.1.097

Lucarelli, B. (2005). Microcredit: A cautionary tale. *Journal of Contemporary Asia*, 35(1), 78–86. DOI: 10.1080/00472330580000051

Mader, P. (2014). Financialisation through Microfinance: Civil Society and Market-Building in India. *Asian Studies Review*, 38(4), 601–619. DOI: 10.1080/10357823.2014.963507

Mader, P. (2015). *The political economy of microfinance : financialising poverty*. DOI: 10.1057/9781137364210

Mahmoud Ali, I. A., & Ghoneim, H. (2019). The effect of microfinance on income inequality: Perspective of developing countries. *Journal of Economics and Management*, 35(1), 40–62. DOI: 10.22367/jem.2019.35.03

Maity, S. (2024). Rawls' difference principle, self-help group, financial inclusion and social cohesion—Lore or actuality? Experience of Central Assam. *Humanities & Social Sciences Communications*, 11(1), 1–13. DOI: 10.1057/s41599-024-02708-z

Maity, S., & Sarania, R. (2017). Does microfinance alleviate poverty and inequality? Studying self-help groups in Bodoland, Assam. *Development in Practice*, 27(7), 1006–1019. DOI: 10.1080/09614524.2017.1355353

Mehta, A., & Bhattacharya, J. (2017). Channels of financial sector development and rural-urban consumption inequality in India. *International Journal of Social Economics*, 44(12), 1973–1987. DOI: 10.1108/IJSE-05-2015-0117

Miled, K. B. H., Younsi, M., & Landolsi, M. (2022). Does microfinance program innovation reduce income inequality? Cross-country and panel data analysis. *Journal of Innovation and Entrepreneurship*, 11(1), 7. DOI: 10.1186/s13731-022-00195-7

Mukhopadhyay, J. P. (2016). Microfinance and consumption inequality: Evidence from a randomized controlled trial in Andhra Pradesh, India. *Journal of Developing Areas*, 50(2), 269–291. DOI: 10.1353/jda.2016.0088

Mushtaq, R., & Bruneau, C. (2019). Microfinance, financial inclusion and ICT: Implications for poverty and inequality. *Technology in Society*, 59, 101154. https://doi.org/https://doi.org/10.1016/j.techsoc.2019.101154. DOI: 10.1016/j.techsoc.2019.101154

NABARD. (2023). *Status of Microfinance in India 2022-23*. 1–272. www.nabard.org

Naguib, C. (2015). *The relationship between inequality and GDP growth: An empirical approach*. LIS Working Paper Series.

Neuhuber, T., & Schneider, A. E. (2024). The role of public social expenditure for mitigating local income inequality: An investigation across spatial scales in Austria. *Journal of Regional Science*, 64(5), 1647–1679. DOI: 10.1111/jors.12722

Nolan, B., Richiardi, M. G., & Valenzuela, L. (2019). THE DRIVERS OF INCOME INEQUALITY IN RICH COUNTRIES. *Journal of Economic Surveys*, 33(4), 1285–1324. https://doi.org/https://doi.org/10.1111/joes.12328. DOI: 10.1111/joes.12328

Omar, M. A., & Inaba, K. (2020). Does financial inclusion reduce poverty and income inequality in developing countries? A panel data analysis. *Journal of Economic Structures*, 9(1), 37. DOI: 10.1186/s40008-020-00214-4

Polacko, M. (2021). *Causes and Consequences of Income Inequality – An Overview. 12*(2), 341–357. https://doi.org/doi:10.1515/spp-2021-0017

Purba, B., Masbar, R., Maipita, I., & Jamal, A. (2019). The Effect of Capital Expenditure and Gross Fixed Capital Formation on Income Disparity in West Coast Region of North Sumatera. *IOP Conference Series. Earth and Environmental Science*, 260(1), 12022. DOI: 10.1088/1755-1315/260/1/012022

Ravallion, M. (2014). Income inequality in the developing world. *Science*, 344(6186), 851–855. DOI: 10.1126/science.1251875 PMID: 24855260

Saïdou, N, Pam, Z, & Kimseyinga, S. (2013). Access to Microcredit and Income Inequality in Burkina Faso. *African Scientific Journal*, 135–153. DOI: 10.1126/science.1251875 PMID: 24855260

Sanyal, P. (2015). Group-based microcredit & emergent inequality in social capital: Why socio-religious composition matters. *Qualitative Sociology*, 38(2), 103–137. DOI: 10.1007/s11133-015-9301-8

Sawadogo, R., & Semedo, G. (2021). Financial inclusion, income inequality, and institutions in sub-Saharan Africa: Identifying cross-country inequality regimes. *International Economics, 167*, 15–28. https://doi.org/https://doi.org/10.1016/j.inteco.2021.05.002

Singh, M. K., & Lee, J. (2020). Social inequality and access to social capital in microfinance interventions. *The International Journal of Sociology and Social Policy*, 40(7/8), 575–588. DOI: 10.1108/IJSSP-01-2020-0024

Sinha, A., Parida, P. C., & Baurah, P. (2012). The impact of NABARD's Self Help Group-Bank Linkage Programme on poverty and empowerment in India. *Contemporary South Asia*, 20(4), 487–510. DOI: 10.1080/09584935.2012.737306

Subramaniam, Y., Masron, T. A., Wahab, M. A., & Mia, M. A. (2021). The impact of microfinance on poverty and income inequality in developing countries. *Asian-Pacific Economic Literature*, 35(1), 36–48. https://doi.org/https://doi.org/10.1111/apel.12326. DOI: 10.1111/apel.12326

Tabash, M. I., Elsantil, Y., Hamadi, A., & Drachal, K. (2024). Globalization and Income Inequality in Developing Economies: A Comprehensive Analysis. In *Economies* (Vol. 12, Issue 1). DOI: 10.3390/economies12010023

Taylor, M. (2011). 'Freedom from Poverty is Not for Free': Rural Development and the Microfinance Crisis in Andhra Pradesh, India. *Journal of Agrarian Change*, 11(4), 484–504. https://doi.org/https://doi.org/10.1111/j.1471-0366.2011.00330.x. DOI: 10.1111/j.1471-0366.2011.00330.x

Ucal, M., Haug, A. A., & Bilgin, M. H. (2016). Income inequality and FDI: Evidence with Turkish data. *Applied Economics*, 48(11), 1030–1045. DOI: 10.1080/00036846.2015.1093081

van der Hoeven, R. (2019). In Nissanke, M., & Ocampo, J. A. (Eds.), *Income Inequality in Developing Countries, Past and Present BT - The Palgrave Handbook of Development Economics: Critical Reflections on Globalisation and Development* (pp. 335–376). Springer International Publishing., DOI: 10.1007/978-3-030-14000-7_10

Walujadi, D., Indupurnahayu, I., & Endri, E. (2022). Determinants of income inequality among provinces: Panel data evidence from Indonesia. *Calitatea*, 23(190), 243–250.

Chapter 6
Towards a Policy Framework for Microfinance:
Innovative Financial Solutions for Sustainable Development

Maybel Fernandez-Vallado
https://orcid.org/0009-0000-1039-1322
University of the Philippines Visayas, Philippines

ABSTRACT

Innovations in clean technology provide a dual advantage by reducing environmental impact and improving the quality of life for users. These technologies empower micro-entrepreneurs by cutting operational costs, boosting productivity, and expanding their market opportunities. Through inclusive financing mechanisms and capacity-building initiatives, microfinance institutions cultivate a culture of sustainability among entrepreneurs, driving the adoption of environmentally conscious practices and products. The Grounded Theory approach and secondary research analysis was employed here. Stakeholders can create inclusive ecosystems that empower individuals and communities to participate in the formal economy while preserving natural resources. This study advocates collaborative efforts among governments, financial institutions, technology providers, and social enterprises to scale innovative solutions that promote both economic growth and environmental protection globally. Thus, a Policy Framework for Microfinance is hereby proposed.

DOI: 10.4018/979-8-3693-6622-6.ch006

1. INTRODUCTION

Financial inclusion, the access of affordable financial services by individuals and business, especially women, is necessary for fostering economic growth and reducing poverty worldwide. Microfinance as a key instrument in financial inclusion, has evolved to incorporate sustainable entrepreneurship and clean technology, catalyzing impacts on both economic development and environmental sustainability.

The possibilities of ensuring sustainable development through microfinance using clean technology is endless. The potential of creating a world where poor and underprivileged people can thrive is now possible. We need to provide opportunities for financial freedom and eventually enable a holistic growth for communities.

A transformative opportunity for sustainable development is the intersection of microfinance and clean technology. Microfinance institutions (MFI) can play a vital role in fostering innovation and promoting sustainability by providing financial resources to entrepreneurs in the clean technology sector. This collaboration only supports economic growth of the community, but also contributes to the global efforts to mitigate the effects of climate change. (FasterCapital, 25 Mar, para 18)

Microfinance and Clean Technology includes:

1. Financial Inclusion and Environmental Impact
2. Education and Capacity Building
3. Market Creation and Expansion
4. Innovation and Adaptation
5. Partnerships for Scale and Reach

Problems and Objectives

What are some of the challenges faced in microfinance for clean technology? How can these challenges be solved? Some challenges and solutions in microfinance or clean technology include: a) Accessibility; b) Affordability; c) Awareness; d) Adaptability; and, e) Assessment.

What are some innovative ideas in microfinance and clean technology? Innovations in microfinance and clean technology include: a) Innovative Financing Models; b) Empowerment through Education; c) Green Micro-Entrepreneurship; d) Partnerships for Scale; e) Data driven approaches: leveraging data analytics; and, f) Regulatory tailwinds.

Significance of the Study

Microfinance should be able to fuel sustainable entrepreneurship. The convergence of microfinance and clean technology has become a pivotal role catalyzing the growth of eco-friendly entrepreneurship in sustainable development. This empowers individuals at the grassroots level and advocates the global agenda for environmental stewardship forward. Microfinance institutions (MFIs) become instrumental in adopting clean technologies when access is granted to people who are excluded from conventional banking systems. Ranging from solar panels to improved cookstoves, these technologies offer a dual benefit. They lessen the ecological footprints and enhance the quality of life of people who use them.

Financial inclusion and technology is the way to go for development to be sustainable and replicable. Ensuring a sustainable future can be achieved by providing financial freedom to poor communities and enabling them to have clean technology that can be replicated across the whole community.

2. REVIEW OF RELATED LITERATURE

2.1. Microfinance and Sustainable Development

Microfinance has been widely recognized as a powerful tool for promoting sustainable development. According to the United Nations (2015), financial inclusion is a critical component of the Sustainable Development Goals (SDGs), particularly Goal 1, which aims to eradicate poverty in all its forms. Access to financial services enables individuals to invest in education, healthcare, and entrepreneurship, thereby improving their overall quality of life (Pitt & Khanker, 1998; WorldBank, 2015).

The role of microfinance in empowering women is particularly noteworthy. Studies have shown that microfinance can significantly enhance women's economic participation, leading to positive social outcomes (Kabeer, 2005). Women who access microfinance are more likely to invest in their families' health and education, contributing to long-term development outcomes. Furthermore, financial inclusion for women is associated with increased decision-making power within households, and communities, fostering social and equity empowerment (UN Women, 2018)

Microfinance and clean technology is providing support for entrepreneurs. Giving relatively larger loans to the non-poor and near-poor entrepreneurs is the response of the MFIs toward the demand of existing and potential clients of inclusive financial growth. Opponents on the other hand, are likely to consider responses such as mission drift by the MFIs. This study attempts to measure the effectiveness of such microenterprise loans on increasing entrepreneurs' incomes and innovation.

Findings support the proponents of giving loans to entrepreneurs. Findings suggest that larger loans increase income, but less innovative practice might threaten such income. Therefore, to ensure the effective utilization of loan capital, we recommend that microenterprise loans associated with proper business skills, information, and technologies can be provided by MFIs with careful screening and monitoring. (Ferdousi, 2015)

Revolution in the business environment has crucial growing changes on the most globalized markets. Numerous organizations are necessitating towards producing more proactive entrepreneurs with dynamic teams who can run and steer their business to victory. Revolutionizing business strategy and entrepreneurial skills also implementing innovation and practices to enhance performance are necessary for these organizations to be more cost-efficient and increase their efficiency. The study aims to clarify issues of whether measurement has a positive effect on different aspects of innovation and best practices. The study contributes to the current understanding in three ways; firstly, by presenting the important aspects of organizational innovation and best practices. Secondly, it shows the importance of measurement in promoting different aspects of innovation and best practices. And thirdly, it examines the link between innovation, best practices and sustainability in microfinance. The study used qualitative research of the microfinance industry. A representative of management and employees in each company was selected through an invitation to participate in getting information for data collection purposes in the study. The study contains a comprehensive description of the impacts of measurement has positive effects on issues related to innovation and best practices. The measurement for several aspects of innovation and best practices has good potential in microfinance industries. Additionally, measurement on innovation and best practices are positively related to each other to enhance organization performance. The study suggests that both academics and practitioners should focus on the development of new methods and practices to describe and scrutinize further understanding for measuring issues which are related to innovation and best practices, in order to better develop the aspect of innovation and best practices toward sustainability. This effort would not only contribute to the firm's success, but also toward the development of the nation in developing countries. (Rahman, Hassan and Said, 2015)

Another research aims to address the problem of financial inclusion and resilience in the recent sustainable development framework. The development agenda designs access to finance a human right and a prior strategy to achieve Sustainable Development Goals (SDGs). Microfinance can play a decisive role in smoothing the risk of adverse events. It acts as a resilience policy tackling vulnerability and poverty, empowering people and vulnerable categories and improving and enlarging their capabilities. This work explores the existing connections between the development agenda and microfinance as a strategy to foster financial access. To this end, summative content analysis is performed on the United Nations General Assembly Resolution A/RES/69/315 - fulfilling a research gap. This inquiry handles 6 selected SDGs, ascribable to 3 dimensions, detecting 5 subdimensions and 16 domains. Analyzing Millennium Development Goals and SDGs, the study also finds increased importance attributed to the topic, key issues and policy strengths, and limitations. Importantly, the analysis shows that the environmental dimension is still neglected in the analyzed corpus, not appearing in any of the examined SDGs. The findings suggest investing in these channels, drafting governance patterns and modeling resilience and development policy to vehiculate improved ecological and institutional results and concerts. (Gato and Sadik-Zada, 2022).

Lastly, it is undeniable that the emergence of microfinance programs in India in the late 1990s led to a significant portion of rural women being able to link with banking services today. As SHG (Self-Help Group) members, poor women now have access to bank deposits and loans. At present, more than 8 core women are linked with microfinance institutions in India, and a total credit low of Rs 17,342 core has been generated with SHGs. (Barman, 2022, p.11) Previously destitute and a problem in society and the state, these proletarians are now a viable economic force in their own right. The country has made commendable progress in the areas of population control, average life expectancy, infant mortality rate, abolition of child marriage, rate of girls enrolled in school and social health awareness. Microfinance has a considerable impact on encouraging women entrepreneurs, in addition to farming and housework today. Rural females work in a wide range of micro-enterprises, including banking, dairy farming, trading rice, grooming, tailoring, raising goats, running petty businesses, manufacturing bamboo wood products and so on. Their contributions include an increase in family income, raising household savings, empowering women, reducing poverty, investing in children;s health and education, housing, clean water, improved sanitation, creating new jobs, increasing Gross Domestic Product (GDP), and so on. Thus, the development of the country through rural poor women entrepreneurs is not just a temporary development, it is a sustainable development. (p.15)

2.2. Green Technology and Microfinance

The concept of Green Technology encompasses a wide range of innovations aimed at reducing environmental impact and promoting sustainability. These technologies can include renewable energy solutions, sustainable agricultural practices, waste management systems, and eco-friendly construction methods (Bocken et al., 2014). As climate change and environmental degradation become increasingly pressing issues, the integration of green technology into microfinance presents an opportunity to address these challenges while promoting economic development.

Research indicates that financing for green technologies can enhance livelihoods and reduce dependence on fossil fuels (Khan, et al., 2018; World Bank, 2017). For instance, solar energy solutions can provide electricity to underserved communities, improving quality of life and reducing reliance on kerosene lamps. Similarly, financing for sustainable agricultural practices can enhance food security and promote environmentally friendly farming methods.

Another study looks into energy efficiency and electrification. The study aims to analyze the feasibility of having policies on preserving the environment in cooking activities in Kyenjojo District in Uganda in terms of sustainability performance. The study conducted a yield survey with 63 households. It also analyzes the causes of the lagging transition to clean energy use in cooking. Besides behavioral and taste aspects, affordability and level of education play an important role in the context of the household-level energy transitions. Education is a significant factor in this issue. Poor rural people have not been educated about environmental protection and paves the way for new explorations, bottom-up projects, sustainable development policies and energy transition modeling. Access to electricity is needed to ensure basic human activities and is a direct measure of energy poverty. Significant steps for rural electrification have been done by intergovernmental organizations to ensure energy security for all, especially rural people, the poor and the vulnerable. Cooking is a basic daily household activity and related to energy security as well. However, in most developing countries and the rural world, cooking is still done through polluting, ineffective and dangerous kerosene stoves and animal manure and primordial tools. (Sadik-Zada, Gatto & Blick, 2022)

Taking microfinance to the next level of effectiveness and impact will require addressing the criticisms leveled against it in recent times, even if many of them are exaggerated and politically motivated. In addition, it can go much further in leveraging its human and physical infrastructure, market knowledge and client relationships to create value for clients and where possible address larger societal problems. In so doing, it will use its unique strengths to solve the proverbial "last mile problem" that has frustrated efforts to bring new ideas, technological advances and business models to the poor in a way that they can take advantage of them for their socio-economic improvement. Two areas that can be prioritized are bringing clean energy solutions - especially solar home systems, improved cooking stoves and solar lanterns with mobile phone charging capabilities - and information about agricultural best practices to the poor and others in the rural areas of the developing world. Microfinance institutions' field staff and clients are positioned to play the role of "trusted intermediaries" who can bring products and knowledge to those who need it and provide financing as required. There are already some promising models showing how this can be done. Incremental financing for these client expenditures may be more productively may be more productively invested than many micro-loans at present. In providing these services, the global issues of climate change and the food crisis will be positively impacted, though these actions by no means constitute a complete solution to these complex problems. Using microfinance as a platform to address these issues while creating value for clients could be a model for other approaches to addressing issues such as health care, education, democratic participation, environmental stewardship, and nutrition, to name a few. New models to create value for clients and help solve multiple problems facing humankind will go a long way to elevating the microfinance brand that has been tarnished in recent times. (Arnold, et al., n.d.)

2.3. Fintech (Financial Technology) Innovations

Fintech combines finance and technology to revolutionize financial services, with global market growth projected from $209.7 billion in 2024 to $644.6 billion by 2029 (Market Data Forecast), driven by innovations like digital payments, block-chain, and AI. These advancements enhance efficiency, security, accessibility, and financial inclusion, reshaping the industry. (Mouka, 2024).

(1) **Mobile-Only Banking:** A key trend is the rise of mobile-only banking, or neobanks, such as Chime, Monzo, and Nubank. These digital-first platforms offer convenient, low-cost services, streaming processes like onboarding and KYC (Know Your Customer). They are particularly impactful in underserved regions and are expected to grow rapidly, with a forecasted CAGR of 46.5% (2020-2026). Neobanks are setting new standards for user experiences and expanding access to financial services globally.

(2) **Open Banking/Open Finance:** Open banking and open finance enable consumer-authorized access to financial data across accounts, driving advancements in fraud prevention, payment initiation, and workflows like tax filing. Companies like Plaid and Yodlee lead this trend, facilitating seamless integration with new financial products.

In the U.S., open banking is widely adopted, providing insights into financial behavior for credit assessments, fraud detection, and financial management. Globally, adoption varies, with growth in LATAM and APAC, while regulatory challenges slow progress in Europe. Despite regional differences, open banking continues to foster innovation and efficiency in the financial sector.

(3) **Real-Time Payments:** Real-time payments enable zero-cost domestic transactions, transforming financial systems in both developed and emerging markets. Countries like the UK, Australia, and Singapore have adopted these systems widely, replacing traditional methods like checks and cash.

In emerging markets, the impact is greater. India's UPI has driven massive adoption, with transactions growing from 1 million in 2016 to 83.7 billion in 2023, representing 75% of all digital payments. Similarly, Brazil's Pix system has enhanced financial inclusion, making instant payments the norm. Real-time payments are democratizing financial access, driving economic participation and growth globally.

(4) **Blockchain and IoT:** Blockchain and the Internet of Things (IoT) are transformative technologies reshaping fintech. Blockchain ensures secure, transparent transactions without intermediaries, with applications like supply chain finance enabling real-time tracking and cost reduction. IoT complements blockchain by collecting and sharing data, enabling innovations like smart contracts and digital assets.

In insurance, these technologies support smart policies and automate claims and payouts based on sensor data, reducing fraud and delays. Future potential includes applications in asset management and decentralized finance (DeFi), promising greater transparency, security and efficiency, and driving continued financial innovation.

(5) **Low Code Platforms:** Low-code platforms are revolutionizing fintech by enabling ra[id development of financial applications with minimal coding. Using visual interfaces and pre-built components, they empower non-developers to create tools like digital banking apps, lending solutions, and chatbots.

These platforms democratize software development, allowing financial institutions to adapt quickly to market changes and customer needs. They are expected to drive a surge in tailored fintech solutions, boosting agility and reducing time to market. BY 2025, 70% of new enterprise applications are predicted to use low-code or no-code technologies.

(6) **Gamification:** Gamification integrated game-like features into financial services to boost user engagement and motivation. It uses rewards, challenges, and interactive tools to make financial management engaging and educational.

Apps like Acorns and Flourish Savings exemplify this approach. Acorns invests spare change from purchases, while Flourish Savings offers incentives for achieving financial goals. Gamification enhances financial literacy, wellness, and habit-building through feedback and social features. As fintech evolves, gamification is poised to become a standard feature, making financial apps more accessible, engaging, and effective.

(7) **Regulatory Technology (Regtech):** Regulatory technology (TegTech) is revolutionizing compliance management for financial institutions by using advanced technologies like data aggregation, machine learning, and natural language processing. It automates regulatory processes, reducing complexity, costs, and non-compliance risks.

Key applications include regulatory reporting, which ensures accurate and timely submissions, and compliance tools for risk assessment and policy management to meet evolving regulations. RegTech also provides regulatory intelligence, keeping firms informed about changes and trends to adapt proactively. As regulations grow more complex, the adoption of RegTech is expected to rise, enhancing compliance efficiency and risk management.

(8) **Embedded Finance:** Embedded finance integrates financial services into non-financial platforms, creating seamless user experiences and driving customer engagement. Companies like Amazon exemplify this trend with services like Amazon Pay for fast transactions and Amazon Lending for small business loans based on sales data.

This transformative model opens new revenue streams across industries and is expected to grow significantly, with the embedded finance market projected to reach $7.2 trillion by 2030.

(9) **AI and Machine Learning:** AI and machine learning are transforming financial services by enhancing decision-making, customer experience, and operational efficiency. These technologies power applications like fraud detection, data analysis, and automated customer service, including chatbots and AI-driven financial advisory.

Their integration in fintech continues to grow, enabling personalized services, improved risk management, and greater operational efficiency, driving innovation across industry.

(10) **Peer-to-Peer (P2P):** Peer-to-peer lending enables individuals and businesses to borrow money directly from others, bypassing traditional financial intermediaries. This model offers better interest rates for both borrowers and lenders and democratizes access to credit.

Platforms like Funding Circle and Prosper Marketplace match borrowers with investors, providing transparent processes and thorough credit assessments. As demand for alternative financing grows, P2P lending platforms are expected to expand and improve risk assessment, enhancing financial inclusion and fostering a more competitive, diverse lending market.

Fintech innovations are transforming the financial sector, enhancing efficiency, security, and inclusivity. Advancements such as mobile-only banking, real-time payments, blockchain, and embedded finance are establishing new industry benchmarks. Looking ahead, the ongoing development of these technologies is expected to bring even more significant changes. To remain competitive and address changing consumer needs, financial institutions must adopt these innovations. (Mouka, 2024).

2.4 Gaps in Literature

Despite the growing recognition of the potential synergies between microfinance and green technology, there remains a limited understanding of how effectively microfinance can promote the adoption of green technologies. Existing literature often focuses on traditional microfinance practices, leaving a gap in knowledge regarding the integration of environmental sustainability within microfinance frameworks. Further research is needed to examine the impact of green technology financing on financial inclusion, community empowerment, and environmental sustainability.

3. RESEARCH METHODS

This study employs a qualitative research approach, utilizing case studies to examine integration of green technology into microfinance practices.

Using secondary research analysis and case methods, this research looks into possible connections between microfinance and clean technology and how entrepreneurs are able to use their financial freedom to create a lasting impact not only to their families and communities, but to the environment as well, creating a well-balanced and sustainable future.

3.1. Data Collection

Data for this chapter were collected from academic articles, reports from microfinance institutions, and reputable sources in the field of sustainable development. The analysis focuses on the impact of these initiates on financial inclusion, community empowerment, and environmental sustainability.

3.2. Data Analysis

The data collected were analyzed using thematic analysis, focusing on key themes that emerged from the case studies, including the impact of green technology financing on poverty alleviation, community empowerment, and environment sustainability.

Additionally, challenges faced by MFIs in integrating green technology into their product offering were identified and discussed.

3.3 Conceptual Framework

The study adopted the Grounded Theory approach, both a theory and method used in making sense of massive amounts of data to reduce the bulk of information, identify patterns and construct a framework for revealing the essence of the data (Patton, 1990:371).

Using the Grounded Theory approach, this Chapter will show how a development initiative such as financial inclusion using clean technology can empower entrepreneurs, especially women to be financially independent and provide for their families. These initiatives likewise helped the community and encouraged others to also be financially adept in using technology to benefit not only their families but the overall well being of their communities and help in environmental protection and preservation.

Figure 1. Conceptual framework grounded theory approach to financial inclusion using clean technology to empower women entrepreneurs

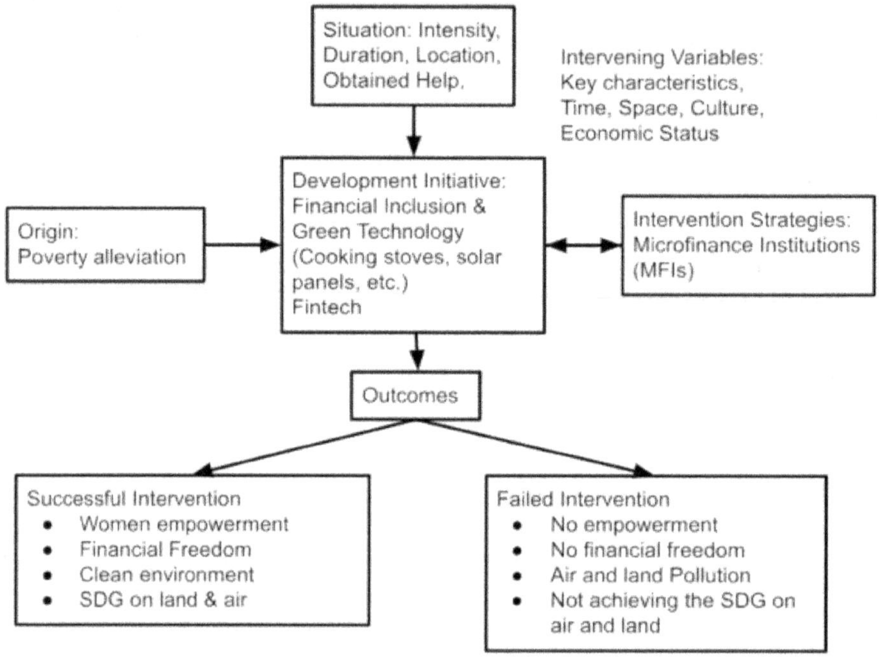

Figure 1: **Conceptual Framework of the Grounded Theory Approach to Financial Inclusion Using Clean Technology to Empower Women Entrepreneurs**

Using the Grounded Theory approach to social science research and adopting the Conceptual Framework *"Communication Dynamics of Women Involved in Microfinance Projects as a Model for Women Empowerment: Microfinance Projects for Poverty Alleviation in the Philippines,"* (Vallado, 2023) the relationship between and among variables are hereby illustrated. These are namely: *origin* (Poverty Alleviation), *development initiative* (Financial inclusion and green technology), *situation* (Intensity, Duration, Location, and Obtained help), *intervening variables* (Key characteristics, Time, Space, Culture, Economic Status), *intervention strategies* (MFIs), and *outcomes* (Empowerment or No empowerment of women & Success or Failure in microfinance projects).

Figure 2. Conceptual framework "Communication Dynamics of Women Involved in Microfinance Projects as a Model for Women Empowerment: Microfinance Projects for Poverty Alleviation in the Philippines" (Vallado, 2023, pp. 18-50)

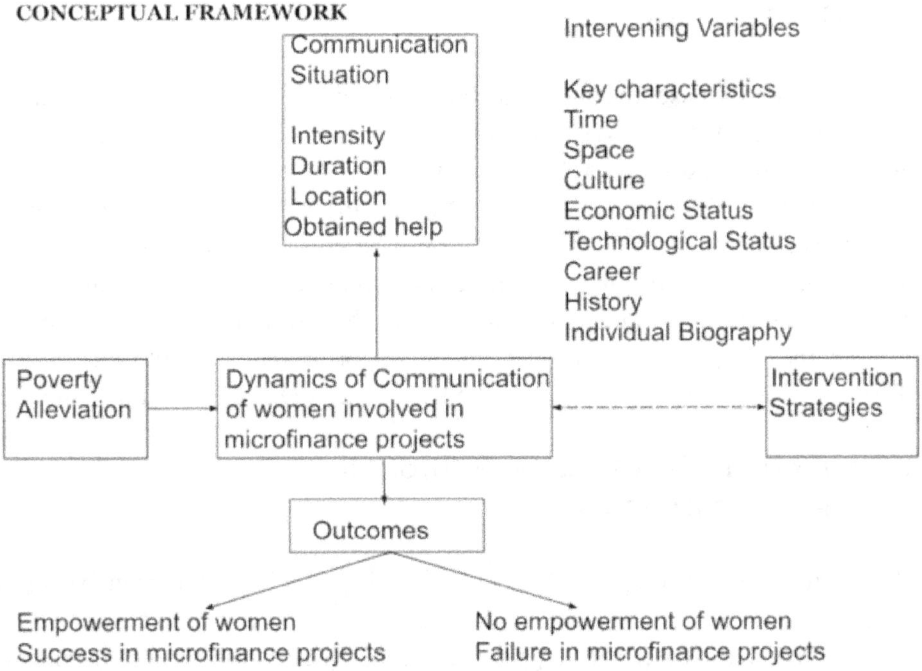

The study of Vallado (2023), discusses the communication dynamics of women involved in microfinance projects that contribute to the success or failure of the projects in three cases; and specifically, (1) identifies the factors that lead to the success or failure of the projects; (2) identifies the the micro-enterprise development (MED) lending methodology used in each case by presenting the key characteristics of the three cases, and (3) presents the communication dynamics of women involved in these microfinance projects in the context of culture as a model for women empowerment. Using the paradigm model of the Grounded Theory approach to social science research, the study shows the relationship between and among different variables, as illustrated in the Conceptual Framework. These are namely: *origin* (Poverty Alleviation), *development initiative* (Dynamics of Communication of Women involved in Microfinance Projects), *situation* (Intensity, Duration, Location, and Obtained help), *intervening variables* (Key characteristics, Time, Space, Culture, Economic Status, Technological Status, Career, History, Individual Biography), *intervention*

strategies (MED), and *outcomes* (Empowerment or No empowerment of women & Success or Failure in microfinance projects)

4. RESULTS AND DISCUSSION

This Chapter discusses the interconnected dynamics between financial inclusion, microfinance, clean technology, and entrepreneurship. These will delve into topics such as definitions and scope of financial inclusion, the evolution of microfinance, the integration of clean technology in entrepreneurial ventures, the principles of sustainable entrepreneurship, and the synergies between these domains.

Comprehensive details, analysis and case studies to illustrate the significance of the research and its implications for sustainable development are presented. Moreover, the Chapter examines challenges, opportunities, and future directions for further research and exploration in the field. The selected case studies include:

4.1. Promotion of Clean Energy through Microfinance in Ethiopia

This initiative in Ethiopia focuses on fostering resilient and inclusive green growth by promoting clean energy technologies via microfinance sector development. Spearheaded by MicroEnergy International (MEI), the project introduced a replicable financing model that allows households and small to medium-sized enterprises (SMEs) to access clean energy technologies (CET) through microcredit. A business model was created for three Ethiopian microfinance institutions (MFIs), which collectively serve over 200,000 clients.

The project, conducted from 1 November 2014, to 30 April 2017, aimed to mitigate climate change by reducing greenhouse gas emissions through the replacement of unsustainable energy sources with renewable alternatives. It developed a full supply chain for high-quality CET targeting low-income markets and provided training to microfinance institutions and CET providers on the new credit mechanism.

Funded by the Nordic Climate Facility, MEI was responsible for overall project management, from planning and implementation to evaluation, including design and optimization of energy products and services, ensuring that financial instruments meet the needs of both businesses and end-users. (MEI, n.d.)

4.2. M-KOPA Solar

M-KOPA Solar in Kenya is a pay-as-you-go solar energy financing model. M-KOPA has emerged as a leading example of microfinance supporting green technology in Kenya. The Company's innovative pay-as-you-go solar energy financing model allows low-income households to access clean, renewable energy. By offering affordable daily payments, M-KOPA has made solar energy accessible to millions of families who previously relied on expensive and harmful kerosene lamps (M-KOPA, 2020).

Figure 3. PAYG concept (IRENA, 2020, Figure 3)

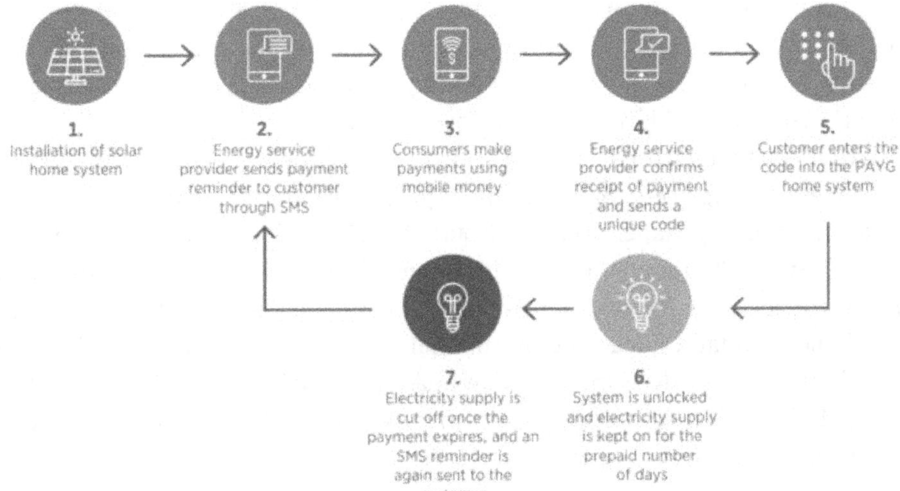

Based on: Energypedia (*n.d.*).

4.2.1. Impact of Solar Energy Financing

The impact of solar energy financing through M-KOPA has been significant. According to the Global Off-Grid Lighting Association (2018), M-KOPA has enabled over 750,000 households to transition from solar lighting, improving health outcomes and reducing carbon emissions. Families that have adopted solar energy report increased savings on energy costs, enhanced quality of life, and improved educational opportunities for children, as they can study at night without the risk of fire hazards associated with kerosene lamps.

Moreover, M-KOPA's model has demonstrated the potential for microfinance to drive economic growth. By investing in solar technology, households are empowered to allocate their savings toward other productive activities, such as starting small businesses or investing in education (M-KOPA, 2020). This ripple effect underscores the broader economic benefits of integrating green technology in microfinance.

4.2.2. Challenges and Lessons Learned

Despite the successes of M-KOPA, challenges remain. The initial cost solar systems can be a barrier for some households, even with the pay-as-you-go model. Additionally, the lack of awareness about the benefits of solar energy may limit adoption rates in certain communities. Future efforts should focus on enhancing education and outreach to potential customers, as well as providing targeted financial products that cater to different income levels.

M-KOPA announced that it has surpassed 5 million customers, with two million of these having come onboard in the past 15 months. Customers come from Kenya, Uganda, Nigeria, GHana and South Africa. Their innovative model makes affordable smartphones embedded with financial services available to 'Every Day Earners' (majority of AFrican adults who earn daily income but struggle to afford smartphones and fail to qualify conventional financial services). According to the World Bank, 75% of adults in Sub Saharan Africa remain excluded financially and to date, M-KOPA has supported its customers with more than 1.5 billion US dollars in financing. Key impact highlights from the 2024 report include:

- 92% confirm that M-KOPA's financing has made technology more affordable.
- 80% of customers report an improved quality of life thanks to M-KOPA's products.
- 70% credit M-KOPA with helping them achieve their financial goals, demonstrating the company's contribution to financial empowerment.
- 62% use their M-KOPA product to generate income.

It has a major impact in improving digital access in Africa. Nearly 2 million customers are first-time internet users and 40% are women. M-KOPA is working to increase its percentage of female customers to 50%, to reduce its carbon footprint by making circularity central to its smartphone supply chain, and to continue pioneering green products like electric motorbikes that contribute to health and sustainability of the communities where it operates. (M-KOPA, 2024)

4.3. A Framework for Regulating Microfinance Institutions: The Experience in Ghana and the Philippines

"A Framework for Regulating Microfinance Institutions," (Gallardo & Randhawa, 1999) sought to provide a framework for addressing regulatory issues which impact the operations and the institutional development of MIs. It was a work in progress in which further developments could be made, based on analysis of selected country experiences from the field. Two countries, Ghana and the Philippines were selected for field testing, having a wide range of informal, semi-formal and formal MFIs providing financial services to the poor, but have legal systems and regulatory frameworks which differ in how financial intermediation activities by MFIs are regulated and/or supervised. In-depth work on issues in developing sustainable rural/microfinance in Indonesia presented an opportunity to deepen the assessment of how the legal and regulatory environment is important to sustainable microfinance. The focus of the assessment and comparative analysis is on key issues in the legal system and judicial processes. It also includes the regulatory and supervisory environment or microfinance which are addressed by governments and microfinance stakeholders in the countries. The Philippines, Ghana and Indonesia all provide microfinance services. Their legal and regulatory environment has, in many years, permitted the establishment of specialized banking and financial institutions with limited financial intermediation services to geographical areas with defined limits.

Table 1 below, shows *Selected Characteristics of 64 Financially Self-Sufficient MFIs* in Gallardo (2001, p. 6):

Table 1. Selected Characteristics of 64 Financially Self-sufficient MFIs (In %)

Organizational formats	Capital/ assets	Operating self-sufficiency	Dollar average loan	Depth*	External funds/ loans F
Bank	21.0	118.6	527	62.5	166.6
Non-bank	27.4	110.4	958	62.4	70.3
Credit union	42.1	122.5	1,306	91.6	88.6
NGO	58.5	130.8	490	38.8	26.6

*Depth = Average loan balance per borrower GNP per capita.
F External funds/loans = borrowed funds @ commercial rates/average loan portfolio.
Source: The MicroBanking Bulletin, Issue No.6 (April 2001), Tables C & D.

Regulatory Thresholds for Activities of MFIs are presented in Table 2, below (p.8):

Table 2. Regulatory thresholds for activities of MFIs

Type of institution	Ownership	Main sources of funds for operations & loans	Activities that trigger regulation	Form of external regulation	Regulatory authority
Informal Community-based Thrift and Credit Self-Help Group - funding from community members and loans from NGOs and MFIs	Community and village members	- Fees and assessments on members - Member's savings deposited with SGH	None	None	None
Category A: Other People's Money (NGO) - Funding from donor funds	Local and foreign donors through a Trust	Grants and donated funds	None - provided microfinance loans do not exceed donated funds	Registration as Non-Profit Society or Trust	Registrar of Societies and/or Trusts
Category A: Other People's Money (Microfinance NGO) - Added funding via commercial loans/ securities issues	Grants and donations converted to share capital	- Grants and donated funds - Concessional and commercial borrowings (wholesale deposit instruments)	- Generating liabilities from commercial - Concessional sources to fund operations and loans	- Registration as limited liability company - Rating by Credit Rating Agency -Licencing by bank authority as non-bank finance company	- Registrar of companies -Central bank authority or superintendency -Securities regulatory agency

continued on following page

Table 2. Continued

Type of institution	Ownership	Main sources of funds for operations & loans	Activities that trigger regulation	Form of external regulation	Regulatory authority
Category B: Members' Money - funding from members' contribution	Members joined by recognized closed common bond	Share capital contributed and savings deposited by members	Accepting deposits from members, and making loans to members	Registration as a financial cooperative [Large institutions may fall under jurisdiction of Banking Law]	- Registrar of Cooperatives, or of Societies or - Central bank authority/ superintendency for larger cooperative institutions
Category C - The Public's Money - funding from retail public deposits	Individual and institutional investors and shareholders	- Contributed share capital - Commercial borrowings - Wholesale deposits - Retail public deposits	- Accepting wholesale - Retail public deposits or intermediation into loans and investments	- Registration as limited liability company - Licensing by banking authority as NBFI, or limited service or full service bank	- Registrar of companies - Central bank authority or superintendency

Source: Adapted from Chart 1 and Table 2, H. van Greuning, J. Gallardo, B. Randhawa, A Framework for Regulating Microfinance Institutions. World Bank Policy Research Working Paper No. 2061, Washington, D.C., February 1999.

Table 3 below, shows a comparison of the *Regulatory Framework for Ghana and the Philippines* (p.24).

Table 3. Regulatory Framework for Ghana and the Philippines

	Ghana	*Philippines*
Continuum of MFIs	Wide range of unregulated and regulated MFIs REGULATED/LICENSED MFIs ● Finance Companies ● Community/Rural Banks ● S & L Companies ● CFIs (Credit Unions) UNREGULATED/UNLICENSED MFIs ● NGOs ● Susu Clubs & Collectors ● ROSCAs and ASCAs	Wide range of unregulated and regulated MFIs REGULATED/LICENSED MFIs ● Thrift Banks ● Rural Banks ● Cooperative Banks ● Private Lending Investors ● Pawnshops UNREGULATED/LICENSED MFIs ● NGOs ● Credit Unions/Savings and Credit units of Cooperatives ● Village "banks" (Solidarity Groups) ● ROSCAs and ASCAs
Strategy for Developing Sustainable Microfinance	● Adopted National Strategic Framework for the Microfinance Sector (1999-2000) ● Established Central Policy Coordination Office at Ministry of Finance ● Introducing amendments to banking laws and regulations responsive to microfinance (minimum capitalization & adequacy requirements, liquidity management standards; loan collateral, classification and loss provisioning guidelines) ● Simplifying (1) reporting standards, chart of accounts; (2) external audit requirements; (3) microfinance manual for Central Bank examiners and inspectors	● Adopted National Policy on Microfinance (a997-98) ● Established Central Policy Coordination Office and at Department of Finance and at Banko Sentral ● Introducing amendments to banking laws and regulations responsive to microfinance (minimum capitalization and adequacy requirements; liquidity management standards; loan collateral, classification, and loss provisioning guidelines) ● Simplifying (1) reporting standards, chart of accounts; (2) external audit requirements; (3) microfinance manual for Central Bank examiners and inspectors
MIssing Links and Regulatory Weaknesses	● Community ownership of rural banks obstructs internal prudential governance and management controls ● Need to regulate unregulated/ unlicensed MFIs into payments infrastructures ● Accelerate capacity building or staff and RegulatoryAuthority and MFIs	● Fragmented regulatory framework: Cooperative financial Institutions are outside (1) Central Bank jurisdiction, (2) formal deposit insurance system ● Need to integrate unregulated/ unlicensed MFIs into payments infrastructure ● Accelerate capacity building for staffs of Regulatory Authority and MFIs

Table 4 below, shows *Financial Profile of Selected MFIs* (p. 26)

Table 4. Financial Profile of Selected MFIs (In%)

Region	*Capital/assets*	*Operating self-sufficiency*	*External funds/ loans*
Africa	51.6%	88.8%	51.7%
Asia	48.5	109.8	40.7
Latin America	44.2	113.8	44.4
Eastern Europe	54.2	107.4	146.5
Organizational formats			
Bank	20.3	107.6	106.0
Non-Bank FI	46.5	96.4	52.2
Credit Union	34.7	109.3	67.7
NGO	59.5	106.4	41.6

Φ External Funds/Loans = Funds @ commercial rates / Average Loan Portfolio
Source: The MicroBanking Bulletin, Issue No.6 (April 2001), Tables A and B

4.4. Effects of Banking Sector Reforms on Microfinance Sustainability in Ghana

Looking into the pivotal role of microfinance institutions (MFIs) in poverty reduction and inclusive development has garnered recognition, promoting extensive research into their economic sustainability. While existing studies focus on institutional and client factors, there's a notable gap regarding impact of regulatory factors on economic sustainability. The recent microfinance sector clean-up by the Bank of Ghana, provided an opportunity for this investigation. Using independent t-tests, the study assessed improvements in operating cost, operating income, and operating profit post-clean-up. Results reveal a lack of significant enhancement in operating costs and income, with a decline in operating profit. This suggests that regulatory measures in Ghana have not yet effectively promoted economic sustainability in the microfinance sector, emphasizing the need for a nuanced understanding of regulatory dynamics in fostering lasting impact (Essiam, 2023, Abstract) The evaluation of financial sustainability involves two aspects: operational sustainability and financial sel-suiciency. Operational sustainability means the institution can fund ists day-to-day expenses solely from operating income, regardless of subsidies (Meyer 2002). On the other hand, financial self-sufficiency signifies that microfinance institutions can autonomously cover operational and borrowing costs, even with market-rate subsidies, using their internally generated revenue. It is crucial to acknowledge that an MFI demonstrating subpar financial performance cannot be considered financially sustainable. Similarly, a profit-generating MFI dependent on subsidized services to cover specific costs would also lack financial sustainability.

True financial sustainability necessitates complete self-sufficiency and the ability to thrive without external financial support. The study highlights nuance trends in financial performance of microfinance institutions in Ghana following the Bank Cleaning era. The unexpected decline in operating profits, the stability of operating income, and the lack of significant change in operating costs underscore the complexity of the post-clean-up financial landscape for these institutions. The main objective of the study is to investigate the aftermath of the Banking Sector Cleanup on Microfinance Sustainability in Ghana. In this attempt the Ex Post Facto Design was adopted to assess how sustainable the 137 microfinance institutions that survived the clean-up exercise have become. This was done by comparing key sustainability variables like operating cost, operating income, and operating profit. After applying an independent sample t-test technique, it was found out that: operating income and operation cost remained statistically the same over the period of study. This could be the result of the short period after the regulatory change. The expectation was that operating profit would also remain the same statistically. Although the short period could be a factor as monetary policies usually have pronounced lags, there is a cause or worry as operating profit of the microfinance institutions have significantly fallen. With operating income and operating cost being statistically the same, the only variable that would account for this fall in operating profit is the provision of risk (including charge-offs). Policy makers should therefore ensure that the proposed measures to be implemented after the clean-up in the microfinance sector that were out by BOG (2019) are followed. This will help avoid the clean-up exercise, a worthless activity. (Essiam, 2023)

Table 5 below, shows descriptive statistics for operating profit, separated into two categories: period prior to and the period following the microfinance institutions' clean-up.

Table 5. Description statistics of operating profit

	Bank Clean-up	**N**	**Mean**	**Standard Deviation**	**Standard Error**
	Before Bank Clean-up	1192	-3739.83	96050.95	2782.04
Operating Profit					
	After Bank Clean-up	1264	-21452.12	197404.45	5552.43

Table 5 reveals that the operating profit of the remaining 137 microfinance institutions did not improve following the clean-up. In fact, the average operating profit declined, dropping from -3,739.84 in the ten months prior to the clean-up to -21,452.12 in the ten months afterward.

Table 6 below, is provided to assess whether this observed difference in the average operating profit is statistically significant.

Table 6. Descriptive statistics operating profit

		Levene's Test for Equality of Variances		T-test for equality of means			
		F	**Sig**	**t**	*df*	**Sig. (2-tailed)**	**Std. Error Difference**
	Equal variances not assumed	13.066	0.0	2.801	2454	0.005	6323.85
Operating profit							
	Equal variances not assumed			2.852	1852.91	0.004	6210.41

Levene's test for equality of variances in Table 6 indicates that the two samples do not have equal variances, as the -test is statistically significant at the 5% level. Consequently, the t-test was performed under the assumption of unequal variances.

According to Table 6, the t-test is also statistically significant at the 5% level, suggesting that the difference in mean operating profits observed in Table 1 is not due to random chance. Therefore, the operating profits of microfinance institutions in the ten months following the clean-up have declined compared to the ten months prior to the exercise.

Table 7 below, shows that the operating income of microfinance institutions was higher in the ten months prior to the clean-up exercise, reaching 71,600.40, compared to 64,619.78 in the ten months following the exercise.

Table 7. Descriptive Statistics of Operating Income

	Bank Clean-up	N	Mean	Standard Deviation	Standard Error
	Before Bank Clean-up	1192	71600.40	14519.99	4272.80
Operating Profit					
	After Bank Clean-up	1264	64619.78	144480.11	4063.82

Levene's test of equality of variance is not significant, allowing the analysis to proceed under the assumption, the t-test is not statistically significant, indicating that the observed difference in Table 6, is due to chance. As a result, the operating income has remained unchanged following the Bank of Ghana's microfinance sector clean-up.

Table 8. T-test of equality of means for Operating Income

		Levene's Test for Equality of Variances		T-test for equality of means			
		F	**Sig**	**t**	*df*	**Sig. (2-tailed)**	**Std. Error Difference**
	Equal variances not assumed	0.258	0.611	1.185	2454	0.236	5893.13
Operating Income							
	Equal variances not assumed			1.184	2438.56	0.237	5896.73

Table 9 below, indicates that the operating costs of microfinance institutions in Ghana decreased slightly from 63,321.29 in the ten months before the clean-up to 62, 872.55 in the ten months following the exercise.

Table 9. Descriptive statistics of operating cost

	Bank Clean-up	N	Mean	Standard Deviation	Standard Error
	Before Bank Clean-up	1192	63321.29	114134.14	3305.90
Operating Profit					
	After Bank Clean-up	1264	62872.55	119442.51	3359.58

Table 10 below, shows the significance level of this difference in the mean.

Table 10. T-test of equality of means of operating cost

		Levene's Test for Equality of Variances		T-test for equality of means			
		F	**Sig**	**t**	*df*	**Sig. (2-tailed)**	**Std. Error Difference**
	Equal variances not assumed	0.25	0.875	0.095	2454	0.924	4719.57
Operating Cost							
	Equal variances not assumed			0.095	2453.52	0.925	4713.29

Table 10 indicates that the variances are unequal, as Levene's test is significant at the 5% level. Based on this, the t-test are not significant at the 5% level, meaning the means are equal. Therefore, there is no statistical evidence to suggest that operating costs for microfinance institutions in Ghana decreased after the Bank of Ghana's clean-up exercise. This implies that operating costs have remained unchanged post-clean-up.

The study reveals complex trends in the financial performance of microfinance institutions in Ghana following the clean-up. These include the unexpected decline in operating profits, the stability of operating costs, illustrating the nuanced financial landscape for these institutions after the reforms.

The main goal of this study was to examine the impact of the Banking Sector Cleanup on the sustainability of microfinance institutions in Ghana. To achieve this, an Ex Post Facto Design was used to evaluate the sustainability of the 137 microfinance institutions that survived the clean-up by comparing key sustainability variables like operating cost, income, and profit.

Using the independent sample t-test, it was found that operating income and costs remained statistically unchanged throughout the study period. This could be attributed to the short time frame following the regulatory changes, as monetary policies often have delayed effects. It was expected that operating profit would also remain stable. However, the significant decline in operating profit is concerning. Given both operating income and costs remained constant, the decline in profit is likely due to increased provisions or risks, including charge-offs.

Policymakers should ensure that the post-clean-up measures proposed by the Bank of Ghana (2019) are properly implemented to prevent the clean-up from becoming ineffective.

4.5. Reinventing Microfinance to Address the "Last Mile Problem": Delivering Clean Energy and Actionable Information to the Poor

For microfinance to reach its full potential and address recent criticisms – many of which are exaggerated or politically motivated – it needs to evolve. Beyond financial services, microfinance can leverage its infrastructure, market knowledge, and client relationships to create more value for clients and tackle broader societal challenges. By capitalizing on its strengths, microfinance can help solve the "last mile problem," which has hindered efforts to deliver new ideas, technologies, and business models to the poor in ways that foster socio-economic improvement.

Two key areas for this expansion are bringing clean energy solutions, such as solar home systems, improved cooking stoves, and solar lanterns with mobile phone charging capabilities, and disseminating agricultural best practices to rural communities in developing countries. Microfinance institutions' field staff and clients are well placed to act as "trusted intermediaries," connecting people with products and knowledge and providing the necessary financing. There are already successful models demonstrating how this can work, and incremental financing or such expenditures could prove more impactful than many traditional microloans.

By offering these services, microfinance can contribute to global issues like climate change and the food crisis, although these efforts alone will not fully solve these complex problems. However, using microfinance as a platform to assess such issues, while simultaneously creating value for clients, could serve as a model for tackling other challenges, such as healthcare, education, democratic participation, environmental sustainability, and nutrition. Developing new models that solve multiple problems while benefiting clients could help restore the reputation of microfinance, which has faced criticism in recent years.

The rise of microfinance programs in India during the late 1990s has undeniably enabled a significant number of rural women to access banking services today. As members of Self-Help Groups (SHGs), these women who previously lacked financial access, can now benefit from bank deposits and loans. Currently, over 80 million women in India are connected to microfinance institutions, with SHGs generating a credit low of Rs 17,342 crore. Microfinance has played a crucial role in encouraging rural women to become entrepreneurs and start small businesses. Alongside their responsibilities in farming and household tasks, many poor rural women now operate microenterprises, including baking, dairy farming, and poultry farming. Their efforts have led to increased family incomes, improved household savings, women's empowerment, poverty reduction, and investments in children's health, education, housing, clean water, sanitation, job creation, and overall GDP growth. These women entrepreneurs are thus driving the alternative economy in India.

4.6. Gender and Renewable Energy Integration: The Mediating Role of Green-Microfinance

Women's empowerment is a key aspect of the fifth Sustainable Development Goal (SDG 5), gender equality, and is influenced by various factors. In East Sumba, the development of renewable energy, as part of the seventh Sustainable Development Goal (SDG 7: Affordable and Clean Energy), presents both opportunities and challenges for empowering women. Rural microfinance institutions (MFIs) play a crucial role in increasing women's empowerment by facilitating energy management. This study examines both the direct and indirect (mediated) effects of renewable energy on women's empowerment through green MFIs. Using Partial Least Square-Structural Equation Modeling (PLS-SEM) with bootstrapping and Sobel test to assess the mediation effect, the findings reveal a direct relationship between renewable energy and green MFIs. The study confirms that green MFIs, which operate under a gender mainstreaming integration model in the renewable energy sector, contribute to sustainable women's empowerment. The results suggest that local government gender policies, combined with the availability of renewable energy, support the development of green MFIs.

The Triple Bottom Line theory suggests that a business is considered sustainable when it achieves three key goals: economic prosperity (profit), social justice (people), and environmental quality (planet) (Elkington, 1998). These three elements are interconnected, interdependent, and sometimes in conflict. To achieve the Triple Bottom Line, a business must adopt innovative thinking and operate across seven dimensions: markets, values, transparency, life-cycle technology, partnerships, time perspective, and corporate governance (Jeurissen, 2000).

This research was carried out at Tapa Walla Badi MFI group in Mbatakapidu, East Sumba, Indonesia. According to Atahau, Huruta, and Lee (2020), microfinance institutions (MFIs) serving older women have maintained their operations for over two decades. The local government of East Sumba plans to develop a hydroelectric power plant in Mbatakapidu as part of the renewable energy initiative under the Sumba Iconic Island project.

Female respondents slightly outnumbered male respondents by 8%. The majority of women were homemakers, accounting for 37.3%. Nearly 35% of the respondents were over 40 years old, and a significant portion had low education levels, with 32% having no formal education. This suggests that more than half of the respondents were housewives with limited education.

The study demonstrates that the availability of renewable energy supports the transformation of MFIs into green MFIs. It shows that improved green loan conditions encourage members to pursue eco-friendly businesses, such as biogas equipment and micro-hydropower plants. The research also highlights a strong connection between green MFIs and women's empowerment, with women empowerment scoring the highest among the variables studied. (Atahau, A., *et al.* 2021)

4.7. GVS Biogas

GVS Biogas is another exemplary initiative that highlights the integration of green technology with microfinance. The company has facilitated the installation of biogas systems for more than 200,000 households in India, transforming agricultural waste into renewable energy (GVS Biogas, 2019). This initiative not only provides clean cooking energy but also contributes to waste management and improved sanitation.

4.7.1. Benefits of Biogas Financing

Financing biogas production systems has several environmental and social benefits. By converting organic waste into biogas, households can reduce greenhouse gas emissions and improve their health by eliminating the need for traditional cooking fuels, such as firewood and kerosene. Biogas systems also generate organic fertilizers, promoting sustainable agricultural practices and enhancing soil health (GVS Biogas, 2019)

4.7.2. Impact on Community Empowerment

The impact of GVS Biogas extends beyond individual households. By promoting the adoption of biogas technology, GVS contributes to community empowerment and environmental sustainability. Local farmers who have implemented biogas systems report increased income from the sale of excess biogas and organic fertilizers, leading to improved livelihoods and enhanced food security.

4.7.3. Challenges and Future Directions

While GVS has achieved significant success, challenges persist. The initial investment required for biogas systems can be a barrier for low- income households, necessitating innovative financing solutions to enhance affordability. Additionally, education and awareness campaigns are essential to promote the benefits of biogas technology and address misconceptions.

4.8. BRAC (Bangladesh Rural Advancement Committee)

BRAC, one of the largest non-government organizations in the world, has implemented a microfinance program in Bangladesh that provides loans for sustainable agriculture practices (BRAC, 2020). By enabling farmers to adopt eco-friendly farming techniques, BRAC promotes environmental sustainability while enhancing food security.

4.8.1. Sustainable Agricultural Practices

BRAC's microloans are designed to support sustainable agricultural practices, such as organic farming, agroforestry, and integrated pest management. These practices not only improve crop yields but also minimize environmental impact. Research has shown that farmers who adopt sustainable practices experience increased income and resilience to climate change (BRAC, 2024).

4.8.2. Social Impact and Empowerment

BRAC's approach to microfinance emphasizes social impact and community empowerment. By providing financial support to women farmers, BRAC promotes gender equity and enhances women's decision-making power with households. Women who participate in BRACs programs report improved economic status and increased confidence in their ability to contribute to their families' livelihoods (BRAC, 2020)

4.8.3. Barriers to Adoption

Despite its successes, BRAC faces challenges in expanding its microfinance program. Limited access to markets, lack of information on sustainable practices, and inadequate infrastructure can hinder farmer's ability to implement eco-friendly techniques. Addressing these barriers requires a holistic approach that includes capacity building, market access, and ongoing support for farmers. (BRAC, 2024)

Figure 4. Timeline of regulatory changes and MFI clean technology integration

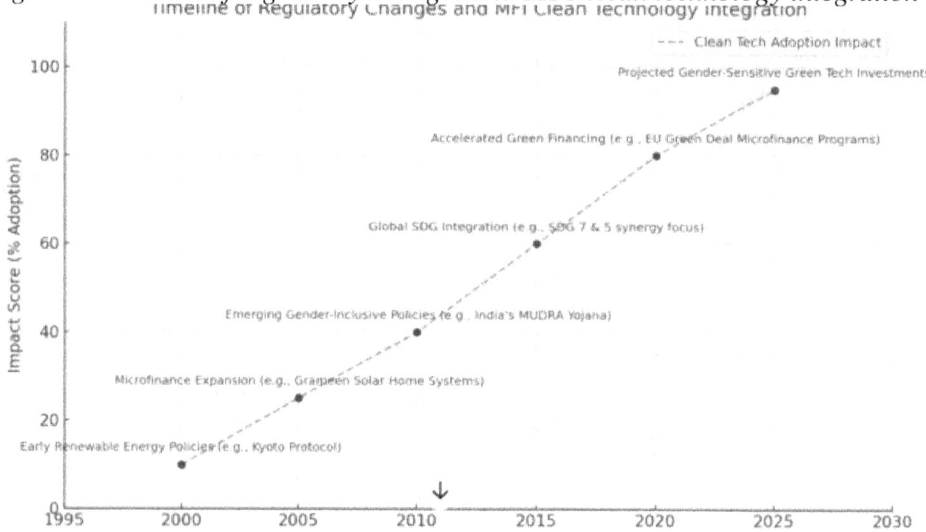

Figure 4, shows the Timeline of Regulatory Changes and MFI Clean Technology Integration: Early Renewable Energy Policies (e.g. Kyoto Protocol) in 2000; Microfinance Expansion (e.g. Grameen Solar Home Systems) in 2005; Emerging Gender-Inclusive Policies (e.g. India's MUDRA Yojana) in 2010; Global SDG Integration (e.g. SDG 7 & 5 synergy focus) in 2015; Accelerated Green Financing (e.g. EU Green Deal Microfinance Programs) in 2020; Projected Gender-Sensitive Green Tech Investments in 2025.

Challenges in the Microfinance Sector

While the case studies illustrate the potential of microfinance to promote green technology, significant barriers persist within the sector that can undermine its effectiveness.

1. Over-Indebtedness

One of the most pressing challenges in the microfinance sector is over-indebtedness. Many borrowers, especially those engaged in income-generating activities, often take out multiple loans from different MFIs to meet their financial needs. This can lead to financial distress and an inability to repay loans (MIcrofinance Gateway, 2015). Policymakers must implement regulations to prevent predatory lending practices and promote responsible lending.

2. Lack of Regulation

The absence of a regulatory framework can result in unethical practices within the microfinance sector. Unregulated MFIs may prioritize profit over social impact, leading to exploitative lending practices. Establishing guidelines for transparency and accountability is essential for protecting borrowers' rights and ensuring that microfinance serves its intended purpose (Rhyne, 2009).

3. Limited Product Offerings

The focus on microcredit has often overshadowed the need for diverse financial products that support green technology. Many MFIs primarily offer traditional microloans without considering the unique financing needs of clients interested in green technology. Encouraging MIs to expand their product offerings can enhance the impact of microfinance on sustainable development.

5. CONCLUSION

The chapter highlights the critical role of microfinance in promoting sustainable development through the financing of green technologies. The case studies of M-KOPA Solar, GVS Biogras, BRAC and others, illustrate how microfinance can empower marginalized communities while addressing environmental challenges. Through innovative financing solutions, these organizations demonstrate that microfinance has the potential to contribute to both economic growth and environmental sustainability.

Despite positive outcomes, significant barriers remain within the microfinance sector. Over-indebtedness, lack of regulation, and limited product offerings pose challenges that must be addressed to optimize the impact of microfinance on sustainable development. A comprehensive policy framework should prioritize regulation and oversight, capacity building for MFIs, and diversification of financial products to include green technology financing.

The Chapter explores the intricate relationship between financial inclusion, microfinance, clean technology, and entrepreneurship as drivers of sustainable development. Through an in-depth analysis of their interconnected dynamics, I have highlighted the importance of collaboration and innovation in harnessing their collective potential to address global challenges and achieve sustainable development goals.

From providing access to financial services for the unbanked and underserved to promoting sustainable business models and clean technology adoption, financial inclusion, microfinance, clean technology, and entrepreneurship offer pathways to inclusive growth, economic resilience, and environmental sustainability. By leveraging synergies, fostering partnerships, and embracing innovative solutions, stakeholders can work together to build inclusive ecosystems that empower individuals and communities to thrive in a rapidly changing world.

Microfinance has the potential to serve as a catalyst for sustainable development when aligned with innovative financial solutions that promote green technology. By fostering financial inclusion and environmental sustainability, microfinance can empower communities and contribute to a more sustainable future.

As we look to the future, it is imperative that we continue to explore emerging trends, overcome barriers, and embrace opportunities for collaboration and innovation in the pursuit of sustainable development. Through collective action and commitment, we can create a more equitable, resilient, and sustainable future for all.

Framework for Integrating Microfinance to Green Technology

1. Policy Objectives
    - 1.1. **Promote Financial Inclusion:** Ensure that marginalized communities have access to financial services tailored to their needs, including microloans for green technologies.
    - 1.2. **Encourage Environmental Sustainability:** Foster the adoption of green technologies that reduce environmental impact and enhance resilience to climate change.
    - 1.3. **Empower Communities:** Support community-driven initiatives that empower individuals, particularly women, through access to financial resources and sustainable practices
2. Key Components of the Framework
    - 2.1. Regulatory Framework
        - 2.1.1. **Establish Clear Regulations:** Create comprehensive regulations that govern microfinance activities, ensuring ethical lending practices and consumer protection.
        - 2.1.2. **Promote Transparency and Accountability:** Require MFIs to disclose information about interest rates, loan terms, and environmental impact of financed projects.
        - 2.1.3. **Encourage Collaboration:** Facilitate partnerships between MFIs, government agencies, and non-governmental organizations (NGOs) to share best practices and resources.
    - 2.2. Product Diversification

2.2.1. **Develop Tailored Financial Products:** Design microfinance products specifically for green technologies, such as low-interest loans for solar energy systems, biogas installations, and sustainable agricultural practices.

2.2.2. **Flexibility Payment Options:** Offer flexible schedules that align with the cash flow cycles of borrowers, ensuring affordability and reducing the risk of over-indebtedness.

2.2.3. **Incentives for Green Investments:** Provide incentives, such as interest rate reductions or subsidies, for borrowers who invest in environmentally friendly technologies.

2.3. Capacity Building and Education

2.3.1. **Training Programs for Borrowers:** Implement training programs that educate borrowers on the benefits of green technologies and how to utilize financing effectively.

2.3.2. **Support for MFIs:** Provide capacity-building initiatives for MFIs to enhance their understanding of green technologies and how to integrate them into their financial offerings.

2.3.3. **Community Awareness Campaigns:** Conduct outreach campaigns to raise awareness about the importance of sustainability and the benefits of adopting green technologies.

2.4. Monitoring and Evaluation

2.4.1. **Impact Assessment Framework:** Establish a robust framework for monitoring and evaluating the impact of microfinance on sustainable development, focusing on both social and environmental outcomes.

2.4.2. **Data Collection and Analysis:** Regularly collect and analyze data on the adoption of green technologies, borrower livelihoods, and environmental metrics to inform policy adjustments and improve program effectiveness.

2.4.3. **Feedback Mechanism:** Create channels for feedback from borrowers and communities to identify challenges and areas for improvement in microfinance services.

3. Implementation Strategies

3.1. Public-Private Partnerships

3.1.1. **Engage Stakeholders:** Involve various stakeholders, including government bodies, MFIs, NGOs, and the private sector, to collaboratively develop and implement the framework.

3.1.2. **Leverage Resources:** Utilize resources from different sectors to enhance the capacity and reach of microfinance initiatives focused on green technology,

3.2. Financial Incentives and Support

3.2.1. **Government Funding and Support:** Secure government funding to support MFIs in developing green finance products and expanding their reach to underserved communities.

3.2.2. **Access to International Funding:** Facilitate access to international funding sources, such as climate finance initiatives, to bolster microfinance efforts in promoting green technologies.

4. Expected Outcomes
    4.1. **Increased Access to Green Technologies:** Enhanced access to affordable financing for low-income households to adopt green technologies.
    4.2. **Empowerment of Marginalized Communities:** Improved livelihoods and economic stability for borrowers, particularly women and marginalized groups
    4.3. **Environmental Benefits:** Reduction in carbon emissions and improved sustainability through the widespread adoption of green technologies.
    4.4. **Resilient Communities:** Enhanced resilience of communities to climate change and environmental degradation through sustainable practices.

5. CONCLUSION

This framework provides a comprehensive approach to integrating microfinance with green technology, addressing the pressing challenges of poverty and environmental degradation. BY promoting financial inclusion, supporting sustainable practices, and empowering communities, (especially women), this framework has the potential to drive significant positive change in both social and environmental dimensions. Policymakers, MFIs and stakeholders are encouraged to adopt and adapt this framework to suit their specific contexts, ensuring that microfinance remains a viable tool for sustainable development in the face of evolving global challenges.

Relationship Between Variables

1. Policy Objectives
    - Influences:
        - Regulatory Framework
        - Capacity Building
    - Outcome of:
        - Increased Access to Green Technologies
        - Empowerment of Marginalized Communities
2. Regulatory Framework
    - Influences:
        - Product Diversification
        - Monitoring and Evaluation

- Outcome of:
    - Environmental Benefits
3. Product Diversification
    - Influences:
        - Capacity Building
    - Outcome of:
        - Increased Access to Green Technologies
4. Capacity Building
    - Influences:
        - Monitoring and Evaluation
    - Outcome of:
        - Empowerment of Marginalized Communities
        - Resilient Communities
5. Monitoring and Evaluation
    - Influences:
        - Regulatory Framework
        - Product Diversification
    - Outcome of:
        - Environmental Benefits

Visual Representation (Conceptual)

If you visualize this in a two-dimensional layout, you could create a diagram with arrows connecting each of these elements to show the influence and relationships. Here's how you can conceptualize it:

Figure 5. Policy Framework: A Comprehensive Approach to Sustainability

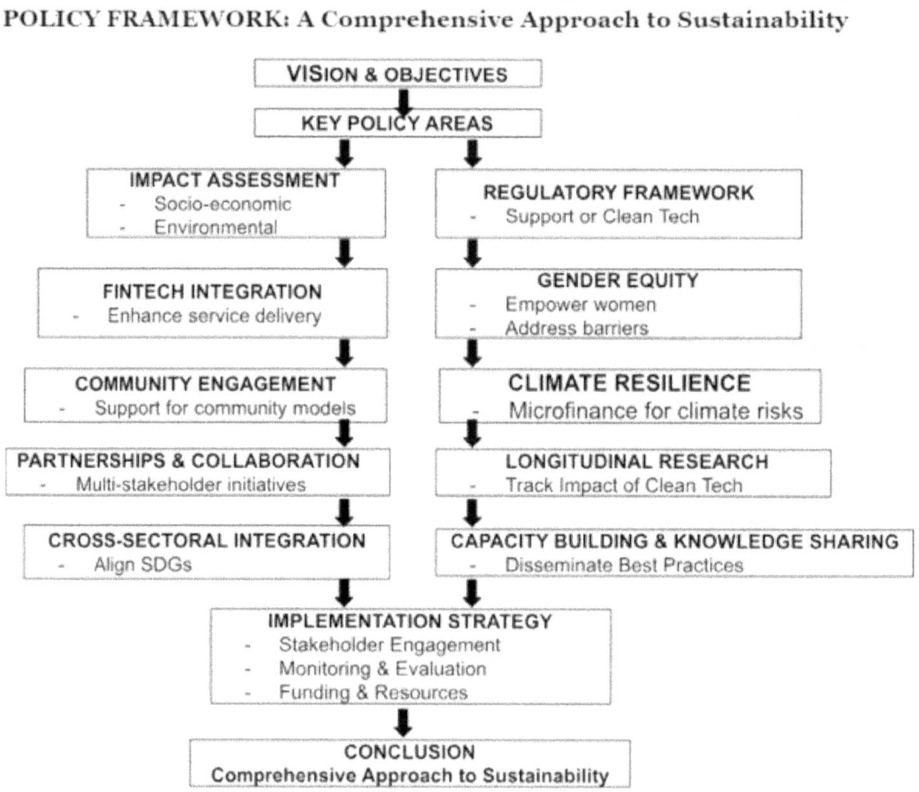

To process the relationships among the variables in the framework for integrating microfinancing and green technology you can follow a systematic approach that involves several steps, including data collection, analysis, implementation, and evaluation. Below is a breakdown of how each component interacts and gets processed:

1. Data Collection
    - **Gather Information:** Collect qualitative and quantitative data related to microfinance, green technology, and community needs. This can involve surveys, interviews, case studies, and secondary data from existing research.
    - **Stakeholder Engagement:** Involve stakeholders such as MFIs, policymakers, community leaders, and beneficiaries to gather insights on their perspectives and experiences related to microfinance and green technology.
2. Analysis of Relationships

- **Mapping Relationships:** Use tools like flow charts or diagrams to visualize how the various components (e.g. Policy Objectives, Regulatory Framework) are interconnected. This helps identify key pathways for influence.
- **Identity Indicators:** Define specific indicators for each variable to measure progress. For example:
    - Policy Objectives: Number of policies implemented supporting green technology
    - Regulatory Framework: Number of regulations established to ensure ethical lending practices.
    - Product Diversification: Variety of financial products offered for green technology.

3. Implementation
    - **Develop Action Plans:** Create detailed plans to implement strategies for each component of the framework. For example, outline steps to develop new financial products or enhance training programs for borrowers.
    - **Allocate Resources:** Ensure that appropriate resources, including funding, human capital, and technology, are allocated to support the implementation of each component.
4. Monitoring and Evaluation
    - **Establish Monitoring Systems:** Develop systems to track progress against denied indicators. This could involve regular data collection and analysis to assess how well each component is functioning.
    - **Evaluate Outcomes:** Assess the impact of the framework on achieving the desired outcomes (e.g. increased access to green technologies, empowerment of marginalized communities) through pre-and post-implementation studies.
    - **Feedback Mechanisms:** Create channels for stakeholders to provide feedback on the effectiveness of the framework. This can inform adjustments and improvements.
5. Continuous Improvement
    - **Refine Processes:** Based on evaluation indians, refine the strategies and processes to better align with objectives. This may involve re-evaluating the regulatory framework or modifying product offerings.
    - **Scale Successful Initiatives:** Identify successful initiatives within the framework and explore opportunities to scale them to reach a broader audience.

Example of Processing Steps

1. **Collect Data:** Conduct a survey of microfinance clients to assess their access to green technology.
2. **Analyze Relationships:** Create a Flowchart mapping the impact of increased access to green technologies on community empowerment.
3. **Implement Training:** Develop a training program for MFIs on how to offer green finance products.
4. **Monitor Outcomes:** Use defined indicators to track changes in community livelihoods and environmental benefits.
5. **Evaluate and Adjust:** Assess the impact of the training program and adjust it based on participant feedback.

By following this structured approach to processing the relationships among variables in the framework, stakeholders can ensure that the integration of microfinance and green technology effectively promotes sustainable development. This continuous cycle of data collection, analysis, implementation, monitoring, and evaluation allows for adaptive management, leading to better outcomes for communities and the environment.

6. RECOMMENDATIONS FOR FURTHER RESEARCH

These recommendations aim to inspire further research and collaboration in advancing our understanding of the complex interactions between financial inclusion, microfinance and clean technology, and entrepreneurship, and their transformative potential for building a more equitable, resilient, and sustainable future.

1. **Impact Assessment of Clean Technology Adoption in Microfinance:** Conduct comprehensive studies to evaluate the socio-economic and environmental impact of integrating clean technology solutions, such as solar-powered microgrids and energy efficient appliances, in microfinance initiatives. Assess the implications for micro-entrepreneurs' productivity, income generation, carbon footprint reduction.
2. **Policy Analysis of Financial Inclusion and Clean Technology:** Investigate the effectiveness of policy frameworks and regulatory incentives in promoting financial inclusion and clean technology adoption in the microfinance sector. Examine the role of government, policies, subsidies, and regulatory support in creating an enabling environment for sustainable entrepreneurship and clean energy investment.

3. **Role of Fintech in Advancing Financial Inclusion:** Explore the potential of financial technology (fintech) innovations, such as mobile banking, digital payments, and blockchain technology, in enhancing financial inclusion outwork.
4. **Gender Perspectives in Microfinance and Clean Technology:** Investigate gender dynamics on male and female entrepreneurs. Assess the barriers and opportunities for women's participation in microfinance initiatives and the role of clean technology in promoting gender equality and women's economic empowerment.
5. **Community-Based Approaches to Sustainable Entrepreneurship:** Explore community-based models of sustainable entrepreneurship and clean technology adoption, such as cooperative enterprises and community-owned renewable energy projects. Investigate the socio-economic benefits, governance structures, and scalability of community-driven initiatives in promoting inclusive development and environmental stewardship.
6. **Climate Resilience and Microfinance:** Examine the role of microfinance institutions in building climate resilience among vulnerable communities through innovative financial products and risk management strategies. Assess the effectiveness of microinsurance systems, climate-smart agricultural practices, and disaster risk financing mechanisms in enhancing resilience to climate change impacts.
7. **Partnerships for Scaling Impact:** Study successful partnerships and collaborations between microfinance institutions, clean technology providers, NGOs, and government agencies in scaling up innovative solutions for sustainable development. Analyze the factors contributing to successful partnerships, such as shared objectives, mutual trust, and effective resource mobilization.
8. **Longitudinal Studies on Sustainable Entrepreneurship:** Conduct longitudinal studies to track the long-term performance and sustainability of micro-enterprises that have adopted clean technology and embraced sustainable business practices. Evaluate the economic, social and environmental outcomes over time and identify factors influencing enterprise resilience and growth.
9. **Cross-Sectoral Integration of Sustainable Development Goals:** Explore the interlinkages between financial inclusion, microfinance, clean technology, and other sustainable development goals (SDGs), such as poverty alleviation, climate action, and gender equality. Assess the potential for integrated approaches to achieving multiple SDGs simultaneously and the synergies between different sectors and initiatives.
10. **Capacity Building and Knowledge Sharing:** Develop capacity-building programs and knowledge-sharing platforms to disseminate best practices, lessons learned, and innovative solutions in the fields of financial inclusion, microfinance, and clean technology, foster collaboration among researchers,

practitioners, policymakers, and community stakeholders to accelerate progress towards sustainable development goals.

These recommendations highlight the need for comprehensive and interdisciplinary research to better understand the dynamics of green technology in microfinance and its potential to drive sustainable development and empower women in underbanked and underserved communities. By addressing these areas, researchers can contribute to the formulation of effective principles and practices that promote equity, sustainability, and economic growth.

REFERENCES

Arnold, J., Alam, M. N., Thorne, H., & Armacost, N. (n.d.). *Towards Reinventing Microfinance Through Solving the "Last Mile Problem": Bridging Clean Energy Solutions and Actionable Information to the Poor* [Abstract]. Researchgate.

Atahau, A., Sakti, I. M., Huruta, A. D., & Kim, M.-S. (2021). Gender and renewable energy integration: The mediating role of green-microfinance. *Journal of Cleaner Production*, 318(October), 128536. DOI: 10.1016/j.jclepro.2021.128536

Barman, C. B. (2022). Microfinance, Rural Women Entrepreneurs and Sustainable Development. In *Sustainable Entrepreneurship*. DOI: DOI: 10.31674/book.2002se.002

Bocken, N. M. O., Shirt, S. W., Rana, P., & Evans, S. (2014). A literature and practice review to develop sustainable business model archetypes. *Journal of Cleaner Production*, 65, 42–56. DOI: 10.1016/j.jclepro.2013.11.039

BRAC. (2024). *BRAC Microfinance Annual Report 2020.*https://www.brack.net

Capital, F. (25 Mar 2024). Microfinance clean technology: The Role of Microfinance in Fueling Sustainable Entrepreneurship. https://fastercapital.com/content/Microfinance-clean-technology--The-Role-of-Microfinance-in-Fueling-Sustainable-Entrepreneurship.html

Essiam, E. (2023). Empirical Investigation into the Consequences of the Banking Sector Cleanup on Microfinance Sustainability in Ghana. *International Journal of Applied Research in Business and Management*, 4(3), 181–199. DOI: 10.51137/ijarbm.2023.4.3.10

Ferdousi, F. (2015). Impact of microfinance on sustainable entrepreneurship development. [Abstract]. *Development Studies Research*, 2(1), 51–63. https://www.tandfonline.com/doi/full/10.1080/21665095.2015.1058718. DOI: 10.1080/21665095.2015.1058718

Gallardo, J. (November 2001). A Framework for Regulating Microfinance Institutions: The Experience in Ghana and the Philippines. *The World Bank*. Financial Sector Development Department. DOI: 10.1080/21665095.2015.1058718

Gateway, M. (2015). Over-Indebtedness in Microfinance: Causes and Solutions https://www. microfinancegateway.org

Gatto, A., & Sadik-Zada, E. R. (2022) Access to microfinance as a resilience policy to address sustainable development goals: A content analysis. 8(10): e10860. DOI: . https://www.ncbi.nlm.nih.gov/pmc/articles/PMC9578961/DOI: 10.1016/j.he;iyon.2002.210860

Global Off-Grid Lighting Association. (2018). *The Off-Grid Solar Market Report*. https://gogla.org

GVS Biogas. (2019). Biogas Solutions for Rural India. https://www.gvsbiogas.com

IRENA. (2020). *Innovation landscape brief: Pay-as-you-go models*. International Renewable Energy Agency.

Kabeer, N. (2005). Is microfinance a "magic bullet" for women's empowerment? *Women Studies International Forum, 28*(1), 13-32. DOI: 10.1016/j.wsif.2005.01.007

Khan, M. A., Iqbal, N., & Ashraf, M. (2018). Green Technology and sustainable development: A review of microfinance and renewable energy. *Sustainable Development*, 26(4), 289–298. DOI: 10.1002/sd.1692

Ledgerwood, J. (1999). *Microfinance Handbook: An Institutional and Financial Perspective*. World Bank Publications.

M-KOPA. (2020). *Impact Report 2020*. https://www.M-KOPA.com

M-KOPA. (2024)."Leading Fintech African M-KOPA Reaches 5 Million Customers, Unlocking $1.5bn in Credit Across 5 Markets." *Impact Report 2024*.https://s24.q4cdn.com/538403808/files/doc_news/Leading-Fintech-African-M-KOPA-Reaches-5-Million-Customers-Unlocking-1.5bn-in-Credit-Across-5-Markets-2024.pdf

Meyer, J. 2002. "Track record of financial institutions assessing the poor in Asia," ADB research institute paper, N. 49 [Online}. http://www.esocialsciences.com/articles (30 September 2011) MicroEnergy International (MEI) (n.d.) Clean Energy Promotion through Microfinance in Ethiopia. https://www. climate-change.org/en/best-practices/clean-energy-promotion-through-microfinance-in-ethiopia/

Mouka, Marina. (2024, 15 July). Top 10 fintech innovations transforming the financial sector. *bobsguide*. bobsguide.com/top-10-fintech-innovations-transforming-the-financial-sector/

Pitt, M. M., & Khaddker, S. R. (1998). The impact of group-based credit programs on poor households in Bangladesh: Does the gender participants matter? *Journal of Political Economy*, 106(5), 958–996. DOI: 10.1086/250037

Rahman, N. A. A., Hassan, S., & Said, J. (2015). Promoting Sustainability of Microfinance via Innovation Risks, Best Practices and Management Accounting Practices. *Procedia Economics and Finance*, 31, 470–484. https://www.sciencedirect.com/science/article/pii/S2212567115011806. DOI: 10.1016/S2212-5671(15)01180-6

Rhyne, E. (2009). *Filling the Financial Services Gap: A Guide for Funders and Investors in Microfinance*. The Microfinance Gateway.

Sadik-Zada, E. R., Gatto, A., & Blick, N. (2022). Rural Electrification and Transition to Clean Cooking. The Case Study of Kanyegaramire and Kyamugarura Solar Mini-Grid Energy Cooperatives in the Kyenjojo District of Uganda. In: Leal Filho, W. Vidal, D.G. Dinis, M,A.P., Dias, R.C, (eds) *Sustainably Policies and Practices in Energy, Environment and Health, World Sustainability Series.* Springer, Cham. DOI: 10.1007/978-3-030-86304-3_32

Vallado, M. F. (2023). Communication Dynamics of Women in Microfinance Projects as a Model for Women Empowerment: Microfinance Projects for Poverty Alleviation in the Philippines. In Alhassan, Y., & Nwagbara, U. (Eds.), *Empowering Women Through Microfinance in Developing Countries* (pp. 18–50)., DOI: 10.4018/978-1-6684-8979-6.ch002

Women, U. N. (2018). Turning promises into action: Gender equality in the 2030 Agenda for Sustainable Development. https://www.unwomen,org.

World Bank. (2015) Global Financial Inclusion Database. https://www.worldbank.org

World Bank. (2017). Financial Inclusion: The Global Findex Database 2017. https://www.worldbank.org

World Economic Forum. 10 January 2024. How innovative financial solutions can build climate resilience. https://www.weforum.org/agenda/2024/01/innovative-financial-solutions-climate-resilience/

KEY TERMS AND DEFINITIONS

Cleantech or Clean Technology: Use of innovative technology that does not make use of fossil fuel nor causes pollution

Community Engagement: Participation of individuals in local activities to foster social and environmental development

Environmental Impact: The effect of activities on the environment, focusing on practices that contribute to ecological health

Financial Literacy: Knowledge and skills to manage finances effectively, including budgeting, saving, and investing

Fintech or Financial Technology: Combines finance and technology to revolutionize financial services driven by innovations like digital payments, blockchain, and AI; these advancements enhance efficiency, security, accessibility, and financial inclusion, reshaping the industry

Green Technology Adoption: incorporating eco-friendly technologies (e.g., solar energy, sustainable farming) to reduce environmental impact.

Microfinance: Availability of small loans and financial services for underserved individuals, particularly women

Microfinance Access: Availability and ability of individuals in underserved communities to obtain financial services from financial institutions (MFIs), including access to small loans, savings accounts, and insurance products that are tailored to the needs of low-income individuals; crucial for empowering women entrepreneurs and enabling them to invest in sustainable technologies and practices

Policy Support: Regulations and initiatives that promote green technology and microfinance access for sustainable growth

Sustainable Development: Development that meets present needs without compromising future generations' ability to meet their needs

Sustainable Entrepreneurship: Entrepreneurs do not seek profit but address ecological challenges; use microfinance as a tool to offer renewable energy solutions, waste reduction, and water conservation, for a greener economy.

Three Main Principles in Microfinance: a. Poor people need not only loans, but also savings, insurance and money transfer services b. Microfinance must be useful to poor households: helping them raise income, buildup assets and or cushion themselves against external shocks c. Microfinance services are designed to reach excluded customers who are poorer segments of the population, socially marginalized, or geographically isolated to help them become self-sufficient.

Women Empowerment: enhancing women's social, economic and political power to make informed decisions and lead their communities

Chapter 7

The Impact of FinTech Integration on the Accessibility and Sustainability of Microfinance Institutions: A Case Study Approach

Yahaya Alhassan
https://orcid.org/0000-0001-6700-635X
University of Sunderland in London, UK

Uzoechi Nwagbara
University of Sunderland in London, UK

Lawrence C Bellamy
University of Staffordshire, UK

ABSTRACT

This chapter investigates the impact of FinTech integration on the accessibility and sustainability of microfinance institutions (MFIs) using a case study approach and secondary data. The chapter examines how the use of FinTech solutions by MFIs have enhanced the accessibility of microfinance services by the poor and financially excluded individuals and groups. The chapter also evaluates the potential impact of FinTech integration on the financial sustainability and operational efficiency of MFIs. The chapter identifies key challenges of microfinance-FinTech integration such as high initial investment costs, cybersecurity risks, regulatory complexities,

DOI: 10.4018/979-8-3693-6622-6.ch007

and the potential for over-indebtedness. This investigation provides insights into the opportunities and challenges that MFIs face in adopting FinTech solutions to achieve their aim of enhancing financial inclusion and long-term sustainability in the evolving digital landscape.

1. INTRODUCTION

The impact of financial technology (FinTech) integration on the accessibility and sustainability of microfinance institutions is the focus of this chapter. Evidence from existing literature (Cull and Hartarska, 2023; Oluwaseun and Olaitan, 2021) suggests that microfinance plays a vital role in promoting financial inclusion by extending financial services to underserved populations across the world, particularly in developing countries. Microfinance as a concept has been defined as a financial service offered to low-income individuals or groups who typically lack access to traditional banking services (Visconti, 2016). Fundamentally, it involves providing small loans, savings accounts, insurance, training, and other basic financial services to empower individuals economically and socially to help them out of poverty and improve their quality of life. Evidence of how microfinance has been used to promote financial inclusion has been reported by various studies. For example, Visconti (2016) have shown that microfinance provides access to credit for individuals who lack collateral or credit history to obtain loans from traditional banks. The implication of this is that by providing small loans, microfinance institutions (MFIs) enable the poor to start or expand small businesses, leading to income generation and economic growth. Microfinance institutions have also been shown to be promoting financial inclusion through savings mobilization. For instance, evidence from Alias (2024) suggests that microfinance institutions encourage individuals to save money regularly, fostering a culture of saving among low-income populations. By doing this, microfinance institutions provide opportunities for low-income people to build financial reserves for emergencies, education, or investment in income-generating activities. There is also evidence that services provided by microfinance institutions have contributed positively to mitigating financial risks associated with illness, crop failure, or natural disasters. The outcomes of Oppong, et al. (2024) for example, suggests that the insurance services offered by microfinance institutions provide a safety net for vulnerable households, protecting them from falling deeper into poverty due to unforeseen events. Perhaps it is in this context that Mosley (2009) posits that microfinance institutions promote financial inclusion through offering insurance policies designed for the unbanked and low-income people in the developing world. Another evidence of how microfinance institutions are promoting financial inclusion is through women empowerment. Microfinance services have been shown to have a significant impact on women's empowerment by providing them with access to financial resources and decision-making power (Lamichhane, 2020). In this regard, Malamsha (2023) concludes that women comprise a large proportion of microfinance clients and often use loans to invest in their families' well-being, such as education and healthcare. The most significant evidence of how microfinance institutions are promoting financial inclusion is the positive contribution to poverty reduction reported by various studies. For example, Sulemana, et al. (2023) argues that by providing small loans and promoting entrepreneurship among the poor, microfinance contributes to poverty reduction at the grassroots level. This is consistent with Salgotra, et al. (2021) who have shown that access to financial services enables the poor to invest in productive assets, improve their livelihoods, and break the cycle of poverty.

Certainly, as demonstrated above, the significance of microfinance in promoting financial inclusion is enormous. The question however is "how can the adoption of FinTech solutions help microfinance institutions deepen this financial inclusive drive and improve their services to the underserved populations?" A review of existing literature suggests that there is limited evidence of how the adoption of FinTech solutions, such as mobile banking, blockchain-based transactions, or AI-driven credit scoring, affects the operations and outcomes of microfinance institutions. Financial technology (FinTech) is defined as the innovative use of technology such as blockchain, artificial intelligence and machine learning to deliver financial services more efficiently, conveniently, and cost-effectively (Alam, et al., 2019). It encompasses a wide range of applications and platforms that leverage advancements in digital technology, data analytics, and connectivity to transform various aspects of the financial sector. The role of FinTech in the financial services industry is growing. For instance, FinTech has revolutionised payment systems by introducing digital payment solutions that offer greater convenience and security compared to traditional cash-based transactions (Yadav, et al., 2024). Mobile payment apps, e-wallets, and peer-to-peer payment platforms have gained widespread adoption, facilitating seamless transactions anytime, anywhere. FinTech platforms have also disrupted traditional lending models by offering alternative sources of credit to individuals and businesses (Anand and Mantrala, 2019). For example, peer-to-peer lending platforms connect borrowers directly with investors, bypassing traditional financial intermediaries. Moreover, algorithm-based lending platforms utilise big data and machine learning algorithms to assess creditworthiness and offer personalized loan products. FinTech has also played a significant role in personal finance management. Currently, FinTech tools and apps have been used to empower individuals to manage their finances more effectively by providing real-time insights into spending patterns, budgeting, and saving goals (Agarwal and Ann, 2024.). These cutting-edge personal finance apps offer features such as expense tracking, goal setting, and investment advice, helping users make informed financial decisions and improve their financial well-being (Jie, 2024).

Given the high promise of FinTech and its impact across the financial services sector, small firms are leveraging this technology to provide innovative products and services that is promoting financial inclusion and enhancing the efficiency and accessibility of financial services (Elsaid, 2023). For instance, startups are leveraging FinTech to modernise the insurance industry by streamlining policy management, claims processing, and risk assessment (Singhal, et al., 2024). Besides, digital insurance platforms offer on-demand insurance products, usage-based pricing, and customised coverage options, enhancing customer experience and increasing market efficiency (Jha and Sahoo, 2022). Blockchain technology, the underlying technology behind cryptocurrencies like Bitcoin, has helped to revolutionise various aspects of the financial sector, including payments, asset tokenisation, and smart contracts. This technology (blockchain) enables secure, transparent, and decentralised transactions without the need for intermediaries, leading to increased efficiency and reduced costs (Javaid, et al., 2022). Various firms have also been reported to be developing regulatory compliance solutions to help financial institutions navigate complex regulatory requirements more efficiently and cost-effectively using FinTech applications (Liu and Lyons, 2024). These FinTech solutions leverage technologies such as artificial intelligence, machine learning, and big data analytics to automate compliance processes, detect financial crimes, and enhance risk management (Abikoye, et al., 2024).

Despite the significant positive contribution of FinTech across the financial services sector, the burgeoning literature on financial development and the effect of microfinance has focused on how microfinance alleviate poverty and empower women (Bent, 2019). Less attention has been paid to the impact of FinTech integration on the accessibility and sustainability of microfinance institutions (see evidence of a critical review of this literature; Arner, et al., 2020; Abis, et al., 2024). Implicitly, ignoring FinTech integration a critical enabler for promoting financial inclusion and enhancing the efficiency and accessibility of financial services. The benefit of FinTech integration by MFIs is likely to be its ability to improve the reach of MFIs services to underserved populations, cost-effectiveness, risk management, and overall financial inclusion (Thomas and Hedrick-Wong, 2019). Therefore, it is important to understand the impact of FinTech integration on the accessibility and sustainability of microfinance institutions since such integration is likely to foster financial inclusion, enhance accessibility and sustainability of microfinance institutions.

Against this backdrop, this chapter addresses a critical gap in the literature by examining the impact of FinTech integration on the accessibility and sustainability of microfinance institutions. The chapter specially aims to achieve four objectives. First and foremost, the chapter seeks to evaluate the extent of FinTech integration in selected microfinance institutions. Secondly, the chapter examines the impact of FinTech integration on the accessibility of microfinance services. Assessing the sustainability of microfinance institutions following FinTech integration is another important objective of this chapter. Last but not the least, the chapter seeks to identify the challenges associated with FinTech integration in microfinance.

The rest of the chapter proceeds as follows. Section 2 outlines the background to the chapter focusing on existing literature on microfinance impact and challenges, evolution of FinTech and the relationship between FinTech and microfinance. Section 3 examines the impact of FinTech integration on microfinance, while section 4 presents the conclusions.

2. BACKGROUND AND LITERATURE REVIEW

Microfinance is the provision of financial services to low-income individuals or groups who typically lack access to traditional banking services (Visconti, 2016). Primarily, it involves the provision of small loans, savings accounts, insurance, training, and other basic financial services to empower individuals economically and socially to help them out of poverty and improve their quality of life. It is therefore reasonable to conclude that microfinance plays a crucial role in advancing financial inclusion by extending financial services to underserved populations and empowering them to participate in the formal economy (Cull and Hartarska, 2023). Besides, by addressing the financial needs of the poor, microfinance contributes to broader development goals, including poverty reduction, women empowerment, and sustainable economic growth. To aid our understanding of the contribution of microfinance, existing literature on microfinance and its impact on poverty alleviation and women empowerment is discussed next.

2.1 Microfinance Impact on Poverty Alleviation

The significance of microfinance in fostering economic growth and reducing poverty is colossal and widely reported in development finance literature. A study conducted by Visconti (2016) for example concludes that microfinance provides financial services, such as credit, savings, and insurance, to individuals who lack access to traditional banking systems. By offering small loans without collateral, microfinance enables the poor to invest in income-generating activities, such as small businesses or farming activities, thereby increasing their income and assets. This is consistent with Bent (2019) who have also shown that microfinance empowers the poor by providing them with opportunities for economic self-sufficiency. This empowerment can lead to broader socio-economic improvements, such as increased self-confidence, improved social status, and greater participation in community development initiatives (Lamichhane, 2020).

Microfinance has a particularly significant impact on women, who often face greater barriers to accessing financial services in most developing countries. By targeting women as key beneficiaries, microfinance institutions not only contribute to poverty reduction within households but also promote gender equality and women's empowerment. Studies (Al-Shami, et al., 2018; Lamichhane, 2020) have shown that women who participate in microfinance initiatives experience increased income and greater decision-making power within their households. The contribution of microfinance institutions to asset building and resilience of the poor has also been reported in microeconomics literature. For example, Ullah and Khan (2017) have demonstrated that microfinance helps vulnerable populations build assets and resilience to economic shocks. These authors argue that by providing access to savings and insurance products, microfinance institutions enable the poor to mitigate risks associated with illness, crop failure, or natural disasters. This asset accumulation and risk management contribute to long-term poverty alleviation. Microfinance has also been shown to facilitate collective decision-making and mutual assistance among borrowers, leading to broader community empowerment and sustainable development outcomes (Akhter and Cheng, 2020).

Overall, it is important to note that while microfinance has demonstrated considerable potential in alleviating poverty and promoting inclusive economic growth, it is essential to know that its impact can vary depending on factors such as the nature of the microfinance experiment, capacity of the microfinance institution, and the broader socio-economic contexts of the beneficiaries.

2.2 Microfinance Impact on Women Empowerment

The contribution of microfinance to women empowerment has also been reported by various studies. For instance, the outcomes of Lamichhane (2020) suggests that microfinance plays a crucial role in promoting financial inclusion for women, who often face greater barriers to accessing formal financial services compared to men. The implication of this finding is that by providing women with access to savings accounts and credit facilities, microfinance institutions empower women to manage their finances, invest in income-generating activities and build assets over time.

Evidence of a positive relationship between microfinance and women entrepreneurship and economic participation has been reported by previous studies. Indeed, Sulemana, et al. (2023) have demonstrated that microfinance enables women to start or expand small businesses, thereby increasing their economic participation and contributing to household income. Other studies (Bent, 2019; Lamichhane, 2020) have shown that women who receive microfinance services experience greater entrepreneurial success, increased income, and improved economic self-sufficiency. Perhaps, it is in this context that Oppong, et al. (2024) argues that this economic empowerment can lead to broader socio-economic benefits, such as improved nutrition, healthcare, and education for women and their families.

Receipt of microfinance services have also been shown to enhance women's decision-making power within their households and communities. For example, Visconti (2016) have shown that by providing women with control over financial resources and decision-making processes, microfinance fosters greater autonomy and self-confidence among female borrowers. This increased decision-making power can lead to improvements in women's social status and community leadership roles.

Overall, the literature suggests that microfinance can be a powerful tool for women's empowerment, with positive impacts on economic participation, decision-making and social empowerment. However, it is essential to understand that the effectiveness of microfinance interventions in promoting women's empowerment can vary depending on factors such as the nature of the microfinance services, cultural context, and the broader socio-economic environment of the community or country.

2.3 The Role of Microfinance in Promoting Financial Inclusion

Microfinance plays a critical role in extending financial services to the poor, particularly in low-income and rural areas where traditional banking infrastructure is limited or nonexistent. By providing savings accounts, credit facilities and insurance services, microfinance institutions enable individuals and communities to access financial services that were previously inaccessible to them (Cull and Hartarska, 2023). Evidence from Visconti (2016) indicates that by offering small loans without collateral and providing financial literacy training, microfinance institutions enable individuals and groups to invest in income-generating activities, build assets and improve their economic well-being. This empowerment can lead to broader socio-economic improvements, including increased self-confidence, social inclusion and participation in economic activities (Lamichhane, 2020).

Access to financial services through microfinance, as demonstrated elsewhere in this chapter, can help alleviate poverty by providing individuals with the means to invest in education and livelihood opportunities (Salgotra, et al., 2021). Studies (Sulemana, et al., 2023; Oppong, et al., 2024) have shown that microfinance interventions contribute to increased household income and improved living standards among the poor and marginalised groups. By promoting entrepreneurship and asset accumulation, microfinance plays a vital role in poverty reduction efforts worldwide. There is also evidence in existing literature that suggests that some microfinance institutions often focus on gender inclusion by targeting women as key beneficiaries. In this regard, women, who are often disproportionately affected by financial exclusion, benefit from microfinance interventions that provide them with access to credit and savings products tailored to their needs (Parwez and Patel, 2022). By promoting women's economic empowerment and financial independence, microfinance institutions contribute to gender equality, leading to broader socio-economic development outcomes (Khursheed, 2022).

Overall, the literature suggests that microfinance plays a crucial role in promoting financial inclusion by providing access to financial services to the poor. By empowering individuals, reducing poverty and promoting gender equality, microfinance contributes to broader development goals and creates pathways for inclusive economic growth and prosperity.

2.4 Challenges and Limitations of Microfinance

Certainly, there are some challenges and limitations associated with microfinance. For example, Wondirad (2022) have shown that many microfinance institutions charge relatively high interest rates on loans which impacts negatively on borrowers. While these interest rates may be necessary for microfinance institutions to sustain their operations, they can also contribute to over-indebtedness among borrowers and impact negatively on loan repayments (Mjuza and Ntsalaze, 2019). Another constraint associated with microfinance experiments is that microfinance institutions often offer a limited range of services, primarily focusing on microcredit and savings products. This lack of product diversification has been shown to constrain beneficiaries' ability to meet diverse financial needs (Satar and Kassim, 2020). Consequently, potential clients of MFIs may turn to informal or unregulated financial services to address their financial needs, exposing them to greater risks.

Studies (Shaikh, 2021; Zhao and Han, 2020) have also shown that several microfinance institutions face challenges related to sustainability and scalability. Simatele and Dlamini (2020) for example, argues that microfinance experiments are often designed to balance financial sustainability of MFIs with their social mission of serving low-income clients, which can be challenging in the absence of sufficient capital. Besides, scaling microfinance interventions to reach larger numbers of beneficiaries often requires significant investments in infrastructure and technology posing barriers to expansion and outreach (Shaikh, 2021).

There are also some narratives in existing literature that suggests that microfinance beneficiaries, particularly those with limited financial literacy or entrepreneurial experience, may be vulnerable to credit risk and over-indebtedness. For example, Mjuza and Ntsalaze (2019) have shown that excessive borrowing can lead to debt traps, where microfinance beneficiaries struggle to repay multiple loans and may resort to informal or exploitative financial service providers to meet their repayment obligations. Certainly, these unintended consequences associated with microfinance experiments can undermine the positive impact of microfinance on poverty alleviation and economic empowerment.

2.5 The Evolution of FinTech and its Applications in Financial Services

Prior research (Sahabuddin, et al., 2023; Chakraborty, 2018) highlights the evolutionary trajectory of FinTech, tracing its roots back to the emergence of online banking, electronic payments and algorithmic trading in the late 20th century. Evidence from Sahabuddin, et al. (2023) suggests that early developments in FinTech focused on improving efficiency, reducing costs and enhancing convenience in financial transactions through digital innovations. The consensus emerging from extant literature is that the evolution of FinTech has been driven by technological advancements, market demand for innovative solutions and shifts in consumer behavior towards digital banking and mobile finance (Taherdoost, 2023).

Overall, evidence from existing literature suggests that FinTech has revolutionised various financial services sectors, including banking, payments, lending, wealth management, insurance, and capital markets. In the banking sector for example, FinTech innovations such as online banking platforms, mobile banking apps and digital wallets have transformed the way customers access and manage their accounts, enabling seamless transactions and real-time monitoring of financial products. In payments, FinTech solutions like mobile payment apps, peer-to-peer (P2P) payment platforms and blockchain-based cryptocurrencies have disrupted traditional payment systems, offering faster, cheaper and more secure alternatives to cash and traditional banking channels. With regards to the lending sector, evidence from Nguyen, et al. (2023) indicates that FinTech platforms utilise artificial intelligence (AI) and machine learning algorithms to streamline loan application and underwriting processes, expanding access to credit for underserved borrowers and businesses.

In addition to the above, FinTech has also been shown to play a significant role in wealth management, insurance and capital markets. In wealth management, Grealish and Kolm (2021) have demonstrated that FinTech startups and robo-advisors leverage technology to offer algorithmic investment advice, portfolio management and automated financial planning services, aimed at digitally savvy investors seeking low-cost, user-friendly investment solutions. In the insurance sector, various firms have leveraged data analytics, Internet of Things (IoT) devices and telematics to enhance risk assessment, pricing, and claims processing (Zanke, 2021). Finally, in the capital markets, FinTech platforms have been designed to facilitate crowdfunding, peer-to-peer lending and algorithmic trading, democratising access to investment opportunities and liquidity in financial markets (Cai, 2018).

Evidence of the impact of FinTech on financial inclusion and economic development has also been reported by previous studies. For example, Anakpo, et al. (2023) found that digital payment solutions, mobile banking apps and digital lending platforms have enabled millions of individuals and small businesses to access credit, make payments and build savings, fostering economic empowerment. FinTech innovations have also fostered entrepreneurship and job creation, driving economic growth and development in rural and poor communities (Ediagbonya and Tioluwani, 2023).

2.6 The Relationship between FinTech and Microfinance

Previous studies (Dang and Vu, 2020; Shaikh, 2021) that have examined the relationship between FinTech and microfinance have contributed to our understanding of how technological innovations are reshaping the microfinance landscape. For instance, Agarwal and Zhang (2020) found that FinTech solutions, such as mobile banking, digital payments and peer-to-peer lending platforms, have improved access to financial services for underserved populations. Aboelenein (2023) have also demonstrated that FinTech-enabled microfinance models, such as mobile-based lending and digital savings accounts, have expanded microfinance outreach to remote communities, overcoming barriers related to physical distance, documentation requirements, and high transaction costs.

In the area of efficiency and cost reduction, Chuc, et al. (2023) have demonstrated that FinTech adoption has improved operational efficiency and scalability for microfinance institutions, enabling them to reach larger client bases, streamline processes and lower transaction costs. Evidence from Mhlanga (2024) indicates that FinTech adoption has led to the introduction of algorithmic credit scoring, which has expedited loan processing times and reduced administrative overheads, enhancing MFIs profitability and sustainability. Similarly, Kumar, et al., 2021) have demonstrated that FinTech solutions, such as alternative credit scoring models, machine learning algorithms and big data analytics, can improve credit risk assessment and portfolio management for microfinance institutions. Perhaps, it is in this context that Nguyen, et al. (2023) argues that by leveraging non-traditional data sources, such as mobile phone usage patterns, social media data and transaction histories, FinTech-enabled credit scoring models enhance predictive accuracy and reduce default rates for microfinance institutions.

In summary, while prior studies have shed light on the potential benefits of FinTech adoption for microfinance institutions and their clients, there are notable gaps in the literature concerning long-term sustainability and ethical considerations. Most studies have focused on short-term outcomes and immediate impacts of FinTech adoption in microfinance, overlooking the long-term implications for MFIs sustainability. In this regard, further research is needed to assess the sustainability of FinTech-enabled microfinance models over extended time horizons and how FinTech interventions can be designed and implemented in a manner that upholds ethical principles.

3. IMPACT OF FINTECH INTEGRATION ON MICROFINANCE

FinTech innovations encompass a diverse range of technologies, including mobile banking, digital payments, blockchain, and artificial intelligence, among others (Hendershott, et al., 2021). The use of these cutting-edge technologies has transformed the operations of MFIs helping them to expand their services to previously inaccessible markets. MFIs capacity to assess the creditworthiness of borrowers has significantly improved due to the integration of FinTech innovations such as digital platforms and data analytics tools designed for efficient credit scoring (Martinčević, et al., 2020). These innovative practices by MFIs have been shown to impact positively on financial inclusion. The contribution of FinTech to financial inclusion is therefore significant. The use of mobile money platforms, in particular, have helped MFIs expand their services to individuals and groups in remote communities (Kandpal, 2023). The integration of FinTech innovations has also helped MFIs to be more efficient and productive, leading to cost savings (Manta, 2018). For instance, the adoption of automated loan approval processes has reduced paperwork and expedited loan approvals. Besides, the use of FinTech applications such as digital repayment channels have enhanced repayment tracking and reduced the incidence of delinquencies. Furthermore, MFIs are now able to monitor client behaviour and trends in real-time due to the integration of FinTech-enabled data analytics applications (Gomber et al., 2018).

Overall, the adoption of FinTech solutions in the microfinance sector has contributed positively to financial inclusion and provides MFIs the opportunity to expand their reach by providing financial services to the unbanked population more efficiently. While there are some challenges, the integration of FinTech in the provision of microfinance services has the potential to foster socioeconomic development and promote financial empowerment amongst the unbanked population. Consistent with the objective of this chapter, the next section examines the extent of FinTech integration in selected microfinance institutions.

3.1 FinTech Integration in Selected Microfinance Institutions

Given the desire by MFIs to deepen financial inclusion across poor communities around the world, the adoption of FinTech solutions in the microfinance industry has grown rapidly. The integration of FinTech applications and tools is also driven by the need to reduce MFIs operational costs and ensure sustainability of these institutions. However, the scale of the integration of these financial technologies varies significantly and depends on the size and innovative capacity of the MFI. This section of the chapter examines the scope of FinTech integration in selected microfinance institutions (MFIs) in different countries and the type of FinTech applications and tools adopted by the MFIs.

The Grameen Bank for the Poor: Grameen Bank focuses on providing microcredit to the poor with the aim of alleviating poverty and empowering the marginalized poor in Bangladesh (Grameen Bank, 2024). Although the Grameen Bank was originally set up to provide small loans to the poor using a direct and personal approach, the organisation has recently started adopting FinTech solutions aimed at improving operational efficiency. Evidence from the 2022 annual report of the MFI for example suggests that the integration of FinTech applications in Grameen's operations largely involves the use of mobile phones for loan disbursement and repayments (Grameen Bank, 2022). The use of these mobile platforms has helped the organisation to reach clients in rural areas where the MFI has no branches. In collaboration with mobile money services like bKash, the Grameen bank has digitalise its loan disbursement and payment collection processes, however, the organisation is yet to integrate cutting edge financial technologies like blockchain and artificial intelligence.

BRAC (Bangladesh): BRAC is another microfinance institution that has integrated FinTech solutions in its operations. Compared to the Grameen Bank, BRAC started scaling up its operations early on, and technology quickly became a powerful enabling force - to ensure efficiency, overcome the challenges of distance, reduce time in administrative duties and inform decision-making (BRAC, 2021). The organisation has adopted mobile financial services and untilising digital platforms and other FinTech innovations to extend its services to rural clients. BRAC has also adopted FinTech driven innovations such as mobile wallets and digital loan repayment applications to provide financial services to clients in locations where the organisation has no physical branches (BRAC, 2021). Furthermore, BRAC has strengthen its credit scoring system by integrating FinTech applications to collect alternative data about clients without formal credit history.

Jumo (South Africa): Jumo is a microfinance institution operating in several countries in Africa. This microfinance institution mainly provides digital financial services (loans and savings) to unbanked population using mobile phone applications. Jumo solely relies on FinTech solutions to deliver financial services to clients in several locations and countries in Africa, enabling real-time access to funds at the lowest possible operating cost (Jumo, 2024). Evidence from the organisation's website suggests that the MFI use artificial intelligence and machine learning to build accurate credit scores and targeted financial products for people who don't have a formal financial identity, collateral or credit record. Jumo works with several mobile phone operators which enable them to reach clients that other MFIs cannot reach. Overall, Jumo use a range of financial technologies, including mobile banking, digital payments, machines learning and artificial intelligence to provide financial services to clients in several locations across the African continent.

FINCA Impact Finance (Global): FINCA Impact Finance operates in over 20 countries and serves low-income populations through a variety of financial services, including savings, loans, and insurance. FINCA has integrated various FinTech solutions in its operations including mobile banking, digital loans and cashless payment systems in various countries around the world. The adoption of FinTech solutions has significantly helped FINCA to expand its reach and increased efficiency across its operations. The extract from the 2021 annual report of the organisation provides evidence of the MFI's investment and integration of FinTech solutions in its operations. "Today Armenian customers can make loan payments effortlessly through mobile wallets, Ugandan customers open accounts online and Tajik customers living abroad are able to send remittances directly to FINCA using bank cards" (FINCA, 2021). FINCA's FinTech integration focuses on enhancing access to financial services, particularly in rural areas. The adoption of FinTech applications by the MFI has enabled customers to access financial services remotely and improved the organisation's risk management and loan disbursement processes.

Bank Andara (Indonesia): Bank Andara is a microfinance bank set up to improve the lives of millions of low-income Indonesians by enabling access to a wide range of financial services (Crunchbase, 2024). The bank has fully embraced FinTech by developing AndaraLink, a platform that enables MFIs and cooperatives to access a centralized core banking system (Metre, 2013). Through AndaraLink, participating MFIs can digitize their processes, enabling real-time transaction monitoring, digital loan disbursement, and improved client servicing. Bank Andara's FinTech integration has been highly successful in improving operational efficiency and providing MFIs with the tools to expand their client base. The platform reduces costs for small MFIs and offers a digital infrastructure that they would otherwise be unable to afford. Overall, Bank Andara's FinTech drive has focused on core banking technology integration for MFIs, real-time transaction processing, and digitised loan servicing.

Kiva (Global): Kiva is a nonprofit organization that operates as a global microfinance platform connecting lenders to low-income entrepreneurs (Lee, 2017). Kiva's integration of FinTech has taken a unique approach through Kiva Protocol, a blockchain-based identity system (Wang and De Filippi, 2020). Kiva Protocol is designed to provide individuals in developing countries with secure, verifiable identities that can be used to access credit and financial services, even without formal identification documents (Kshetri, 2023). Kiva's use of blockchain technology ensures that the personal data of borrowers is securely stored and easily verifiable, enabling them to access services across a variety of financial institutions. Kiva's digital platform also allows lenders from around the world to provide small loans directly to entrepreneurs, leveraging a peer-to-peer lending model that reduces costs and increases access. The key focus of Kiva's FinTech integration is on blockchain technology for digital identity verification, global peer-to-peer lending, and digital platforms to expand access (Kshetri, 2023).

3.2 Impact of FinTech Integration on the Accessibility of Microfinance services

The use and substantial integration of FinTech solutions into the processes of providing microfinance services has transformed the landscape of financial inclusion significantly. MFIs are now able to provide financial services for previously underserved populations. The provision of microfinance services has traditionally been associated with high operational costs and inefficient processes (Siwale and Godfroid, 2022). However, the recent integration of FinTech solutions such as digital platforms, mobile technology, machine learning and blockchain have helped to reduce these high costs and significantly increasing the accessibility and efficiency of microfinance services (Pal, et al., 2023). The most apparent evidence of the effect of FinTech integration in the provision of microfinance services is the improved reach of MFIs and the enhanced client experience (Chuc, et al., 2023). Below are some of the notable effects of FinTech integration on accessibility of microfinance services:

Expanding Geographical Reach: One major contribution of FinTech to the microfinance sector and financial inclusion is the ability to extend services to remote and rural communities around the world (Goswami, et al., 2022). The provision of microfinance has traditionally been caried out in branch offices through in-person interactions, which often makes it difficult to provide financial services to people in remote parts of the world. Fintech, particularly mobile technology, has eliminated the need for physical branches, allowing MFIs to serve clients in even the most remote locations (Visconti, 2019). For instance, FinTech solutions like mobile banking and digital wallets have played a key role in extending microfinance services to underserved populations. In many parts of Africa, Asia, and Latin America, mobile money platforms such as M-Pesa (Kenya) and bKash (Bangladesh) have enabled individuals to access financial services without the need for a traditional bank account or branch (Islam, et al., 2022). A major impact example is M-Pesa, which has helped millions of Kenyans in rural areas to access financial services through mobile phones (Abdulhamid, 2020; Mulili, 2022). Hence, the integration of FinTech solutions in the microfinance sector has made it easier for MFIs to disburse loans and collect repayments through digital technology, significantly improving accessibility for the unbanked population (Chuc, et al., 2023).

Lowering Transaction Costs: FinTech integration has also been shown to have contributed to reducing the cost of providing microfinance services and therefore making it more affordable to people around the world (Thomas and Hedrick-Wong, 2019). Velnamby and Ajanthan (2021) have demonstrated that traditional microfinance often involves high operational costs due to the use of mainly manual operational processes, which has led to high interest rates for borrowers. By contrast, FinTech solutions automate and digitise many of the core processes involved in microfinance, reducing overhead and improving cost efficiency (Hoque, 2022). For instance, clients can now apply for loans and receive disbursements digitally, which saves both time and money (Pal, et al., 2023). Besides, the use of mobile platforms for loan repayments reduces the need for costly in-person collections (Benami and Carter, 2021). One impact example in the Philippines is the integration of GCash in the provision of microfinance to provide cashless payment options for borrowers (Zawya, 2024). This has enabled beneficiaries to make loan repayments more conveniently and at a lower cost.

Faster and More Efficient Service Delivery: The adoption and integration of FinTech solutions in the provision of microfinance has significantly improved the speed and efficiency of microfinance services. The provision of microfinance services has often been done using extensive paperwork and in-person visits to designated locations. However, the use of FinTech solutions to automate these processes has helped to reduce waiting times and streamlined user experience (Pytkowska and Korynski, 2017). For example, the use of digital lending platforms and mobile phone applications allow for near-instant loan disbursement and repayments. In India for example, platforms like PaySense and Capital Float provide instant, small-ticket loans to individuals and businesses by leveraging AI and digital underwriting processes (Trodos Investment Management, 2019). These platforms have reduced the traditional loan approval time from several days to just a few minutes, improving access to credit for underserved populations.

Personalised Financial Products: The provision of personalised microfinance products is another benefit of the integration of FinTech innovations in the microfinance sector. Using data analytics, FinTech platforms are used by MFIs to analyse client behaviour, financial habits, and preferences to develop customised loan products, savings plans, and insurance policies to unbanked population (Dang and Vu, 2020). For example, BRAC, one of the largest MFIs in the world, has integrated FinTech innovations to develop more client-centric financial products. In this regard, BRAC is able to offer personalised loan products that meet the specific needs of its clients, such as short-term loans for farmers or flexible repayment plans for small businesses.

Empowering Women and Marginalized Groups: FinTech has played a significant role in increasing the accessibility of microfinance services for women who have historically faced problems in accessing formal financial services. In many regions, women are less likely to have bank accounts, access to credit, or formal employment. However, Ediagbonya and Tioluwani (2023) have demonstrated that FinTech solutions, particularly mobile banking and digital lending, have enabled women to access financial services more independently. For example, FinTech has empowered women by providing them with direct access to financial services through mobile phones. Besides, mobile money services, digital lending platforms, and peer-to-peer lending networks have given women access to financial products and opportunity to start businesses, invest in education, or improve their households (Kofman and Payne, 2021). In Tanzania for example, the FinTech platform Tigo Pesa has been integrated into microfinance services to provide women entrepreneurs with access to digital loans and savings accounts (Lowe, 2023). Women who previously relied on informal financial networks are now able to access formal financial services through their mobile phones, allowing them to grow their businesses and contribute to the local economy.

3.3 Sustainability of Microfinance Institutions following FinTech Integration

The integration of FinTech into microfinance institutions (MFIs) has transformed the way these organisations operate. The adoption of FinTech solutions has specifically opened new avenues for the provision of microfinance services and improved efficiency of service delivery within the sector (Pal, et al., 2023). However, while FinTech offers numerous advantages, its impact on the long-term sustainability of MFIs must be critically assessed. Sustainability, in this context, refers to the capacity of MFIs to maintain their operations, fulfil their social mission, and ensure financial viability over time (Sinha and Gosh, 2022). The contribution of FinTech innovations to the sustainability microfinance institutions are discussed below.

Operational Sustainability: One of the most significant contributions of FinTech to MFIs is the enhancement of operational efficiency. Evidence from Thomas and Hedrick-Wong (2019) for example suggests that by digitising key processes, FinTech reduces the cost of operations, enabling MFIs to reach more clients at lower costs. FinTech has also been shown to enable MFIs to automate their processes, such as loan applications, credit assessments, and repayments thereby helping to reduce administrative costs which has traditionally been one of the significant expenses for MFIs (Siwale and Godfroid, 2022). The use of mobile banking and digital payment systems by MFIs has reduced the need for physical branches and in-person interactions (Mulili, 2022). In this regard, MFIs can now reach clients in remote areas without the costly infrastructure of maintaining a branch network. For example, FINCA, a major player in the microfinance industry has embraced digital transformation through mobile banking and digital payment solutions (FINCA, 2024). By integrating these FinTech applications, FINCA has reduced operational costs and improved its ability to scale services in remote and underserved areas, thus enhancing its operational sustainability.

Financial Sustainability: While FinTech integration can improve operational efficiency, its impact on the financial sustainability of MFIs is more complex. According to Githaiga, et al. (2023) financial sustainability is the ability of a microfinance institution to generate enough revenue to cover its costs and invest in future growth. The adoption of FinTech has been shown to improve MFIs financial sustainability. For instance, FinTech expands the reach of MFIs, allowing them to serve a larger client base (Thomas and Hedrick-Wong, 2019). This increased client base has been shown to translate into higher revenues and therefore financial sustainability of MFIs (Pazarbasioglu, et al., 2020). The adoption of FinTech solutions also enables MFIs to provide a variety of financial products and services, which create new revenue streams, which is important for financial sustainability, especially in competitive markets (Githaiga, 2022).

Social Sustainability: Microfinance institutions are often set up to achieve financial sustainability and fostering financial inclusion. FinTech integration has the potential to enhance the social sustainability of MFIs by improving and deepening financial inclusion. For instance, the use of FinTech applications has enabled MFIs to expand their services for millions of individuals who were previously excluded from the formal financial system. People in rural areas and low-income communities are able to access financial services through mobile technology and digital platforms as a result of the integration of FinTech tools in the operations of MFIs (Thomas, 2021). This contributes to the social sustainability of MFIs, as they are better able to fulfil their mission of providing financial services to those who need them most.

Environmental Sustainability: The integration of FinTech solutions offers MFIs the opportunity to reduce carbon footprint associated with traditional banking practices, such as paper-based transactions and physical branches. One of the environmental benefits of FinTech integration is the shift to paperless transactions (Arner, et al., 2020). By digitising loan applications, repayments and associated processes, MFIs have reduced their reliance on paper, which has positive environmental implications. On the other hand, the increased use of digital platforms can contribute to higher energy consumption, particularly through the use of data centres and servers. Moreover, the rapid turnover of electronic devices, such as smartphones and laptops, can contribute to electronic waste. MFIs will need to adopt environmentally sustainable practices in their digital operations to ensure they are not contributing to environmental degradation.

3.4 Challenges Associated with FinTech Integration in Microfinance

The integration of financial technology (FinTech) into microfinance institutions (MFIs) has transformed financial services, particularly for underserved and unbanked populations (Pal, et al., 2023). As discussed above, FinTech enables MFIs to enhance their operational efficiency, broaden their reach, and offer more personalised and accessible financial products. However, the success of this integration depends on various factors and challenges that need to be addressed. These challenges are discussed below.

High Initial Investment Costs: The initial investment required to develop, integrate, and maintain FinTech solutions can be a significant barrier for many MFIs, particularly smaller institutions with limited financial resources (Ediagbonya and Tioluwani, 2023). For example, developing mobile applications, setting up digital platforms, and investing in cybersecurity all require substantial capital outlays. Beyond initial investment, Ng and Pan (2024) have demonstrated that FinTech platforms require continuous maintenance, upgrades, and innovation to remain competitive. However, the rapid pace of technological advancements can make it difficult for MFIs to keep up without incurring additional costs.

Digital Literacy Gap: In many regions, MFI clients may not have the digital literacy necessary to fully benefit from FinTech services. Without adequate training and support, clients may struggle to navigate mobile banking apps or digital lending platforms, leading to low adoption rates and underutilization of services. In this regard, Dang and Vu (2020) suggests that MFIs may need to invest heavily in client education and training schemes to ensure that clients can use FinTech platforms effectively. This can be costly, especially in communities with low levels of literacy or limited access to technology.

Data Privacy and Security Concerns: As MFIs move toward digital platforms, they become more vulnerable to cybersecurity threats, including hacking, data breaches, and fraud (Nwankwo, et al., 2023). Protecting sensitive client information is critical, and failure to do so can lead to financial losses and a loss of trust among clients. In many countries, data privacy regulations are either lacking or underdeveloped. In this regard, MFIs must navigate complex regulatory environments to ensure they are compliant with data protection laws, which can be challenging (Quartey and Kotey, 2019).

Over-Indebtedness Risk: FinTech platforms has been shown to streamline the loan approval process, enabling faster disbursement of credit (Dang and Vu, 2020). While this improves accessibility, it also increases the risk of over-indebtedness if clients take on more loans than they can repay. MFIs must ensure that proper credit assessments are conducted, even with digital lending platforms. Furthermore, MFI clients with limited financial literacy may not fully understand the terms and conditions of digital loans, leading to poor financial decision-making. This can increase default rates and negatively impact the financial sustainability of MFIs.

Regulatory and Compliance Challenges: The regulatory environment for FinTech is still evolving in many countries, and MFIs often face challenges in navigating new laws related to digital finance (Macchiavello, 2017). Evidence from Chen, et al., (2021) suggests that regulatory frameworks around mobile banking, digital lending, and alternative credit scoring are not always clear, and non-compliance can result in penalties or loss of licenses. Besides, MFIs operating in multiple countries may struggle to comply with different regulatory requirements across jurisdictions. This can slow down FinTech integration and increase operational complexity.

Infrastructure Gaps: In many developing countries, especially in rural areas, mobile network coverage and internet access are inconsistent. Without reliable connectivity, MFI clients may not be able to access FinTech services, limiting the effectiveness of digital financial inclusion efforts. Besides, the success of FinTech in microfinance is often dependent on partnerships with telecom providers (Beck, 2020). However, in some countries, these providers may not have the infrastructure or incentives to support mobile banking solutions, further complicating FinTech integration efforts.

4. CONCLUSION

This chapter concludes that the extent of use of FinTech solutions and applications in the provision of microfinance services varies significantly. While microfinance institutions such as Grameen Bank are slowly integrating FinTech solutions, other organisations like Jumo and Kiva utilise fully FinTech-driven operations. The overall conclusion on the extent of FinTech integration is that most organisations in the microfinance industry are in a transitional phase, integrating FinTech solutions and applications gradually to enhance financial inclusion.

The integration of FinTech into the provision of microfinance services has significantly improved the accessibility of financial services for underserved populations around the world. By leveraging FinTech solutions like mobile phone applications and digital payment systems MFIs have expanded their reach, allowing millions of individuals and businesses to access financial products. Despite challenges related to digital literacy, infrastructure, and regulation, FinTech offers a transformative opportunity to enhance financial inclusion and improve the lives of low-income populations globally.

The integration of FinTech into microfinance institutions has also improved the sustainability of MFIs by improving operational efficiency and expanding client reach. However, while FinTech can reduce costs and increase revenue streams, it also presents challenges such as high initial investment costs, regulatory compliance issues, and the need for ongoing technological upgrades. Besides, digital literacy and data security challenges are critical areas that need to be addressed to ensure long-term sustainability. MFIs must also consider the environmental impact of their digital operations as they move towards a more sustainable future.

In addition to the above, the integration of FinTech solutions into the provision of microfinance services presents significant opportunities for enhancing financial inclusion and service delivery. However, challenges such as high upfront costs, digital literacy gaps and regulatory hurdles must be addressed to ensure the long-term sustainability and effectiveness of FinTech in the microfinance sector. For FinTech to reach its full potential in the microfinance sector, microfinance institutions must navigate these challenges while continuing to innovate and adapt to the rapidly evolving financial landscape.

The future of FinTech-microfinance integration has enormous potential for advancing financial inclusion and driving sustainable development. By embracing cutting edge technologies like AI, ML and blockchain MFIs can leverage FinTech to transform their operations and achieve their mission of enhancing financial inclusion. However, realising this vision requires continuous innovation and a commitment to addressing the challenges inherent in FinTech-microfinance integration to ensure that the benefits of technology are accessible to all.

REFERENCES

Abdulhamid, N. A. 2020. Disruptive Technology, Mobile Money, and Financial Mobilization in Africa: M-Pesa as Kenya's Solution to Global Financial Exclusion? *Disruptive technologies, innovation and development in Africa*, pp.187-202.

Abikoye, B. E., Adelusi, W., Umeorah, S. C., Adelaja, A. O., & Agorbia-Atta, C. (2024). Integrating Risk Management in Fintech and Traditional Financial Institutions through AI and Machine Learning. *Journal of Economics. Management and Trade*, 30(8), 90–102.

Abis, D., Pia, P., & Limbu, Y. (2024). FinTech and consumers: A systematic review and integrative framework. *Management Decision*.

Aboelenein, A.A., 2023. Technology Effects on Emerging Economies' Financial Services and Economic Development: The case of Egypt and India.

Agarwal, S., & Ann, T. C. 2024. Personal Finance Applications of Fintech. In *The Emerald Handbook of Fintech: Reshaping Finance* (pp. 235-248). Emerald Publishing Limited. DOI: 10.1108/978-1-83753-608-520241029

Agarwal, S., Kigabo, T., Minoiu, C., Presbitero, A. F., & Silva, A. F. (2023). Serving the underserved: Microcredit as a pathway to commercial banks. *The Review of Economics and Statistics*, 105(4), 780–797. DOI: 10.1162/rest_a_01117

Agarwal, S., & Zhang, J. (2020). FinTech, lending and payment innovation: A review. *Asia-Pacific Journal of Financial Studies*, 49(3), 353–367. DOI: 10.1111/ajfs.12294

Agyekumhene, C., de Vries, J. R., van Paassen, A., Macnaghten, P., Schut, M., & Bregt, A. (2018). Digital platforms for smallholder credit access: The mediation of trust for cooperation in maize value chain financing. *NJAS Wageningen Journal of Life Sciences*, 86(1), 77–88. DOI: 10.1016/j.njas.2018.06.001

Al-Shami, S. S. A., Razali, M. M., Majid, I., Rozelan, A., & Rashid, N. (2016). The effect of microfinance on women's empowerment: Evidence from Malaysia. *Asian Journal of Women's Studies*, 22(3), 318–337. DOI: 10.1080/12259276.2016.1205378

Alam, N., Gupta, L., & Zameni, A. 2019. *Fintech and Islamic finance*. sl: Springer International Publishing. DOI: 10.1007/978-3-030-24666-2

Alias, N. A. L. 2024. Microfinance Institutions: Catalysts for Improved Personal Financial Behavior. *Available atSSRN* 4845920. DOI: 10.2139/ssrn.4845920

Anand, D., & Mantrala, M. (2019). Responding to disruptive business model innovations: The case of traditional banks facing fintech entrants. *Journal of Banking and Financial Technology*, 3(1), 19–31. DOI: 10.1007/s42786-018-00004-4

Arner, D. W., Buckley, R. P., Zetzsche, D. A., & Veidt, R. (2020). Sustainability, FinTech and financial inclusion. *European Business Organization Law Review*, 21(1), 7–35. DOI: 10.1007/s40804-020-00183-y

Beck, T. 2020. *Fintech and financial inclusion: Opportunities and pitfalls* (No. 1165). ADBI working paper series.

Benami, E., & Carter, M. R. (2021). Can digital technologies reshape rural microfinance? Implications for savings, credit, & insurance. *Applied Economic Perspectives and Policy*, 43(4), 1196–1220. DOI: 10.1002/aepp.13151

Bent, B. B. (2019). The impact of microfinance on poverty reduction and women empowerment. In *Rais collective volume–Economic science* (pp. 72–86). Scientia Moralitas Research Institute.

Björkegren, D., & Grissen, D. (2020). Behavior revealed in mobile phone usage predicts credit repayment. *The World Bank Economic Review*, 34(3), 618–634. DOI: 10.1093/wber/lhz006

BRAC. 2021. Annual report 2021. [Online] Available at https://www.brac.net/annual-reports-and-publications [Accessed 26 September 2024].

Cai, C. W. (2018). Disruption of financial intermediation by FinTech: A review on crowdfunding and blockchain. *Accounting and Finance*, 58(4), 965–992. DOI: 10.1111/acfi.12405

Chakraborty, S., 2018. Fintech: evolution or revolution. *Business analytics research lab India*. DOI: 10.1111/acfi.12405

Chuc, A. A. M., Atayah, A. A., & Özer, S. Q. (2023). Impact of Financial Technology (Fintech) on Financial Performance of Micro Finance Institutions in Bahrain. *African Journal of Emerging Issues*, 5(17), 1–11.

Crunchbase, 2024. *About Bank Andara*. [Online] Available at https://www.crunchbase.com/organization/bank-andara [Accessed 26 September 2024].

Cull, R., & Hartarska, V. (2023). Overview of microfinance, financial inclusion, and development. In *Handbook of microfinance, financial inclusion and development* (pp. 2–19). Edward Elgar Publishing. DOI: 10.4337/9781789903874.00006

Dang, T. T., & Vu, H. Q. (2020). Fintech in Microfinance: A new direction for Microfinance institutions in Vietnam. *Asian Journal of Business Environment*, 10(3), 13–22. DOI: 10.13106/jbees.2020.vol10.no3.13

Ediagbonya, V., & Tioluwani, C. (2023). The role of fintech in driving financial inclusion in developing and emerging markets: Issues, challenges and prospects. *Technological Sustainability*, 2(1), 100–119. DOI: 10.1108/TECHS-10-2021-0017

Elsaid, H. M. (2023). A review of literature directions regarding the impact of fintech firms on the banking industry. *Qualitative Research in Financial Markets*, 15(5), 693–711. DOI: 10.1108/QRFM-10-2020-0197

FINCA. 2021. *Annual report 2021*. [Online] Available at https://cdn.finca.org/wp-content/uploads/20221020102204/FINCA-2021-Annual-Report-4.pdf [Accessed on 27 September 2024].

FINCA. 2024. *Fintech Innovations and Solutions Across the Network*. [Online] Available at https://finca.org/en-gb/our-work/microfinance/innovations-and-technology [Accessed 28 September 2024].

Gambacorta, L., Huang, Y., Qiu, H., & Wang, J. (2024). How do machine learning and non-traditional data affect credit scoring? New evidence from a Chinese fintech firm. *Journal of Financial Stability*, 73, 101284. DOI: 10.1016/j.jfs.2024.101284

Githaiga, P. N. (2022). Revenue diversification and financial sustainability of microfinance institutions. *Asian Journal of Accounting Research*, 7(1), 31–43. DOI: 10.1108/AJAR-11-2020-0122

Githaiga, P. N., Soi, N., & Buigut, K. K. (2023). Does intellectual capital matter to MFIs' financial sustainability? *Asian Journal of Accounting Research*, 8(1), 41–52. DOI: 10.1108/AJAR-06-2021-0080

Goswami, S., Sharma, R. B., & Chouhan, V. (2022). Impact of financial technology (Fintech) on financial inclusion (FI) in Rural India. *Universal Journal of Accounting and Finance*, 10(2), 483–497. DOI: 10.13189/ujaf.2022.100213

Grameen Bank. 2022. *Annual report*. [Online] Available at https://grameenbank.org.bd/archives/annual-report [Accesses 25/09/2024].

Grameen Bank. 2024. *Welcome to Grameen Bank*. [Online] Available at https://grameenbank.org.bd/ [Accessed 25/09/2024].

Hendershott, T., Zhang, X., Zhao, J. L., & Zheng, Z. (2021). FinTech as a game changer: Overview of research frontiers. *Information Systems Research*, 32(1), 1–17. DOI: 10.1287/isre.2021.0997

Hoque, M. M. 2022. *Microfinance challenges and the potential benefits of blockchain technology and mobile money* (Doctoral dissertation, Queensland University of Technology).

Islam, A. H., Basher, S. A., & Enamul Haque, A. K. (2022). The impact of mobile money on long-term poverty: Evidence from Bangladesh. *Journal of Social and Economic Development*, 24(2), 436–455. DOI: 10.1007/s40847-022-00194-0 PMID: 36034405

Javaid, M., Haleem, A., Singh, R. P., Suman, R., & Khan, S. (2022). A review of Blockchain Technology applications for financial services. *BenchCouncil Transactions on Benchmarks. Standards and Evaluations*, 2(3), 100073.

Jha, R. S., & Sahoo, P. R. (2022). Technology Shaping Models of "Personalization" in Insurance. In *ICT Systems and Sustainability: Proceedings of ICT4SD 2022* (pp. 237–246). Springer Nature Singapore.

Jie, T. J. 2024. Unlocking Potential: The Impact of Financial Technology (FinTech) on Financial Inclusion and Personal Economic Security. *Available atSSRN* 4847463. DOI: 10.2139/ssrn.4847463

Jumo, 2024. Innovation is all it takes. [Online] Available at https://jumo.world/ [Accessed 27 September 2024].

Kandpal, V., Chandra, D., Dalei, N. N., & Handoo, J. (2023). Expanding financial inclusion through Fintech and e-governance. In *Financial inclusion in circular economy: A bumpy road towards sustainable development* (pp. 103–129). Springer International Publishing. DOI: 10.1007/978-3-031-22723-3_6

Kayongo, S., & Mathiassen, L. 2020, September. Dynamic capabilities in microfinance innovation: A case study of the Grameen Foundation. In *The Tenth International Conference on Engaged Management Scholarship*. DOI: 10.2139/ssrn.3687792

Kofman, P., & Payne, C. 2021. Digital financial inclusion of women: An ethical appraisal. *Handbook on ethics in finance*, pp.133-157.

Kshetri, N. (2023). Blockchain in the Global South: Key Issues and Current Status. In *Blockchain in the Global South: Opportunities and Challenges for Businesses and Societies* (pp. 1–28). Springer Nature Switzerland. DOI: 10.1007/978-3-031-33944-8_1

Kshetri, N. (2023). *Blockchain in the Global South*. Springer Books. DOI: 10.1007/978-3-031-33944-8

Kumar, A., Sharma, S., & Mahdavi, M. (2021). Machine learning (Ml) technologies for digital credit scoring in rural finance: A literature review. *Risks*, 9(11), 192. DOI: 10.3390/risks9110192

Lamichhane, B.D., 2020. Microfinance for women empowerment: A review of best practices. *Interdisciplinary journal of management and social sciences, 1*(1), pp.13-25. DOI: 10.3390/risks9110192

Lee, W., 2017. Microfinance: Models and implications for social entrepreneurship. *Educating social entrepreneurs, 2*. DOI: 10.3390/risks9110192

Liu, F., & Lyons, A. C. 2024. Use Cases in Fintech. In *The Emerald Handbook of Fintech: Reshaping Finance* (pp. 43-64). Emerald Publishing Limited. DOI: 10.1108/978-1-83753-608-520241005

Lowe, 2023. *Mobile money in Tanzania: Unveiling the vision ofTigo Pesa.* [Online] Available at https://www.gsma.com/solutions-and-impact/connectivity-for-good/mobile-for-development/blog/mobile-money-in-tanzania-unveiling-the-vision-of-tigo-pesa/ [Accessed 28 September 2024].

Macchiavello, E. (2017). *Microfinance and financial inclusion: The challenge of regulating alternative forms of finance*. Routledge. DOI: 10.4324/9781315623962

Malamsha, C., 2023. Effectiveness of microcredits provision by women development fund on enhancing household wellbeing in Tanga City, Tanzania. *East Africa Journal of Social and Applied Sciences (EAJ-SAS), 5*(1). DOI: 10.3390/risks9110192

Manta, O. (2018). Financial Technologies (FinTech), Instruments, mechanisms and financial products. *Internal Auditing & Risk Management*, 52(4), 78–102.

Martinčević, I., Črnjević, S., & Klopotan, I. (2020). FinTech revolution in the financial industry. *ENTRENOVA-ENTerprise REsearch InNOVAtion*, 6(1), 563–571.

Metre, K. (2013). [) in Indonesia: Opportunities and Challenges.]. *Information and Communication Technologies for Development*, IC, T4D.

Mhlanga, D. (2024). *FinTech, Financial Inclusion, and Sustainable Development: Disruption, Innovation, and Growth.* Taylor & Francis. DOI: 10.4324/9781032657981

Mjuza, N., & Ntsalaze, L. (2019). Over-indebtedness of microfinance borrowers in South Africa. *African Review of Economics and Finance*, 11(2), 98–128.

Mohanasundaram, T., Sathyanarayana, S., & Rizwana, M. 2021. Disruptions on India's FinTech landscape: The 5G wave. In *ITM Web of Conferences* (Vol. 37, p. 01008). EDP Sciences.

Mosley, P. (2009). *Assessing the success of microinsurance programmes in meeting the insurance needs of the poor*. Financing for Overcoming Economic Insecurity.

Mulili, B. M. (2022). Digital Financial Inclusion: M-PESA in Kenya. In *Digital Business in Africa: Social Media and Related Technologies* (pp. 171–191). Springer International Publishing. DOI: 10.1007/978-3-030-93499-6_8

Ng, E., & Pan, S. L. (2024). Competitive strategies for ensuring Fintech platform performance: Evidence from multiple case studies. *Information Systems Journal*, 34(3), 616–641. DOI: 10.1111/isj.12406

Nwankwo, C., Kanyangale, M., Anoke, A. F., & Eze, S. U. (2023). Effect of Cyber Security on Business Sustainability of Listed Microfinance Banks in Nigeria. *The Arab Journal of the Social Sciences*, 22(1), 79–106. DOI: 10.29138/ijebd.v6i5.2279

Oluwaseun, A.M., & Olaitan, M.R., 2021. Microfinance banking services and financial inclusion in rural communities of Nigeria. *Trailblazer International Journal of Educational Research*, 1(1). DOI: 10.29138/ijebd.v6i5.2279

Oppong, E. O., Yu, B., & Mazonga Mfoutou, B. O. (2024). The effect of microinsurance on the financial resilience of low-income households in Ghana: Evidence from a propensity score matching analysis. *The Geneva Papers on Risk and Insurance. Issues and Practice*, 49(3), 1–27. DOI: 10.1057/s41288-024-00325-0

Pal, A., Dey, S., Nandy, A., Shahin, S., & Singh, P. K. (2023). Digital Transformation in Microfinance as a Driver for Sustainable Development. In *Handbook of Sustainability Science in the Future: Policies, Technologies and Education by 2050* (pp. 251–271). Springer International Publishing. DOI: 10.1007/978-3-031-04560-8_74

Parwez, S., & Patel, R. (2022). Augmenting women empowerment: A systematic literature review on microfinance-led developmental interventions. *Journal of Global Responsibility*, 13(3), 338–360. DOI: 10.1108/JGR-01-2021-0005

Pazarbasioglu, C., Mora, A.G., Uttamchandani, M., Natarajan, H., Feyen, E., & Saal, M., 2020. Digital financial services. *World Bank, 54*, pp.1-54. DOI: 10.1108/JGR-01-2021-0005

Pytkowska, J., & Korynski, P. (2017). *Digitalizing microfinance in Europe*. Microfinance Centre.

Quartey, J. A., & Kotey, B. (2019). The effect of regulations on ability of MFIs to provide sustained financial services to small business. *Small Enterprise Research*, 26(3), 235–252. DOI: 10.1080/13215906.2019.1670236

Sahabuddin, M., Sakib, M. N., Rahman, M. M., Jibir, A., Fahlevi, M., Aljuaid, M., & Grabowska, S. (2023). The evolution of FinTech in scientific research: A bibliometric analysis. *Sustainability (Basel)*, 15(9), 7176. DOI: 10.3390/su15097176

Salgotra, A. K., Kandari, P., & Bahuguna, U. (2021). Does access to finance eradicate poverty? A case study of Mudra beneficiaries. *The Journal of Asian Finance, Economics and Business*, 8(1), 637–646.

Satar, N., & Kassim, S., 2020. Issues and challenges in financing the poor: Lessons learned from Islamic microfinance institutions. *European Journal of Islamic Finance*, (15).

Shaikh, S. A. (2021). Using Fintech in scaling up Islamic microfinance. *Journal of Islamic Accounting and Business Research*, 12(2), 186–203. DOI: 10.1108/JIABR-10-2019-0198

Simatele, M., & Dlamini, P. (2020). Finance and the social mission: A quest for sustainability and inclusion. *Qualitative Research in Financial Markets*, 12(2), 225–242. DOI: 10.1108/QRFM-02-2019-0024

Singhal, N., Goyal, S., & Singhal, T. (2024). Decentralized Insurance Platforms: Innovation and Technology for Trust and Efficiency. In *Potential, Risks, and Ethical Implications of Decentralized Insurance* (pp. 95–163). Springer Nature Singapore. DOI: 10.1007/978-981-97-5894-4_3

Sinha, S., & Ghosh, K. (2022). Organizational sustainability and performance improvement in microfinance institutions (MFIs): Managerial insights of what, why and how. *Social Responsibility Journal*, 18(2), 240–265.

Siwale, J., & Godfroid, C. (2022). Digitising microfinance: On the route to losing the traditional 'human face'of microfinance institutions. *Oxford Development Studies*, 50(2), 177–191. DOI: 10.1080/13600818.2021.1998409

Sulemana, M., Fuseini, M. N., & Abdulai, I. A. (2023). Effects of microfinance and small loans centre on poverty reduction in Wa West District, Ghana. *Heliyon*, 9(12), e22685. DOI: 10.1016/j.heliyon.2023.e22685 PMID: 38107329

Taherdoost, H. 2023. Fintech: Emerging trends and the future of finance. *Financial technologies and DeFi: a revisit to the digital finance revolution*, pp.29-39.

Thomas, H., & Hedrick-Wong, Y. 2019. How digital finance and fintech can improve financial inclusion. In *Inclusive Growth: The Global Challenges of Social Inequality and Financial Inclusion* (pp. 27-41). Emerald Publishing Limited. DOI: 10.1108/978-1-78973-779-020191004

Thomas, K. P. 2021, October. Use of Digital Channels by Micro Loan Customers in India. In *The 2018 International Conference on Digital Science* (pp. 342-357). Cham: Springer International Publishing.

Trodos Investment Management. 2019. *Capital Float: revolutionising the loan market in India*. [Online] Available at: https://www.triodos-im.com/articles/2019/case-study-capital-float-revolutionising-the-loan-market-in-india [Accessed 28 September 2024].

Ullah, I., & Khan, M. (2017). Microfinance as a tool for developing resilience in vulnerable communities. *Journal of Enterprising Communities: People and Places in the Global Economy*, 11(2), 237–257. DOI: 10.1108/JEC-06-2015-0033

Velnamby, T., & Ajanthan, A. (2021). Efficiency and financial sustainability of microfinance institutions: A study of Jaffna district. *ACADEMICIA: An International Multidisciplinary Research Journal*, 11(4), 545–561. DOI: 10.5958/2249-7137.2021.01053.3

Visconti, R. M. (2016). Microfinance vs. traditional banking in developing countries. International. *Journal of Financial Innovation in Banking*, 1(1-2), 43–61. DOI: 10.1504/IJFIB.2016.076613

Visconti, R. M. 2019. Microfintech: Outreaching financial inclusion with cost-cutting innovation. *Available atSSRN* 3533873. DOI: 10.2139/ssrn.3533873

Wang, F., & De Filippi, P. (2020). Self-sovereign identity in a globalized world: Credentials-based identity systems as a driver for economic inclusion. *Frontiers in Blockchain*, 2, 28. DOI: 10.3389/fbloc.2019.00028

Wondirad, H. A. (2022). Interest rates in microfinance: What is a fair interest rate when we lend to the poor? *Quality & Quantity*, 56(6), 4537–4548. DOI: 10.1007/s11135-022-01320-0

Yadav, P., Lohani, V. J., Sharma, S., & Choudhary, S. (2024). Transforming Transactions: The Evolution of Fintech in Indian Banking Sector. [IRJAEM]. *International Research Journal on Advanced Engineering and Management*, 2(07), 2179–2194.

Zanke, P. (2021). Enhancing Claims Processing Efficiency Through Data Analytics in Property & Casualty Insurance. *Journal of Science and Technology*, 2(3), 69–92.

Zawya, 2024. *GCash loans surpass $2.7bln mark in Philippines*. [Online] Available at https://www.zawya.com/en/markets/bonds-and-loans/gcash-loans-surpass-27bln-mark-in-philippines-xu55cxbm [Accessed 28 September 2024].

Zhao, M., & Han, J. (2020). Tensions and risks of social enterprises' scaling strategies: The case of microfinance institutions in China. *Journal of Social Entrepreneurship*, 11(2), 134–154. DOI: 10.1080/19420676.2019.1604404

KEY TERMS AND DEFINITIONS

AI: Artificial intelligence
APIs: Application programming interfaces
DeFi: Decentralised finance
FinTech: Financial technology
ML: Machine learning
MFIs: Microfinance institutions

Chapter 8
Impact of Digital Payment Trends:
Unraveling Consumer Behavior Patterns (Pre- and Post-COVID-19)

Ananya Chaturvedi
Christ University, India

Shruti Ranjan
https://orcid.org/0000-0002-0655-8801
Christ University, India

ABSTRACT

The COVID-19 pandemic has accelerated the adoption of digital payments worldwide, fundamentally altering consumer behavior patterns. This study investigates the impact of digital payment trends on consumer behavior, comparing pre- and post-pandemic scenarios. It delves into the factors which drove the shift towards digital payments, exploring the changing preferences and perceptions of consumers. The study examines the influence of demographics, socio-economic factors, and technological advancements on consumer adoption of digital payment methods. It also analyzes the effect of the pandemic on e-commerce, online shopping, and mobile payments, highlighting the emergence of new trends and preferences. The findings provide valuable insights into the evolving landscape of digital payments and consumer behavior, offering implications for businesses, policymakers, and researchers

DOI: 10.4018/979-8-3693-6622-6.ch008

1. INTRODUCTION

As the title suggests, this chapter analyzes the impact of digital payment trends on behavior patterns and the changes that took place during Covid. This chapter, section 1, is introduced by the background of the study. This study was intended to investigate the impact of digital payment trends on behavior patterns. By providing the reader with a detailed literature on the topic of study, it sets the scene for the research. Then the focus of the study is provided. This study aimed to find out whether there existed any significant impact of the digital payment trend on consumer behavior and what changes were made to payment and spending habits. Later on the purpose of the study is also prescribed to give the reader a clear indication why I undertook such a research. The main purpose was clearly stated to investigate the impact of digital payment trends on behavior patterns, understand consumer behavior, and establish how digital payment has impacted on such behavior. Subsequently, the scope of the study is outlined. This is important as the reader expects a description of the range of the study. This gives background information to help understand and evaluate the research. The potential areas, however, to be covered under the scope include the impact of digital payment trend on behavior pattern, impact of digital payment trend on spending patterns, and impact on merchants and businesses. Such will offer much guidance as the reader will understand the issues addressed in the whole study. By identifying and later fulfilling these aspects as per the scope, it would be easier to comprehend the results of the research. On the other hand, the reader may keep questioning what the research intended to address.

2. LITERATURE REVIEW

Digital payment methods have witnessed rapid growth and adoption in recent years, reshaping the way individuals conduct financial transactions globally. The emergence of various digital payment platforms, coupled with advancements in technology, has revolutionized traditional payment systems. Understanding the impact of these digital payment trends on consumer behavior is crucial for businesses, policymakers, and researchers alike, particularly in light of the COVID-19 pandemic, which accelerated the shift towards cashless transactions.

1. **Digital Payment Adoption and Consumer Behavior:** Numerous studies have explored the factors influencing the adoption of digital payment methods and their subsequent impact on consumer behavior. Venkatesh et al., (2003) proposed the Unified Theory of Acceptance and Use of Technology (UTAUT), which identifies key determinants such as perceived usefulness, ease of use,

and social influence in predicting consumer acceptance of new technologies, including digital payment systems. Subsequent research by Luarn and Lin (2005) and Liao et al., (2007) further validated the UTAUT model and highlighted the importance of trust and perceived risk in shaping consumer attitudes towards digital payments.

2. **COVID-19 and Acceleration of Digital Payment Trends:** The onset of the COVID-19 pandemic led to unprecedented changes in consumer behavior, with widespread adoption of contactless and online payment methods to mitigate the risk of virus transmission through physical currency. Research by McKinsey & Company (2020) revealed a significant surge in digital payment transactions during the pandemic, driven by factors such as safety concerns, convenience, and government mandates promoting cashless payments. This rapid acceleration of digital payment trends underscores the dynamic interplay between external shocks and consumer behavior.
3. **Impact on Spending Patterns and Financial Management:** The shift towards digital payments has not only transformed the way consumers make transactions but also influenced their spending habits and financial management practices. A study by Statista (2021) found that individuals using digital wallets and mobile payment apps tend to spend more frequently and impulsively compared to those using traditional payment methods. Moreover, digital payment platforms often offer personalized recommendations and budgeting tools, empowering consumers to track their expenses and make informed financial decisions.
4. **Challenges and Opportunities for Merchants and Businesses:** While digital payments offer numerous benefits for consumers, merchants and businesses face both challenges and opportunities in adapting to this evolving landscape. Research by Capgemini Research Institute (2020) highlighted concerns among retailers regarding transaction fees, security risks, and the need for technological infrastructure to support digital payment acceptance. However, businesses that effectively leverage digital payment technologies can enhance customer engagement, streamline operations, and gain competitive advantage in an increasingly digital marketplace.

3. DIGITAL PAYMENT TREND ANALYSIS

The aim of this section is to assess and analyze the digital payment trends. These trends are studied through detailed interviews and surveys conducted among consumers. The reports from Accenture and McKinsey have also been considered. The chapter provides insights about how the trends have been found to change pre and post the onset of the outbreak of COVID-19. The aim of this study was to get understanding from the experts in the field regarding what they thought were the reasons as to why the digital payment trends can be shown to have changed and what they believed were the possible future implications. By studying the reports, the authors aimed to understand the current state of the payment trends and how these can be potentially used to devise future strategies by merchants and corporations. Also, the experts' opinion provided another level of qualitative data which can be used to provide rationality to the studies.

3.1. Pre-Covid Scenario

One of the major challenges posed by the digital payment trend was the lack of awareness and reluctance to switch to the new payment mode. There was only a small percentage of people who were using digital money. In a recent survey, only 14% of respondents used cash for most of their payments. Further, the analysis of payment behavior on a typical day showed that digital money accounted for only 2 out of 10 recorded transactions. The main reasons attributed to the low penetration of digital payments included lack of awareness or familiarity with the digital payment systems, general resistance to change and the perception of better record keeping with traditional cash transactions. Most people were not aware that the convenience of digital payment included, among others, ease of money transfer, efficiency and attractive bonuses that most service providers offer. The analysis showed that personal contact with the service provider would significantly influence a change to digital payment services. In particular, there was a need to identify and address the existing gaps that deter the switch to digital novels and innovative ways.

3.2. Post-Covid Scenario

Our lives were changing rapidly right from the beginning of 2020. The impacts of Covid-19 were mainly felt from March that year. The Indian government had to enforce a nationwide lockdown to prevent the spread of the Covid-19 virus. This lockdown had severe effects on the country's economy and a lot of people suffered. There were a lot of challenges in making financial transactions during and after the lockdown, mainly due to the fear of infection and the ban on crowded places. Also, most of the people were staying at home and they needed to pay utility bills or buy groceries. However, as a result of the pandemic, we witnessed exponential growth in the use of digital payment platforms like Paytm, Google Pay, etc. These payment gateways incorporated many technological features into their systems and launched many marketing strategies to attract new users. Also, these platforms focused on integrating lots of software functions, which can collectively help to manage, analyze, and automate all the payments, customer service, and transactions. As a result, more and more people started to trust and use these platforms for their daily transactions. This scenario clearly reflects the significance of digital platforms as each merchant and biller means a lot of potential consumers.

3.3. Key Players

It is extremely important to understand who the stakeholders were in defining and shaping the digital payments trends that we have observed in both the pre and post-Covid periods. First and foremost, it is evident that digital payment solutions that are provided by technology companies have continued to emerge and receive significant traction within the industry. Established giants like Google and Apple, as well as newer players such as PayTM and Samsung, who have developed digital wallets, continue to drive this innovation. These organizations are involved in providing a spectrum of digital payment methods and infrastructure that is both broad and diverse. Furthermore, digital payment solutions provided by FinTechs have gained significant traction and representation amongst the major payment trends within both the pre-Covid and post-Covid periods. For instance, a coalition of digital payment providers which includes popular players like PayPal, PayU and VISA, have been established to provide a singular marketplace solution for digital payment infrastructure. VISA came up again as a major market player as one of the world's largest digital payment organizations: which appears to be driving the narrative that card payments as a whole are going to overtake both legacy and emerging methods of digital/mobile payments. It is also very staggering to note that established banks and financial institutions played a leading role in championing various types of digital payment methods and cashless strategies in the pre-Covid period.

3.4. Market Trends

The market has seen major shifts in recent trends, with driving factors such as open banking, biometrics and blockchain offering respite for the growth of the digital payment industry. This trend is expected to continue. It is predicted that by 2023, the digital payment market will be worth USD 10.07 billion, growing at a CAGR of 23.8%. Furthermore, real-time payment volume is expected to increase by five times. This showcases a major shift from the traditional payment methods to digitalization. Such real time payment adoption was also seen in the recent months. For instance, in the United States, the real time payments have exploded by over 40% year on year in 2020, with 3.24 billion real time payments made. On the other hand, traditional payment methods, such as cash or cheques, have seen decreasing trends. The use of cash has been termed as a great mode of disease transmission. As a result of the fear of contracting the disease through cash, there has been a decrease in the willingness of people to use cash. In China, over 90% of people are comfortable to go out with no cash as digital payments have become the most popular means to pay for goods and services. Also, in the United Kingdom, the contactless transactions surged in the global pandemic, hitting a record of 1.2 billion in the seven months leading up to September 2020, despite the overall sharp decline in the use of cash.

4. OBJECTIVE OF THE STUDY

1. To assess the extent of digital payment adoption.
2. To identify key drivers of digital payment usage.
3. To examine changes in consumer spending patterns.
4. To evaluate consumer satisfaction and perceived benefits.
5. To investigate challenges and barriers to adoption.

5. HYPOTHESIS

1. **Hypothesis 1:** There is a significant difference in consumer behavior patterns before and after the COVID-19 pandemic, indicating a shift towards increased adoption of digital payment methods post-pandemic.
2. **Hypothesis 2:** Demographic factors such as age, income, and education level significantly influence the adoption of digital payment methods among consumers, with younger, higher-income, and more educated individuals showing greater propensity for digital payments.
3. **Hypothesis 3:** Technological advancements significantly influence the adoption of digital payment methods among consumers, with the availability of convenient and secure digital payment platforms leading to increased adoption rates.
4. **Hypothesis 4:** There is no significant difference in consumer behavior patterns related to digital payment adoption between urban and rural populations.
5. **Hypothesis 5:** The COVID-19 pandemic has played a significant impact on the overall volume and frequency of digital payment transactions, with an increase in digital transactions observed during and after the pandemic period due to safety concerns and changes in consumer behavior.

6. METHODOLOGY

Type of Research

The proposed research is descriptive and analytical research and exploratory in nature. The descriptive analysis includes survey and fact-finding information. The main objective of descriptive research is to describe the present population, situation and phenomena. It is providing information about the relevant characteristics and related to study.

Analytical research uses already available facts or information for analysis and critical evaluation of the material. Analytical research is primarily concerned with testing hypotheses and understanding the significance of the information already available.

Scope of the Study

Population of the study consist the Delhi NCR region consumers and stratified random sampling method is used for sampling.

Sample size- 100

Data Collection Methods

Primary data collection – Questionnaire method will be used for survey of the consumer.

Data Results

Figure 1.

Data analysis:

1. Gender (Male: Female)

Sr no	Particulars	No of respondent (%)
1	Male	47
2	Female	53

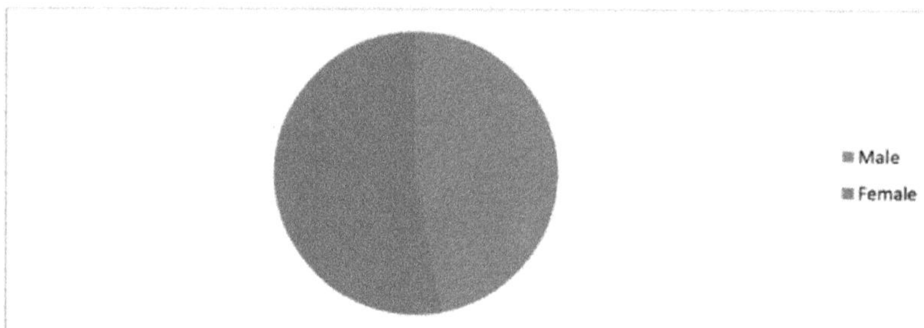

2. Marital status

Sr no	Particulars	No of respondent (%)
1	Married	49
2	Single	51

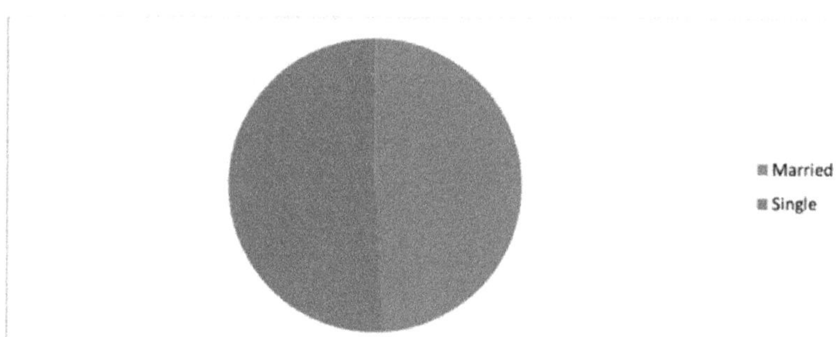

Figure 2.

3. Education

Sr no	Particulars	No of respondent (%)
1	Post graduate	62
2	Graduate	38

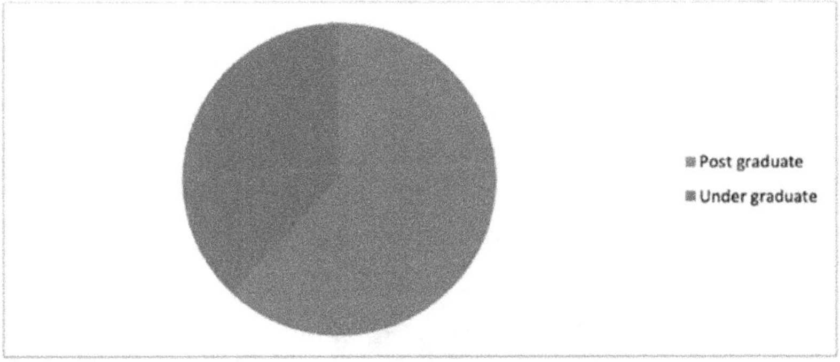

4. Occupation

Sr no	Particulars	No of respondent (%)
1	Salaried	40
2	Professional	39
3	Self employed	15
4	Student	4
5	House wife	2

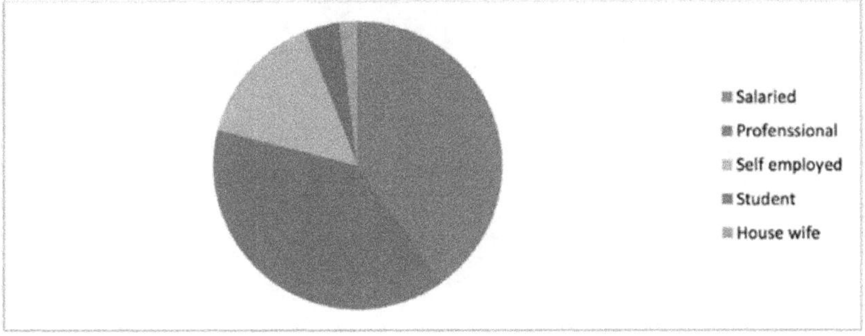

Figure 3.

5. Age

Sr no	Particulars	No of respondent (%)
1	Below 20 years	5
2	20-30 years	68
3	30-40 years	21
4	Above 40 years	6

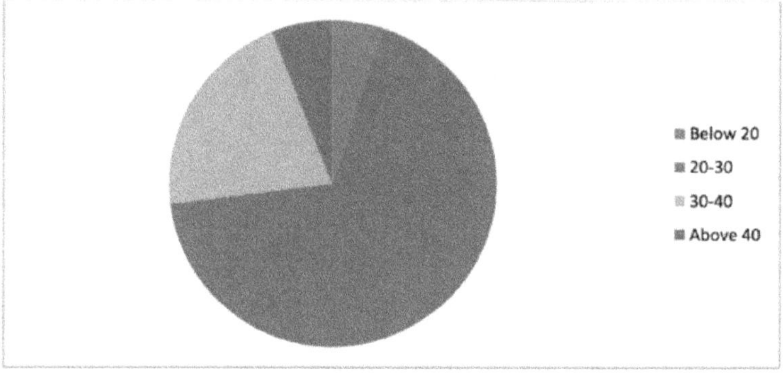

Figure 4.

6. Duration of using digital payment system

Sr no	Particulars	No of respondent (%)
1	Less than 1 year	5
2	01-05 years	80
3	05-10 years	11
4	More than 10 years	4

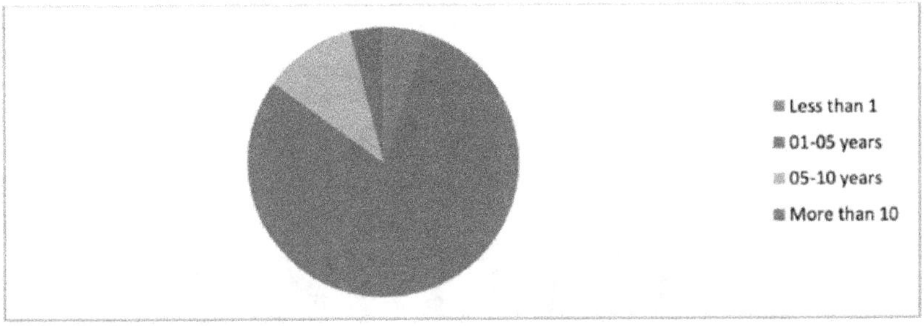

Interpretation:

80% of people are using digital payment system for 01-05 years.

Where 11% of people are using it for 05-10 years.

7. Different digital payment methods used by the customers.

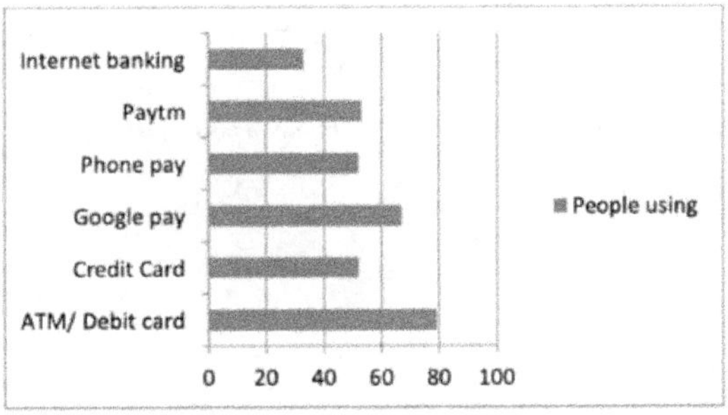

Interpretation:

Maximum People prefer ATM/Debit card for the digital payments method and at second place people prefer google pay. Very few people are using internet banking.

Figure 5.

8. After the impact of Covid-19, the usage rate of digital payments for the following transactions.

Sr no	Particulars	Very less	Less	Neutral	High	Very High
1	Electricity bill	9	3	16	32	40
2	Grocery bills	3	8	28	44	17
3	Gas bills	2	6	35	35	22
4	Credit card bills	5	9	27	44	15
5	Mobile bills	4	5	20	38	33
6	Other	1	7	29	43	20

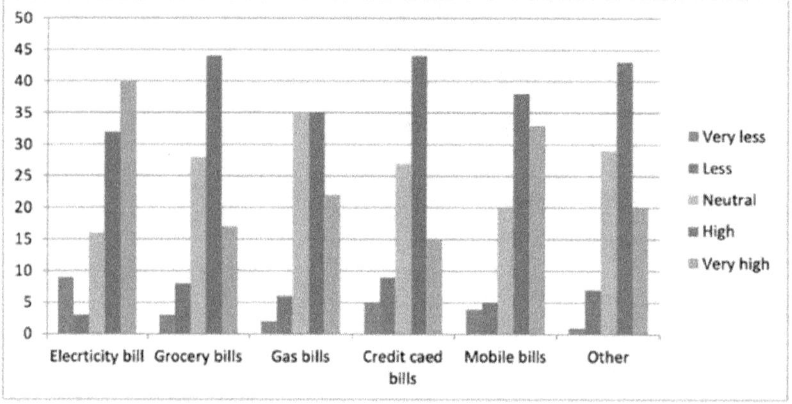

Interpretation:

Maximum number of people using digital payments for the payment of grocery bills and credit card bills.

Figure 6.

9. The benefits of using digital payment systems to the customers.

Sr no	Particulars	Strongly disagree	Disagree	Neutral	Agree	Strongly agree
1	Convenient	9	5	16	30	40
2	Saves time	3	11	16	50	20
3	24*7	3	7	35	32	23
4	Easy to use	3	9	26	44	18
5	Flexibility	6	6	22	28	38
6	Increase prestige	1	13	28	42	16
7	Cashless payments	3	9	30	31	27
8	Non banking hours also can get the benefit	2	9	24	48	17

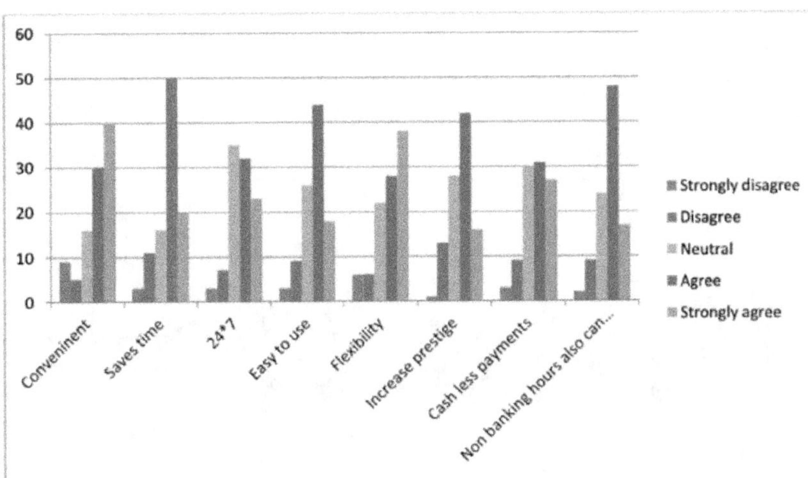

Interpretation:

Maximum numbers of people are being agreed with the benefit of using digital payments system. Only the few people are strongly disagree with the benefits.

Figure 7.

10. The difficulties faced by the customers from digital payment systems.

Sr no	Particulars	Strongly disagree	Disagree	Neutral	Agree	Strongly agree
1	Server problems	10	5	24	23	38
2	Lack of knowledge	2	14	27	44	13
3	Technical errors	2	8	43	30	17
4	Fear of fraud	2	10	34	41	13
5	Hidden charges	5	6	29	28	32
6	Connectivity	1	9	31	42	17
7	Lack of up to date information	4	10	46	22	18
8	Lack of security	2	14	24	41	15
9	Fear of losing money	5	8	31	24	32
10	Complicated instructions	2	12	32	36	18

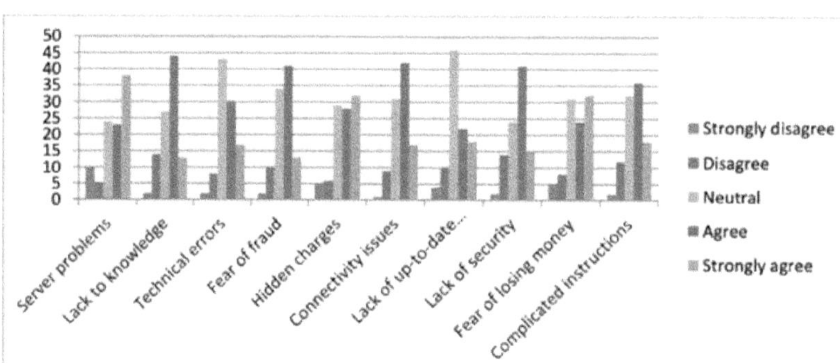

6. BEHAVIOR PATTERNS SHIFT (ANALYSIS)

The widespread use of digital payment methods have been seen impacting lifestyle and behavior. Online shoppers do not need to step out of their house to buy anything; as long as they have internet and bank accounts, then the transaction can be done within a few seconds. The usage of these cashless methods is usually related to convenience and pace of everyday life; people in big cities favor digital payment methods rather than cash as it's more convenient and faster. Millennials and younger generations appear to be leading in the adoption of digital payment methods, but many more people of all demographics from elderly to teenagers have now made at least one type of digital payment method. The pandemic has escalated the adoption rate of contactless and digital payments. Markets have seen an increase in awareness and use of digital payments with consumers looking for cleaner and more hygienic solutions. Thanks to the current situation, digital methods are expected to gradually shift society's perspective on reliance on cash and digital inclusiveness. Industries would expect a rapid digitalization and change of business model and operation. When cashless is becoming a common phenomenon around the globe, technological transfer and cooperation among different markets will be intensified; if any, expertise and experience will be better shared and utilized. On the other hand, the social and cultural transformation brought by the digitalization of payment methods should not be disregarded. It is foreseeable that the relationship among fellow beings would experience a new dimension as transaction and exchange of value is fundamentally underpinned by the world of digital interactivity and decentralization.

6.1. Pre-Covid Behavior

Consumers were so used to traditional payment methods and hardly a small percentage of the population preferred cashless. The main reason that people still trust the traditional method of payment is because they are used to it whereas there is a lack of trust in new technology on digital payment. The social issue of the payment divide is significant in current society. They are non-tech savvy and people from the age above 40 would have problems adapting to this new technology. They still trust the traditional method while the world moves on to the new trend of digital payment. Also, the issue of the digital divide, meaning that separate societal groups have unequal access to the technology. The number of retailers that accept digital payment was relatively low and, in most cases, it limits to the fast-food outlets, convenience stores and also the entertainment industry. Most of the retailers' fear having payment fraud issues and complicated procedures on setting up the account for digital payment for their business. As a result, only some of them provide the digital payment option and it is not convenient for most of the people to go cashless at any time when most of the places only accept cash. Most people in cities rely on using cashless payment because they have more access and the environment is more conductive for cashless payment compared to the rural area. As in rural areas, the retailer that accepts digital payment is even lower. Most of them only accept cash and the geographical issue also contributes to the low desire in using digital payment. They feel that it is unnecessary to go for digital payment as it may expose to another type of fraud where digital fraud could be harder to prove than the stolen account information nowadays.

6.2. Post-Covid Behavior

Fueled by the concern of getting Covid-19 through physical money, the digital payment trend accelerated in the wake of the Covid-19 pandemic. As a response to safety and hygiene concerns, the share of digital wallet payment methods, compared to cash, has increased by approximately 4%. The findings further highlight that this shift was pronounced in urban populations, with a 7% increase in digitized payments as compared to rural areas. However, the gender dimension in uptake on digital modes of payments narrowed as a result of the pandemic. Traditionally, there existed some gender disparity in the use of digital payment modes; with men being more likely to use digital modes compared to women. However, the Covid-19 pandemic period experienced a larger increase in the use of digital modes by women compared with men, reducing the gender gap by half. The uptake on digital payments was high among women due to concerns over security of handling physical money, especially among urban female dwellers who recorded an 11% increase in the use of digital payment methods. Analysis of the data from consumers interviewed in the wake of the pandemic reveals that consumers have adopted and integrated more digital payment options in their everyday payments and purchases. Although about half still prefer using traditional modes of payments, the percentage of those that exclusively use digital modes saw an increase (Chen 2020). 58% of the people that participated in the study noted that they had increased the use of contactless payments because of the pandemic, as they try to avoid the risk of handling physical money. This behavioral transformation is prevalent in cities more than rural areas, with a 12% increase in the uptake of newer and digitized payments.

6.3. Impact on Society

The digital payment trend has significantly affected the lifestyle and living of many people. Society today is full of digitization and modernization. In the era of digitalization, many people in society prefer online services hence the digital payment. Technology has changed how people used to transact in society. There are many digital business platforms that have been set up in society making online payment become more common. This is because digital payment has enabled them to do so through their phones. Also, a farmer in the rural area has access to a wide market due to the digital innovation such as mobile banking app which he and the buyers can use to transact. This has made him increase his production to meet the demand of the vast market which goes beyond his locality. Also, the growth of the digital markets and businesses has led to employment of many youths in the society. On the other hand, digital payment has led to some negative impact in society. Digital payments could possibly wipe out the tax and revenue for the small businesses who operate under cash and checks.

7. CONSUMER PREFERENCES

After analyzing the data obtained, a majority of the respondents outlined the convenience of using a certain service-based digital transaction while also indicating that travel time to a payment location and availability of digital financial options played a major role in their preferred mode of payment. Conventional methods like the use of checks are also slowly being replaced by the advancement in digital services and there are more preferences to the use of electronic payments like e-wallets, direct deposits and mobile money. 87.4% of the respondents use some form of digital payment while only 12.6% indicated that they do not use electronic means in any form of payment (World bank 2020). The availability of digital options was considered to be an insignificant challenge to take up by respondents who slightly use digital payment services while those who majorly and always use digital payment appeared to be critical on its availability. These preferences and such sentiments were registered across all the age categories; the older generation slightly use digital payments as compared to the majority and the young population. These results suggest that new technologies like the use of artificial intelligence and detection solutions will define the trends in consumer preferences seeing that most respondents indicated that they prefer a given mode of service-based digital payment due to its reliability when it comes to security when compared to PIN and chip cards. Such a mode of digital payment that was most preferred was the newer adoption in the form of near-field communication and mobile initiated transactions which allow for provision of one-time payment numbers, innovative encryption and blocking of unauthorized applications. With the continuous trend in the advancement of digital technologies and the emergence of disruptive technologies championed by cybersecurity experts such as the use of biometrics and Blockchain solutions, the above preferences may change since most of the technological advancements currently have been framed to address todays and the future security threats. Well, it is anticipated that the revolution of consumer preferences over the services based digital payment will take a new phase with the adoption of modern technologies in preventing potential payment security threats. The data also indicated that gender, income and education do not have significant contributing factors in individual consumer preference for a given mode of digital payment in services and opportunities. These results, however, do not translate to the consumer behavioral adaptation to the advancement in financial industries and increased digital options given that the data was obtained from exploring shallow information held by the current customer base.

8. ECONOMIC IMPLICATIONS

The pre-digital economic era, the choice of substituting to digital payment trends in the modern world would seem impractical to many. However, this kind of transition is not only feasible, but inevitable. The social security payment system was initially using a labor-intensive and costly process in making monthly payments to beneficiaries. The traditional process was highly susceptible to fraud thus calling for additional cost in setting up measures to minimize the fraud cases. However, the wage payment system will result in lower bank charges on the account of large electronic transaction volume. This is due to the fact that electronic systems are cheaper as compared to the expensive traditional banking methods. Additionally, banks will likely reduce the bank account charges for these beneficiaries. The accrued savings to the banks will be passed on the customers in order to stay competitive in business. Also, the beneficiaries will realize the time value of money. This is because they will have access to cash as soon as the payments are made. On the other hand, under the traditional wage payment system, wage-earners will get a low interest income since they are not able to deposit their wage into an interest-yielding account for the period preceding wage payment. As the benefits of the trend are realized and with the continuous innovation, a wider economic modernization is expected. The shift from the traditional payment systems to mobile and digital payment systems will allow for the leveraging of business opportunities in local and international markets. The growth of digital payments may suit the government's agenda of creating a cashless economy. This is a very noble economic prospect. An electronic or digital payment system will realize a reduction in the liquidity preference of the people. Modern theories of money have elucidated more on money demand and its relation to the interest rate.

8.1. Cost Savings

After using mobile payment to replace credit cards or cash for transactions, cost savings are evident. As Carder (2019) posits, credit cards are expensive to use for business-to-business transactions and they often come with 'maintenance fees, set-up fees, transaction fees and even penalties for failing to reach a certain usage level. With digital payment using mobile phones, these additional costs associated with credit card transactions are eliminated or substantially reduced. According to Evans (2017), mobile payment transactions cost less than $0.21 in fees compared to 2-4% charges for credit card transactions. As a result, businesses or consumers who use mobile payments are incentivized by the significant cost savings. These cost savings can be substantial. Using big data analytic tools available in the market nowadays, businesses can turn the data generated from mobile payment transactions into business insights that can help cut unnecessary costs, improve efficiency and results, and eventually lead to better products and services for consumers (Carder, 2019). For example, by analyzing the digital receipts and payment history, retailers can send personalized offers to customers based on their purchase history, preferences, and even the best time for them to receive marketing information (Carder, 2019, para 15). This not only reduces the costs related to conventional marketing, but also provides values and convenience to both the businesses and consumers. In essence, from these examples, it is apparent that mobile payment does not only save costs for both businesses and consumers, but also has the potential to improve the very processes and methods of conducting business so as to make it more effective and consumer-oriented.

8.2. Growth Opportunities

Clearly, the digital payments ecosystem can be expected to continue to play an increasingly important role in economies worldwide as the COVID-19 pandemic eases and ultimately recedes. This is for several reasons. First, there will be an influx of fresh customer capital entering the electronic payments market. Many of those who either began using digital payment tools for the first time during the pandemic, or who significantly increased their use of such tools, will be potential users in the longer term. As these user segments mature, providers of digital payment services will be able to tap into the improved data liquidity they provide to develop and market tailored and value-add products. This will, in turn, feed a cycle of further increasing user numbers and provider profitability as the value proposition of digital payments continues to improve relative to traditional methods. Dynamic markets in parts of the world such as the Asia-Pacific region and Africa, where the economic use of digital payment tools is gathering momentum, could see rapid expansions in customer numbers and investments in payment infrastructure. Moreover, product and service innovations in the digital payments space – such as novel interfaces, distributed ledger technology, and the integration of artificial intelligence to provide personalized services – will become more prevalent as a result of new investment drawn in by a growing user base. This, in turn, will play a critical role in both maintaining the interest of end users and maximizing the potential benefits to be gained from the digitalisation of the payments process – for example, enhancing data security and protection, improving transaction speed, and facilitating easier compliance with anti-money laundering and counter-terrorism financing regulations. Indeed, in some cases, digital payments could become the backbone of infrastructure projects designed to take advantage of blockchain and other distributed technologies, including in the areas of "smart cities" or the Internet of Things.

9. TECHNOLOGICAL ADVANCEMENTS

Over the past few years, we've seen major technological advancements in digital payments. From the introduction of contactless cards to the growing prevalence of mobile wallets, it is clear that these innovations have changed the way that people make payments. It was found that in recent years, these innovations are increasingly being directed towards improving the digital wallet experience. For example, mobile wallets are becoming a popular method of payment for consumers and the growing capacity for these wallets to store a wider variety of loyalty cards and transport tickets is making them more appealing.

9.1. Innovations in Digital Payments

Digital payments have progressed from desktops to smart devices in the last couple of years. The mobile payment methods like Apple Pay and Google Pay have made transactions easier and faster by just placing the device against the payment terminal. The latest inclusion in the digital payment methods is the introduction of biometric authentication. Biometric authentication is the process of matching the live biometric data with the stored biometric data. In this method, facial recognition and fingerprints are used to confirm one's identity before making a purchase. Customers are not required to enter their personal identification numbers (PIN) or other passwords when using biometric authentication methods, therefore providing a faster and secure payment using digital methods. The market for wearable payment devices has also grown larger in recent years. These devices may come in the form of wristbands, key fobs or stickers and usually connected to credit card accounts. Major finance companies like Mastercard, Barclays and Fitbit have already introduced and promoted the use of wearable payment devices in making contactless payments. Such devices rely on a secure digital platform called tokenization. When the card information is initially entered and verified, the card's primary account number is replaced with a series of randomly generated numbers that are used to process the payment. This method does not only help to prevent fraud but also protect the actual card information from being exposed to the merchants. With the advanced technologies in digital payments, the development of application programming interfaces (API) for open banking has helped many startup fintech companies rapid and secure access to banking and financial information. Open banking allows the consumer's financial data to be shared securely between the banks and other financial service providers. By doing so, it paves the way for the development of innovative payment and other financial services - designed to offer more choices to consumers and small businesses. All these digital payment methods are aimed at providing quicker, secure and convenient payment to the consumers in their everyday life. Such innovations and technological advancements in the digital payment landscape reflect how customer behavior and preferences have changed drastically since the integration of technology, in particular with the start of the mobile era. The constant need for wireless technology and faster and better mobile devices have been recognised by many players in the digital payment industry. Not only has this improved the overall quality of digital payment methods and point of sale transactions for the benefit of all parties involved, it has also shaped the way merchants and industries explore and adopt into more digitized and modernized business models.

9.2. Impact on User Experience

An important development in the digital payments ecosystem has been the rise of mobile payment technology. This technology uses a mobile phone to allow secure payments. Once users have added their card details, they can enjoy several advantages such as contactless payments, one-touch payments and the ability to carry out remote transactions. Recently, solutions like Apple Pay, Google Pay and Samsung Pay have become widely accepted. As per recent research, the global mobile payment market is expected to grow at a CAGR of 26% during 2020-2023 and reach a value of $12.06 trillion (McKinsey, 2020). This engagement with these newer forms of payment could be because they offer the ideal mix of security, efficiency and ease of use. For example, by having the facility to use a mobile to complete a contactless payment the potential market size of those who can use this technology is increased to include anyone who has a compatible phone. It is estimated that by 2025 the smartphone industry will have penetrated 29% of the total market (Statista 2020). As more people use digital payment systems and the platforms benefit from greater revenue and customer involvement, it might be expected that the companies behind these solutions will use some of the profits to engage in corporate social responsibility activities. For example, from September 2020, Apple donates a portion of the profits from Apple Pay transactions to support global public health and economic development. So, from these benefits, including the ability to make traveling easier and more secure, to charitable acts on the part of these companies, digital payment technologies have begun to exert considerable influence on the user and the market. It is these kinds of transformative digital experiences and catalysts of social change that really solidify the relationship between the user and the technology. The more that technology can simplify our lives and solve our everyday problems both efficiently and securely, the more we may find our attitudes and actions shifting in favor of integrating that technology into our behaviors and practices.

10. CHALLENGES AND RISKS

The inculcation of digital payment tools and techniques in the deployment of financial transactions has expedited the swiftness and expediency of the fund transfer and settlement system. The transaction that is done through online mode is always on the radar of cyber criminals owing to the fact that the transactions are done through the internet and every activity is traced and tracked. Routinely, hackers attack the transactions carried out in the e-commerce industry and money laundering activities are performed with the connivance of unknown sellers and buyers. It has been usually observed that personal information of the customers is used by the sellers without taking any consent of such registered individuals. Many companies sell the information of the online purchasers to the next companies who, in turn, use such information in an illegal practice of spamming and sending unsolicited emails to the respective purchasers. Moreover, clauses related to the terms and conditions provide that the location of servers and data of the customers are situated and stored within the international jurisdiction. The access, control and display of the data is secured but due to the diversified and dynamic nature of the cyber laws and constant changes in the market, the risk of data leakage or theft is always there. Sophisticated, relentless, disproportionately large online cyber assaults on the infrastructure can destabilize the company and impede the ability to meet the expectations of customers. Also, prolonged and substantial data breach of financial information can lead to business discontinuance, as well as significant financial costs in reparation and manifold actions stemming from the same attack. The threat of transaction data theft is omnipresent but also hard to resolve. This is because the data is most vulnerable when it is 'at rest', that is stored in some form in a server or other device. Cyberattackers are typically, but not excursively, interested in 'at rest' transaction data and seek to exfiltrate that data for their fraudulent purposes.

10.1. Cybersecurity Threats

Given that all financial transactions and data stored are digitally interfaced and stored, the industry has become a lucrative target for cyber criminals. Cybersecurity is the technique of protecting against encroachment by malicious adversaries seeking to gain from interrupting digital business operations. A data breach occurs when sensitive, confidential or otherwise protected data is accessed or disclosed in an unauthorized way. Specially designed malware used to attack autonomous digital networks to compromise or destroy information; notably, the malware does not need human intervention to execute the attack. On the other hand, ransomware is becoming more prevalent in which a type of malware designed to deny access to a computer system or data until a ransom is paid. Viruses and worms indeed affect a number of critical infrastructure sectors worldwide. They can be spread through a number of tools such as phishing, which is the fraudulent practice of sending emails purporting to be from reputable sources in order to induce individuals to reveal personal information. Spreading a virus could therefore be a staged act of destruction by an identified critical infrastructure adversary. Cyberattacks are stealthy as they enable antagonists to take more time to plan a long-term attack on critical infrastructure facilities. A cyberattack is any sort of attack launched by means of cyberspace through the use of computers against a state or its population.

10.2. Data Privacy Issues

Even though digital payments offer convenience, there is a general concern over the risk that the personally identifiable information of an individual will be exposed to the possibility of unauthorized use when records are stored. The right of privacy is often discussed because the digital payment trends mean that every transaction is recorded in a digital format and the concept of privacy will definitely be affected. Meta data i.e. data about data or any other information linked with the respective data in a digital payment record becomes at risk to exposure. This means the history of the usage of the digital data can be traced or certain assumptions to the transaction can be made by any party who has access to this data. When relating this risk to big data and the IoT (internet of things) technology, the exposure of personally identifiable information becomes a real threat to a person's privacy. Take for example, the convenience of the digital payment trend has also allowed the emergence of mobile payment where a person may find the need of using certain health apps provided by the respective mobile company. Posting a record in the social media of certain favorable health issues may defeat the purpose of anonymity in using health apps and big data might be used by the respective company to analyze the digital data to look for any latest trends in health. For instance, if a case is recognized where the patients of the same condition are using the mobile payment at the same time of the year, the personal identity of that person could be confirmed by cross checking the meta data in the digital payment record and the substance of the social media posting. It is not unknown that companies who are managing the big data are providing the service free and they generate profit by selling the digital payment history data of the users to interested commercial parties.

10.3. Fraudulent Activities

The increasingly digital landscape offers innumerable benefits, not only for the consumers, but also for businesses and governments. Nevertheless, by extensively reviewing numerous academic and industry-level works, it emerged that potential fraudulent activities such as hacking, phishing and identity theft are significant risks when digital payments are concerned. Firstly, despite the numerous security measures that are usually implemented by financial service providers, such as end-to-end encryption, fraud monitoring tools, and two-factor authorizations, hackers have been quite inventive in finding ways to deceive those mechanisms. For instance, it was highlighted by Solomatine et al., (2019) that malware - a kind of software that is specifically designed to damage or disrupt a system - is becoming increasingly used by fraudsters to steal sensitive data like user credentials and personal financial information. This is due to the fact that malware can operate in various ways such as exploiting known weaknesses in the hardware or operating systems, or taking advantage of the common practice of disregarding the hundreds of security notices that an average user gets daily on the internet (Lyons et al., 2012). Fraudulent activities are usually more prevalent in digital payments where the process of conducting a transaction is shorter as compared to traditional card-based payments that require PIN verifications or original signatures.

11. FUTURE OUTLOOK

As life becomes more and more comfortable and of course digitized through the implementation of advanced technology and the provision of the simplest solution to humankind, the demand and needs of digital payment solutions will be required to be customized and expanded more than ever. The trend of cashless or digital payment solution tools, initiatives and services, in general, will likely be dominated by more biometric fingerprint payment options along with the smartphone digital wallet solutions. Adapting to the future society trend, emphasis and improvisation may have to be given to include wearables payment solutions as part of the development efforts not only from methodological aspects but also from consumer adaptability research and strategy areas. On the other hand, the improvement in artificial intelligence, big data analytics, machine learning and cybersecurity and privacy measures will continue to reshape the future trends of digital payment solutions. These enabling digital technologies will lead the future landscape of digital payment solutions as we could foresee that big data and machine learning analytics could be more effectively used as the emerging trend of customer-preferable personalized payment experience and promotion. Also, such amazing advancement in cybersecurity and privacy measures will definitely motivate the public and financial institutions in adopting more digital payment solutions as the worries and concerns of financial fraud cases and privacy leak relevant to digital payment methods will be adequately and continuously addressed by the technology experts and professionals. It is highly expected that the future digital payment solution trends will move towards methods that provide easier and more personalized consumer experiences coupled with obligatory needs of adapting to biometric and smart digital signature security measures. Such technology trends based on big data, artificial intelligence, cybersecurity and biometric methods will be truly benefited and implemented in personalized and futuristic payment experiences like smart city initiative and long-term usability.

11.1. Emerging Trends

Understanding consumer behavior is the key to successful strategies as well as long term survival of the business in the modern world. The trends that have been emerging in the digital world have a considerable impact on the consumer behaviors, and business strategies need to accommodate the changes in the market and thus changes in consumer behaviors. This chapter provides a comprehensive review on emerging trends on digital consumer behavior such as social media commerce. Social media is quickly becoming an alternative to the cumbersome methods used around the long-established traditional methods such as the use of credit cards that involve actually going through a long process to make a payment. The context of the study involves understanding this emerging trend in digital consumer behaviors as a result of the growing trend of using social media as a new platform for making payments. Social media is a growing market and digital platforms such as Facebook or Twitter have actually become more than just means of communication among people but as a way of carrying out e-commerce marketing. As such, social media platform operators such as Facebook, which now have services such as the 'Facebook store' for digital marketing, can actually take advantage of the changing trends discussed in this chapter. And because technology keeps evolving, the society itself may also continue to adapt to the new practices in the pictures so it is quite likely that the shared economy on social media and social media as a new payment platform will only continue to grow in the future.

12. FINDINGS

The upward trajectory in digital payment methods is set to continue and in fact accelerate. The actual figures to be reached in terms of total payment value is not possible to accurately predict, due to the volatile economic climate, although predictions from various financial institutions have it surpassing 150,000 billion Euros by 2025. It will come as a very welcome sign for merchants and clients alike, particularly in planned spending, and shows that in the long term there's scope for real change in the type of payment methods society as a whole uses. Security will always be the main concern for clients, and even though the adoption of new methods in the payment industry is traditionally slow, the recent pandemic and requirement for more remote based transactions have greatly accelerated the switch to digital. This coincides with a new shift in the balance of power in terms of accepted payment methods, with younger generations growing up more with technology-based solutions as compared to long-established card and cash methods through consumer habits. This could mean that the accepted and most widely used payment methods in years to come could be radically different to what they are today. Is it another financial revolution in the making such as the birth of credit and debit cards? Only time will tell.

13. LIMITATIONS

The study would be taking into account the previous patterns before the COVID-19 era and the effects and the expectations in the future. In this way, the study would be covering the years before 2020 and the possible ways that digital payment behavior may take. Also, the individuals to take into account will be included, that is, those who were previously indexed for any electronic payments and the new technology savvy population that might be embracing digital payments. By doing so, the study will take into account two categories of people and the general expectations along the two divisions. This will also apply for the digital payments explored. There were several ways of digital payments previously and according to the findings, the analyses will involve the latest methods of digital payments and the effect on society. This has been necessitated by the quick developments in the cyber world and therefore there are several new payment options. In some of the digital payment companies, the most recent methods of payment have been indicated in the respective sites at which the users get comparisons and reviews. In order to prove the impact of digital payments in society, this study will take into account. Some methods that are currently being used and trending among different population segments will be studied to see how digital payments have really influenced people and the possible future. Also, the knowledge that is passed to the users and benefits of embracing electronic payments will be taken to see if it really has influenced society. This brings out the scope of the investigation on the impact of the digital mode of currency on social behavior and in general to members of the public.

REFERENCES

Accenture. (2021). Global payments trends report 2021. Retrieved from https://www.accenture.com/us-en/insights/banking/global-payments-report

Carder, B. (2019). A positive approach. *Quality Progress*, 52(4), 24–29.

Chen, J., & See, K. C. (2020). Artificial intelligence for COVID-19: Rapid review. *Journal of Medical Internet Research*, 22(10), e21476. DOI: 10.2196/21476 PMID: 32946413

Chen, Y., & Dubinsky, A. J. (2020). The impact of COVID-19 on the U.S. payment system: A new dataset. SSRN Electronic Journal. https://doi.org/DOI: 10.2139/ssrn.3649999

Evans, G. W. (2017). Artificial intelligence: where we came from, where we are now, and where we are going.

Lee, J., & Kim, J. (2020). Exploring the factors influencing consumer adoption of digital payment systems: A comparative analysis pre and post COVID-19. *Journal of Retailing and Consumer Services*, 61, 102542. DOI: 10.1016/j.jretconser.2020.102542

Liao, S. H., Fei, W. C., & Chen, C. C. (2007). Knowledge sharing, absorptive capacity, and innovation capability: An empirical study of Taiwan's knowledge-intensive industries. *Journal of Information Science*, 33(3), 340–359. DOI: 10.1177/0165551506070739

Luarn, P., & Lin, H. H. (2005). Toward an understanding of the behavioral intention to use mobile banking. *Computers in Human Behavior*, 21(6), 873–891. DOI: 10.1016/j.chb.2004.03.003

Lyon, D. (2012). *Surveillance after snowden*. John Wiley & Sons.

McKinsey & Company. (2020). COVID-19: Implications for business. Retrieved from https://www.mckinsey.com/business-functions/risk/our-insights/covid-19-implications-for-business

Reserve Bank of India. (2020). Digital payments in India: Trends, issues, and challenges. Retrieved from https://www.rbi.org.in/Scripts/PublicationReportDetails.aspx?UrlPage=&ID=996

Sharma, R., & Dhir, A. (2020). The rise of digital payment methods amid COVID-19 pandemic: A consumer perspective. *Journal of Public Affairs*, 20(4), e2161. DOI: 10.1002/pa.2161

Statista. (2020). COVID-19 impact on digital payments worldwide. Retrieved from https://www.statista.com/statistics/1105552/covid-19-impact-on-digital-payments-worldwide/

Venkatesh, V., Morris, M. G., Davis, G. B., & Davis, F. D. (2003). User acceptance of information technology: Toward a unified view. *Management Information Systems Quarterly*, 27(3), 425–478. DOI: 10.2307/30036540

Verma, R., & Mishra, P. (2020). Understanding the impact of COVID-19 on digital payments in India. *Journal of Public Affairs*, 20(4), e2175. DOI: 10.1002/pa.2175

World Bank. (2020). Digital payments and the COVID-19 pandemic: A cross-country analysis. Retrieved from https://www.worldbank.org/en/topic/digitalpayments/brief/digital-payments-and-the-covid-19-pandemic-a-cross-country-analysis

World Economic Forum. (2020). Advancing digital payment systems in the post-COVID era. Retrieved from https://www.weforum.org/reports/advancing-digital-payment-systems-in-the-post-covid-era

Chapter 9
Financial Literacy Theory of Financial Inclusion

Peterson K. Ozili
https://orcid.org/0000-0001-6292-1161
Central Bank of Nigeria, Nigeria

ABSTRACT

This article proposes a financial literacy theory of financial inclusion. It also presents the different possible scenarios of the relationship between financial literacy, financial illiteracy, financial inclusion and financial exclusion using a grid. The theory argues that financial literacy can influence the level of financial inclusion, and it projects low level of financial literacy as a potential cause of low level of financial inclusion. It showed that people who are financially illiterate and are financially included may not be able to maximise their welfare in the formal financial system because they lack financial literacy. By providing financial literacy programs and other incentives to join the formal financial system, many financially illiterate people will be willing to join the formal financial system and use existing formal financial services to meet their needs. The theory is significant because it explains a major reason why the level of financial inclusion in low in some countries.

1. INTRODUCTION

The purpose of this article is to propose a financial literacy theory of financial inclusion. It explains how financial literacy affects financial inclusion, the sources of financial literacy, and proposes a grid analysis which shows the possible scenarios of the relationship between financial literacy, financial illiteracy, financial inclusion, and financial exclusion. This study contributes to the existing theories of financial inclusion by analyzing how financial literacy enables an individual to

DOI: 10.4018/979-8-3693-6622-6.ch009

transition from being unbanked (or financially excluded) to becoming banked (or financially included).

Financial inclusion is defined as access and use of formal financial services to improve the welfare of individuals and businesses (Cámara and Tuesta, 2014; Ozili, 2021). Financial literacy, on the other hand, refers to the ability to use knowledge and skills to manage financial resources effectively for a lifetime to improve one's financial well-being (Hung, Parker, Yoong, 2009). Financial literacy – or the opposite of it, financial illiteracy – is a determinant of financial inclusion. For instance, Grohmann, Klühs and Menkhoff (2018) showed that financial literacy has positive benefits for financial inclusion across diverse income levels. Morgan and Long (2020) examined the impact of financial literacy on financial inclusion and savings behavior in Laos and found that high level of financial literacy has a detrimental impact on both financial inclusion and savings. They also found that individuals with high financial literacy rating were more likely to have savings in both formal and informal forms than those who have low financial literacy ratings, irrespective of income level or level of education. Fanta and Mutsonziwa (2021) document evidence from 6,029 individuals in Kenya and Tanzania and found that financial illiteracy (or literacy) is a significant determinant of financial inclusion in the two countries. Mutamimah and Indriastuti (2023) observed that financial literacy moderates the effect of fintech on financial inclusion for 202 small and medium scale enterprises (SMEs) in Indonesia. Although the empirical literature links financial literacy to financial inclusion, there is insufficient theoretical understanding of the mechanisms through which financial literacy affects financial inclusion.

There is a need to understand financial literacy in the context of a theory that explains how financial literacy affects the level of financial inclusion. Establishing a theory is important because such theory can demonstrate the mechanisms through which financial literacy influences financial inclusion, and it can advertise the need to consider financial illiteracy as a potential cause of financial exclusion, and present financial literacy as an immediate solution for financial inclusion. This study is not the first attempt to develop a theory of financial inclusion. Many theories of financial inclusion exist in the literature, such as the institutional theory and the vulnerable group theory of financial inclusion (Ozili, 2020). But the existing theories have not considered the effect of financial literacy on financial inclusion outcomes. Therefore, it is important to understand the unique approach which the financial literacy theory of financial inclusion offers. This study addresses this issue by exploring how financial literacy affects financial inclusion, identifying the sources of financial literacy, and proposing a financial literacy-inclusion grid.

This study contributes to the literature in several ways. First, the study contributes to existing theories of financial inclusion by analyzing how financial literacy enables an individual to transition from being unbanked (or financially excluded) to becoming banked (or financially included). Second, the study contributes to the literature that examines the determinants of access to formal financial services. Third, the study contributes to the literature that examines the determinants of financial inclusion by identifying financial literacy as a factor that enables financial inclusion. This is an important contribution to the literature because it proposes that policymakers and financial institutions need to invest in financial literacy programs for prospective and existing users of formal financial services.

The rest of the article is structured as follows. Section 2 presents the financial literacy theory of financial inclusion. Section 3 presents a grid analysis. Section 4 presents the implications of the theory and suggests some directions for further research. Section 5 presents the conclusion.

2. UNDERSTANDING THE FINANCIAL LITERACY THEORY OF FINANCIAL INCLUSION

The theory draws on numerous already accepted ideas in the financial literacy literature. It consolidates these ideas into a general explanatory model of financial inclusion which is based on financial literacy. The first generally accepted idea, which the theory builds on, is that financial inclusion works on the basis of demand and supply of formal financial services (Yangdol and Sarma, 2019; Mukhopadhyay, 2016; Singh, 2021; Fahmy and Ghoneim, 2023). The second generally accepted idea is that the demand for formal financial services is significantly affected by the level of financial literacy (Raina, 2014; Ramakrishnan, 2011). This means that if people are unaware of existing financial services and do not know how to use available financial services to improve their welfare, they will not demand formal financial services. As a result, financial inclusion will not take place.

These two widely accepted ideas in the literature are the two foundations guiding the theoretical model developed in this article.

The financial literacy theory of financial inclusion states that financial literacy is a necessary condition for people to access and use formal financial services in a meaningful way and in a way that improves their welfare (Ozili, 2020). This is because financial literacy will increase people's readiness to join the formal financial sector by giving them knowledge about basic financial services, knowledge about basic financial management concepts, knowledge on how to use digital technology to access financial services, and increase their awareness of available financial products and services which will enable them to access and use credit and other financial resources to start a business and generate income to improve their welfare and livelihoods (Ozili, 2020). When financially excluded people become financially literate, they will be willing to join the formal financial system, and they will seek formal financial services wherever they can find it. This suggests that high level of financial literacy will lead to greater demand for formal financial services and lead to high level of financial inclusion. Conversely, low level of financial literacy can lead to low demand for formal financial services, and lead to a decrease in the level of financial inclusion. There are six assumptions underlying the financial literacy theory of financial inclusion.

1. Every country has a segment of the population that is financially excluded, and the majority of them are financially illiterate.
2. The financially illiterate unbanked adults are unaware of available formal financial products, services, and digital technologies that exist.
3. Even when they become aware of it, financially illiterate unbanked adults will be less interested in financial products, services, and digital technology if they do not understand how to use it – they will not use what they do not understand.
4. Financially illiterate individuals can only transition to become financially literate through financial literacy programs of any type[1].
5. Financially illiterate unbanked adults have a "*what's in it for me*" attitude. They are self-interested just as everyone else. Therefore, an incentive or benefit must be provided to motivate them to be formally included. The incentive should be so good to entice financially illiterate unbanked people to join the formal financial sector and to remain in the formal financial sector. The incentive can be anything ranging from the need to pay utilities through a bank account, the need to receive frequent government-to-person (G2P) social welfare transfers, access to non-interest overdraft, high interest paid on savings deposit, free debit cards, etc.
6. Financial literacy programs, together with an incentive, will provide a strong motivation for them to join the formal financial system, and it will increase the level of financial inclusion. The provision of financial literacy programs without an incentive may not provide a strong motivation for them to join the formal financial system.

These assumptions are intuitive and emphasize that financially excluded people who are financially illiterate will be motivated to join the formal financial system if they have financial literacy and are given an incentive. When they become financially literate and are aware of available financial products, services, digital technologies, and are given an incentive to join the formal financial system, they will seek formal financial services wherever they can find it (Ozili, 2020), thereby increasing the demand for formal financial services and increasing the level of financial inclusion through increase in formal account opening and increase in the use of payment, credit, savings and insurance products. Several empirical studies have used the financial literacy theory of financial inclusion, initially developed in Ozili (2020), to explain financial inclusion in different contexts. These studies include Bashiru et al (2023), Kobugabe and Rwakihembo (2022), Okeke et al (2023) and Al-Smadi (2023).

Moving on to the model formulation, the propositions of the theory lead to the formulation of a model that encapsulates the idea of the financial literacy theory of financial inclusion. In the model, financial inclusion is a function of financial literacy and some control variables, as shown in equation 1. The variables in the model include the size of the unbanked population, the number of unbanked adults who are financially illiterate, the nature and type of financial literacy program, the incentive provided to unbanked adults, and supply of formal financial services.

$$Financial\ inclusion = f\,(financial\ literacy\ \ ;\ control\ variables) ----- Equation\ 1$$

Expanding equation 1, the financial inclusion variable is any indicator of access and usage of formal financial services. The financial literacy variable refers to any formal or informal financial literacy program of any type. The control variables are the number of unbanked adults in the population[2]; the number of unbanked adults who are financially illiterate, the incentive provided to unbanked adults; and the level of supply of formal financial services.

The expanded functional model is specified below:

Financial inclusion

= f (provision of financial literacy programs of any type; number of unbanked adults in the population; number of unbanked adults who are financially illiterate; the incentive provided to unbanked adults; level of supply of formal financial services.) --------- Equation 2

The model proposes a linear relationship between financial literacy and financial inclusion. However, the relationship may be non-linear if the assumptions underlying the financial literacy theory of financial inclusion are violated or if we take into account the exceptions of the theory. For instance, there could be cases where financially illiterate people can become financially included even without receiving any incentive and without having good knowledge of how to use existing financial services to maximise their welfare. There are also cases where financial literate people may choose to stay outside the formal financial system for personal reasons. This demonstrates that the relationship between fina6ncial literacy and financial inclusion may not be linear. In the next section, I use a grid to identify the exceptions that could introduce non-linearities into the relationship between financial literacy and financial inclusion.

3. GRID ANALYSIS

The grid in table 1 presents a good depiction of the different possible scenarios of the relationship between financial literacy, financial illiteracy, financial inclusion and financial exclusion

The grid '***Row A x Column A***' describes financially excluded people who are financially illiterate. This category of people will not join the formal financial system because, one, they lack the basic financial literacy that is needed to know how to access and use available formal financial products, services, and digital technology; and two, no incentive is given to them to motivate them to learn about financial services or to join the formal financial system. Therefore, this category of people will likely remain financially excluded.

The grid '***Row A x Column B***' describes the case where financially excluded and financially illiterate people are given incentives to join the financial system. The provision of incentives could make them consider joining the formal financial system if the incentive is attractive, but they still lack knowledge on how to use formal financial services to maximize their welfare. Therefore, this category of people may remain financially excluded despite being offered an incentive to join the formal financial system.

The grid '***Row B x Column A***' describes the case where people who are financial literate voluntarily do not want to be financially included until they receive an incentive or see a tangible benefit of financial inclusion. Without an incentive, they will not join the formal financial system. This category of people will remain financially excluded.

The grid '***Row B x Column B***' describes the case where people who are financially literate voluntarily do not want to be financially included for different reasons. They will not join the formal financial system even if they are offered an incentive to join the formal financial system. This category of people will remain financially excluded.

The grid '***Row A x Column C***' describes financially illiterate people who become financially included even without receiving an incentive and without having knowledge of how to use formal financial services to maximise their welfare. People in this category include newly banked adults who open a formal account and do not perform any financial transaction on the formal account until the formal account becomes dormant and closed due to account inactivity. With the account becoming dormant, they may exit the formal financial system.

The grid '***Row A x Column D***' describes people who are financially illiterate but are financially included people and are incentivized. This category of people will join the formal financial system but knowledge of how to use formal financial services to maximise their welfare despite receiving incentives to join the formal financial system.

The grid '***Row B x Column C***' describes financial literate people who are financially included but did not receive an incentive to join the formal financial system. After being financially included, and in the absence of any incentive, people in this category may exit the formal system at any time if they do not see a clear benefit of joining the formal financial system.

The grid '***Row B x Column D***' describes people who are financial literate, financially included people and are incentivized. This category of people will remain in the formal system for as long as they can due to the incentives they have received and their sound knowledge of how to use formal financial services to maximise their welfare.

Table 1. Grid showing the relationship between financial literacy and financial inclusion

		Financially excluded people		Financially included people	
		Column A	**Column B**	**Column C**	**Column D**
	Levels of financial literacy	**Without Incentives**	**With Incentives**	**Without Incentives**	**With Incentives**
Row A	**People who are financially illiterate**	People in this category will not join the formal financial system because there is no incentive to join, and they lack basic financial literacy skills. This will lead to financial exclusion	Due to the provision of incentives, people in this category will consider joining the formal financial system even though they lack knowledge on how to use formal financial services to maximize their welfare	People in this category are already financially included and financially illiterate. This means that financially illiterate people can join the formal financial system even without receiving any incentive and without having knowledge of how to use formal financial services to maximise their welfare.	People in this category are already financially included and financially illiterate. This means that financially illiterate people can join the formal financial system after receiving an incentive even though they lack knowledge of how to use formal financial services to maximise their welfare.
Row B	**People who are financial literate**	People in this category will not join the formal financial system until they receive an incentive or see a tangible benefit for being formally included. Without an incentive, they will not join the formal financial system	Due to some reasons, people in this category will not join the formal financial system even if they receive an incentive to join the formal financial system.	People in this category are already financially included and financially literate. However, in the absence of incentives to remain in the financial system, they are willing to exit the formal financial system at any time if they do not see a benefit of joining the formal financial system	People in this category are already financially included and financially literate. Due to the provision of incentives, people in this category will remain in the formal system for as long as they can

4. IMPLICATION OF THE THEORY FOR RESEARCH AND AREAS FOR FUTURE RESEARCH

The financial literacy theory of financial inclusion has some implications for research which are highlighted in this section. This section also suggests some areas for future research to expand the financial literacy theory of financial inclusion.

4.1. Implications for Research

One implication of the theory is that it provides a framework to understand how financial literacy increases level of financial inclusion, and it projects low levels of financial literacy as a potential cause of low level of financial inclusion. The theory also used a grid to emphasize that people who are financially illiterate and are financially included will not be able to maximise their welfare in the formal financial system because they lack financial literacy. The financial literacy theory of financial inclusion can expand ongoing debates about the relationship between financial literacy and financial inclusion. The theory adds to the broad finance and development literature by introducing financial literacy as a factor that agents of financial inclusion should take into consideration when offering financial services to underserved customer segments. Researchers can use the financial literacy theory of financial inclusion to enrich the literature that examines how financial literacy affects the different dimensions of financial inclusion. Another important implication of the theory is that it can stimulate the need to empirically test whether financial literacy significantly affects the level of financial inclusion. This implies that the financial literacy theory of financial inclusion can be validated or refuted using existing data. Researchers can use existing data to validate or refute the propositions of the financial literacy theory of financial inclusion. Such evaluation will help to assess whether the propositions of the theory are supported by real world data. The theory should also be tested and re-tested using empirical data and qualitative data obtained from a single subject or multiple subjects across time, countries and regions. The outcome of such evaluation can lead researchers to accept the theory, refine the theory or refute the theory.

4.2. Directions for Further Research

This study offers several avenues for further research. Future studies can investigate whether gender-related financial literacy is important for financial inclusion. Such studies should investigate whether financial literacy programs for women are more effective in increasing financial inclusion than financial literacy programs for men. Such research is important because it can provide insights into whether gender differences affect the relationship between financial literacy and financial inclusion. It can also reveal whether financially illiterate women are more likely to be financially excluded than financially illiterate men. Another important area for future research is to examine the role of government intervention in increasing financial literacy in the population to promote financial inclusion. Such studies should examine whether government intervention can increase financial literacy in the population and increase unbanked people's readiness to join the formal financial system. Future studies can also empirically investigate whether the level of financial inclusion is lower in countries that have a high number of financially illiterate population.

5. CONCLUSION

This study explored the financial literacy theory of financial inclusion. It provided an elaborate discussion of the relationship between financial literacy and financial inclusion using a grid. The study offered some important implications for further research. The study showed that financial literacy can influence the level of financial inclusion, and it projects low level of financial literacy as a potential cause of low level of financial inclusion. It showed that people who are financially illiterate and are financially included may not be able to maximise their welfare in the formal financial system because they lack financial literacy. Therefore, financial literacy is essential for financial inclusion. Consequently, all stakeholders should work together to ensure that agents of financial inclusion prioritize financial literacy when reaching the unbanked population. National strategies and policy efforts aimed at increasing the level of financial inclusion should consider the role of financial illiteracy and financial literacy in influencing the level of financial inclusion. Researchers also have a role to play by developing frameworks that show how financial literacy may influence the level of financial inclusion in different country contexts.

REFERENCES

Al-Smadi, M. O. (2023). Examining the relationship between digital finance and financial inclusion: Evidence from MENA countries. *Borsa Istanbul Review*, 23(2), 464–472. DOI: 10.1016/j.bir.2022.11.016

Bashiru, S., Bunyaminu, A., Yakubu, I. N., & Al-Faryan, M. A. S. (2023). Drivers of Financial Inclusion: Insights from Sub-Saharan Africa. *Economies*, 11(5), 146. DOI: 10.3390/economies11050146

Cámara, N., & Tuesta, D. (2014). Measuring financial inclusion: A muldimensional index. *BBVA Research Paper*, (14/26).

Fahmy, M., & Ghoneim, H. (2023). Financial inclusion demand-side determinants: analysis from Egypt. *Management & Sustainability: An Arab Review*. DOI: 10.3390/economies11050146

Fanta, A., & Mutsonziwa, K. (2021). Financial literacy as a driver of financial inclusion in Kenya and Tanzania. *Journal of Risk and Financial Management*, 14(11), 561. DOI: 10.3390/jrfm14110561

Grohmann, A., Klühs, T., & Menkhoff, L. (2018). Does financial literacy improve financial inclusion? Cross country evidence. *World Development*, 111, 84–96. DOI: 10.1016/j.worlddev.2018.06.020

Hung, A., Parker, A. M., & Yoong, J. (2009). Defining and measuring financial literacy. DOI: 10.1016/j.worlddev.2018.06.020

Kobugabe, C., & Rwakihembo, J. (2022). Financial Literacy and Financial Inclusion: A positivist view of Proprietors of Small and Medium Enterprises in Fort Portal City, Western Uganda. *American Journal of Finance*, 7(2), 1–12. DOI: 10.47672/ajf.1014

Morgan, P. J., & Long, T. Q. (2020). Financial literacy, financial inclusion, and savings behavior in Laos. *Journal of Asian Economics*, 68, 101197. DOI: 10.1016/j.asieco.2020.101197

Mukhopadhyay, J. P. (2016). Financial inclusion in India: A demand-side approach. *Economic and Political Weekly*, •••, 46–54.

Mutamimah, M., & Indriastuti, M. (2023). Fintech, financial literacy, and financial inclusion in Indonesian SMEs. *International Journal of Entrepreneurship and Innovation Management*, 27(1-2), 137–150. DOI: 10.1504/IJEIM.2023.129331

Okeke, C. T., Ifebi, O. E., & Ekesiobi, C. S. (2023). Financial Inclusion and Unemployment in Nigeria. *Journal of Advanced Research in Economics and Administrative Sciences*, 4(4), 28–47. DOI: 10.47631/jareas.v4i4.639

Ozili, P. K. (2020). Theories of financial inclusion. In *Uncertainty and challenges in contemporary economic behaviour* (pp. 89–115). Emerald Publishing Limited. DOI: 10.1108/978-1-80043-095-220201008

Ozili, P. K. (2021). Financial inclusion research around the world: A review. *The Forum for Social Economics*, 50(4), 457–479. DOI: 10.1080/07360932.2020.1715238

Raina, N. (2014). Financial literacy and credit counselling a demand-side solution to financial inclusion (A study of initiatives by select scheduled commercial banks in India). *Journal of Commerce and Management Thought*, 5(4), 659–675. DOI: 10.5958/0976-478X.2014.00013.5

Ramakrishnan, D. (2011). Financial literacy-the demand side of financial inclusion. *Available atSSRN* 1958417.

Singh, A. (2021). Exploring demand-side barriers to credit uptake and financial inclusion. *International Journal of Social Economics*, 48(6), 898–913. DOI: 10.1108/IJSE-04-2020-0234

Yangdol, R., & Sarma, M. (2019). Demand-side factors for financial inclusion: A cross-country empirical analysis. *International Studies*, 56(2-3), 163–185. DOI: 10.1177/0020881719849246

ENDNOTES

1 'Financial literacy refers to the ability to understand and effectively use various financial skills to make informed decisions regarding money. The skills include personal financial management, budgeting, and investing. Financial literacy, financial education and financial knowledge are used interchangeably.

2 This is a simple proxy for the number of financially illiterate people.

Chapter 10
Business Transformation Towards Sustainability:
Integration of Islamic Finance Principles in the Global Business Context

Early Ridho Kismawadi
https://orcid.org/0000-0002-9420-5212
IAIN Langsa, Indonesia

Mohammad Irfan
https://orcid.org/0000-0002-4956-1170
Business School, NSB Academy, India

ABSTRACT

This research aims to explore the integration of Islamic finance principles in sustainable business practices. The main focus is to understand how the principles can be applied holistically and inclusively to support economic and environmental sustainability goals. Using a qualitative approach and in-depth descriptive analysis, this study reveals that the integration of Islamic finance principles into business practices is able to create a solid foundation for sustainable and inclusive business growth. The results of the analysis show that these principles help companies face complex economic and environmental challenges in a more ethical and sustainable way. The implications of this research are particularly relevant for business practitioners in designing more sustainable financial strategies, as well as for policymakers in formulating regulations that support the development of Islamic finance. A key contribution of the study lies in a deeper understanding of the transformational potential of integrating Islamic finance principles in shaping a more sustainable business overall.

DOI: 10.4018/979-8-3693-6622-6.ch010

1. INTRODUCTION

In today's global business context, sustainable financial management has become one of the top priorities (Chang et al., 2022; Pang et al., 2022; Wang et al., 2022). Increasingly complex economic challenges and threats to the environment require companies to adopt sustainable business practices (Di Vaio et al., 2020; Fatimah et al., 2020; Leng et al., 2020). This is not only important for the continuity of the company's own operations, but also for maintaining the sustainability of the planet. The complexity of economic challenges faced by companies around the world, including fluctuations in raw material prices, market uncertainty, and global competitive pressures, further emphasizes the importance of sustainable financial management(Ishaq et al., 2022; Pe'er et al., 2020; Yadav et al., 2020). Meanwhile, threats to the environment such as climate change, pollution, and declining natural resources add urgency to shift business practices towards more sustainable models.

In this situation, the integration of Islamic finance principles offers a holistic and ethical approach (Harahap et al., 2023; Yesuf & Aassouli, 2020). Both Islamic finance principles (e.g., no usury (riba), no uncertainty (gharar), benefit for society (haram) and sustainability targets complement each other. Usury bans, for instance, support corporate abstinence from predatory and harmful financial practices while impact investments bolster companies' engagement in social enterprises. By incorporating Islamic finance principles, not the least of which is ethical and environmentally cognizant business models, this approach to sustainability would be a hope for the world. As a result, this provides an undeniably solid foundation for the company when moving forward with its sustainability goals over the long term that benefits their local community and environment. Good financial management is no longer just the responsibility of a company to allow the sustainability of its business, but it is part of social responsibility and an input from us in the positive transformation towards sustainability here on our little planet. Incorporation of Islamic finance principles is a key strategy to realize this objective.

The rapid growth of Islamic finance in recent decades marks an increasingly strong presence of alternative financial systems at the global level (Mukhlisin et al., 2023; Qanas & Sawyer, 2022). Indeed, this trend marks the reaction of more responsible financial behaviour and sustainability in the face of an increasingly sophisticated challenge by traditional financial setups. The Sharia principles on which Islamic finance is based have been growing in popularity as a viable and more stable alternative to the conventional financial system. Interest, or usury, is forbidden under Islamic finance. In traditional finance interest is considered the fundamental origin of earning while in Islamic finance it is an unethical and harmful practice known as riba. The benefits of the ban on usury are important because it leads to a better way for businesses to avail themselves of more equitable and sustainable ways when those seek access to provide their resources in funding the development of projects.

The principles of Islamic finance also emphasize better risk management through uncertainty. The concept of uncertainty or gharar emphasizes the importance of transparency, fairness, and responsibility in every financial transaction (Jatmiko et al., 2024; Mohd Noh et al., 2024). In business practice, the goal is to reduce uncertainty so as to ensure that organizations are able to continue their activities into the long term, while managing risks related to market or environmental fluctuations. Moreover, the fundamentals of Islamic finance also advocate for investments in social projects. More than being profitable, a sustainable business keeps in mind their broader impact on society and the planet. Islamic finance fosters the optimal use of capital to grow a more inclusive and sustainable business ecosystem by supporting investment in projects that enhance social and environmental well-being.

Figure 1. Issuers of green and sustainability sukuk in the Gulf Cooperation Council between 2019 and 2022, by value (in million U.S. dollars)

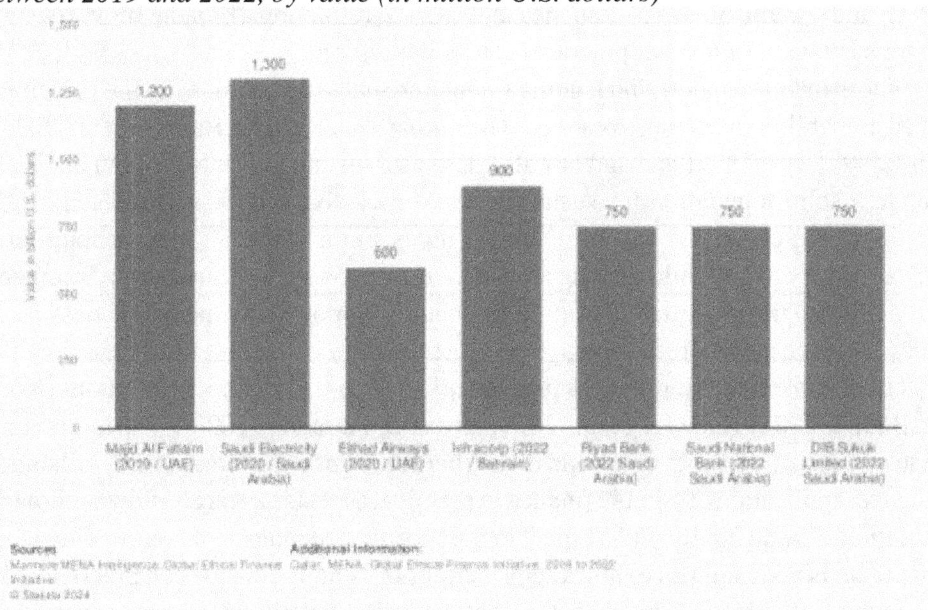

There has been significant activity in the issuance of green and sustainability sukuk by issuers in the GCC region over 2019-22, especially from Saudi Arabia. The following year, Saudi National Bank issued $750 million worth of green and sustainable Islamic bonds (sukuk) which were guaranteed; a significant contribution in 2022. This issuance was an extension of a trend in which Saudi Arabia led from the front!

Across the GCC, Saudi Arabia has been the most active issuer of green and sustainable sukuk between 2018 and H1 2022. This was the fourth issuance under this format by the country in a short period, indicating its commitment to sustainable finance. In line with the Saudi Vision 2030 aiming for economic diversification and seeking more sustainable ways to operate, this highlights a welcome focus in achieving those objectives.

Sukuk like these are designed to comply with the principles of Islamic finance and are particularly interesting for investors seeking Shariah-compliant opportunities with additional ESG dimension. The increasing interest of the GCC in green and sustainable sukuk underlines the growing recognition by the region of its responsibility to meet standards achieved in developing countries, whereby financial instruments are developed and directed toward environmental and social projects. Contributions from institutions such as the Saudi National Bank mean that in the 2019-2022 period, Saudi Arabia has accounted for the overwhelming majority of green and sustainable sukuk issuance in the GCC, reflecting a broader move towards more sustainable financial practices across the region.

The principles underlying Islamic finance are naturally in line with the principles of sustainability in business practices (Kunhibava et al., 2020; Rubbab et al., 2024). They not only offer ethical and fair alternatives to managing finances, but also help create a solid foundation for sustainable and inclusive business growth. By integrating these principles into business practices, companies can achieve long-term sustainability goals while making a positive impact on society and the environment.

Although the potential of Islamic finance to support sustainable business practices has been widely recognized, there is still a void in the literature regarding the practical implementation of these principles in day-to-day business operations (Khan & Badjie, 2022; Rabbani et al., 2021; Yesuf & Aassouli, 2020). While previous research has given more emphasis in the theoretical or conceptual issues of Islamic finance, application of Islamic finance in practical aspects has rarely drawn scholarly attention. The difficulty with respect to the broader acceptance of Islamic finance is that there is no insight as to how the principles of Islamic finance can practically be integrated into everyday business transactions. Although these principles are widely understood, the specifics of how to translate them into action often remain nebulous. This consequently makes it difficult for practitioners and business decision makers to apply these principles in actual business practices.

Previous research has not fully explored the impact of integrating Islamic finance in business operations (E R Kismawadi, Irfan, M., Al Muddatstsir, U. D., & Abdulkarim, 2023). Although it is believed that these principles will help to make business more sustainable and yield positive effects on societies and the environment, there is a dearth of substantial empirical evidence supporting these contentions. Shortage of data and limited case studies: It is challenging to assess how much Islamic finance implementation contributes to sustainable business practices since there is very little data available. This indicates that the literature must be developed in this area, and here is required talking about more research. A deeper empirical understanding of how Islamic finance can be integrated in business operations creates potential points for practitioners and business decision makers. The findings may also help encourage greater acceptance and stronger justification of the wider endorsement, that could stem from Islam Finance principles in comprehensive business sustainability decision-making process, for achieving enterprise overall sustainability performance and SDGs.

Well, this is our way of trying to understand how the principles of Islamic finance can be powdered into sustainable practices. This relates to the role of Islamic finance principles as part of a holistic integrated method in tackling clean energy and sustainability projects, including how these principles can address economic and environmental aspects. In providing a comprehensive view Unpacking is a step further placed within the broader context of principles Islamic finance aims to avoid, in this case among business operations yet holistically including as opposed simply parts these norms. It just explains these principles to be utilized in different business-oriented works as financial management, risk management and other investment strategies.

The purpose of this study is to explore the conceptual framework of Islamic finance and its role in economic sustainability, as well environmental sustainability. It evaluates the impact of operationalising Islamic finance principles on achieving the objective of sustainability such as inclusive economic growth, poverty reduction, narrow socio-economic disparities and environmental protection. Accordingly, besides a critical examination of how principles of Islamic finance can be applied as the blueprint for sustainable business practices, this research seeks to demonstrate how the implementation of these principles could be transformative in influencing a more sustainable environment and economy overall. Consequently, we believe that this research will add considerably to the ongoing debate of Islamic Finance sustainability and sustainable business practices.

We will use a qualitative approach in this study emphasizing on in-depth descriptive analysis. This will enable us to dig deep into the means in which these Islamic finance principles are integrated on a functional basis too. To achieve a high degree of insight into the concrete ways in which the principles delineated above are actualized in business practice we will apply diverse qualitative techniques, such as participatory observation and document analysis. This approach will be both inductive and qualitative, allowing exploration of the business practices context of implementing Shariah principles through depth rather than breadth. We will also intention to split what elements of the commercial surroundings have an effect on those standards deeply. In this respect, we are able to provide a clear, context-specific discussion of how corporate practices can be framed in Islamic finance principles, and discuss the effectiveness of such implementation towards sustainability objectives 1.

One of the major contributions of this research is explaining how integrative approach Islamic finance principles are advance to the context such as modern global business environment which is full with delicate economic and environmental issues. The principle of usury prohibition and investment in services that are supportive of the welfare of the society can be integrated by enterprises to carry out more ethical and sustainable actions on financial management utilizing Islamic finance. But those who say, what is the need of this integration, does not understand how continuity of such integration interfaces should be an integral part of the operations for the company as well as making sure that life on earth continues in a sustainable way. Islamic financial principles also promote other types of investments with social returns - for instance community infrastructure or environment projects. In doing so, the company not only wants to drive more income, but as well helps in impacting society and nature positively. These actions establish a better platform for business growth that is sustainable and inclusive, built on the understanding that societal health and environmental well-being are two sides of the same coin. The findings have implications for practitioners and policy makers within business as well as in academia. The exercise of embedding Islamic finance principles into a business model is not merely for financial returns but also serves to maximise economic, social and environmental good. Thus, it contributes to the development of a new course that more ethically, inclusively and sustainably the planet to do business in such a complex global context.

The article will be divided in to six main blocks that showcase the best practices in terms of integrating Islamic finance principles with sustainable business practices. The Introduction will present the background of the research topic, research problem, objectives, and scope of the research. They will be followed by a review of related literature discussing the knowledge of Islamic finance, sustainable business practices, and their interrelations, presenting a conceptual framework for research and pointing out existing research gaps. Research Methodology is where the methodological approach used, data collection and analysis techniques will be explained. Results: These will include the outcomes of data analysis and empirical data to support the findings of the research. The discussion will interpret the findings in the light of literature, and give a detailed perspective on how these findings affect the outcome. The free-form responses will be ordered by most commonly coded item, and the conclusion will summarize key points in the free-form data and confirm practical and scholarly implications with recommendations for practitioners and scholars. This:

provides readers with a structure that will facilitate comprehensive understanding of how Islamic finance is also essential in adopting sustainable business practices.

2. METHODOLOGY

This study uses a systematic review of the literature to develop an evidence-based model. Introduction - the framework: This section clarifies the integration processes between Islamic business principles and modern digital marketing practices and presents a set of theoretical speculations that inspire our empirical inquiry.

The research follows literature review with a case study method analysing a sample of Islamic companies adopting digital marketing strategies successfully. These insightful case studies provide perspectives on how the theoretical insights can be operationalised in practice and the interaction dynamics between Islamic business ethics and modern-day digital marketing tools.

The insights by the case studies and the literature review are then scrutinized, synthesized into a long list of metadata. This study aims to generate practical recommendations on how digital marketing strategies should be structured in line with Islamic business ethics, compelling ethical behaviour. This methodological rigor not only bolsters the theoretical underpinning of the research, but also complements it with empirical evidence facet developing holistic insights into how other scholars and marketing managers would be able to understand better the incorporation of Islamic principles in digital marketing practice.

3. INTEGRATING ISLAMIC FINANCE IN SUSTAINABLE BUSINESS MODELS

The integration of Islamic finance principles in sustainable business models offers a promising approach to addressing complex economic and environmental challenges (Kismawadi et al., 2024; Ridho Kismawadi et al., 2023). Islamic finance, which is governed by Sharia law, necessitates the prohibition of usury, uncertainty (gharar), and investment in socially detrimental activities, which inherently encourage ethical and sustainable practices (Abasimel, 2023; Saiti & Abdullah, 2015). This article examines the holistic and inclusive approach that Islamic finance can offer, taking into account the ethical, social, and environmental impacts that are essential for sustainable development.

First, One, there is a strong ethic involved in the ban on usury. While traditional finance frequently funds interest-based loans, Islamic finance seeks out alternative routes, such as profit-sharing. This method will help simplify the way trading occurs in order for it to be done efficiently, and to prevent borrowers from being exploited, and lenders only to offer loans responsibly. This reduces the level of debt-related risk that companies are subject to by steering clear of interest-based transactions, benefiting long-term financial stability. However, the ethical investment practices that are encouraged by these usury bans also have the knock-on effect of encouraging those investments to be projects that must benefit society and the economy in real terms, rather than simply speculative ventures.

Figure 2. Distribution of Islamic financial asset value worldwide in 2022, by country (in billion U.S. dollars)

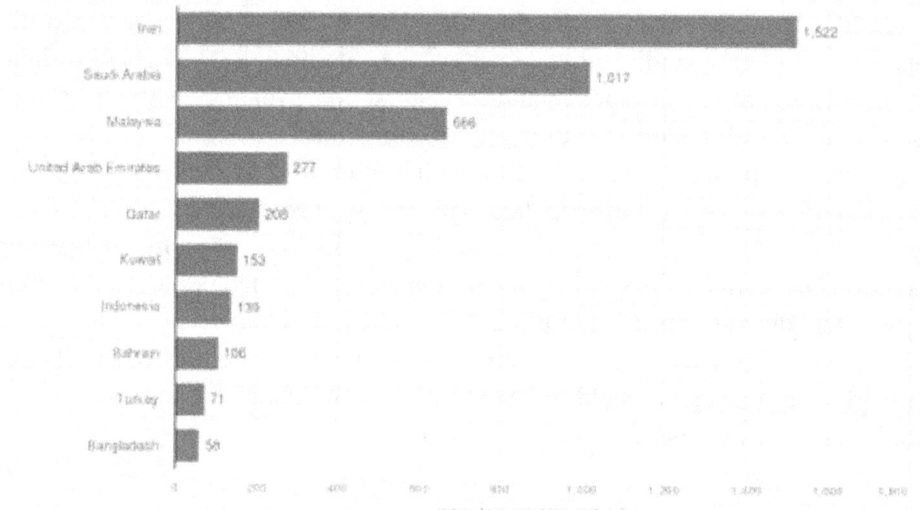

Source: ICD, Graphics by Statista

Global Islamic finance assets distribution in 2022 (to the nearest whole figure by country) Debt management fund in 2022, the Islamic finance assets of Iran reached \$1.5 billion Islamic finance assets worldwide grew to 4.5 trillion US dollars during the same year. This distribution is an indication that Iran represents less than a fraction of global total Islamic financial assets. Despite a long tradition of Islamic finance in Iran - where its \$1.5 billion contribution would make up only a sliver of the broader global market, which is estimated to be worth more than trillions of dollars. The global Islamic finance market is based on a variety of instruments like Islamic banking, sukuk (Islamic bonds), and Islamic investment funds, but the most popular type is the takaful which is an Islamic insurance. Saudi Arabia, Malaysia, and the United Arab Emirates also claim a large portion of Islamic financial assets around the world representing different institutions that comply with sharia law. The growth of the asset value of Islamic finance is attributable to not only the increased demand for Sharia compliant financial products but also increasing recognition and acceptance of responsible investing practices globally.

Also, some Islamic finance puts the emphasize on conscience investing and corporate social responsibility (CSR), which are parts of their businesses. Community development must focus on organization and infrastructure as well as environmental sustainability. In Islamic finance, CSR is not treated as voluntary but fundamental to the very operation of any business. CIE works of this nature may have significant implications for the promotion of community development through raising the living standards, education, and health services in at a disadvantaged geographic setting (Faruq Ahmad et al., 2022; Shabbir et al., 2018). In addition, the allocation of funds to green projects means that money is going towards a better environment and companies' cut off their carbon emissions. These socially responsible investments and CSR behave the company to instill goodwill and improve relations, it furthermore acts as a catalyst and will ensure that they have a sustainable growth of the business.

In terms of sustainability, a comparative analysis against conventional practices shows the more tangible benefits of Islamic finance. Traditional finance often focuses on short-term profits, often ignoring the moral aspects, whilst Islamic finance considers both profit motives and ethical and social responsibility Islamic finance, which gives much greater emphasis on asset-based financing and risk sharing than conventional finance, is less likely to create the speculative bubbles that are often the source of financial crises. Islamic finance is a method to promote financial inclusion which also targets people who, because of their strict credit terms, cannot benefit from conventional banking. This broader, more inclusive approach helps to support broader economic stability and development.

Therefore, the harmonization of sustainable business models with principles of Islamic finance outlines a coherent tool to counter varying economic and environmental changes into account in the 21st century (Schulte & Hallstedt, 2018; Yang & Lee, 2020). Finally, Islamic finance is an ethical system based on prohibition of usury making a positive external economical influence due to investments in priority sectors more likely achieved by following the corporate social responsibility policy, this features Islamic finance as a potentially very attractive alternative to the traditional financial system. This integrated wholeness not only assists companies to reach long-term sustainable goals but also ensures that one make a valuable contribution towards social & environmental well-being. The results and lessons from this study highlight the importance of conducive policy environments, public-private partnerships and awareness-building to help catalyse Islamic finance into playing a bigger role in supporting sustainable development.

3.1 Risk Management in Islamic Finance: A Sustainable Approach

Islamic finance management take a sounder and more sustainable route of risk management as opposed to the conventional that all hinge on disclosure, transparency, neutrality to eventually reducing uncertainty and managing market and environmental risks (Al Rahahleh et al., 2019; Alhammadi et al., 2020; Shahar et al., 2020). In Islamic Finance, Gharar, or uncertainty which is the presence of uncertainty in a contract is a matter of central importance as mutuality (and voluntary) is made difficult to determine where gharar effects the sale etc. This way, everyone participating to the transaction would have all the information they need and reduce the fraud or uncertainty. This study examines the application of these principles in the risk management practices adopted by Islamic financial institutions and its contribution to long-run business sustainability.

Experience based on case studies from Islamic financial institutions indicates that operational risk management can improve the stability and durability of business practices. For instance, some Islamic banks have managed to implement profit-sharing mechanisms that limit credit risk by splitting profits and losses between banks and depositors. This significantly enhances transparency, but more importantly means Dieu funding projects with a very high chance of success as all the parties in the transaction have skin in the game.

The merger of risk management function with business functions should not be purely financial but also include the environmental risks. This phenomenon also abides to the sustainability principle of avoiding investment in industries that harm the environment, where Islamic finance is often concerned. Therefore, in addition to risk management practices, Islamic financial institutions support environmentally sustainable financing by bankrolling green and environmentally friendly projects. The idea today is the practice of ethical business and long-term thinking in alignment to the principles of Shariah, which is very alien to conventional investor who focusses on shortcuts and immediate results.

Islamic finance risk management, which is based on principles of equity, transparency and sustainability provides a more ethical and responsible model for addressing economic and environmental risks. The study offers a distinctive understanding of how these principles can be put into practice and are employed in real- term business conduct which leads to long lasting stability and sustainability. Thus, these implications propose that the inclusion of Shariah governance in risk management not only could be a way to manage risks, but also as an initiative in pushing for more ethical and sustainable business conduct.

3.2 Islamic Finance as a Catalyst for Inclusive Economic Growth

Islamic Finance therefore has an enormous potential to serve as a catalyst for inclusive economic growth, operating in a manner so distinct from conventional finance as it is grounded by ethical principles guided by Sharia law (Kismawadi, 2024). Islamic finance offers access to financing for small and medium-sized enterprises (SMEs) who are often not served or under-served by traditional finance as it avoids use of interest-based mechanism. It is a win-win arrangement where there are no huge interest payments for SMEs that can constrain their growth and future liquidity with the Share-at-Risk system in Islamic finance, just an opportunity cost. This methodology allows Islamic finance to contribute significantly to the reduction of economic discrepancies and help strengthen inclusive growth by extending access to financial services across neglected segments of society.

Figure 3. Value of Islamic finance assets distribution worldwide in 2022, by type (in billion U.S. dollars)

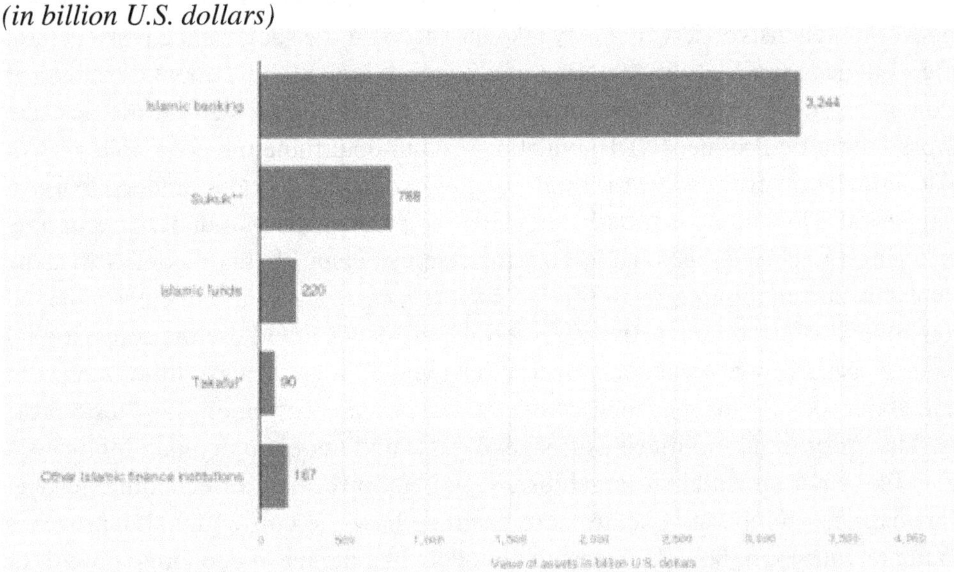

Source: ICD, Graphics by Statista

By asset type, Islamic banking accounts for the largest share of the value of Islamic financial assets worldwide in 2022. The value of global assets in the Islamic banking industry amounted to 3.2 trillion US dollars, corresponding to 71% of the total value of Islamic financial assets, which reached 4.5 trillion US dollars Islamic banking assets are deposits, financing and investments that are managed by Islamic banks in compliance with sharia principles. Another key tool in Islamic finance market is sukuk or Islamic bonds, which are used to fund infrastructure projects by governments and companies assuming a more discrete value than the described example for a decade. Islamic investment funds and takaful (Islamic insurance) are also integral to the sharia economy, with investment funds operating portfolios compliant to sharia law and takaful providing avatars of insurance also in line with sharia principles. In addition, this world Islamic finance market involves furthermore financial instruments such as Islamic microfinance and Islamic leasing to offer moral and sustainable monetary variations. The sheer size of Islamic banking assets (which account for more than 80% of all Islamic finance assets) underscores the significance of banking as the backbone of the Islamic finance industry, as other products complement and catalyse its expansion and diversification.

Traditional finance theory emphasises short term gain and often overlooks social impact arising from financial activity when compare to some of the traditional economic growth model. Comparative analysis with traditional economic growth models means comparing theoretical approaches that are traditionally held in economics, that tend to value economic growth as a measure of well-being, with a more comprehensive view that may take into account the social and environmental effects of economic activity. So, first of all, we are going to talk about the classical economic growth model. These models are generally predicated on metrics like Gross Domestic Product (GDP) which is used to determine the economic growth of a nation as determined by the total value of goods and services produce in a certain period. This model is usually targeted at improving the output of the economy by trying to achieve sustainable growth. One criticism of this model is that the emphasis on economic growth often comes at a cost of social and environmental components of economic activity. As few examples we could use the conventional finance scenario where financial institutions and companies have little interest to care about social impact of their activities, instead of focusing on short-term profits. They may trend too much as financial goals and not enough along food-saved lines like environmental sustainability, social empowerment or economic justice. This calls for comparative analysis to examine how the conventional approaches compare with more holistic alternative models like inclusive economic growth or sustainable development. For finance, this iteration looks to the effects financial activities might have on society at large, or as ATTN: puts it "that are good for the economy, but also good for people, and planet. Such actions could involve responsible financial practices, socially and environmentally responsive investments or funding of projects that encourage sustainable development. This comparative analysis offers an insight into how traditional finance is generally short-sighted, focusing on short-term gains as opposed to more holistic frameworks for the social and environmental consequences of financial activity.

Instead, Islamic finance emphasizes fairness, transparency, and social responsibility, which can help create more balanced and sustainable economic growth (bin Md Nor et al., 2024; Khalidin et al., 2023). Traditional growth models often result in greater economic inequality, as access to financing tends to be limited to individuals and large corporations with good credit. In this context, Islamic finance offers a more inclusive alternative solution, by ensuring that financial benefits also bring broader social benefits.

Policies that support Islamic finance can play an important role in increasing economic inclusivity (Franzoni & Allali, 2018; Ledhem & Mekidiche, 2022; Naz & Gulzar, 2023). Policymakers can develop frameworks that encourage financial institutions to adopt Islamic finance principles, such as profit-sharing based financing and usury avoidance. The government can provide incentives for financial institutions that support projects that benefit the wider community, such as infrastructure development, education, and health. Thus, Islamic finance not only serves as a tool to achieve economic stability but also as a mechanism to promote social welfare.

Figure 4. Value of green Sukuk issuances worldwide in 2020, by Sukuk name (in million U.S. dollars)

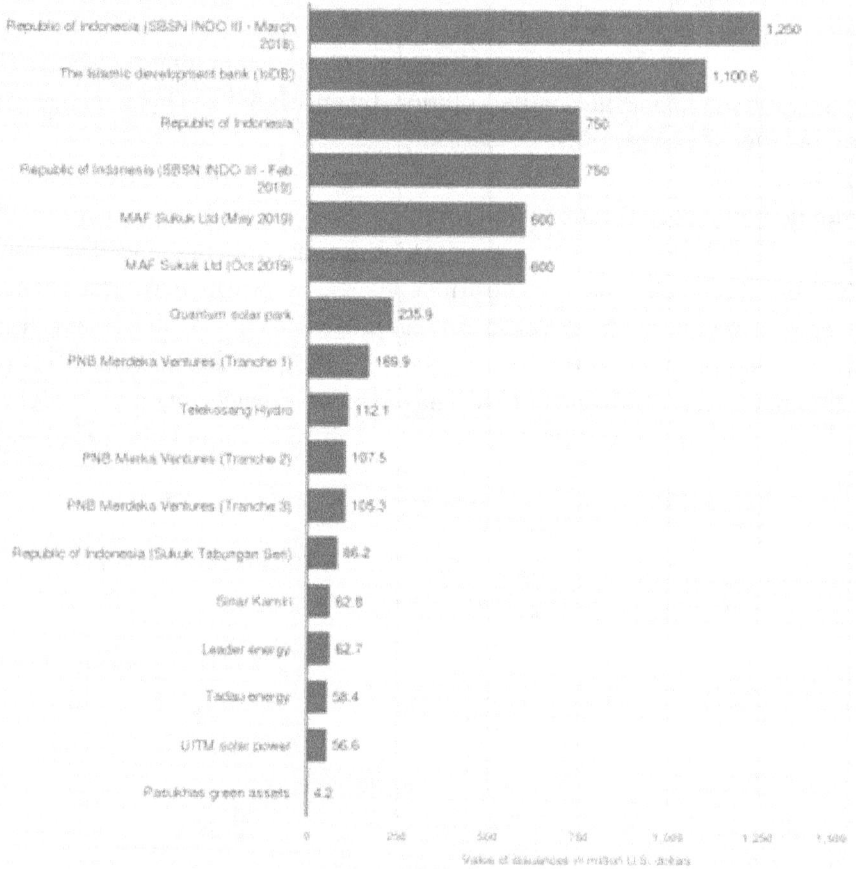

Sources: ICD, Alpen Capital, Graphics by Statista

In July 2020, the largest issuance of green sukuks globally was a bond issued by the Republic of Indonesia (SBSN INDO III) dated March 2019 in value around USD 1.25 billion. A size of the global Islamic finance market in 2020, based on total asset value 2.88 trillion US dollars. The issuance of this green sukuk shows Indonesia's dedication to sustainable finance and it has a significant role in the global Islamic finance market, such as in issuing financial securities that support green projects.

Figure 5. Number of exchanges who offered environmental, social, and governance (ESG) products in 2023, by product type

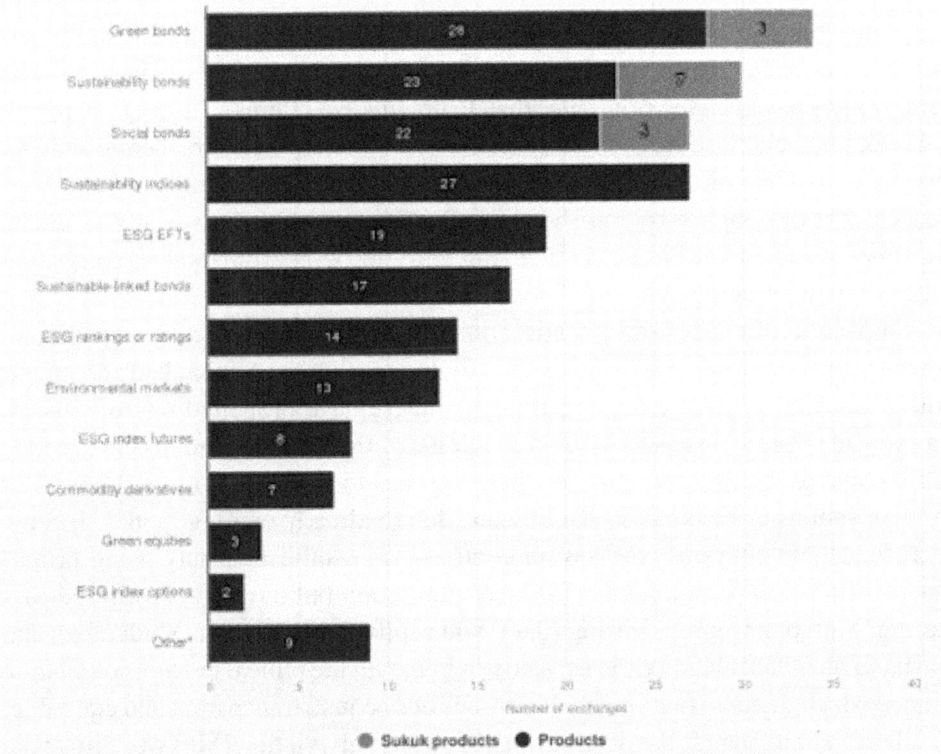

Source: WFE, Graphics by Statista

In 2024, the product most popular in the ESG category to be offered by the exchange is going to be green bonds. Across the street, sustainability bonds were number two in ESG product preference. Sustainability index and social bond (3 of 8) Growth of green bonds illustrates a growing investor dedication to funding opportunities which ensure environmental protection and reduce climate change. Sustainability bonds, which tend to be targeted at positive impact projects (environmental & social), are also experiencing a strong increase of issuance volumes. On the other hand, the sustainability index, offers guidance for investors wishing to assess how companies perform from an ESG angle and social bonds help finance projects supporting social welfare. For their part, the ESG products allow markets all around the world to assess this as a matter of urgency, providing investment propositions that underpin sustainable development.

3.3 Islamic Finance and Poverty Alleviation: Sustainable Solutions

Islamic finance which follows the principles of Sharia presents a distinct perspective on combating socio-economic issues including poverty eradication. The framework is based on the principles that do not involve interests (usury), share risk and seek for social justice, eventually enabling an inclusive financial environment. The article - "Islamic Finance and Poverty Alleviation: Sustainable Solutions" - provides a thorough look into how Islamic finance, with its varying financial instruments and moral bases, has the capability to be instrumental in combating poverty and facilitating economic inclusion.

Islamic microfinance is an essential component of the Islamic finance model and to synergetic relationship serves as a vital tool in reaching out unbanked and underbanked population. While organizations like these have propelled microfinance a long way in its promise to serve the poor, more traditional organizations have tended to see some problems, particularly when it comes to doing so with high levels of familiar options to help clients avoid loans due to already owning money. Islamic microfinance institutions (IMFIs), in contrast, are established only using principles that do not depend on interest-based transaction but based on profit-and-loss sharing, Murabaha, qardh, leasing (ijara) and capital participation (Mudarabah and Musharakah). The dual mode is perfectly in line with the ethical precepts of Islamic finance which demand that financial transactions be just, transparent and equitable.

Islamic microfinance has diverse roles in poverty alleviation IMFI works to make it possible for entrepreneurs to start or grow their businesses, provide employment and earn a living by providing access to capital. This is of particular significance in remote and underserved regions where many people cannot access the services of a traditional bank. Islamic microfinance supports financial inclusion, with a range of savings and insurance products that help the poor handle financial shocks and manage risk. Furthermore, some mechanisms such as takaful (Islamic insurance) introduce a mutual basis of shared direct financial liability which also entails a sense of contribution and assist that not only with managing the risk but also because it would encourage social and community cohesion. Successful poverty alleviation programs funded by Islamic finance serve as case studies that demonstrate the transformational aspects of these initiatives. For instance, the Baitul Maal wat Tamwil (BMT) is an institution in Indonesia that plays a critical role catering for Islamic finance to marginalized communities (Ascarya & Sakti, 2022; Maulana et al., 2018; Rahayu, 2020). These institutions are a mix between a bank and a social welfare institution, as they provide financial services in the form of a cooperative based system with money raised by zakat and alms for social services like education or health. This whole approach addresses the complexity of poverty, securing a least that money empowerment is merged through greater social well-being.

Several strategies serve as policy recommendations to increase the effectiveness of Islamic finance in alleviating poverty. One, I see is a conducive regulatory environment required for growth and sustainability of Islamic finance entities. Regulators must be vigilant as well to ensure that these banks operate within shariah principles besides being prudential and consumer interests' protection agents. Governments and spat lists must collaborate to promote financial literacy programmes to make aware the public about Islamic finance, its benefits and principles. Better awareness and understanding lead to higher acceptance and use of Islamic financial services.

Technology plays a key role in Islamic finance and can extend its reach and efficiency. The idea is to use digital and mobile banking platforms to reach people in remote or underserved areas who may have fallen through the cracks when traditional banks announced their relief packages, thus making finance more accessible. Islamic finance-focused Fintech solutions could help and make processes more efficient, reduce costs, and provide new products that are catered to the least privilege. Else there is a roll of the Islamic financial institutions with aid groups that is of great importance. International development agencies, nongovernmental organizations (NGOs), local communities, etc., will make these poverty alleviation programs more effective on the ground. By partnering, we can share knowledge, secure resources, and ensure our collective investment in poverty reduction is scaled up and the lessons learned are implemented.

Adopting social finance instruments like zakat, waqf and sukuk into poverty reduction strategy allows for an additional supply of finance for development projects. The Zakat and waqf, on the other hand, has a large potential to finance the social safety net programs as well as developing physical infrastructure in areas of underdevelopment. Innovative deployment of sukuk can bring investment to projects with positive financial and social returns. In conclusion, Islamic finance is an efficient way to assist the poor improved on an ethical base and is using various types of compromise instruments for that purpose which could be effective as well. Among these is the role played by Islamic microfinance in fostering financial inclusion and economic empowerment through enhanced access to finance for the unbanked (Abdullahi & Othman, 2021; Hussein Kakembo et al., 2021; Nik Azman et al., 2021). Various successful country case studies indicate that there is a great potential of Islamic finance to bring about significant development impacts in the lives of the poor. To capitalize on this opportunity, policy makers, financial institutions and development organizations need to strengthen the enabling environment, increase financial literacy programs, use technology, as well as take advantage of social finance tools. Islamic finance can provide valuable assistance to the global fight against poverty and for a more fair and meaningful life of all world citizens.

Moreover, when one delves into the nuances of the workings of the Islamic finance, it becomes evident that it has a lot in store to help us tackle the age-old systematic inequalities mainly prevalent within the conventional financial ecosystem. Islamic finance creates a more inclusive economic landscape by emphasizing equity and risk-sharing in lieu of debt-based financing. This becomes apparent in the Mudarabah and Musharakah modalities as the business relationships are on the basis of partnership and sharing of profits. Find of basis the on and a pre-agreed shares profit takes place in and entrepreneur manages expertise on with capital provides financier, The contract Mudarabah a tie. However, the burden of losses falls entirely on financers, which promotes trust and cooperation. Partnership (Musharakah): Partner invests with other partners in a business, sharing profits and losses, promoting risk taking and investment in ethical ventures.

One of the notable benefits of cost-benefit based profit-losses sharing provision is its support for small and medium enterprises (SMEs), which are essential in local economy growth and employment gathering especially in developing countries (Badaj & Radi, 2018; Dalimunthe et al., 2019). Traditional bank financing is out of reach for most SMEs who find the collateral requirements too strict and interest rates scary. Islamic finance can offer another path: equity-based financing that is more in line with what SMEs need as well as their ability to make money. He believed that it could create jobs and help the local economy, thus reducing unemployment while increasing quality of living.

It is further established a fact that the social prong of Islamic finance reinforces its help in poverty alleviation. The instrument of zakat, waqf, and qard al-hasan are not only financial but it has also imbued with social responsibility and ethical imperative (Ascarya, 2022; Kuanova et al., 2021; Tahiri Jouti, 2019). Zakat is also one of the Five Pillars of Islam and requires Muslim people have to tithe to help the poor and needy. Thus, a well-managed zakat fund can deploy different poverty alleviation initiatives from direct cash transfers to supporting education and health services ensuring that both short- and long- term needs of the poor are tackled.

Another great support for social development: waqf, or waqf Endowments have long invested in public goods, like schools or hospitals or infrastructure, resulting in lasting social and economic good. Applications of Endowments: Modern applications of endowments can be used in the setting up microfinance banks, clinics, and awarding scholarships for special education thus reaching out to underserved areas. Such objectives may serve to trigger a nexus of investment in human capital, forming a virtuous cycle which can facilitate economic development.

Islamic finance's dedication to investment based on ethics and social justice is also consistent with the sustainable development ingredients (Bagheri, 2021; Paltrinieri et al., 2019). By prohibiting investment in business fields targeted as detrimental to society (i.e., those related to alcohol, gambling and tobacco, among others), the determination for greater good and moral-related activities are maintained within financial activities. Such an alignment with ethical investing could attract socially responsible investors, particularly those interested in combining financial returns with beneficial social effects.

They must not lose sight of the power of sukuk (Islamic bonds) as a way to finance major infrastructure projects. Unlike traditional bonds, sukuk qualifies as an asset developed on the basis of real assets or systems and thus providing transparency in terms of having a genuine economic activity to support its investments. Sukuk backed by assets hence less speculation and more sustainability. Sukuk can also be issued by governmental and development agencies to provide funding for infrastructure projects, projects related to renewable energies, as well other development programs that are financially rewarding and socially desirable. By doing so, it can attract much desired capital for development - from within and outside the country.

Several challenges must be overcome if the full potential of Islamic finance in poverty reduction is to be realised. Wrong, with more stringent standardization and harmonization of Shariah interpretations between jurisdictions. This could be due to different interpretations of Shariah ruling would create ambiguity and therefore, limit the scalability options for Islamic products. International standards and a stronger role of regulatory bodies such as AAOIFI to ensure consistency of practices can affirm credibility in the system of Islamic finance.

3.4 Capacity Development is Essential in the Islamic Finance Sector

This will not only in training financial professionals in Shariah-compliant practices, but also building expertise in Islamic financial products and enhancing the capacity of regulators. Academic institutions and industry associations can contribute to creating curricula and certification programs to train individuals with the right skills and knowledge.

Encourage research and innovation in the realm of Islamic finance. Introducing provisions for the development of new products and services that target the needs of poorer, less fortunate communities can enhance the role Islamic finance plays. Developing micro-takaful products, such as creating a pocket-friendly insurance for low-income households could shield the poor from economic and unexpected uncertainties. Also, technology can be harnessed towards creating mobile banking solutions and digital platforms that extend the penetration of Islamic finance to remote disadvantaged areas.

Islamic finance provides a holistic and ethical manner to uproot poverty by providing sustainable financing solutions. With unique principles and instruments like profit and loss sharing, zakat, waqf and sukuk, it presents viable alternatives to conventional finance which could promote economic empowerment, financial inclusion and social justice. Islamic finance has been proven - in real case studies from the ground, such as Indonesia and Pakistan - to change the game in ways that drastically improve the lives of poor people. Nonetheless, realising its potential would require the concerted efforts of clinics like ASRM and those seeking to overcome existing barriers through safe regulation, appearance of a capacity for manufacturing, and drive towards innovation. If Islamic finance takes advantage of this strategy, it has a critical role to play in the global alleviation of poverty and the transformation of society into a fairer and more prosperous one.

3.5 Sustainable Development Goals (SDGs) and Islamic Finance: Synergies and Strategies

Islamic finance is a plausible framework in the context of advancing the United Nations Sustainable Development Goals (SDGs) as it is built on ethical investment, social justice and sustainability. In the article "Sustainable Development Goals (SDGs) and Islamic Finance: Synergies and Strategies" it seeks to examine the vis-a-vis between Islamic finance principles and SDGs as well provide practical ways in which these can be leveraged strategically to foster sustainable development across various sectors.

Islamic finance, as a system that prohibits interest (usury) and promotes risk sharing, social welfare, zakat (alms), endowment waqf, and Islamic bonds sukuk at its core (Alaeddin et al., 2021; Mohammed et al., 2020; Zain & Muhamad Sori, 2020). These principles are also closely aligned with a programs and targets under SDGs 1, 5, and 8 targeting inequality reduction, sustainable economic development, and social inclusion. Islamic finance profit-sharing mechanisms, such as Mudarabah (partnerships) and Musharakah (joint ventures), for example, directly contribute to the achievement of SDG 8 (Decent Work and Economic Growth) by promoting entrepreneurship and improving access to finance for small and medium enterprises (SMEs). These instruments facilitate the investment of SME in growth and job creation by offering a risk capital with shared profit between both parties.

Moreover, IDB capitalizes its Islamic finance principles of social justice, fair distribution and SDG 10 (Reducing Inequality) in tandem. It uses zakat and waqf as instruments to redistribute wealth back to society for the needs of poor and marginalised. Compulsory almsgiving (Zakat) is a form of tax that can support educational, health service or safety line programs for the needy and hence an anti-inequality initiative. Public goods and services - like schools and hospitals - which are essential if we are to address socio-economic inequality, have historically been funded by endowments capable of deploying such long-term social infrastructure.

In the framework of SDG 7 (Affordable and Clean Energy), sukuk is potentially an effective mechanism for fund raising (Mohd Daud et al., 2021). One such type of bond is green sukuk, which is a sharia-compliant bond that would be used to finance renewable energy and other green projects. Green sukuk assists in attracting investment in the construction of clean energy infrastructure to reduce carbon dioxide emissions, and to promote sustainable solutions-energy sources (Noordin et al., 2018). Both Malaysia and Indonesia were the first to issue the green sukuk which other countries followed suit. Fostering investment in renewable energy through Islamic finance, these initiatives present the potential of Islamic finance to support global action on climate mitigation.

Sustainable Cities and Communities (SDG 11) Islamic finance can also make a significant difference in Sustainable Cites and Communities. The principles of ethical investment and social responsibility associated with Islamic finance provoke the emergence of inclusive, safe, resilient and sustainable human settlements. Sukuk & Waqf: Islamic financial institutions can deploy instruments such as sukuk and waqf to fund affordable housing projects, sustainable infrastructure, community development initiatives etc. Urban development sukuk, for instance, funds urban projects that could be integral in improving living standards of city dwellers like transport systems, parks and waste projects ultimately building up sustainable cities.

Selected policy recommendations and strategies to amplify the effect of Islamic finance on the SDGs include fostering an enabling regulatory environment balancing sharia compliance with innovation and inclusivity. Global sharia standards need to be more seamlessly adopted to accommodate cross-border Islamic financial transactions and regulators are expected to play a large part in this. National development plans are a strategic entry point for the integration of Islamic finance principles towards greater alignment with financial policies and Sustainable Development Goals.

This is besides spreading more awareness and knowledge around Islamic finance among the stakeholders. Professional education and training programs for professionals in the finance, policy making, governance and general public can offer the tools necessary to make practical use of Islamic finance instruments in sustainable development. Moreover, cultivating linkages between Islamic financial institutions and global development agencies can help to raise resources and include best practices.

To this end, it is worth promoting research and innovation within Islamic finance to create new financial products that target certain SDGs. For example, developing micro-takaful (Islamic insurance) products can ensure low-income households affordably manage social risks, protect them from losing livelihoods due to economic shocks and assist with SDG 1 (No Poverty). Studies also suggested that building digital platforms for Islamic microfinance development will improve financial inclusion, even in remote and less serviced areas, fulfilling SDG 9 (Industry, Innovation, and Infrastructure).

The compatibility of Islamic finance with the SDGs also offers an important potential tool to enhance sustainable development globally (AliE-mail, 2020; Endri et al., 2022; Khan, 2019; Khan & Badjie, 2022). Indeed, through the mapping of Islamic finance principles to individual SDGs and harnessing the powers of relevant instruments such as the zakat, waqf and sukuk, an array of development actions from economic to social and environmental will be able to receive support from Islamic finance. Real examples in this regard are complemented by country-specific case studies demonstrating the actual advantages that Islamic finance brings about in the realization of these goals. While approaches to leverage this potential can vary depending on country circumstances, their optimal utilization generally requires three main areas of action: conducive regulations; enhanced financial education; and innovation incentives. Islamic finance thus has a critical role to play in the realization of the SDGs and helping towards creating a fairer, more sustainable future.

3.6 Islamic Finance and Circular Economy: Pathways to Sustainable Business

Rooted in Sharia principles and practices, Islamic finance is underpinned by the concepts of social justice and environmental sustainability and prohibits riba (interest) or gharar (uncertainty) (Jatmiko et al., 2024; Jelili Amuda & Alabdulrahman, 2023; Putriana, 2024). All these principles related to a Circular Economy which focuses on reducing the amount of waste and retaining usage of resources in economy, system recycling, recovery and regeneration. Whereas the traditional approach to the economy is take, make, discard, the circular economy offers a new economic model based on reducing materials usage. But circular economy focuses on preserving the value of products, materials and resources as long as possible so that it can help to reduce environmental impact and improve resource efficiency. Principles are based on durable, repairable, and recyclable products which are the cornerstones of Islamic finance to promote responsible consumption and sustainable resource usage.

Circular economy projects financed by Islamic finance: Case studies They could finance various types of projects that focus on renewable energy, waste management etc. (Ibrahim & Shirazi, 2020; Khan, 2019). For example, in some Muslim countries there is also a green sukuk issuance for solar panel development issued. In Malaysia, the issuance of green sukuk has funded the development of world-class wastewater purification plants and solar panels. They not only help to sustain the circular economy by reducing waste and ensuring the effective use of our resources, but they also deliver significant social value by creating jobs and improving the quality of life for those living in surrounding communities.

This idea can also be suffused into the concept of the waqf used to push for projects that are meant to spoon from the circular economy. However, endowments as public-good endowments can finance initiatives that go beyond these such those in the recycling, renewables and resource conservation sectors. It could do this by establishing endowments to finance the construction of environmentally sustainable waste management infrastructure, or fund research and development in green technology. Endowments as financial instruments for sustainability goals and a circular economy

One of the strategic frameworks that have been outlined in order to adopt circular economy within Islamic finance is shown below. The first thing that should be done is to define the standards and guidelines that ensure projects funded through resources generated by Islamic financial instruments indeed support the goals of circular economy. Such regulations target to ensure that the capital is channeled into projects which provide the maximum resource efficiency and minimal adverse environmental impacts in its respective category, underpinned with performance-based requirements such as green standards for sukuk and socially responsible investments.

Two, stakeholders in Islamic finance must be informed about the advantages and principles of various aspects of the Circular Economy. To do this, training programs, workshops and seminars linking the theory and practice of the circular economy with Islamic finance principles. This will help financial professionals, policymakers and businesses to understand how they can support the transition in the circular economy through Islamic finance.

The third is that there must be active collaborations between Islamic financial institutions and stakeholders including governments and private sectors to foster, prioritize, and finance circular economic initiatives Such partnerships can also enable the flow of knowledge, technology and resources required for a wide-scale deployment of circular economy practices. In a circular economy developed with Islamic finance instruments, governments could offer incentives in the form of tax breaks, or else subsidies on external projects.

Islamic finance integrated with the circular economy will be a promising way ahead for sustainable business. The principles that back Islamic finance also take an interest in prudent resource consumption, and environmental preservation - a perfect fit with the objectives of circular economy. Several case studies from around the world indicate that circular economy projects financed by Islamic finance can provide good support to the objectives of a greener economy with lower environmental footprints while delivering numerous social benefits. If a sound strategic framework is developed to enable such an integration, Islamic finance will be in the driving seat of global sustainability-which will secure the sustainable future that we all envision.

3.7 Technological Innovations in Islamic Finance for Sustainable Development

The landscape of technology innovation in Islamic finance is widespread and spans a spectrum of digital solutions that are changing the way financial services are delivered and consumed. As one such innovation, Fintech brings in a plethora of applications which are designed to make financial processes easier and automated. Take for instance the sharia-based fintech platforms that not only allow for quicker, more transparent peer-to-peer transactions but also can drastically cut both the expense and time needed to complete financial projects. The applications from sharia-compliant and non-bank track are facilitating access to banking services with mobile gate, particularly upscale geographical areas where the financial technology providers do not have a presence.

One such application in Islamic finance is blockchain - a technology best known for its ability to create a transparent and immutable record of transactions (Iskandar et al., 2022; Wanke et al., 2022). With platform blockchain, it becomes possible the records of financial contracts like sukuk and Mudarabah to be verifiable and transparent which ultimately ensure Sharia adherence as well as reduces fraud risk and avoiding uncertainty. Blockchain-based smart contracts are a type of self-executable digital contracts, built on the blockchain thus providing an automated mechanism to initiate the terms of any agreement which in turn reduces human-error and increases operational-efficiency.

The dissemination of cases applying fintech to Islamic finance has illustrated the transformative power of technology in financial acts over the course while delivering individual examples of marked successes. Certainly, the sharia-based crowdfunding model has already funded numerous small and medium-sized enterprise (SME) projects in the United Arab Emirates - where many such businesses struggle to obtain financing through conventional channels. This provides the opportunity for retail investors to participate in Sharia-compliant ventures, to diversify their portfolios and contribute to infusion of capital into regional economies.

On the other hand, in Malaysia with the implementation of blockchain technology to cover sukuk issuance this gives a better clarity and efficiency in the issuance process (Eletter, 2024; Fernando et al., 2023; Nazeri et al., 2023). Since all transactions and shareholders are written on the blockchain, thanks to the assurance mechanism that surrounds it, all stakeholders can benefit from verifying information in real-time contrary to waiting on statements that can arrive days after every transaction, a practice that generates this kind of error and generates mistrust about this media for investors. It would bring more credibility and reduce the risk associated with these financial instruments leading to more investment in Islamic means of finance.

Nevertheless, future efforts to couple technology with Shariah-compliant finance for sustainability may not pan out without a struggle. It is tough to follow and implement that all technology solutions are following the sharia principles, this is one of the most imperative challenges. Technology developers are working hand in glove with sharia experts and regulators to ensure the new products are innovative and Islamic compliant. New technologies usually come with expensive initial investments, as well as entail some modifications in the present set-up that smaller finance organizations do not find conducive or appealing.

This obviously has implications for cybersecurity and data protection. If anything, the security of information is unfortunately a bigger fear with digital solutions. Thus, Islamic banks need the highest security and protection over customer data. To tackle these headwinds and harness the overall benefits of technology in Islamic finance, a number of policy maneuvers can be embarked upon. Clear Regulations and Standards of Islamic Financial Technology are Developed First There is a clear consensus that regulators should work with industry to develop frameworks that allow for innovation while being sharia compliant. Secondly, training and education on fintech and blockchain must be improved amongst Islamic finance practitioners so that they become more conversant with these technologies.

International cooperation is a way to share the best practices and experiences of different countries. countries with more established industries can help others in building their technical know-how. Islamic financial institutions that work with technology companies can innovate and deliver more appropriate solutions. Technological innovation has the potential to support these ends in the form of greater transparency and efficiency as well as deepening financial inclusion all three aspects contributing to greater sustainability in Islamic finance. This will enable Islamic finance to tackle its operational issues and reach more of society by accepting fintech, blockchain technology, and other digital innovations. Indeed, technology can underpin more open and effective practices in Islamic financial service provision, as country case studies demonstrate, but issues relating to compliance in Islamic Finance and internet security also require attention. If used in the right way, technological integration can play a critical role towards that end and prepare the landscape for years to come, paving the way for a prosperous and sustainable future through Islamic finance.

3.8. Islamic Finance, Business Ethics, and Sustainable Development

Islamic finance is based on the principles of Maqasid Shari'ah, which is the main goal of Islamic law. These principles aim to promote general well-being and justice by protecting essential elements such as religion, life, intellect, heredity, and property. At its core, Islamic finance seeks to ensure that economic activity contributes to value creation while preventing harm to individuals and society. This is achieved through mechanisms such as risk-sharing contracts (Musharakah, Mudarabah), asset-based financing, and ethical investments that avoid speculation and support real economic growth. Additionally, Islamic finance promotes social welfare through practices such as Zakat and Waqf, which encourage wealth distribution and reduce inequality. Prevention of danger is another important feature, which is manifested through the prohibition of Riba (riba), Gharar (excessive uncertainty), and Maysir (gambling), which are considered exploitative and disrupt stability. These prohibitions ensure that financial transactions are transparent, fair, and based on real economic value, avoiding speculation and unethical profiteering. In addition, Islamic finance emphasizes the importance of alignment with business ethics, encouraging transparency, fairness, and social responsibility in all transactions. It ensures that business practices contribute to long-term sustainability, protect stakeholder rights, and operate within the boundaries of ethical and moral standards, thereby creating a financial system that not only generates profits but also improves the well-being of Society (Abdullah et al., 2024; Hassan, 2024).

Islamic finance principles, such as the prohibition against riba (interest) and the implementation of asset-based financing, contribute significantly to sustainable development and ethical business practices. The prohibition of riba ensures that profits are not obtained through exploitation or unfair interest charging to other parties. In the conventional financial system, interest often causes injustice, especially for the underprivileged, because debt can grow without any real value being created. Islamic finance, by banning riba, focuses on managing the shared risks and profits of real ventures, which promotes sustainable economic growth without incurring social inequality. Additionally, asset-based financing requires that all transactions are backed by real assets, such as property, goods, or commodities, creating a direct link between finance and the real economy. This approach prevents excessive speculation, which is often the cause of economic instability and financial crises. With a focus on productive assets and real economic activity, Islamic finance encourages sustainable and responsible investment. This not only ensures that wealth circulates fairly in society, but also minimizes the risks associated with irresponsible speculative financial practices. The principles also support ethical business practices, by promoting transparency, fairness, and social responsibility. In the Islamic financial system, all parties to a transaction must be treated fairly, with clear rights and obligations, thus creating trust between stakeholders. The prohibition of usury and asset-based financing also ensures that profits are obtained through legitimate and productive ventures, in line with the principles of social justice and general welfare. Therefore, Islamic finance has a role to play in creating a more sustainable and ethical economic system, which prioritizes the well-being of society as a whole as well as ensuring a balance between economic benefits and moral responsibility (Alshaleel, 2019; Kismawadi et al., 2024).

Islamic finance has great potential to mobilize financial resources to achieve the Sustainable Development Goals (SDGs) through instruments such as sukuk (sharia bonds) and waqf (charitable endowments). The sukuk, which operates without interest and is based on real assets, has been used to fund various infrastructure, renewable energy, education, and health projects, which directly support the achievement of the SDGs. One example is green sukuk, which is specifically focused on green projects, such as the development of clean energy and climate change mitigation. Meanwhile, waqf provides a long-term source of funding for social projects through assets that are gifted and managed productively, such as in education, health, and poverty alleviation. Productive waqf management allows these assets to continue to provide benefits without reducing their principal value, creating a sustainable source of funding for SDGs initiatives (Alshaleel, 2019; Haron, 2024).

The Islamic finance industry is increasingly integrating ESG (Environmental, Social, and Governance) factors in planning and investment. The integration aims to assess the impact of investments on the environment, social responsibility, and good governance, in accordance with Islamic principles that emphasize social justice, environmental protection, and transparent governance. By adopting ESG, Islamic finance ensures that investments not only generate financial returns, but also contribute positively to social and environmental well-being. Through the use of instruments such as sukuk and waqf, as well as the incorporation of ESG criteria, Islamic finance can accelerate the achievement of the SDGs, creating a more sustainable, fair, and inclusive future for all (Agrawal et al., 2023; Hassan, 2024).

3.9 Regulatory Framework and Policy Support

The wider adoption of Islamic finance globally faces significant regulatory challenges and requires specific policy measures to address them. One of the main obstacles is the lack of consistent regulation across countries. Islamic finance has unique principles such as the prohibition of riba, gharar, and maysir which are often not comprehensively regulated outside of Muslim-majority countries. In addition, differences in the interpretation of sharia compliance in various jurisdictions create difficulties in creating universally recognized international standards. To overcome this challenge, government support is crucial, including through the development of a legal framework that supports Islamic financial products, such as sukuk and takaful, as well as the provision of tax incentives and the promotion of Islamic financial literacy. In addition, international cooperation is needed to harmonize regulatory standards at the global level, with organizations such as AAOIFI and IFSB playing a role in creating more uniform Islamic financial standards. Economic and technological incentives can also help expand the adoption of Islamic finance, for example by supporting the development of Islamic fintech and digital solutions that facilitate public access to Islamic financial services. As such, collaborative efforts between governments, regulators, and industry players are essential to address regulatory challenges and support the growth of Islamic finance globally.

Region-specific fragmentation and growth are major obstacles to bringing Islamic finance practices together among different countries. Fragmentation occurs because each country, or even each region, has a different approach to interpreting and applying Islamic finance principles. Sharia supervisory boards in different jurisdictions often have different views on financial products, such as sukuk, takaful, and other investment instruments. This results in a lack of uniform standards globally, so financial institutions operating across borders face difficulties in adapting their products to different rules. In addition, the more rapid growth of the Islamic finance industry in some regions, such as the Middle East and Southeast Asia, compared to other regions, has also created a gap in the adoption of Islamic finance practices at the international level (Ahmed et al., 2017). This situation exacerbates fragmentation, as each region is often more focused on local growth than seeking globally acceptable standards. To overcome these obstacles, stronger international cooperation, both among regulators and industry players, is needed to create universal standards that facilitate the harmonization of Islamic financial practices in various countries, so that Islamic finance can develop more evenly and harmoniously at the global level.

The lack of a standardized reporting system that is aligned with Islamic principles as well as international standards is a critical problem in the development of Islamic finance. Current reporting systems often do not fully reflect sharia principles such as the prohibition of riba, gharar, and maysir, which are the main cornerstones of Islamic financial products and services. On the other hand, many Islamic financial institutions must also comply with international standards such as IFRS (International Financial Reporting Standards), which are not always compatible with sharia rules. The absence of a reporting system that can accommodate these two aspects creates difficulties for Islamic financial institutions in compiling financial statements that are transparent, accurate, and in accordance with the demands of the global market. In addition, differences in the interpretation of sharia principles in different jurisdictions exacerbate the situation, as each country or region has a different approach to sharia financial reporting. As a result, financial institutions face challenges in ensuring that they can meet the needs of international regulation while maintaining compliance with sharia. To address this problem, it is necessary to develop a standardized reporting framework, which not only takes into account sharia principles, but is also in line with international standards. This will increase transparency, strengthen market confidence, and allow Islamic finance to expand more widely on a global level (Al-Zaqeba & Basheti, 2024).

Increased involvement of Western regulators and credit rating agencies, the implementation of robust accounting procedures, and better protection for stakeholders in Islamic Financial Institutions (MFIs) are important factors that can influence the growth of the Islamic finance sector. Western regulators, especially in non-Muslim countries, are increasingly interested in accommodating Islamic finance in their financial systems as global demand for sharia products increases. Their involvement helps create a more inclusive regulatory framework and promotes more uniform global standards, so that Islamic financial products can be more accessible in international markets. In addition, credit rating agencies such as Moody's and Standard & Poor's also play an important role by assessing Islamic financial instruments, such as sukuk, which gives global investors' confidence in the stability and compliance of these products with international standards and sharia principles. The implementation of more transparent and consistent accounting procedures is also very important to encourage trust in LKI. Strong accounting standards, both those that follow international standards and those that are in line with Islamic principles, such as those developed by AAOIFI (Accounting and Auditing Organization for Islamic Financial Institutions), will ensure that LKI's financial statements are more reliable and transparent. This is important for strengthening the industry's credibility in the eyes of stakeholders, including investors, regulators, and consumers (Alexakis & Tsikouras, 2009).

CONCLUSION

Islamic finance can serve as a strong instrument to complement sustainable economic development through its ethical precepts based on Sharia law. This research aims to uncover the avenues where technology innovation can better support the sustainability of Islamic finance, it practices. Islamic finance will enhance transparency, efficiency and sustainability by using technologies as fintech, blockchain and other digital solutions. In support of sustainable development, there is a significant role that can be played by technological innovation within Islamic finance. Fintech, an abbreviation for financial technology, is one such area that can help bring marginalized or unbanked communities into the formal economy and promote economic inclusivity. Boosting transparency and bringing a high level of accountability in financial transactions, blockchain can offer better compliance to shariah norms and mechanisms that are designed for real-time monitoring whether the funds are used according to Shariah principles or not.

Islamic Fintech Implementation: Fintech incubation case studies in Islamic finance demonstrate how the technology can be used to yield positive outcomes. For instance, the introduction of Sharia-based fintech platforms has helped Small and Medium-sized Enterprises (SMEs) to access interest-free financing so they can grow and help benefit the domestic economy. In addition to that, the employment of blockchain technology in zakat and endowments has been beneficial alongside the enhancement of their distribution and transparency to sustain better assistance for those in need. Nevertheless, technology integration in Islamic finance is not free of obstacles. However, this information must be kept secure with strict data privacy practices. Islamic finance industry players need to be educated and learn how to use technology. There is a tremendous potential for sustainability enhancement in Islamic finance through the game-changing advancements in technology. Ethically and inclusively deployed, technology can enable fair and inclusionary financial practices that promote sustainable economic development. This research explains at a much deeper level on how technology can be used to blend well with the rules of Islamic Finance and give rise to a fair, transparent, and green financial system.

The policy recommendations and strategies proposed in this paper underline the need for coordination among governments, financial institutions and technology developers to exploit the full potential of technological innovations in Islamic finance. Providing the needed regulatory support and increasing the availability of knowledge can help remove some of these bottlenecks and drive broader adoption levels for tech-enablers in Islamic Finance. Therefore, the adoption of technology in Islamic finance could not only lead to higher efficiency and transparency but could also encourage a more comprehensive and sustainable growth in the economy.

This study, thus, have some significant implications and it paves way for exploring more on the technology-Islamic finance integration. The first is that it broadens the study that addresses the effectiveness of using fintech, blockchain and other digital solution to improve efficiency and accountability in sharia-based financial transactions. Another key implication from the study is that technology can aid financial inclusion by increasing the number of people who have access to financial services, and further research in this area could investigate how technological advances might lessen economic inequality. Third, this research highlights the use of technology to enhance integration in operation and reduce financial transaction costs resulting to the operational efficiency of Islamic financial institutions. Finally, the use of blockchain technologies can also improve transparency and trust in financial transactions - a key requirement to verify that all operations are running following Islamic norms.

Here are some suggestions for future researchers to further this field of research. An area that we need to address early on is to develop a wide-ranging regulatory framework and to facilitate the adoption of technology in Islamic finance. This can be learned from studying best practices from other countries which have adopted the technology effectively. Secondly, researchers are required to raise education and digital literacy programmes for players of the Islamic finance industry so that they could get competent training regarding technology usage and understanding that would efficiently avail tech-based products. Third, research concentrating on the individual case studies on technology and its application in Islamic finance across countries would be called for to delve into the practical angle in generating understandings of what problems and successes encountered. Interdisciplinary collaboration including experts in tech, economics and sharia law is a must to deliver complete and halal solutions. The fifth recommendation is exploring the real possibility of creating new financial products with elements of technology whereby when employed it is possible to adhere to Islamic rules (e.g. using blockchain based smart contracts, and the development of Islamic fintech applications). Therefore, research is required to quantify the social and economic returns on the adoption of technology in Islamic finance, exploring its causes and ramifications, including whether this has any implications for policy towards financial inclusion, poverty reduction or sustainable economic development. These suggestions can in general help researchers make an additional meaningful contribution in the advancement of a tech-ridden Islamic finance that is more efficient, transparent and long-term sustainable.

REFERENCES

Abasimel, N. A. (2023). Islamic Banking and Economics: Concepts and Instruments, Features, Advantages, Differences from Conventional Banks, and Contributions to Economic Growth. *Journal of the Knowledge Economy*, 14(2), 1923–1950. DOI: 10.1007/s13132-022-00940-z

Alaeddin, O., Dakash, M. A., & Azrak, T. (2021). Implementing the Blockchain Technology in Islamic Financial Industry: Opportunities and Challenges. *Journal of Information Technology Management*, 13(3), 99–115. DOI: 10.22059/JITM.2021.83116

bin Md Nor, A. H., Muneeza, A., & Mohsin, M. (2024). What is the insolvency regime applied under Shariah for Islamic banks? *International Journal of Law and Management*. DOI: 10.22059/JITM.2021.83116

Chang, L., Taghizadeh-Hesary, F., Chen, H., & Mohsin, M. (2022). Do green bonds have environmental benefits? *Energy Economics*, 115, 106356. Advance online publication. DOI: 10.1016/j.eneco.2022.106356

Di Vaio, A., Palladino, R., Hassan, R., & Escobar, O. (2020). Artificial intelligence and business models in the sustainable development goals perspective: A systematic literature review. *Journal of Business Research*, 121, 283–314. DOI: 10.1016/j.jbusres.2020.08.019

Eletter, S. F. (2024). The use of blockchain in the insurance industry: A bibliometric analysis. *Insurance Markets and Companies*, 15(1), 12–29. DOI: 10.21511/ins.15(1).2024.02

Endri, E., Hania, B. T., & Ma'ruf, A. (2022). CORPORATE GREEN SUKUK ISSUANCE FOR SUSTAINABLE FINANCING IN INDONESIA. *Environment and Ecology*, 13(1), 38–49. DOI: 10.21511/ee.13(1).2022.04

Fatimah, Y. A., Govindan, K., Murniningsih, R., & Setiawan, A. (2020). Industry 4.0 based sustainable circular economy approach for smart waste management system to achieve sustainable development goals: A case study of Indonesia. *Journal of Cleaner Production*, 269, 122263. Advance online publication. DOI: 10.1016/j.jclepro.2020.122263

Fernando, Y., Tseng, M.-L., Wahyuni-TD, I. S., Sroufe, R., & Mohd-Zailani, N. I. A. (2023). Blockchain technology adoption for carbon trading and energy efficiency: ISO manufacturing firms in Malaysia. *International Journal of Logistics*, 26(11), 1556–1577. DOI: 10.1080/13675567.2022.2090527

Franzoni, S., & Allali, A. A. (2018). Principles of Islamic finance and principles of Corporate Social Responsibility: What convergence? *Sustainability (Basel)*, 10(3), 637. Advance online publication. DOI: 10.3390/su10030637

Harahap, B., Risfandy, T., & Futri, I. N. (2023). Islamic Law, Islamic Finance, and Sustainable Development Goals: A Systematic Literature Review. *Sustainability (Basel)*, 15(8), 6626. Advance online publication. DOI: 10.3390/su15086626

Ibrahim, A.-J., & Shirazi, N. S. (2020). The role of islamic finance in fostering circular business investments: The case of oic countries. *Journal of Economic Co-operation and Development*, 41(1), 89–120.

Ishaq, H., Dincer, I., & Crawford, C. (2022). A review on hydrogen production and utilization: Challenges and opportunities. *International Journal of Hydrogen Energy*, 47(62), 26238–26264. DOI: 10.1016/j.ijhydene.2021.11.149

Iskandar, R. D. M., Maryanti, T., Jayaprawira, A. R., & Sari, S. N. (2022). Indonesian Islamic Banking Fintech Model Strategy: ANP Method. *APTISI Transactions on Technopreneurship*, 4(2), 142–152. DOI: 10.34306/att.v4i2.257

Jatmiko, W., Iqbal, A., & Ebrahim, M. S. (2024). On the Ethicality of Islamic Banks' Business Model. *British Journal of Management*, 35(1), 115–136. DOI: 10.1111/1467-8551.12703

Jelili Amuda, Y., & Alabdulrahman, S. (2023). Reinforcing policy and legal framework for Islamic insurance in Islamic finance: Towards achieving Saudi Arabia Vision 2030. *International Journal of Law and Management*, 65(6), 600–613. DOI: 10.1108/IJLMA-03-2023-0045

Khalidin, B., Musa, A., & Kiawan, A. (2023). MURABAHA FINANCING OF THE INDONESIAN ISLAMIC BANKS UNDER AN ISLAMIC ECONOMIC LAW AND THE FATWA DSN MUI. *Petita: Jurnal Kajian Ilmu Hukum Dan Syariah*, 8(2), 203–218. DOI: 10.22373/petita.v8i2.238

Khan, T. (2019). Reforming Islamic finance for achieving sustainable development goals. *Journal of King Abdulaziz University. Islamic Economics*, 32(1), 3–21. DOI: 10.4197/Islec.32-1.1

Khan, T., & Badjie, F. (2022). Islamic blended finance for circular economy impactful smes to achieve sdgs. *The Singapore Economic Review*, 67(1), 219–244. DOI: 10.1142/S0217590820420060

Kismawadi, E. R., Irfan, M., Al Muddatstsir, U. D., & Abdulkarim, F. M. (2023). Fintech innovations: Risk mitigation strategies in Islamic finance. In *Fintech Applications in Islamic Finance* (pp. 35–58). AI, Machine Learning, and Blockchain Techniques., DOI: 10.4018/979-8-3693-1038-0.ch003

Kismawadi, E. R., Irfan, M., Haron, R., & Masitah, M. (2024). Bridging Finance and Sustainability: Islamic Financial Institutions' Contributions to the Transition to Sustainable Energy. In Irfan, M., Hussainey, K., Bukhari, S. A. C., & Nam, Y. (Eds.), *Issues of Sustainability in AI and New-Age Thematic Investing* (pp. 138–161). IGI Global., DOI: 10.4018/979-8-3693-3282-5.ch009

Kunhibava, S., Mustapha, Z., Muneeza, A., Sa'ad, A. A., & Karim, M. E. (2020). ukūk on blockchain: A legal, regulatory and Sharī'ah review. *ISRA International Journal of Islamic Finance*, 13(1), 118–135. DOI: 10.1108/IJIF-06-2020-0120

Ledhem, M. A., & Mekidiche, M. (2022). Islamic finance and economic growth: The Turkish experiment. *ISRA International Journal of Islamic Finance*, 14(1), 4–19. DOI: 10.1108/IJIF-12-2020-0255

Leng, J., Ruan, G., Jiang, P., Xu, K., Liu, Q., Zhou, X., & Liu, C. (2020). Blockchain-empowered sustainable manufacturing and product lifecycle management in industry 4.0: A survey. *Renewable & Sustainable Energy Reviews*, 132, 110112. Advance online publication. DOI: 10.1016/j.rser.2020.110112

Mohammed, M. M., Tok, M. E., & Ali, S. N. (2020). The potential of islamic finance in reinforcing and regaining economic stability in qatar. *Journal of Economic Cooperation and Development*, 41(4), 191–217. https://www.scopus.com/inward/record.uri?eid=2-s2.0-85108997153&partnerID=40&md5=b6f650421b41a515a9cc8ac6bda4f18c

Mohd Daud, M. A., Rosly, S. A., & Muhamad Sori, Z. (2021). Structuring fund for affordable housing investment in Malaysia: An exploratory research. *International Journal of Housing Markets and Analysis*, 14(2), 260–271. DOI: 10.1108/IJHMA-03-2020-0024

Mohd Noh, M. S., Nor Azelan, S. H., & Zulkepli, M. I. S. (2024). A review on Gharar dimension in modern Islamic finance transactions. *Journal of Islamic Accounting and Business Research*. Advance online publication. DOI: 10.1108/JIABR-01-2023-0006

Mukhlisin, M., al-Falih, A. A., Azid, T., & Shirazi, N. S. (2023). The Indonesian Islamic capital market and achievement of Maqasad Al-sHari'ah: Success or failure. In *Islamic Economic Institutions In Indonesia* (pp. 209–226). Are They Successful In Achieving The Maqasad-al-shari'ah., DOI: 10.1142/9789811272691_0012

Naz, S. A., & Gulzar, S. (2023). Islamic financial development & economic growth: The emergence of Islamic financial market in Pakistan. *Journal of Islamic Accounting and Business Research*, 14(6), 989–1012. DOI: 10.1108/JIABR-09-2022-0222

Nazeri, A. N. N., Nor, S. M., Abdul-Rahman, A., Abdul-Majid, M., & Hamid, S. N. A. (2023). EXPLORATION OF A NEW ZAKAT MANAGEMENT SYSTEM EMPOWERED BY BLOCKCHAIN TECHNOLOGY IN MALAYSIA. *ISRA International Journal of Islamic Finance*, 15(4), 127–147. DOI: 10.55188/ijif.v15i4.568

Noordin, N. H., Haron, S. N., Hasan, A., & Hassan, R. (2018). Complying with the requirements for issuance of SRI sukuk: The case of Khazanah's Sukuk Ihsan. *Journal of Islamic Accounting and Business Research*, 9(3), 415–433. DOI: 10.1108/JIABR-02-2016-0024

Pang, L., Zhu, M. N., & Yu, H. (2022). Is green finance really a blessing for green technology and carbon efficiency? *Energy Economics*, 114, 106272. Advance online publication. DOI: 10.1016/j.eneco.2022.106272

Pe'er, G., Bonn, A., Bruelheide, H., Dieker, P., Eisenhauer, N., Feindt, P. H., Hagedorn, G., Hansjürgens, B., Herzon, I., Lomba, Â., Marquard, E., Moreira, F., Nitsch, H., Oppermann, R., Perino, A., Röder, N., Schleyer, C., Schindler, S., Wolf, C., & Lakner, S. (2020). Action needed for the EU Common Agricultural Policy to address sustainability challenges. *People and Nature*, 2(2), 305–316. DOI: 10.1002/pan3.10080 PMID: 32626843

Putriana, V. T. (2024). Examining a distinctive loan contract "Pagang Gadai" practiced in a Muslim society: An Islamic finance perspective. *Journal of Islamic Accounting and Business Research*. Advance online publication. DOI: 10.1108/JIABR-10-2023-0341

Qanas, J., & Sawyer, M. (2022). Financialisation in the Gulf States. *Review of Political Economy*. Advance online publication. DOI: 10.1080/09538259.2022.2099669

Rabbani, M. R., Bashar, A., Nawaz, N., Karim, S., Ali, M. A. M., Rahiman, H. U., & Alam, M. S. (2021). Exploring the role of islamic fintech in combating the aftershocks of covid-19: The open social innovation of the islamic financial system. *Journal of Open Innovation*, 7(2), 136. Advance online publication. DOI: 10.3390/joitmc7020136

Ridho Kismawadi, E., Irfan, M., & Shah, S. M. A. R. (2023). Revolutionizing islamic finance: Artificial intelligence's role in the future of industry. In *The Impact of AI Innovation on Financial Sectors in the Era of Industry 5.0* (pp. 184–207). DOI: 10.4018/979-8-3693-0082-4.ch011

Rubbab, U.-E., Irshad, M., Abid, S., Ejaz, S., Ejaz, F., & Hossain, M. B. (2024). Examining the impact of Islamic work ethics on employee voice behavior: Mediating effect of felt obligation for constructive change and moderating role of sanctification of work. *Cogent Psychology*, 11(1), 2348860. Advance online publication. DOI: 10.1080/23311908.2024.2348860

Saiti, B., & Abdullah, A. (2015). Sale of goods and sale of debts: A comparative analysis. *Al-Shajarah, 20*(Specialissue), 249–272. https://www.scopus.com/inward/record.uri?eid=2-s2.0-85028459958&partnerID=40&md5=62ee30fdd6ddfcb45946a772fe68324f

Syed Nazim Ali, S. N. A.AliE-mail. (2020). Big Data, Islamic Finance, and Sustainable Development Goals. *Journal of King Abdulaziz University. Islamic Economics*, 33(1), 83–90. DOI: 10.4197/Islec.33-1.6

Wang, L., Wang, Y., Sun, Y., Han, K., & Chen, Y. (2022). Financial inclusion and green economic efficiency: Evidence from China. *Journal of Environmental Planning and Management*, 65(2), 240–271. DOI: 10.1080/09640568.2021.1881459

Wanke, P., Hassan, M. K., Azad, M. A. K., Rahman, M. A., & Akther, N. (2022). Application of a distributed verification in Islamic microfinance institutions: A sustainable model. *Financial Innovation*, 8(1), 80. Advance online publication. DOI: 10.1186/s40854-022-00384-z

Yadav, G., Luthra, S., Jakhar, S. K., Mangla, S. K., & Rai, D. P. (2020). A framework to overcome sustainable supply chain challenges through solution measures of industry 4.0 and circular economy: An automotive case. *Journal of Cleaner Production*, 254, 120112. Advance online publication. DOI: 10.1016/j.jclepro.2020.120112

Yesuf, A. J., & Aassouli, D. (2020). Exploring synergies and performance evaluation between Islamic funds and socially responsible investment (SRIs) in light of the Sustainable Development Goals (SDGs). *Heliyon*, 6(8), e04562. Advance online publication. DOI: 10.1016/j.heliyon.2020.e04562 PMID: 32904259

Zain, N. S., & Muhamad Sori, Z. (2020). An exploratory study on Musharakah SRI Sukuk for the development of Waqf properties/assets in Malaysia. *Qualitative Research in Financial Markets*, 12(3), 301–314. DOI: 10.1108/QRFM-09-2018-0099

Chapter 11
An Econometric Analysis of the Influence of Exchange Rate Volatility on Trade Balance:
A Special Reference to India (2003-2022)

Umang Bhutani
Dev Samaj College for Women, India

Shefali Saini
Chandigarh University, India

ABSTRACT

This paper delves into the pivotal roles of exchange rates and balance of trade, influencing economic policies, trade dynamics, and the broader global market landscape. Focused on the interplay between exports and exchange rates from 2003 to 2022, this study employs a rigorous quantitative methodology. Leveraging the Auto Regressive Distributed Lag (ARDL) model in EViews-12, it meticulously analyzes the long-run relationship between these variables. Additionally, Granger causality tests are applied to unveil short-run dynamics. The findings underscore the substantial and positive impact of India's exports on its exchange rates, highlighting implications for both short-term fluctuations and long-term trends.

DOI: 10.4018/979-8-3693-6622-6.ch011

INTRODUCTION

An economy depends heavily on foreign exchange since the value of a certain currency indicates the strength of a country's economy. Therefore, the most qualified specialists and technocrats, who are typically gathered at the top financial institution, are in charge of managing it rather than leaving it to chance (Segal, 2021). Since the beginning of the floating exchange rate regime in 1973, this corpus of study has expanded tremendously, particularly in the post-Bretton Woods era when the foreign currency rate has been extremely volatile (Mitchell, 2023).

An important metric in economics is the exchange rate, which shows how much one currency can be swapped for another (Roy, Suvendu. 2021). To make payments to other nations for products, services, and interest on loans for investment purposes, foreign currency is needed (*Methods of Payment*, n.d.). In the flexible exchange system, exchange rates are regulated by the interplay between supply and demand. An upsurge in imports generates a heightened demand for the foreign currency of the exporting nation, whereas an upswing in exports results in an increased supply of the same foreign currency (Mishkin, 2007).

The trade policy of India underwent a transformation in 1991 due to its economic liberalisation, resulting in a rise in exports, diversification, and foreign investment(*Indian Economy: An Overview*, n.d.).Between 1957 and 2021, India's Balance of Trade averaged -2.97 USD Billion (D, n.d.). Trade is an essential economic statistic that shows how well a country is performing in global trade. A positive trade balance can result in an increase in the value of a country's currency, whereas a negative balance might affect inflation levels and the ability to borrow money. Policymakers diligently track trade balance data to guide choices, promote sustainable economic expansion, and facilitate India's entrance into the global market (*Global Strategic Institute for Sustainable Development | Department of Economic and Social Affairs*, 2023).

Figure 1. Line graph showing net exports over the years

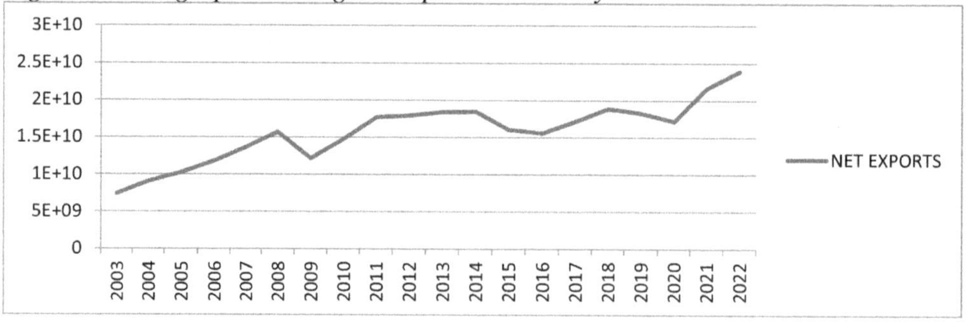

Figure 2. Line graph showing exchange rate over the years

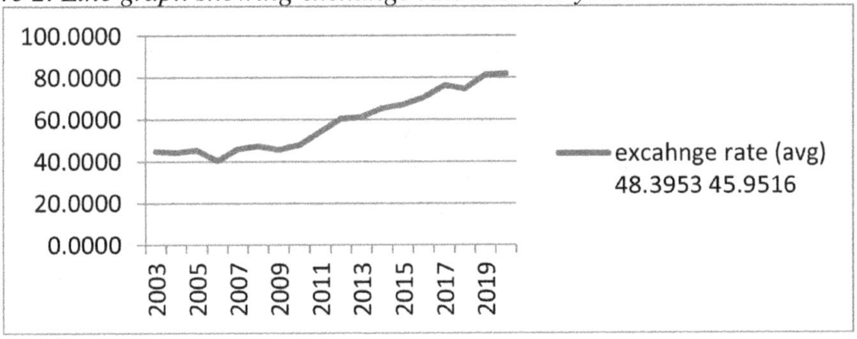

This study looks into whether changes in exchange rates have a noticeable and direct effect on India's trade balances with other countries.

Objective

This study aims to examine the short-term and long-term connection between net exports (expressed as NX) and exchange rates (expressed as XR) in India from 2003 to 2022.

Review of Literature

Thahara et al. (2021) investigated the relationship between the exchange rate and Trade Balance in Sri Lanka for the time period 1977 to 2019. Trade Balance is used as the dependent variable, and the independent variables are Exchange Rate, Gross Domestic Product, and Inflation. Augmented Dickey-Fuller unit root test was adopted to test the stationary property of time series data, Auto Regressive Distributed Lag model was employed to find the long run and short-run relationship and long-run adjustment, Bound test approach, the unrestricted Error Correction Model and Granger Causality Test are used to analyze the data. The research findings suggest that the exchange rate has the adverse effects on Trade balance in the long run.

Oluyemi and Isaac (2017) conducted a study on the effect of exchange rate on imports and exports in Nigeria by using monthly data from the year 1996 to 2015. The study used augmented dickey fuller test to check the stationarity of each of the variables. The results found that the exchange rate have a positive and insignificant effect on imports while have a negative and insignificant effect on exports in Nigeria.

Ahmed et al. (2017) examined a study on the impact of exchange rate on exports in case of Pakistan by using annual time series data from the time period 1970 to 2015. The study used secondary data which is taken from the official site of the international monetary fund and world bank. Augmented dicky fuller test and Phillip-person test is used to test the stationarity and Autoregressive distributive lag model is used to check the relationship between the variables. The results shown that the exchange rate have negative but insignificant impact on exports of Pakistan.

Adam et al. (2017) investigated the dynamic relationship between exchange and the Indonesia's exports by using monthly timeseries data from the time period 2001 to 2015. The data is collected from the central bureau of statistics and vector autoregression, granger causality and ARDL method is used to check the relationship between the variables. The results found the negative relationship between the variables.

Liew et al. (2016) examined a study on the relationship between the exchange rate and trade balance of the ASEAN countries by using yearly time series data from the time period 1986 to 1999. The purchasing power parity theory is used to check the relationship between the variables which concluded that the trade balance has negatively affected on the nominal exchange rate.

Altintas et al. (2011) conducted a study on the impact of exchange rate volatility on Turkish exports by using quarterly time series data from the time period 1993 to 2009. The data is extracted from the online sources of the OECD website and the study used autoregressive distributive lag model for the analysis. The results suggest that exchange rate volatility has positive and statistically significant impact on Turkish exports.

Jian (2007) examined the effect of real exchange rate misalignment of RMB on china's exports using annual data from the time period 1978 to 2005. The study used error correction model to check the analysis, and the results found that the real exchange rate has a negative effect on export.

Oyovwi (2012) studied the effect of exchange rates volatility on economic growth in Nigeria using annual data from 1970 to 2009. Generalized autoregressive conditional heteroscedasticity (GARCH) method is used to test the exchange rate volatility and the findings shown that in the short run, economic growth had positively responsive to exchange rate volatility, while in long run a negative relationship existed between the two variables.

Hypothesis

H0- There is a long-term relationship between the exchange rate and the trade balance.

H1- There is no long-term relationship between the exchange rate and the trade balance.

DATA SOURCES AND METHODOLOGY

Annual time series data is taken from the Handbook on Indian economy by RBI and database of World Bank for the years 2003- 2022.The data has been analysed in E views-12 statistical software. Moreover, for the empirical analyses, the variables are transformed into their natural algorithm to reduce the disturbing influence of the outliers in the extracted data. The study utilized data on net exports and exchange rates collected from 2003 to 2022

Long-Run Analysis: ARDL Bounds testing Approach

The study employed the ARDL Bounds testing technique to analyse the long-term correlation between the variables for the period from 2003 to 2022. The estimation procedure involves the succeeding steps. To test for the presence of a unit root in the variables, the Augmented Dickey-Fuller test(ADF) by D.A. Dickey is used. . Based on the results, in the next step, ARDL Bound testing approach is used to analyse the long-run relationship between the variables and in the last step, Granger's causality test in a multivariate VAR framework has been applied to deduce short-run relationship and direction of causality by using E-views software.

Exchange Rate is expressed as (XR) and balance of trade is expressed as BOT. The regression model of the study is as follows:

$$BOT= f(XR) \qquad (1)$$

Transforming the equation (1) into linear equation

$$BOT_t = \alpha_o + \alpha_1 XR + \varepsilon_{1t} \qquad (2)$$

Where, $\alpha_{o,}$ is a constant, α_1 is a coefficient of BOT and ε_{1t} is the error term in the model which is in the equation (2). All the variables are transformed into their natural logarithms. Therefore, the final description of the model is presented in succeeding equation:

$$lnBOT_t = \alpha_o + \alpha_1 lnXR + \varepsilon_{1t}. \qquad (3)$$

Firstly, the stationarity of the variables is checked as the ARDL method needs variables to be stationary at either I(0) or I(1) levels. Unit root tests are broadly used to check stationarity. The present study has used ADF to check the unit root at both level and at the first difference level. The null hypotheses in the ADF test is that- lnBOT and lnXR have unit root i.e. the series is non-stationary. The results are exhibited in Table 1 and 2.

Table 1. Unit Root Table: ADF, Log XR

Tests	ADF
Level (Intercept)	0.97993
Level (Trend and Intercept)	0.2067
1st Difference (Level)	0.0021**

Note: 1. The results have been computed by using ADF test using EViews software 12.
2. The symbols *, **, and *** signify statistical significance at the 10%, 5%, and 1% levels, respectively.
Source: Computed

Table 2. Unit Root Table: ADF, Log net exports

Tests	ADF
Level (Intercept)	0.1976
Level (Trend and Intercept)	0.1922
1st Difference (Level)	0.0009**

Note: 1. The results have been computed by using ADF test using EViews software 12.
2. The symbols *, **, and *** signify statistical significance at the 10%, 5%, and 1% levels, respectively.
Source: Computed

The results from the tests show that lnXR is stationary at I(1) by using ADF, as depicted in Table 1. The p-value is statistically significant at 0.0021 by using ADF test. Whereas, lnNX is stationary at I(1) by using the ADF test as shown in Table 2 i.e., at 0.0009 at both level and intercept by using ADF. The results qualifies for the usage of ARDL model to deduce the long-run relationship between the variables. In the next step, the existence of long-run relationship will be examined by using the Bounds test approach. Following is the ARDL equation of the model, when BOT is a dependent variable:

$\Delta\ln(BOT)t = \alpha 0 + \sum_{j=1}^{n} bj\Delta\ln(BOT)_{t-1} + \sum_{j=0}^{n} cj\Delta\ln(XR)_{t-1} + \delta 1\ln(BOT)_{t-1} + \delta 2\ln(XR)_{t-1} + \varepsilon_{1t.}$ Where δ1 and δ2 are the long-run multipliers in the ARDL model, while bj and cj are the short-term dynamic coefficients. The null hypothesis, H01: $\delta 1 = \delta 2 = 0$, which assumes no co-integration, is being tested against the alternative hypothesis, H11: $\delta 1 \neq \delta 2 \neq 0$, which suggests the presence of co-integration. Table 3 presents the outcomes of the Bounds test.

Table 3. F- Bounds test

Significance	10%	5%	2.5%	1%
I(0)	3.02	3.62	4.18	4.94
I(1)	3.51	4.16	4.79	5.58

F-Statistic 4.359093
Source: Computed

According to the criterion, we cannot reject the null hypothesis if the f-value is lower than the I(0) bound. Suppose the f-value is higher than the I(1) bound. In that case, we can reject the null hypothesis and accept the alternative hypothesis that there is a long-run co-integration relationship between the variables. If the f-statistic falls between the bounds, the test is inconclusive. The ARDL Bounds test findings indicate that the f-statistic value, 4.359093, exceeds the I(1) Bound value of 4.16, even at a significance level of 5%. This strongly supports the presence of a long-term relationship between the variables. The subsequent phase will involve the analysis of short-term causation through the utilization of VAR Granger causality.

Short-Run Analysis: VAR Granger Causality

The null hypothesis posits no short-term causal relationship between the variables, while the alternative hypothesis posits that there is such a relationship between the variables from 2003 to 2022. According to econometric rules, the null hypothesis is rejected when the p-value is below the 5% threshold.

Table 4. Pairwise Granger Casuality Tests

Null Hypothesis	Obs.	F statistic	Prob
Log XR does not granger cause log BOT	18	1.83623	0.1984
Log BOT does not Granger Cause Log XR		5.64347	0.0172

Source- computed

In the next step, the VAR Granger Causality Test by C. Granger (1969 and 1980) has been applied to analyse the short-run causality between the variables. The results depicted in Table 4 clearly show a uni-directional causality running from lnBOT to lnXR, in the short-period at a 5% level of significance, i.e., 0.0172 < 5% level of significance. Whereas other way causality was not found as the p-value is statistically insignificant i.e., 0.1984 > 5% level of significance.

Residual Testing

Residual testing of the model has been done, and the results are presented in tables 5 and 6. Since the p-value in both cases is above the 5% level of significance i.e., at 0.1823 and 0.6608 respectively for serial correlation and heteroscedasticity. Thus, we conclude that the model is fitted well and is also free from both problems.

Table 5. Breusch-Godfrey Serial Correlation LM Tests

Adjusted R-square	R-square	Prob
-0.065662	0.230355	0.1823

Source- computed

Table 6. Breusch-Godfrey Heteroskedasticity Tests

F-statistic	Prob.
0.542158	0.6608

Source- computed

Normality Testing

Figure 3. Normality test conducted on the dataset

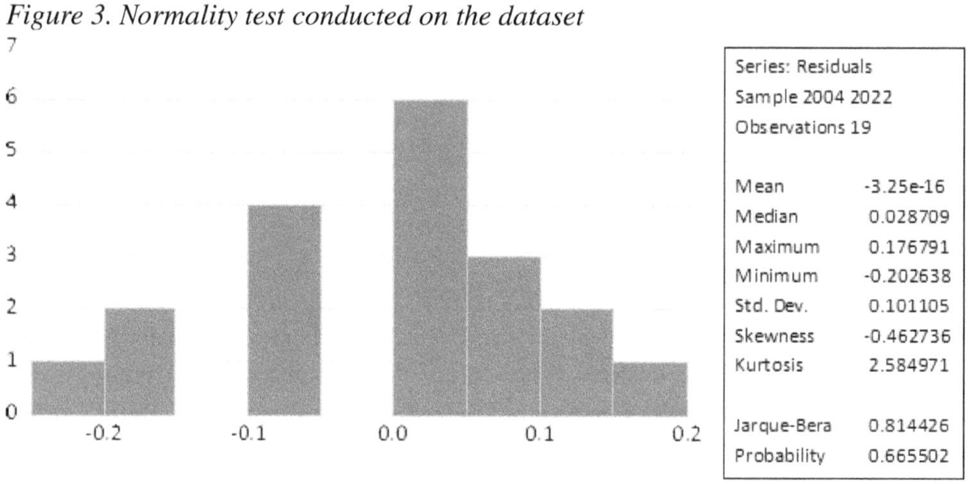

Source: Eviews 12

Figure 3, above depicts the results of the normality test conducted on the dataset. The null hypothesis posits that the data is normally distributed, while the alternative hypothesis suggests otherwise. With a p-value exceeding the 5% significance level ($p = 0.665502$), we fail to reject the null hypothesis. Thus, based on this analysis, we conclude that the data is normally distributed.

CONCLUSION

This study has examined the correlation between fluctuations in exchange rates and the trade balance in India throughout the period of 2003 to 2022. The analysis was performed utilising the ARDL Bounds testing technique and VAR Granger Causality tests.

The study's findings indicate that India's exports exert a substantial and favourable influence on India's exchange rate, both in the short term and the long term. This implies that an increase in exports leads to an appreciation of the Indian rupee against other currencies, while a decrease in exports leads to depreciation.

Additionally, the ARDL Bounds testing approach provides evidence that there is a long-term connection between the volatility of the exchange rate and the trade balance in India.. This suggests that changes in exchange rates have a persistent effect on India's trade balance over time.

Furthermore, the VAR Granger Causality tests indicate a uni-directional causality running from exports to exchange rate in the short run. This implies that changes in India's exports cause changes in the exchange rate, but not vice versa, in the short term.

Overall, these findings enhance the comprehension of the relationship between the fluctuation of currency rates and the trade balance in India. It is recommended that authorities closely monitor the influence of currency exchange rate variations on India's trade balance and take steps to minimise any adverse consequences.

REFERENCES

Adam, P., Nusantara, A. W., & Muthalib, A. A. (2017). A Model of the Dynamic of the Relationship between Exchange Rate and Indonesia's Export. *International Journal of Economics and Financial Issues*, 7(1), 255–261.

Ahmad, D., Afzal, M., & Khan, U. G. (2017). Impact of exports on economic growth empirical evidence of Pakistan. *International Journal of Applied*, 5(2), 9.

Alsanusi, M., Altintaş, H., & Alnour, M.ALSANUSİ. (2022, December 31). The role of real exchange rate in the trade balance between Turkey and Libya: Evidence from nonlinear and wavelet-based approaches. *Journal of Ekonomi*, 4(2), 46–56. DOI: 10.58251/ekonomi.1173205

Altintaş, H., Cetin, R., & Öz, B. (2011). The impact of exchange rate volatility on Turkish exports: 1993-2009. *South East European Journal of Economics and Business*, 6(2), 71–81. DOI: 10.2478/v10033-011-0017-8

Altintas, K. M.Kadir Murat Altintas. (2011, October 28). The dynamics of financial literacy within the framework of personal finance: An analysis among Turkish University Students. *African Journal of Business Management*, 5(26). Advance online publication. DOI: 10.5897/AJBM11.401

Bhat, S. A., & Bhat, J. A. (2020, November 2). Impact of Exchange Rate Changes on the Trade Balance of India: An Asymmetric Nonlinear Cointegration Approach. *Foreign Trade Review*, 56(1), 71–88. DOI: 10.1177/0015732520961328

Brada, J. C., Kutan, A. M., & Zhou, S. (1997, June). The exchange rate and the balance of trade: The Turkish experience. *The Journal of Development Studies*, 33(5), 675–692. DOI: 10.1080/00220389708422489

D, S. K. (n.d.). *Balance of Trade - Indian Economy Notes*. Prepp. https://prepp.in/news/e-492-balance-of-trade-indian-economy-notes

Dogo, M. Y., & Aras, O. N. (2021, September 18). EFFECT OF VOLATILITY IN THE NAIRA - DOLLAR EXCHANGE RATE ON THE VOLUME OF IMPORTS TO, AND EXPORTS FROM NIGERIA. *International Journal of Economics and Financial Issues*, 11(5), 68–73. DOI: 10.32479/ijefi.11799

Dogru, T., Isik, C., & Sirakaya-Turk, E. (2019, October). The balance of trade and exchange rates: Theory and contemporary evidence from tourism. *Tourism Management*, 74, 12–23. DOI: 10.1016/j.tourman.2019.01.014

Global Strategic Institute for Sustainable Development | Department of Economic and Social Affairs. (2023, March 24). https://sdgs.un.org/partnerships/global-strategic-institute-sustainable-development

Indian Economy: An Overview. (n.d.). Invest India. https://www.investindia.gov.in/team-india-blogs/indian-economy-overview

Jian, L. Ü. (2007). Empirical study on the infl uence of RMB exchange rate mis-alignment on China's export. *Frontiers of Economics in China*, 2(2), 224–236. DOI: 10.1007/s11459-007-0012-2

Liew, V. K. S., Tan, W. Y., & Ho, L. S. (2016). The relationship between exchange rate and trade balance in ASEAN countries: Evidence from time series data. *Asian Economic Policy Review*, 11(2), 234–250. DOI: 10.1111/aepr.12157

Lioudis, N. (2023, August 22). *How the Balance of Trade Affects Currency Exchange Rates*. Investopedia. https://www.investopedia.com/ask/answers/041515/how-does-balance-trade-impact-currency-exchange-rates.asp

Mishkin, F. S. (2007, January 1). *The Economics of Money, Banking, and Financial Markets*. Pearson Education. http://books.google.ie/books?id=ni8yiX9JsAsC&printsec=frontcover&dq=10:+0-13-473382-7&hl=&cd=1&source=gbs_api

Mitchell, C. (2023, September 7). *Floating Exchange Rate: What It Is, How It Works, History*. Investopedia. https://www.investopedia.com/terms/f/floatingexchangerate.asp

Oluyemi, O., & Isaac, E. D. (2017). The effect of exchange rate on imports and exports in Nigeria from January 1996 to June 2015. International journal of economics and business management, 3(2), 66-77.

Oyovwi, O. D. (2012). Exchange rate volatility and imports in Nigeria. *Academic Journal of Interdisciplinary Studies*, 1(2), 103–114.

Segal, T. (2021, June 4). *Currency Fluctuations: How they Affect the Economy*. Investopedia. https://www.investopedia.com/articles/forex/080613/effects-currency-fluctuations-economy.asp

Shuaibu, M., & Isah, A. (2020). Exchange Rate Dynamics and Trade Balance in Selected African Countries. *Journal of African Trade*, 7(1–2), 69. DOI: 10.2991/jat.k.201218.001

Thahara, A. F., Rinosha, K. F., & Shifaniya, A. J. F. (2021). The relationship between exchange rate and trade balance: Empirical evidence from Sri Lanka.

Chapter 12
What's Next After Achieving 100% Level of Financial Inclusion?

Peterson K. Ozili
https://orcid.org/0000-0001-6292-1161
Central Bank of Nigeria, Nigeria

ABSTRACT

This study considers a world where it is possible to attain full financial inclusion where full financial inclusion means achieving a 100% level of financial inclusion in whichever way financial inclusion is measured. This study examines the possible course of actions which policymakers can take after achieving full financial inclusion. This study also explores the philosophical nature of this question by casting some light into whether attaining full financial inclusion is a worthwhile goal for policymakers to focus on. The insights offered in this study are useful to scholars and policymakers and those responsible for advancing financial inclusion in their countries.

1. INTRODUCTION

This study examines the possible course of actions which policymakers can take after achieving full financial inclusion. Financial inclusion refers to access and use of affordable formal financial services for every member of the population (Demirgüç-Kunt et al, 2015). Broadly speaking, financial inclusion means that individuals and businesses have access to useful and affordable financial products and services that meet their needs such as credit, current account, savings, payment and insurance products that enable them to participate fully and meaningfully in

DOI: 10.4018/979-8-3693-6622-6.ch012

the formal financial system (Ozili, 2021). Financial inclusion is important because it gives people access to formal credit and other financial products and services which they can use to improve their welfare and live a better life (Demirgüç-Kunt et al, 2015; Ozili, 2021).

In society today, it is easy to see the efforts made by private corporations, governmental organizations, international organizations, and non-governmental organizations to increase the level of financial inclusion in developed and developing countries. Their collective efforts have led to significant increase in formal account ownership, bank branch expansion, increase in ATM penetration, large number of fintech and Bigtech providers, increase in mobile money wallets and the development of national financial inclusion strategies, all of which are aimed at increasing the level of financial inclusion (Ozili, 2021). Among the initiatives introduced to increase financial inclusion, the most notable initiative in most societies today is the use of technological innovations and digital tools to increase financial access, affordability and financial literacy for unbanked and vulnerable people (Kouladoum et al, 2022; Shen et al, 2020; Ambarkhane et al, 2022; Elzahi Saaid Ali, 2022), and it enables them to manage their own financial future independently of others so that they can make decisions that improve their welfare (Pal et al, 2022; Ozili, 2018). These technology-driven initiatives also aim to increase the level of digital financial inclusion to a high point.

This high point is expected to be a 100 percent level of financial inclusion because it is the highest level of financial inclusion that can be attained if we accept the World Bank, IMF, the Gates Foundation, and central banks' approach to measuring financial inclusion which is to measure financial inclusion in terms of a percentage point which lies within the range of 0% to 100% (Demirgüç-Kunt and Klapper, 2012). Under this setting, we can reasonably expect that full financial inclusion is achieved when the level of financial inclusion reaches a 100-percentage point. This idea is supported by evidence from the 2021 Global Findex database which show that several countries are already close to reaching a 100 percent level of financial inclusion. For instance, in 2021, the level of financial inclusion, measured by the percentage of people who reported owning a formal account of any type, reached 99 percent in Australia, Belgium, Estonia, France, Luxembourg, New Zealand, Norway, Slovenia, and Switzerland, while the level of financial inclusion reached a 100 percent in countries like Austria, Canada, Denmark, Finland, Germany, Iceland, Ireland, the Netherlands, the United Kingdom and Sweden according to the 2021 Global Findex database. The countries at the 99 percent level will likely attain a 100 percent level of financial inclusion in the coming years, while policymakers in the countries that have already attained the 100 percent high point will be faced with the question: Where do we go from here? What should we do next? This is the big question which nobody is asking or researching.

The financial inclusion literature is filled with research that proffer strategies for increasing the level of financial inclusion in developing countries (Joshi, 2014; Güngen, 2018; Chandran, 2011). However, the literature is silent on the next steps that countries can take after attaining the highest level of financial inclusion possible. There is a need to gain insights into the next course of actions that policymakers can take after a country has attained the highest level of financial inclusion possible. Such insight can offer a new direction to those responsible for advancing financial inclusion in their countries. This study addresses this question by identifying the possible course of actions that can be taken after a country has achieved full financial inclusion.

This study contributes to the existing literature by offering insights that can guide policymakers in developed countries in determining the next course of actions to take after attaining full financial inclusion. Policymakers need to know the next course of actions to take after attaining full financial inclusion. Without knowing this, they may get carried away by the international accolades and recognition that come with achieving a 100 percent level of financial inclusion. They may become complacent in their financial inclusion efforts and end up achieving a level of financial inclusion that falls below the 100 percent mark, just after attaining the 100 percent mark in the previous period. This event was witnessed in Australia and Norway which attained a 100 percent level of financial inclusion in 2017 but witnessed a decrease in the level of financial inclusion to 99 percent in 2021 according to the 2021 Global Findex database. This event demonstrates how important it is for policymakers to gain insight into the course of actions they need to take after attaining a high level of financial inclusion in order to avoid a downward trend in the level of financial inclusion. Therefore, this study provides insight to guide policymakers on what they need to do after attaining full financial inclusion.

The rest of the study is structured as follows. Section 2 reviews the literature that offer strategies to increase financial inclusion. Section 3 presents a discussion of the next course of action to take after attaining the highest level of financial inclusion. Section 4 presents some criticism of achieving full financial inclusion. Section 5 presents the conclusion of the study.

2. LITERATURE REVIEW

In the literature, several studies suggest ways to increase the level of financial inclusion. For instance, Milana and Ashta (2020) suggest that microfinance is useful for increasing financial inclusion because microfinance gives poor people the funds, they need to engage in entrepreneurial activities that would lift them out of poverty. However, they showed that despite the provision of microcredit by microfinance institutions to poor people, microfinance institutions have not been able to raise the living standard of clients due to the social divide and the inequalities that affect access and use of microfinance. Kumar and Pathak (2022) considered the role of financial awareness in fostering financial inclusion in some states in India. They found that more financial awareness increases the level of financial inclusion. Kim and De Moor (2017), in a survey, showed that crowdfunding can enable financial inclusion by helping to democratise access to capital. It enables people to access little amounts of capital to start a business and to improve their welfare.

Strøm et al (2016) argued that female leaders of microfinance institutions, whether a female CEO, female chair, or female directors, tend to give more priority to poor people in access to, and provision of, credit than male leaders. Their findings imply that female leaders are more effective in promoting financial inclusion for the poor. Aga et al (2014) used data from the World Bank survey of more than 10,000 households in Burkina Faso, Kenya, Nigeria, Senegal, and Uganda, to examine the relationship between international remittances and the financial inclusion of households in Sub-Saharan Africa. The study found that people who receive international remittances are more likely to open a bank account in all the five countries. The findings imply that foreign remittances are important drivers of financial inclusion in some sub-Saharan African countries.

Senou et al (2019) focused on whether digital technology is an enabler of financial inclusion. They examined the role of digital technologies in accelerating mobile phone penetration and internet usage in selected WAEMU countries. They analysed data obtained from the Central Bank of West African States (BCEAO) and the International Telecommunication Union from 2006 to 2017 and found evidence that both mobile phone penetration and Internet usage significantly increase financial inclusion in the WAEMU countries. The authors urge policy makers to use legislation to enhance the ability of mobile financial services providers to increase financial inclusion.

Broekhoff et al (2024) argued that increasing trust in the payment system can enable financial inclusion. However, in their study, they observed that people who have low digital skills and people with financial difficulties have low levels of trust in the payment system. Their findings suggest that increasing digital literacy and increasing financial capacity of people would increase trust in the payment system which, in turn, will increase financial inclusion. Shaikh (2023) was more concerned about whether mobile money can meet the needs of the less privileged people in developing and emerging markets. They examined whether mobile money services are a determinant of digital financial inclusion in Ghana. They found evidence that the credibility of mobile money agents and the quality of their service are factors promoting financial inclusion in Ghana. Ediagbonya and Tioluwani (2023) examine the role of financial technology in accelerating financial inclusion in Nigeria.

They showed that the presence of digital platforms and the use of smartphones are effective in accelerating financial inclusion in Nigeria, even though the gaps in financial inclusion are caused by illiteracy, poor infrastructural facilities, poor electricity supply, and unexplained transaction charges.

Morgan (2022) examined how fintech is driving financial inclusion in the Association of Southeast Asian Nations (ASEAN) member countries and India. They showed that Fintech is contributing to financial inclusion by providing newly banked customers with access to a means for savings, investment, consumption smoothing, and insurance. Fintech is also being used to deliver financial services to consumers and businesses through smartphones. Khan et al (2023) considered the role of cybersecurity in promoting financial inclusion. They found that strong cybersecurity reduces the adverse effect of cyber threats to financial inclusion. The authors suggest the need for banks to enhance their cybersecurity control to reduce the occurrences of cyber-attacks that could hinder financial inclusion. While these studies suggest ways to increase the level of financial inclusion, they do not suggest the next course of actions that countries can take after achieving a 100 percent level of financial inclusion. The present study fills a gap in the literature by offering insights into the course of actions that countries can take after achieving a 100 percent level of financial inclusion.

3. WHAT DOES A 100 PERCENT LEVEL OF FINANCIAL INCLUSION MEAN?

A 100 percent level of financial inclusion, also known as full financial inclusion, means that all individuals and members of society have access to useful and affordable financial products and services that meet their needs such as credit, current account, savings, payment and insurance products that enable them to participate fully and meaningfully in the formal financial system (Ouma et al, 2017). It means that every individual in a country has a formal account or a mobile money account which becomes the access point to the formal financial system and enables them to use savings, payment, credit and insurance products to improve their welfare. A 100 percent level of financial inclusion means that everybody is included in the formal financial system, and nobody is left behind or left out. Having established what a 100 percent level of financial inclusion means, it is important to state what it is not. Achieving a 100 percent level of financial inclusion does not mean that there is no informal economy or that nobody is operating in the informal sector. Rather, it could mean that people in the formal financial sector are also actively participating in the informal sector. This would occur if financially people need some services which are offered in the informal sector, but which are not offered in the formal financial sector. As a result, the informal sector will continue to exist and remain active if formally included people continue to demand services offered in the informal sector which are not available in the formal financial sector. Furthermore, a 100 percent level of financial inclusion does not mean that people are using formal financial services frequently. People who have access to formal credit may choose not to take a loan. People who have a credit card may choose not to use the credit card. People who have access to cheap insurance may choose not to take it, and people who have a bank account may choose not to deposit any money in their account for a long time. This shows that a 100 percent level of financial inclusion does not mean that all financially included people are actively using the formal financial services they now have access to.

4. STEPS TO TAKE AFTER ACHIEVING A 100 PERCENT LEVEL OF FINANCIAL INCLUSION

This section details the steps which those responsible for financial inclusion can take after attaining a 100 percent level of financial inclusion.

4.1. Do Nothing

As bizarre as it sounds, developed countries that have attained a 100 percent level of financial inclusion may do nothing after the achievement. Policymakers in these countries may prefer to do nothing other than to celebrate the achievement. They may organize some events to announce the achievement and to appreciate the public sector and private sector stakeholders that played a significant role in achieving a 100 percent level of financial inclusion. The event will allow stakeholders to express positive feelings about the achievement. After the celebration, the euphoria dims, and nobody does anything due to complacency or the belief that the 100 percent level of financial inclusion will continue forever (Du, 2018). But the rational mind knows that the achievement is only temporary if nothing is done after attaining full financial inclusion.

4.2. Reflect on the Achievement to Learn More

After achieving a 100 percent level of financial inclusion, policymakers and everyone involved in the financial inclusion process should reflect on the achievement. Such reflection would give everyone a positive sense of happiness about everything that was done right, as well as provide them with ideas for the things that can be done better (Matsuo, 2022). Policymakers and other financial inclusion stakeholders should look back at the entire financial inclusion process and the strategies that were adopted to note what was done, the mistakes that were made but were identified early and were corrected, the ideas that worked and those that did not work. Looking back to reflect on the entire financial inclusion strategies that were adopted will provide an opportunity for policymakers and everyone involved in the financial inclusion process to learn about why a 100 percent level of financial inclusion was achieved and what can be done to sustain the efforts that led to the attainment of a 100 percent level of financial inclusion.

4.3. Sustain the Current Effort Put into Achieving Full Financial Inclusion

Policymakers and everyone involved in the financial inclusion process should sustain the efforts they have put into achieving full financial inclusion if they want to maintain the highest level of financial inclusion. This means that sustainability is key. For instance, financial regulators should conduct regular surveillance of the financial ecosystem to identify early any market and non-market barriers to financial inclusion so that those barriers can be removed immediately (Ambarkhane et al, 2022). They should constantly monitor all financial access points in the country to ensure that all financial access points enabling financial inclusion in a fair and consistent manner (Garz et al, 2021). They should also continue to monitor the quality of financial service delivery to customers to ensure that customers are treated fairly by financial services providers and ensure that customers are receiving appropriate financial services. Customers should continue to report to the authorities any unfair and unethical practices of financial service providers that can hinder financial inclusion. Financial service providers should continue to inform the authorities about existing and new policies that might hinder their own efforts to increase financial inclusion for customers so that those policies can be modified or discontinued if they cannot be modified.

4.4. Identify and Close Any Inequality or Disparity in the Use of Formal Financial Services

Once every member of the population has been granted access to formal financial services, there may be unequal use of formal financial services across the population. Some segments of the population will use formal financial services to a greater extent than other segments of the population (Kulkarni and Ghosh, 2021). Therefore, policymakers should assess formal financial services usage data to identify the pattern of usage of formal financial services across all demographic segments of the population (Kulkarni and Ghosh, 2021). The assessment should also identify the areas or segments of the population that are affected by disparities in the use of formal financial services. For example, ethnic minorities, migrants, and low-income people tend to use formal financial services less frequently. The reasons for such disparities should be identified and the authorities responsible for financial inclusion should put measures in place to close any disparity that exists in the use of formal financial services in the population.

4.5. Deepen the Use of Formal Financial Services Across the Population

After every individual in the population has been granted access to formal financial services, policymakers should focus on deepening financial inclusion. Policymakers can deepen the use of formal financial services by supporting the use of existing and new digital technologies to (i) accept payments from customers through debit cards, credit cards and other payment channels, (ii) enable offline payments for cardholders in remote areas and informal economic sectors, (iii) offer more effective banking services, (iv) offer a one-stop shop for financial services which fosters easy access to a variety of financial products and services, (v) deliver tailored financial services to new customer segments, and (vi) encourage specialization in financial services to meet specialized needs (Waema and Omwansa, 2014). At the same time, policymakers should also facilitate interagency policy coordination, upgrade existing supervisory and regulatory frameworks, and update their national financial inclusion strategy to include new infrastructure, technology, products, services and institutions that facilitate the deepening of financial inclusion (Capital, 2019).

4.6. Pursue a Completely Different Goal if There is No Room for Further Improvement in Financial Inclusion

After achieving full financial inclusion, policymakers should consider pursuing another important national goal if there is no room for further improvement after a 100 percent level of financial inclusion has been achieved. The new goal might be to increase the level of social inclusion, economic inclusion, financial development or any other worthwhile goal (Seifert et al, 2021). Policymakers should be willing to pursue a new economic goal or a new development goal especially if they are confident that the attained full financial inclusion can be sustained without further policy support. The new goal should be meaningful, and they should develop strategies for achieving the goal and set a timeframe to achieve the goal.

4.7. Help Other Countries to Increase Their Level of Financial Inclusion

After a country has achieved a 100 percent level of financial inclusion and there is no scope for further improvement in financial inclusion in the country, the country should consider helping other countries to attain a high level of financial inclusion. The country can do this by sharing their financial inclusion strategies with countries experiencing low levels of financial inclusion and offer technical assistance where it is needed. In the process of helping others, the country offering assistance will be able to reinforce what it has learned when attaining full financial inclusion and will learn new things in the process of assisting other countries. Alternatively, a country that has achieved a 100 percent level of financial inclusion can join international consortiums that are set up to assist poor and developing countries in increasing financial inclusion (Stein et al, 2011; Waema and Omwansa, 2014). The country can provide financial support and any other type of group support that would enable the consortium to assist poor and developing countries in increasing their level of financial inclusion.

5. CRITICISMS

Despite learning about what needs to be done after full financial inclusion has been achieved, there will be criticisms about whether achieving full financial inclusion is a worthwhile goal considering the subjective nature of all available financial inclusion indices. The first criticism relates to whether attaining full financial inclusion is a noble target which pursue policymakers should pursue. There could be other more noble causes such as attaining full employment, full economic inclusion and full social inclusion. The second criticism has to do with the belief that attaining a 100 percent level of financial inclusion would lead to a multidimensional improvement in people's lives (Mader, 2018). Some academic studies promote this belief by insinuating that high levels of financial inclusion would lead to significant improvement in people's lives (see, for example, Chakrabarty and Mukherjee, 2022; Mulbah et al, 2022; Omar and Inaba, 2020). This belief is both an illusion and wishful thinking because achieving full financial inclusion, in whichever way it is measured, does not guarantee that people's lives will suddenly improve, it does not guarantee that unemployment will significantly decrease, it does not guarantee that people's income will significantly increase, and it does not guarantee that economic opportunities will suddenly become available for everybody who is financially included (Mader, 2018). Another criticism of attaining full financial inclusion is that it masks the inequality that exists in the use of formal financial services (Ozili, 2018). Once full financial inclusion has been achieved, policymakers may assume that there is equitable use of formal financial services across the population. This may not be the case because some segments of the population will use formal financial services to a greater extent than other segments of the population. Another criticism has to do with how full financial inclusion is measured by the world bank. The measurement is subjective because it is based on people's opinion expressed through surveys. The survey usually reports the percentage of people who consider themselves to be financially included because they have access to a formal account or because they use formal payment methods. These indicators are subjective because a specific financial inclusion indicator may report a 100 percent level of financial inclusion in a country while another financial inclusion indicator can report a percentage that is less than 100 percent for the same country. We see this occurring in Denmark, Finland, Norway and Sweden (see Global Findex data in table 1 in Appendix A).

6. CONCLUSION

This article examined the next course of action which a country can take after achieving full financial inclusion, assuming full financial inclusion represents a 100 percent level of financial inclusion. The study recommends that countries that have achieved full financial inclusion can either (i) do nothing, (ii) reflect on the achievement to learn more, (iii) sustain the current effort put into achieving full financial inclusion, (iv) identify and close any inequality or disparity in the use of formal financial services, (v) deepen the use of formal financial services, (vi) pursue a completely different goal if there is no room for further improvement in financial inclusion, or (vii) help other countries to increase their level of financial inclusion. Policymakers should consider this course of actions after achieving full financial inclusion in their countries.

However, it must be acknowledged that some policymakers do not agree with the idea that a 100 percent level of financial inclusion can be attained because it suggests that the level of financial inclusion can be accurately measured, and the measurement will form the basis for determining whether full financial inclusion has been achieved or not. Also, some scholars do not agree with the idea of measuring financial inclusion in terms of numbers as the World Bank does. They do not think that a concept as broad as financial inclusion should be reduced to a numeric construct such as a percentage point.

There are also criticisms about the subjective nature of any measurement of financial inclusion and there are criticisms about whether achieving full financial inclusion is a worthwhile goal since there are other noble causes which a country can strive to achieve rather than focusing on achieving full financial inclusion. There is also concern that achieving full financial inclusion, in whichever way it is measured, does not guarantee that people's lives will suddenly improve, it does not guarantee that unemployment will significantly decrease, it does not guarantee that people's income will significantly increase, and it does not guarantee that economic opportunities will suddenly become available for every financially included individual or firm. Another concern is that attaining full financial inclusion could mask the inequalities that exist in the use of formal financial services. These criticisms are important, and policymakers should take them seriously in their effort to increase the level of financial inclusion to a high point. However, they should not consider it a thing of pride to attain a 100 percent level of financial inclusion; rather, they should be more concerned about whether achieving full financial inclusion has any tangible benefits to society and for the economy.

REFERENCES

Aga, G., & Martinez Peria, M. S. (2014). International remittances and financial inclusion in Sub-Saharan Africa. World Bank Policy Research Working Paper, (6991).

Ambarkhane, D., Singh, A. S., Venkataramani, B., & Marak, Z. (2022). Overcoming barriers to financial inclusion: Empirical evidence from India. *International Journal of Social Economics*, 49(9), 1302–1323. DOI: 10.1108/IJSE-04-2020-0254

Broekhoff, M. C., van der Cruijsen, C., & de Haan, J. (2024). Towards financial inclusion: Trust in banks' payment services among groups at risk. *Economic Analysis and Policy*, 82, 104–123. DOI: 10.1016/j.eap.2024.02.038

Capital, F. (2019). Strengthening collaboration and sharing lessons learned of financial inclusion initiatives supported by IDRC in Latin America. DOI: 10.1016/j.eap.2024.02.038

Chakrabarty, M., & Mukherjee, S. (2022). Financial inclusion and household welfare: An entropy-based consumption diversification approach. *European Journal of Development Research*, 34(3), 1486–1521. DOI: 10.1057/s41287-021-00431-y

Chandran, D. S. (2011). Financial inclusion strategies for inclusive growth in India. *Available atSSRN* 1930980. DOI: 10.2139/ssrn.1930980

Demirgüç-Kunt, A., Klapper, L. F., Singer, D., & Van Oudheusden, P. (2015). The global findex database 2014: Measuring financial inclusion around the world. *World Bank Policy Research Working Paper*, (7255).

Du, K. (2018). Complacency, capabilities, and institutional pressure: Understanding financial institutions' participation in the nascent mobile payments ecosystem. *Electronic Markets*, 28(3), 307–319. DOI: 10.1007/s12525-017-0267-0

Ediagbonya, V., & Tioluwani, C. (2023). The role of fintech in driving financial inclusion in developing and emerging markets: Issues, challenges and prospects. *Technological Sustainability*, 2(1), 100–119. DOI: 10.1108/TECHS-10-2021-0017

Elzahi Saaid Ali, A. (2022). Overcoming financial inclusion challenges through digital finance. In *Empowering the poor through financial and social inclusion in Africa: An Islamic perspective* (pp. 119–136). Springer International Publishing. DOI: 10.1007/978-3-031-00925-9_8

Garz, S., Giné, X., Karlan, D., Mazer, R., Sanford, C., & Zinman, J. (2021). Consumer protection for financial inclusion in low-and middle-income countries: Bridging regulator and academic perspectives. *Annual Review of Financial Economics*, 13(1), 219–246. DOI: 10.1146/annurev-financial-071020-012008

Güngen, A. R. (2018). Financial inclusion and policy-making: Strategy, campaigns and microcredit a la Turca. *New Political Economy*, 23(3), 331–347. DOI: 10.1080/13563467.2017.1349091

Joshi, D. P. (2014, January). Strategy adopted for financial inclusion. In *Speech Delivered at Workshop on* (Vol. 24).

Khan, A., Mubarik, M. S., & Naghavi, N. (2023). What matters for financial inclusions? Evidence from emerging economy. *International Journal of Finance & Economics*, 28(1), 821–838. DOI: 10.1002/ijfe.2451

Kim, H., & De Moor, L. (2017). The case of crowdfunding in financial inclusion: A survey. *Strategic Change*, 26(2), 193–212. DOI: 10.1002/jsc.2120

Kouladoum, J. C., Wirajing, M. A. K., & Nchofoung, T. N. (2022). Digital technologies and financial inclusion in Sub-Saharan Africa. *Telecommunications Policy*, 46(9), 102387. DOI: 10.1016/j.telpol.2022.102387

Kulkarni, L., & Ghosh, A. (2021). Gender disparity in the digitalization of financial services: Challenges and promises for women's financial inclusion in India. *Gender, Technology and Development*, 25(2), 233–250. DOI: 10.1080/09718524.2021.1911022

Kumar, R., & Pathak, D. C. (2022). Financial awareness: a bridge to financial inclusion. Development in Practice, 32(7), 968-980.Milana, C., & Ashta, A. (2020). Microfinance and financial inclusion: Challenges and opportunities. *Strategic Change*, 29(3), 257–266.

Mader, P. (2018). Contesting financial inclusion. *Development and Change*, 49(2), 461–483. DOI: 10.1111/dech.12368

Matsuo, M. (2022). Reflection on success in promoting authenticity and proactive behavior: A two-wave study. *Current Psychology (New Brunswick, N.J.)*, 41(12), 8793–8801. DOI: 10.1007/s12144-021-01352-z

Morgan, P. J. (2022). Fintech and financial inclusion in Southeast Asia and India. *Asian Economic Policy Review*, 17(2), 183–208. DOI: 10.1111/aepr.12379

Mulbah, F. F., Olumeh, D. E., Mantey, V., & Ipara, B. O. (2022). Impact of financial inclusion on household welfare in Liberia: A gendered perspective. *Review of Development Economics*.

Omar, M. A., & Inaba, K. (2020). Does financial inclusion reduce poverty and income inequality in developing countries? A panel data analysis. *Journal of Economic Structures*, 9(1), 37. DOI: 10.1186/s40008-020-00214-4

Ouma, S. A., Odongo, T. M., & Were, M. (2017). Mobile financial services and financial inclusion: Is it a boon for savings mobilization?. *Review of development finance, 7*(1), 29-35. DOI: 10.1186/s40008-020-00214-4

Ozili, P. K. (2018). Impact of digital finance on financial inclusion and stability. *Borsa istanbul review, 18*(4), 329-340. DOI: 10.1186/s40008-020-00214-4

Ozili, P. K. (2021). Financial inclusion research around the world: A review. *The Forum for Social Economics*, 50(4), 457–479. DOI: 10.1080/07360932.2020.1715238

Pal, M., Gupta, H., & Joshi, Y. C. (2022). Social and economic empowerment of women through financial inclusion: Empirical evidence from India. *Equality, Diversity and Inclusion*, 41(2), 294–305. DOI: 10.1108/EDI-04-2021-0113

Seifert, A., Cotten, S. R., & Xie, B. (2021). A double burden of exclusion? Digital and social exclusion of older adults in times of COVID-19. *The Journals of Gerontology. Series B, Psychological Sciences and Social Sciences*, 76(3), e99–e103. DOI: 10.1093/geronb/gbaa098 PMID: 32672332

Senou, M. M., Ouattara, W., & Acclassato Houensou, D. (2019). Financial inclusion dynamics in WAEMU: Was digital technology the missing piece? *Cogent Economics & Finance*, 7(1), 1665432. DOI: 10.1080/23322039.2019.1665432

Shaikh, A. A., Glavee-Geo, R., Karjaluoto, H., & Hinson, R. E. (2023). Mobile money as a driver of digital financial inclusion. *Technological Forecasting and Social Change*, 186, 122158. DOI: 10.1016/j.techfore.2022.122158

Shen, Y., Hueng, C. J., & Hu, W. (2020). Using digital technology to improve financial inclusion in China. *Applied Economics Letters*, 27(1), 30–34. DOI: 10.1080/13504851.2019.1606401

Stein, P., Randhawa, B., & Bilandzic, N. (2011). Toward universal access: Addressing the global challenge of financial inclusion. *Postcrisis Growth and Development: A Development Agenda for the G, 20*, 439-491. DOI: 10.1080/13504851.2019.1606401

Strøm, R. Ø., D'Espallier, B., & Mersland, R. (2016). Female leaders and financial inclusion. Evidence from microfinance institutions. Evidence from Microfinance Institutions (February 24, 2016). DOI: 10.1080/13504851.2019.1606401

Waema, T. M., & Omwansa, T. K. (2014). Deepening financial inclusion through collaboration to create innovative and appropriate financial products for the poor. DOI: 10.1080/13504851.2019.1606401

APPENDIX

Table 1.

Some indicators used to measure financial inclusion									
S/N	**Country**	**Year**	**Account (% age 15+)**	**Financial institution account (% age 15+)**	**Owns a credit card (% age 15+)**	**Owns a debit card (% age 15+)**	**Owns a debit or credit card (% age 15+)**	**Saved at a financial institution (% age 15+)**	**Borrowed from a formal financial institution (% age 15+)**
1	Denmark	2014	100%	100%	36%	95%	97%	65%	41%
	Denmark	2017	100%	100%	45%	97%	98%	63%	46%
	Denmark	2021	100%	100%	58%	99%	100%	67%	53%
2	Finland	2014	100%	100%	63%	97%	97%	57%	58%
	Finland	2017	100%	100%	63%	98%	99%	55%	54%
	Finland	2021	100%	100%	65%	97%	98%	62%	53%
3	Norway	2014	100%	100%	67%	99%	99%	78%	63%
	Norway	2017	100%	100%	71%	98%	98%	79%	69%
	Norway	2021	99%	99%	67%	98%	98%	81%	67%
4	Sweden	2014	100%	100%	45%	98%	98%	75%	50%
	Sweden	2017	100%	100%	45%	98%	99%	75%	44%
	Sweden	2021	100%	100%	48%	98%	99%	80%	49%

Compilation of References

Abasimel, N. A. (2023). Islamic Banking and Economics: Concepts and Instruments, Features, Advantages, Differences from Conventional Banks, and Contributions to Economic Growth. *Journal of the Knowledge Economy*, 14(2), 1923–1950. DOI: 10.1007/s13132-022-00940-z

Abdulhakim, N. (2020). Determinants of financial sustainability of microfinance institutions in Ethiopia. [HAJBE]. *Horn of African Journal of Business and Economics*, 3(2), 47–59.

Abdulhamid, N. A. 2020. Disruptive Technology, Mobile Money, and Financial Mobilization in Africa: M-Pesa as Kenya's Solution to Global Financial Exclusion? *Disruptive technologies, innovation and development in Africa*, pp.187-202.

Abdullah, S., & Quayes, S. (2016). Do women borrowers augment financial performance of MFIs? *Applied Economics*, 48(57), 5593–5604. DOI: 10.1080/00036846.2016.1181831

Abebe, A., & Kegne, M. (2023). The role of microfinance institutions on women's entrepreneurship development. *Journal of Innovation and Entrepreneurship*, 12(1), 17. DOI: 10.1186/s13731-023-00285-0 PMID: 36968150

Abikoye, B. E., Adelusi, W., Umeorah, S. C., Adelaja, A. O., & Agorbia-Atta, C. (2024). Integrating Risk Management in Fintech and Traditional Financial Institutions through AI and Machine Learning. *Journal of Economics. Management and Trade*, 30(8), 90–102.

Abis, D., Pia, P., & Limbu, Y. (2024). FinTech and consumers: A systematic review and integrative framework. *Management Decision*.

Aboelenein, A.A., 2023. Technology Effects on Emerging Economies' Financial Services and Economic Development: The case of Egypt and India.

About Bharat financial inclusion limited. (n.d.). Bharat Financial Inclusion Limited I. https://www.bfil.co.in/about-us.php

Accenture. (2021). Global payments trends report 2021. Retrieved from https://www.accenture.com/us-en/insights/banking/global-payments-report

Adam, P., Nusantara, A. W., & Muthalib, A. A. (2017). A Model of the Dynamic of the Relationship between Exchange Rate and Indonesia's Export. *International Journal of Economics and Financial Issues*, 7(1), 255–261.

Addae-Korankye, A. (2012). Microfinance: A tool for poverty reduction in developing countries. *The Journal of Business and Retail Management Research*, 7(1), 138–149.

Addae-Korankye, A., 2020. Historical emergence of microfinance and the microfinance sector in Ghana. *Business Management Dynamics, 10*(2).

Administrator. (n.d.). *Our vision & mission*. https://joomlakave.com. https://www.janabank.com/about-us/who-we-are/our-vision-mission//

Adnan, S. A., & Kumar, P. (2021). Role of microfinance in economic development. *Adhyayan: A Journal of Management Sciences, 11*(2), 22-30.

Aga, G., & Martinez Peria, M. S. (2014). International remittances and financial inclusion in Sub-Saharan Africa. World Bank Policy Research Working Paper, (6991).

Agarwal, A. (2012). A Guide to RBI's Weekly Statistical Supplement – II, STDI-Primary Dealer Ltd; 2012 Jan 27. Available from: http://www.stcipd.com/UserFiles/File/A%20Guide%20to%20RBI's%20Weekly% 20Statistical%20Supplement.pdf

Agarwal, S., & Ann, T. C. 2024. Personal Finance Applications of Fintech. In *The Emerald Handbook of Fintech: Reshaping Finance* (pp. 235-248). Emerald Publishing Limited. DOI: 10.1108/978-1-83753-608-520241029

Agarwal, S., Kigabo, T., Minoiu, C., Presbitero, A. F., & Silva, A. F. (2023). Serving the underserved: Microcredit as a pathway to commercial banks. *The Review of Economics and Statistics*, 105(4), 780–797. DOI: 10.1162/rest_a_01117

Agarwal, S., & Zhang, J. (2020). FinTech, lending and payment innovation: A review. *Asia-Pacific Journal of Financial Studies*, 49(3), 353–367. DOI: 10.1111/ajfs.12294

Aghion, B. A., & Morduch, J. (2000). Microfinance beyond group lending. *Economics of Transition*, 8(2), 401–420. DOI: 10.1111/1468-0351.00049

Agyekumhene, C., de Vries, J. R., van Paassen, A., Macnaghten, P., Schut, M., & Bregt, A. (2018). Digital platforms for smallholder credit access: The mediation of trust for cooperation in maize value chain financing. *NJAS Wageningen Journal of Life Sciences*, 86(1), 77–88. DOI: 10.1016/j.njas.2018.06.001

Ahmad, D., Afzal, M., & Khan, U. G. (2017). Impact of exports on economic growth empirical evidence of Pakistan. *International Journal of Applied*, 5(2), 9.

Ahmed, F., Begum, R. A., Siwar, C., Mia, M. S., & Wiboonpongse, A. (2019). Impact of microcredit on income inequality among rural women: The case of Panchagarh district in Bangladesh. *Pertanika Journal of Social Science & Humanities*, 27(4), 2367–2382.

Aithal, P. S. (2024). Influence of Digital Technology on Microfinance Sector: A Study in Kerala. [IJAEML]. *International Journal of Applied Engineering and Management Letters*, 8(2), 186–197.

Akanmu, P. M., Clement, J. O., & Samaila, M. (2018). Impact of cooperative Microfinance on the performance of women entrepreneurship in Kwara state Nigeria. *Financial Markets. Institutions and Risks*, 2(4), 20–28. DOI: 10.21272/fmir.2(4).20-28.2018

Akingunola, R. O., Adekunle, O. A., Adegbesan, K. J., & Aninkan, O. O. (2013). Microfinance banks and entrepreneurship development in Nigeria: A case of Ogun State. *European Journal of Business and Management*, 5(28), 100–110.

Alaeddin, O., Dakash, M. A., & Azrak, T. (2021). Implementing the Blockchain Technology in Islamic Financial Industry: Opportunities and Challenges. *Journal of Information Technology Management*, 13(3), 99–115. DOI: 10.22059/JITM.2021.83116

Alam, N., Gupta, L., & Zameni, A. 2019. *Fintech and Islamic finance*. sl: Springer International Publishing. DOI: 10.1007/978-3-030-24666-2

Al-Azzam, M. (2023). For narrower income inequality: Traditional finance or microfinance? *Applied Economics*, •••, 1–18.

Alemu, S. H., Van Kempen, L., & Ruben, R. (2018). Women empowerment through self-help groups: The bittersweet fruits of collective Apple cultivation in Highland Ethiopia. *Journal of Human Development and Capabilities*, 19(3), 308–330. DOI: 10.1080/19452829.2018.1454407

Alias, N. A. L. 2024. Microfinance Institutions: Catalysts for Improved Personal Financial Behavior. *Available atSSRN* 4845920. DOI: 10.2139/ssrn.4845920

Ali, H. (2024). *Islamic Microfinance: Landscape, Models and Future Prospects.* Walter de Gruyter GmbH & Co KG.

Allet, M. (2014). Why do microfinance institutions go green? An exploratory study. *Journal of Business Ethics*, 122(3), 405–424. DOI: 10.1007/s10551-013-1767-2

Alsanusî, M., Altintaş, H., & Alnour, M.ALSANUSİ. (2022, December 31). The role of real exchange rate in the trade balance between Turkey and Libya: Evidence from nonlinear and wavelet-based approaches. *Journal of Ekonomi*, 4(2), 46–56. DOI: 10.58251/ekonomi.1173205

Al-Shami, S. S. A., Razali, M. M., Majid, I., Rozelan, A., & Rashid, N. (2016). The effect of microfinance on women's empowerment: Evidence from Malaysia. *Asian Journal of Women's Studies*, 22(3), 318–337. DOI: 10.1080/12259276.2016.1205378

Al-Smadi, M. O. (2023). Examining the relationship between digital finance and financial inclusion: Evidence from MENA countries. *Borsa Istanbul Review*, 23(2), 464–472. DOI: 10.1016/j.bir.2022.11.016

Altintaş, H., Cetin, R., & Öz, B. (2011). The impact of exchange rate volatility on Turkish exports: 1993-2009. *South East European Journal of Economics and Business*, 6(2), 71–81. DOI: 10.2478/v10033-011-0017-8

Altintas, K. M.Kadir Murat Altintas. (2011, October 28). The dynamics of financial literacy within the framework of personal finance: An analysis among Turkish University Students. *African Journal of Business Management*, 5(26). Advance online publication. DOI: 10.5897/AJBM11.401

Ambarkhane, D., Singh, A. S., Venkataramani, B., & Marak, Z. (2022). Overcoming barriers to financial inclusion: Empirical evidence from India. *International Journal of Social Economics*, 49(9), 1302–1323. DOI: 10.1108/IJSE-04-2020-0254

Amidžic, G., Massara, M. A., & Mialou, A. (2014). *Assessing countries' financial inclusion standing-A new composite index.* International Monetary Fund.

Anand, D., & Mantrala, M. (2019). Responding to disruptive business model innovations: The case of traditional banks facing fintech entrants. *Journal of Banking and Financial Technology*, 3(1), 19–31. DOI: 10.1007/s42786-018-00004-4

Anandhi, A. K. (2019). Microfinance An Overview. *Think India Journal*, 22(14), 12465–12469.

Anjum, B., & Tiwari, R. (2012). Role of private sector banks for financial inclusion. *Zenith International Journal of Multidisciplinary Research*, 2(1), 270–280.

Appietu, R. K., Dankwa, I. O., & Caesar, L. D. (2021). Exploring the nexus between microfinance activities and economic wellbeing at the grassroots: Evidence from an emerging market economy. *Global Social Welfare : Research, Policy & Practice*, 8(4), 337–349. DOI: 10.1007/s40609-020-00172-6

Ardic, O. P., Heimann, M., & Mylenko, N. (2011). Access to financial services and the financial inclusion agenda around the world: A cross-country analysis with a new data set. *World Bank Policy Research Working Paper*, •••, 5537. DOI: 10.1596/1813-9450-5537

Arifa, L. N. (2021). Banker To the Poor and Its Urgency Based on Indonesian Context (Perceiving the Toughts and Experiences of Muhammad Yunus). *Risâlah. Jurnal Pendidikan Dan Studi Islam*, 7(2), 226–238. DOI: 10.31943/jurnal_risalah.v7i2.188

Armendáriz, B. (2010). *The economics of microfinance*. MIT press.

Arner, D. W., Buckley, R. P., Zetzsche, D. A., & Veidt, R. (2020). Sustainability, FinTech and financial inclusion. *European Business Organization Law Review*, 21(1), 7–35. DOI: 10.1007/s40804-020-00183-y

Arnold, J., Alam, M. N., Thorne, H., & Armacost, N. (n.d.). *Towards Reinventing Microfinance Through Solving the "Last Mile Problem": Bridging Clean Energy Solutions and Actionable Information to the Poor* [Abstract]. Researchgate.

Artige, L., & Cavenaile, L. (2023). Public education expenditures, growth and income inequality. *Journal of Economic Theory*, 209, 105622. DOI: 10.1016/j.jet.2023.105622

Ashta, A., Couchoro, M., & Musa, A. S. M. (2014). Dialectic evolution through the social innovation process: From microcredit to microfinance. *Journal of Innovation and Entrepreneurship*, 3(1), 1–23. DOI: 10.1186/2192-5372-3-4

Atahau, A., Sakti, I. M., Huruta, A. D., & Kim, M.-S. (2021). Gender and renewable energy integration: The mediating role of green-microfinance. *Journal of Cleaner Production*, 318(October), 128536. DOI: 10.1016/j.jclepro.2021.128536

Audu, I., Abubakar, A. M., & Baba, M. (2021). The Role of Microfinance Institutions' Services on the Performance of Small and Medium Entreprises in Gombe State, Nigeria. *Journal of Management Sciences*, 4(1), 500–517.

Avallone, P., & Strangio, D. (2024). Different Forms of Microcredit and Social Business—Microfinance in Global History from the Late Medieval to the Modern. In *Different Forms of Microcredit and Social Business: Microfinance in Global History from the Late Medieval to the Modern* (pp. 1–15). Springer Nature Switzerland. DOI: 10.1007/978-3-031-60942-8_1

Badran, M. A. (2009). *Money Transfer Services* (Doctoral dissertation, Eastern Mediterranean University (EMU)).

Balasubramanian, S. (2013). Why micro-credit may leave women worse off: Non-cooperative bargaining and the marriage game in South Asia. *The Journal of Development Studies*, 49(5), 609–623. DOI: 10.1080/00220388.2012.709618

Banerjee, A., Breza, E., Duflo, E., & Kinnan, C. (2019). Can microfinance unlock a poverty trap for some entrepreneurs? (No. w26346). National Bureau of Economic Research. DOI: 10.3386/w26346

Banerjee, A., Duflo, E., Glennerster, R., & Kinnan, C. (2015). The miracle of microfinance? Evidence from a randomized evaluation. *American Economic Journal. Applied Economics*, 7(1), 22–53. DOI: 10.1257/app.20130533

Banerjee, A., Karlan, D., & Zinman, J. (2015). Six randomized evaluations of Microcredit: Introduction and further steps. *American Economic Journal. Applied Economics*, 7(1), 1–21. DOI: 10.1257/app.20140287

Barman, C. B. (2022). Microfinance, Rural Women Entrepreneurs and Sustainable Development. In *Sustainable Entrepreneurship*. DOI: DOI: 10.31674/book.2002se.002

Bashiru, S., Bunyaminu, A., Yakubu, I. N., & Al-Faryan, M. A. S. (2023). Drivers of Financial Inclusion: Insights from Sub-Saharan Africa. *Economies*, 11(5), 146. DOI: 10.3390/economies11050146

Bateman, M., & Chang, H.J., 2012. Microfinance and the illusion of development: From hubris to nemesis in thirty years. *World Economic Review*, (1).

Beck, T. 2020. *Fintech and financial inclusion: Opportunities and pitfalls* (No. 1165). ADBI working paper series.

Benami, E., & Carter, M. R. (2021). Can digital technologies reshape rural microfinance? Implications for savings, credit, & insurance. *Applied Economic Perspectives and Policy*, 43(4), 1196–1220. DOI: 10.1002/aepp.13151

Bent, B. B. (2019). The impact of microfinance on poverty reduction and women empowerment. In *Rais collective volume–Economic science* (pp. 72–86). Scientia Moralitas Research Institute.

Bernards, N. (2022). *A critical history of poverty finance: Colonial roots and neoliberal failures*. Pluto Press. DOI: 10.2307/j.ctv2tjd6qs

Bhat, S. A., & Bhat, J. A. (2020, November 2). Impact of Exchange Rate Changes on the Trade Balance of India: An Asymmetric Nonlinear Cointegration Approach. *Foreign Trade Review*, 56(1), 71–88. DOI: 10.1177/0015732520961328

Biswas, B., & Sana, A. K. (2015).. . *MICROCREDIT DELIVERY.*, (July), 26–29.

Biswas, M. P., & Rao, M. R. M. (2014). Role of NGO in empowering women through microfinance: A conceptual study. *Journal of Small Business and Entrepreneurship Development*, 2(2), 141–150.

Björkegren, D., & Grissen, D. (2020). Behavior revealed in mobile phone usage predicts credit repayment. *The World Bank Economic Review*, 34(3), 618–634. DOI: 10.1093/wber/lhz006

Black, A. H. (2017). *Capital, saving and credit in peasant societies.* Routledge. DOI: 10.4324/9781315081786

Bocken, N. M. O., Shirt, S. W., Rana, P., & Evans, S. (2014). A literature and practice review to develop sustainable business model archetypes. *Journal of Cleaner Production*, 65, 42–56. DOI: 10.1016/j.jclepro.2013.11.039

Bora, N. M. (2020). Financial inclusion in India: A case study of the north-eastern states. *International Journal of Scientific and Technology Research*, 9(2), 1319–1323.

BRAC. (2024). *BRAC Microfinance Annual Report 2020.*https://www.brack.net

BRAC. 2021. Annual report 2021. [Online] Available at https://www.brac.net/annual -reports-and-publications [Accessed 26 September 2024].

Brada, J. C., Kutan, A. M., & Zhou, S. (1997, June). The exchange rate and the balance of trade: The Turkish experience. *The Journal of Development Studies*, 33(5), 675–692. DOI: 10.1080/00220389708422489

Briggs, C., & Koyama, M., 2012. Pledging and credit markets in medieval England.

Broekhoff, M. C., van der Cruijsen, C., & de Haan, J. (2024). Towards financial inclusion: Trust in banks' payment services among groups at risk. *Economic Analysis and Policy*, 82, 104–123. DOI: 10.1016/j.eap.2024.02.038

Brush, C. G., & Cooper, S. Y. (2012). Female entrepreneurship and economic development: An international perspective. *Entrepreneurship and Regional Development*, 24(1-2), 1–6. DOI: 10.1080/08985626.2012.637340

Bruton, G. D., Khavul, S., & Chavez, H. (2011). Microlending in emerging economies: Building a new line of inquiry from the ground up. *Journal of International Business Studies*, 42(5), 718–739. DOI: 10.1057/jibs.2010.58

Building a better life - About us | Ujjivan small finance bank. (n.d.). Ujjivan Small Finance Bank. https://www.ujjivansfb.in/about-us

Bulut, M., & Korkut, C. E. M. (2019). Ottoman cash waqfs. *Insight Turkey*, 21(3), 91–112.

Cai, C. W. (2018). Disruption of financial intermediation by FinTech: A review on crowdfunding and blockchain. *Accounting and Finance*, 58(4), 965–992. DOI: 10.1111/acfi.12405

Cai, J., Meki, M., Quinn, S., Field, E., Kinnan, C., Morduch, J., & Said, F. (2023). Microfinance. *VoxDevLit*, 3(2), 26.

Cámara, N., & Tuesta, D. (2014). Measuring financial inclusion: A muldimensional index. *BBVA Research Paper*, (14/26).

Capital, F. (25 Mar 2024). Microfinance clean technology: The Role of Microfinance in Fueling Sustainable Entrepreneurship. https://fastercapital.com/content/Microfinance-clean-technology--The-Role-of-Microfinance-in-Fueling-Sustainable-Entrepreneurship.html

Carder, B. (2019). A positive approach. *Quality Progress*, 52(4), 24–29.

Carstens, A. (2019). *Central banking and innovation: partners in the quest for financial inclusion. speech at the Reserve Bank of India.* CD Deshmukh Memorial Lecture.

Carter, S. P., & Skiba, P. M. (2012). Pawnshops, behavioral economics, and self-regulation. *Rev. Banking & Fin. L.*, 32, 193.

Chakrabarty, M., & Mukherjee, S. (2022). Financial inclusion and household welfare: An entropy-based consumption diversification approach. *European Journal of Development Research*, 34(3), 1486–1521. DOI: 10.1057/s41287-021-00431-y

Chandran, D. S. (2011). Financial inclusion strategies for inclusive growth in India. *Available atSSRN* 1930980. DOI: 10.2139/ssrn.1930980

Chang, L., Taghizadeh-Hesary, F., Chen, H., & Mohsin, M. (2022). Do green bonds have environmental benefits? *Energy Economics*, 115, 106356. Advance online publication. DOI: 10.1016/j.eneco.2022.106356

Chatterjee, A., & Patil, K. (2022). Assessing the Impact of Microfinance on Inequality: A Study of Major SAARC Nations Using Panel Causality Analysis. In *Microfinance to Combat Global Recession and Social Exclusion: An Empirical Investigation* (pp. 195–208). Springer. DOI: 10.1007/978-981-16-4329-3_14

Chaturvedi, P. (2022). The role of small finance banks in promoting financial inclusion in India. *International Journal of Multidisciplinary*, 7(5), 8–15. DOI: 10.31305/rrijm.2022.v07.i05.002

Chen, Y., & Dubinsky, A. J. (2020). The impact of COVID-19 on the U.S. payment system: A new dataset. SSRN Electronic Journal. https://doi.org/DOI: 10.2139/ssrn.3649999

Chen, J., & See, K. C. (2020). Artificial intelligence for COVID-19: Rapid review. *Journal of Medical Internet Research*, 22(10), e21476. DOI: 10.2196/21476 PMID: 32946413

Cheston, S., & Kuhn, L. (2002). Empowering women through microfinance. In Daley-Harris, S. (Ed.), *Pathways out of poverty: Innovations in microfinance for the poorest families* (pp. 167–228). Kumarian Press.

Chiazor, I. A., Egharevba, M. E., & Ozoya, M. I. (2016). Widening inequality and poverty in the developing world-micro-financing as a viable solution. In *The Social Sciences* (Vol. 11, Issue 13, pp. 3286–3293). https://doi.org/DOI: 10.3923/sscience.2016.3286.3293

Chikwira, C., Vengesai, E., & Mandude, P. (2022). The impact of microfinance institutions on poverty alleviation. *Journal of Risk and Financial Management*, 15(9), 393. DOI: 10.3390/jrfm15090393

Chintrakarn, P. HERZER, D., & NUNNENKAMP, P. (2012). FDI AND INCOME INEQUALITY: EVIDENCE FROM A PANEL OF U.S. STATES. *Economic Inquiry*, *50*(3), 788–801. https://doi.org/https://doi.org/10.1111/j.1465-7295.2011.00384.x

Chithra, N., & Selvam, M. (2013). Determinants of financial inclusion: An empirical study on the inter-state variations in India. *Available atSSRN* 2296096. DOI: 10.2139/ssrn.2296096

Chliova, M., Brinckmann, J., & Rosenbusch, N. (2015). Is microcredit a blessing for the poor? A meta-analysis examining development outcomes and contextual considerations. *Journal of Business Venturing*, 30(3), 467–487. DOI: 10.1016/j.jbusvent.2014.10.003

Chowdhury, M. J. A. (2000). *Microcredit, enhancement of entitlement and alleviation of poverty: an investigation into the Grameen Bank's role in Bangladesh.*

Chuc, A. A. M., Atayah, A. A., & Özer, S. Q. (2023). Impact of financial technology (fintech) on financial performance of micro finance institutions in Bahrain. *African Journal of Emerging Issues*, 5(17), 1–11.

Chuc, A. A. M., Atayah, A. A., & Özer, S. Q. (2023). Impact of Financial Technology (Fintech) on Financial Performance of Micro Finance Institutions in Bahrain. *African Journal of Emerging Issues*, 5(17), 1–11.

Citaristi, I. (2022). African Development Bank—AfDB. In *The Europa Directory of International*

Colovic, A., & Mehrotra, S. (2020). Lifelong activism and women's entrepreneurship: How a social movement organization improves conditions for self-employed women in India. *European Business Review*, 32(5), 937–958. DOI: 10.1108/EBR-09-2019-0215

Copestake, J. (2002). Inequality and the polarizing impact of microcredit: Evidence from Zambia's copperbelt. *Journal of International Development*, 14(6), 743–755. https://doi.org/https://doi.org/10.1002/jid.921. DOI: 10.1002/jid.921

Cozarenco, A., & Szafarz, A. 2019. Microfinance in the North: Where do we stand? In *A Research Agenda for Financial Inclusion and Microfinance* (pp. 125-137). Edward Elgar Publishing.

Craan, V. 2019. *Entrepreneurial Financing of Micro-Small-Medium Enterprises in Haiti: Barriers and Proposed Solutions* (Doctoral dissertation, Universidad ESAN).

Creedy, J., & Hoang, H. T. (2018). Types of microfinance organisation: A taxonomy. *Third Sector Review*, 24(2), 105–136.

Crépon, B., Devoto, F., Duflo, E., & Parienté, W. (2015). Estimating the impact of microcredit on those who take it up: Evidence from a randomized experiment in Morocco. *American Economic Journal. Applied Economics*, 7(1), 123–150. DOI: 10.1257/app.20130535

Crunchbase, 2024. *About Bank Andara*. [Online] Available at https://www.crunchbase.com/organization/bank-andara [Accessed 26 September 2024].

Cull, R., & Morduch, J. (2018). Microfinance and economic development. *Handbook of Finance and Development*, 550-572. https://doi.org/DOI: 10.4337/9781785360510.00030

Cull, R., Demirgüç-Kunt, A., & Morduch, J. (2009). Microfinance meets the market. *The Journal of Economic Perspectives*, 23(1), 167–192. DOI: 10.1257/jep.23.1.167

Cull, R., & Hartarska, V. (2023). Overview of microfinance, financial inclusion, and development. In *Handbook of microfinance, financial inclusion and development* (pp. 2–19). Edward Elgar Publishing. DOI: 10.4337/9781789903874.00006

Current policy issues, *ADBI Working Paper*, No. 259, Asian Development Bank Institute (ADBI), Tokyo

Cysne, R. P. (2009). On the positive correlation between income inequality and unemployment. *The Review of Economics and Statistics*, 91(1), 218–226. DOI: 10.1162/rest.91.1.218

D, S. K. (n.d.). *Balance of Trade - Indian Economy Notes*. Prepp. https://prepp.in/news/e-492-balance-of-trade-indian-economy-notes

Dang, T. T., & Vu, H. Q. (2020). Fintech in Microfinance: A new direction for Microfinance institutions in Vietnam. *Asian Journal of Business Environment*, 10(3), 13–22. DOI: 10.13106/jbees.2020.vol10.no3.13

Datta, S., & Sahu, T. N. (2022). Livelihood transformation through microfinance: An empirical investigation on tribal entrepreneurs in India. *International Journal of Business Innovation and Research*, 29(1), 127–140. DOI: 10.1504/IJBIR.2022.125671

Demir, A., Pesqué-Cela, V., Altunbas, Y., & Murinde, V. (2022). Fintech, financial inclusion and income inequality: A quantile regression approach. *European Journal of Finance*, 28(1), 86–107. DOI: 10.1080/1351847X.2020.1772335

Demirgüç-Kunt, A., Klapper, L. F., Singer, D., & Van Oudheusden, P. (2015). The global findex database 2014: Measuring financial inclusion around the world. *World Bank Policy Research Working Paper*, (7255).

Department of Financial Services, Ministry of Finance, Government of India. (2024, July 24). *Pradhan Mantri Jan - Dhan Yojana*. Pradhan Mantri Jan Dhan Yojana. Retrieved August 2, 2024, from https://www.pmjdy.gov.in/account

Dhar, P. (2016). Microfinance penetration in India: A state wise analysis. *International Journal of Interdisciplinary Research in science society and culture*, 2(2), 86-96. DOI: 10.1257/app.5.1.163

Di Vaio, A., Palladino, R., Hassan, R., & Escobar, O. (2020). Artificial intelligence and business models in the sustainable development goals perspective: A systematic literature review. *Journal of Business Research*, 121, 283–314. DOI: 10.1016/j.jbusres.2020.08.019

Dogo, M. Y., & Aras, O. N. (2021, September 18). EFFECT OF VOLATILITY IN THE NAIRA - DOLLAR EXCHANGE RATE ON THE VOLUME OF IMPORTS TO, AND EXPORTS FROM NIGERIA. *International Journal of Economics and Financial Issues*, 11(5), 68–73. DOI: 10.32479/ijefi.11799

Dogru, T., Isik, C., & Sirakaya-Turk, E. (2019, October). The balance of trade and exchange rates: Theory and contemporary evidence from tourism. *Tourism Management*, 74, 12–23. DOI: 10.1016/j.tourman.2019.01.014

Dollar, D., & Kraay, A. (2002). Institutions, trade, and growth. *Journal of Monetary Economics*, 50(1), 133–162. DOI: 10.1016/S0304-3932(02)00206-4

Du, K. (2018). Complacency, capabilities, and institutional pressure: Understanding financial institutions' participation in the nascent mobile payments ecosystem. *Electronic Markets*, 28(3), 307–319. DOI: 10.1007/s12525-017-0267-0

Ediagbonya, V., & Tioluwani, C. (2023). The role of fintech in driving financial inclusion in developing and emerging markets: Issues, challenges and prospects. *Technological Sustainability*, 2(1), 100–119. DOI: 10.1108/TECHS-10-2021-0017

Egharevba, M. E., Eguavoen, A., Azuh, D., Iruonagbe, T. C., & Chiazor, I. A. (2016). Microfinance and poverty reduction strategy for promoting national development: The challenge of social/financial inclusion. *Social Sciences*, 11(22), 5373–5386.

Ekpe, I. (2011). Women entrepreneurs and economic development in Nigeria: Characteristics for success. *International Journal of Business and Social Science*, 2(1).

Eletter, S. F. (2024). The use of blockchain in the insurance industry: A bibliometric analysis. *Insurance Markets and Companies*, 15(1), 12–29. DOI: 10.21511/ins.15(1).2024.02

El-Nasharty, H. (2022). The Role Of Microfinance In Poverty Reduction: Countries Experiences by Regions 2000-2018. *Innovation Journal of Social Sciences and Economic Review*, 4(1), 1–09. DOI: 10.36923/ijsser.v4i1.101

Elsaid, H. M. (2023). A review of literature directions regarding the impact of fintech firms on the banking industry. *Qualitative Research in Financial Markets*, 15(5), 693–711. DOI: 10.1108/QRFM-10-2020-0197

Elzahi Saaid Ali, A. (2022). Overcoming financial inclusion challenges through digital finance. In *Empowering the poor through financial and social inclusion in Africa: An Islamic perspective* (pp. 119–136). Springer International Publishing. DOI: 10.1007/978-3-031-00925-9_8

Endri, E., Hania, B. T., & Ma'ruf, A. (2022). CORPORATE GREEN SUKUK ISSUANCE FOR SUSTAINABLE FINANCING IN INDONESIA. *Environment and Ecology*, 13(1), 38–49. DOI: 10.21511/ee.13(1).2022.04

Esquivias, M. A., Sethi, N., & Iswanti, H. (2021). Dynamics of income inequality, investment, and unemployment in Indonesia. [JPSS]. *Journal of Population and Social Studies*, 29, 660–678. DOI: 10.25133/JPSSv292021.040

Essiam, E. (2023). Empirical Investigation into the Consequences of the Banking Sector Cleanup on Microfinance Sustainability in Ghana. *International Journal of Applied Research in Business and Management*, 4(3), 181–199. DOI: 10.51137/ijarbm.2023.4.3.10

Evans, G. W. (2017). Artificial intelligence: where we came from, where we are now, and where we are going.

Fanta, A., & Mutsonziwa, K. (2021). Financial literacy as a driver of financial inclusion in Kenya and Tanzania. *Journal of Risk and Financial Management*, 14(11), 561. DOI: 10.3390/jrfm14110561

Fatimah, Y. A., Govindan, K., Murniningsih, R., & Setiawan, A. (2020). Industry 4.0 based sustainable circular economy approach for smart waste management system to achieve sustainable development goals: A case study of Indonesia. *Journal of Cleaner Production*, 269, 122263. Advance online publication. DOI: 10.1016/j.jclepro.2020.122263

Ferdousi, F. (2015). Impact of microfinance on sustainable entrepreneurship development. *Development Studies Research*, 2(1), 51–63. DOI: 10.1080/21665095.2015.1058718

Fernando, Y., Tseng, M.-L., Wahyuni-TD, I. S., Sroufe, R., & Mohd-Zailani, N. I. A. (2023). Blockchain technology adoption for carbon trading and energy efficiency: ISO manufacturing firms in Malaysia. *International Journal of Logistics*, 26(11), 1556–1577. DOI: 10.1080/13675567.2022.2090527

Field, E., Pande, R., Papp, J., & Rigol, N. (2013). Does the classic microfinance model discourage entrepreneurship among the poor? Experimental evidence from India. *The American Economic Review*, 103(6), 2196–2226. DOI: 10.1257/aer.103.6.2196

FINCA. 2021. *Annual report 2021*. [Online] Available at https://cdn.finca.org/wp-content/uploads/20221020102204/FINCA-2021-Annual-Report-4.pdf [Accessed on 27 September 2024].

FINCA. 2024. *Fintech Innovations and Solutions Across the Network*. [Online] Available at https://finca.org/en-gb/our-work/microfinance/innovations-and-technology [Accessed 28 September 2024].

Fox, L., & Romero, C. (2017). In the mind, the household, or the market? Concepts and measurement of women's economic empowerment. *Policy Research Working Papers*. https://doi.org/DOI: 10.1596/1813-9450-8079

Franzoni, S., & Allali, A. A. (2018). Principles of Islamic finance and principles of Corporate Social Responsibility: What convergence? *Sustainability (Basel)*, 10(3), 637. Advance online publication. DOI: 10.3390/su10030637

Fritz, H., & Lang, G. (2012). *Microcredit, Human Capital, and Personal Income Distribution: Empirical Evidence from Greater Cairo*.

Fuentes, M.P., 2023. Unveiling the Constraints: Exploring Limiting Factors for Microfinance Institutions Effectiveness in Fostering Women's Empowerment in India.

Gambacorta, L., Huang, Y., Qiu, H., & Wang, J. (2024). How do machine learning and non-traditional data affect credit scoring? New evidence from a Chinese fintech firm. *Journal of Financial Stability*, 73, 101284. DOI: 10.1016/j.jfs.2024.101284

Garikipati, S. (2008). The impact of lending to women on household vulnerability and women's empowerment: Evidence from India. *World Development*, 36(12), 2620–2642. DOI: 10.1016/j.worlddev.2007.11.008

Garz, S., Giné, X., Karlan, D., Mazer, R., Sanford, C., & Zinman, J. (2021). Consumer protection for financial inclusion in low-and middle-income countries: Bridging regulator and academic perspectives. *Annual Review of Financial Economics*, 13(1), 219–246. DOI: 10.1146/annurev-financial-071020-012008

Gateway, M. (2015). Over-Indebtedness in Microfinance: Causes and Solutions https://www. microfinancegateway.org

Gatto, A., & Sadik-Zada, E. R. (2022) Access to microfinance as a resilience policy to address sustainable development goals: A content analysis. 8(10): e10860. DOI: . https://www.ncbi.nlm.nih.gov/pmc/articles/PMC9578961/DOI: 10.1016/j. he;iyon.2002.210860

Gatto, A. (2018). Historical roots of microcredit and usury: The role of Monti di Pietà in Italy and in the kingdom of Naples in XV–XX centuries. *Journal of International Development*, 30(5), 911–914. DOI: 10.1002/jid.3386

Geisst, C. R. (2013). *Beggar thy neighbor: A history of usury and debt*. University of Pennsylvania Press. DOI: 10.9783/9780812207507

Geleta, T. E., Mengistu, A. A., & Gesese, S. A. (2019). Determinants of rural households' participation in microfinance services: The case of Cheliya District, West Shoa Zone, Oromia National Regional State, Ethiopia. *Journal of Development and Agricultural Economics*, 11(2), 24–32. DOI: 10.5897/JDAE2018.1008

Gitaharie, B. Y., Soelistianingsih, L., Djutaharta, T., Nursamsu, S., Hastiadi, F. F., Panennungi, M. A., & Listya, R. (2014). *Financial inclusion: Household access to credit in Indonesia (No. 201401)*. Faculty of Economics, University of Indonesia.

Githaiga, P. N. (2022). Revenue diversification and financial sustainability of microfinance institutions. *Asian Journal of Accounting Research*, 7(1), 31–43. DOI: 10.1108/AJAR-11-2020-0122

Githaiga, P. N., Soi, N., & Buigut, K. K. (2023). Does intellectual capital matter to MFIs' financial sustainability? *Asian Journal of Accounting Research*, 8(1), 41–52. DOI: 10.1108/AJAR-06-2021-0080

Global Off-Grid Lighting Association. (2018). *The Off-Grid Solar Market Report*. https://gogla.org

Global Strategic Institute for Sustainable Development | Department of Economic and Social Affairs. (2023, March 24). https://sdgs.un.org/partnerships/global-strategic-institute-sustainable-development

Goel, D. V. (2020). Microfinance and Experiences in Measuring Income and Inequality : Evidence From an Indian State. *International Journal of Management*, 11(10), 1651–1664. DOI: 10.34218/IJM.11.10.2020.150

Goetz, A. M., & Gupta, R. S. (1996). Who takes the credit? Gender, power, and control over loan use in rural credit programs in Bangladesh. *World Development*, 24(1), 45–63. DOI: 10.1016/0305-750X(95)00124-U

Gomathy, M. (2015). An overview of financial inclusion and rural development in India. *IOSR Journal of Business and Management (IOSRJBM), 17*(8), 06-11. DOI: 10.1016/j.sbspro.2012.03.281

Goswami, S., Sharma, R. B., & Chouhan, V. (2022). Impact of financial technology (Fintech) on financial inclusion (FI) in Rural India. *Universal Journal of Accounting and Finance*, 10(2), 483–497. DOI: 10.13189/ujaf.2022.100213

Grameen Bank. 2022. *Annual report.* [Online] Available at https://grameenbank.org.bd/archives/annual-report [Accesses 25/09/2024].

Grameen Bank. 2024. *Welcome to Grameen Bank.* [Online] Available at https://grameenbank.org.bd/ [Accessed 25/09/2024].

Grohmann, A., Klühs, T., & Menkhoff, L. (2018). Does financial literacy improve financial inclusion? Cross country evidence. *World Development*, 111, 84–96. DOI: 10.1016/j.worlddev.2018.06.020

Guha, S., & Gupta, G. (2005). Microcredit for income generation: The role of RoSCA. *Economic and Political Weekly*, •••, 1470–1473.

Guirkinger, C., & Boucher, S. R. (2008). Credit constraints and productivity in Peruvian agriculture. *Agricultural Economics*, 39(3), 295–308. DOI: 10.1111/j.1574-0862.2008.00334.x

Güngen, A. R. (2018). Financial inclusion and policy-making: Strategy, campaigns and microcredit a la Turca. *New Political Economy*, 23(3), 331–347. DOI: 10.1080/13563467.2017.1349091

GVS Biogas. (2019). Biogas Solutions for Rural India. https://www.gvsbiogas.com

Haile, H. B., Bock, B., & Folmer, H. (2012, July). Microfinance and female empowerment: Do institutions matter? [). Pergamon.]. *Women's Studies International Forum*, 35(4), 256–265. DOI: 10.1016/j.wsif.2012.04.001

Haini, H., Musa, S. F. P. D., Wei Loon, P., & Basir, K. H. (2023). Does unemployment affect the relationship between income inequality and food security? *The International Journal of Sociology and Social Policy*, 43(1/2), 48–66. DOI: 10.1108/IJSSP-12-2021-0303

Hannig, A., & Jansen, S. (2010). Financial inclusion and financial stability: Henegar, D., Ilie , G. L., Mure an, I. C., Poru iu, A. R., Arion, I. D., & Arion, F. H. (2024). Customers' perception of microfinance services as a tool for rural development: a Romanian case study. *Agriculture*, 14(7), 1087.

Harahap, B., Risfandy, T., & Futri, I. N. (2023). Islamic Law, Islamic Finance, and Sustainable Development Goals: A Systematic Literature Review. *Sustainability (Basel)*, 15(8), 6626. Advance online publication. DOI: 10.3390/su15086626

Hashemi, S. M., Schuler, S. R., & Riley, A. P. (1996). Rural credit programs and women's empowerment in Bangladesh. *World Development*, 24(4), 635–653. DOI: 10.1016/0305-750X(95)00159-A

Hendershott, T., Zhang, X., Zhao, J. L., & Zheng, Z. (2021). FinTech as a game changer: Overview of research frontiers. *Information Systems Research*, 32(1), 1–17. DOI: 10.1287/isre.2021.0997

Henrekson, M., & Johansson, D. (1999)... *Small Business Economics*, 12(1), 11–23. DOI: 10.1023/A:1008002330051

Hermes, N. (2014). Does microfinance affect income inequality? *Applied Economics*, 46(9), 1021–1034. DOI: 10.1080/00036846.2013.864039

Hermes, N., & Lensink, R. (2020). Microfinance and development. In *Contemporary issues in development finance* (pp. 51–72). Routledge. DOI: 10.4324/9780429450952-3

Heshmati, A. (2006). The world distribution of income and income inequality: A review of the economics literature. *Journal of World-systems Research*, •••, 61–107. DOI: 10.5195/jwsr.2006.372

High Mark, C. R. I. F. (January 25, 2024). Portfolio outstanding of microfinance industry in India from financial year 2020 to 2023 (in trillion Indian rupees) [Graph]. In Statista. Retrieved June 21, 2024, from https://www.statista.com/statistics/1344112/india-microfinance-industry-portfolio-outstanding/

Hilson, M. (2018). The International Co-operative Alliance and the consumer co-operative movement in northern Europe, c. 1860–1939. In *The International Co-operative Alliance and the consumer co-operative movement in northern* [Manchester University Press.]. *Europe*, c, 1860–1939.

Hollis, A., & Sweetman, A. 1996. THE EVOLUTION OF AMicrocredit INSTITUTION: THE IRISH LOAN FUNDS, 1720-1920. *Department of Economics University of Toronto Working Paper.*

Hollis, A., & Sweetman, A. (1998). Microcredit in prefamine Ireland. *Explorations in Economic History*, 35(4), 347–380. DOI: 10.1006/exeh.1998.0702

Hoque, M. M. 2022. *Microfinance challenges and the potential benefits of blockchain technology and mobile money* (Doctoral dissertation, Queensland University of Technology).

HR. U., & KN, R. (2013). The role of SHGS in financial inclusion. A case study. *International Journal of Scientific and Research Publications, 3*(6).

Hsu, B. Y. (2014). Alleviating poverty or reinforcing inequality? Interpreting micro-finance in practice, with illustrations from rural C hina. *The British Journal of Sociology*, 65(2), 245–265. DOI: 10.1111/1468-4446.12076 PMID: 24784017

Huang, K., Sim, N., & Zhao, H. (2020). DOES FDI ACTUALLY AFFECT INCOME INEQUALITY? INSIGHTS FROM 25 YEARS OF RESEARCH. *Journal of Economic Surveys*, 34(3), 630–659. https://doi.org/https://doi.org/10.1111/joes.12373. DOI: 10.1111/joes.12373

Hunt, J., & Kasynathan, N. (2002). Reflections on microfinance and women's empowerment. *Development Bulletin (Canberra)*, 57, 71–75.

Ibrahim, A.-J., & Shirazi, N. S. (2020). The role of islamic finance in fostering circular business investments: The case of oic countries. *Journal of Economic Co-operation and Development*, 41(1), 89–120.

Illangakoon, A. G., Azam, S. M., Khatibi, A., & Sudasinghe, S. (2021). Women empowerment in microfinance: Poverty alleviation tool. *South Asian Journal of Social Studies and Economics*, 12(4), 159–172. DOI: 10.9734/sajsse/2021/v12i430324

Indian Economy: An Overview. (n.d.). Invest India. https://www.investindia.gov.in/team-india-blogs/indian-economy-overview

IRENA. (2020). *Innovation landscape brief: Pay-as-you-go models*. International Renewable Energy Agency.

Ishaq, H., Dincer, I., & Crawford, C. (2022). A review on hydrogen production and utilization: Challenges and opportunities. *International Journal of Hydrogen Energy*, 47(62), 26238–26264. DOI: 10.1016/j.ijhydene.2021.11.149

Iskandar, R. D. M., Maryanti, T., Jayaprawira, A. R., & Sari, S. N. (2022). Indonesian Islamic Banking Fintech Model Strategy: ANP Method. *APTISI Transactions on Technopreneurship*, 4(2), 142–152. DOI: 10.34306/att.v4i2.257

Islam, A. H., Basher, S. A., & Enamul Haque, A. K. (2022). The impact of mobile money on long-term poverty: Evidence from Bangladesh. *Journal of Social and Economic Development*, 24(2), 436–455. DOI: 10.1007/s40847-022-00194-0 PMID: 36034405

İstekli, M., & Ustaoğlu, M. (2020). Monte di Pietà. In *The Evolution of Interest and Debt* (pp. 86–96). Routledge. DOI: 10.4324/9781003041245-9

Jack, W., Kremer, M., De Laat, J., & Suri, T. (2016). *Borrowing requirements, credit access, and adverse selection: Evidence from kenya* (No. w22686). National Bureau of Economic Research.

Jacobs, M., & Mazzucato, M. (Eds.). (2016). *Rethinking capitalism: Economics and policy for sustainable and inclusive growth*. John Wiley & Sons.

Jalil, M. F. (2021). Microfinance towards micro-enterprises development in rural Malaysia through digital finance. *Discover Sustainability*, 2(1), 55. DOI: 10.1007/s43621-021-00066-3 PMID: 35425910

Jatmiko, W., Iqbal, A., & Ebrahim, M. S. (2024). On the Ethicality of Islamic Banks' Business Model. *British Journal of Management*, 35(1), 115–136. DOI: 10.1111/1467-8551.12703

Javaid, M., Haleem, A., Singh, R. P., Suman, R., & Khan, S. (2022). A review of Blockchain Technology applications for financial services. *BenchCouncil Transactions on Benchmarks. Standards and Evaluations*, 2(3), 100073.

Jelili Amuda, Y., & Alabdulrahman, S. (2023). Reinforcing policy and legal framework for Islamic insurance in Islamic finance: Towards achieving Saudi Arabia Vision 2030. *International Journal of Law and Management*, 65(6), 600–613. DOI: 10.1108/IJLMA-03-2023-0045

Jha, R. S., & Sahoo, P. R. (2022). Technology Shaping Models of "Personalization" in Insurance. In *ICT Systems and Sustainability: Proceedings of ICT4SD 2022* (pp. 237–246). Springer Nature Singapore.

Jian, L. Ü. (2007). Empirical study on the infl uence of RMB exchange rate misalignment on China's export. *Frontiers of Economics in China*, 2(2), 224–236. DOI: 10.1007/s11459-007-0012-2

Jie, T. J. 2024. Unlocking Potential: The Impact of Financial Technology (FinTech) on Financial Inclusion and Personal Economic Security. *Available atSSRN* 4847463. DOI: 10.2139/ssrn.4847463

Joshi, D. P. (2014, January). Strategy adopted for financial inclusion. In *Speech Delivered at Workshop on* (Vol. 24).

Jumo, 2024. Innovation is all it takes. [Online] Available at https://jumo.world/ [Accessed 27 September 2024].

Kabeer, N. (2005). Is microfinance a "magic bullet" for women's empowerment? *Women Studies International Forum, 28*(1), 13-32. DOI: 10.1016/j.wsif.2005.01.007

Kabeer, N. (2001). Conflicts over credit: Re-evaluating the empowerment potential of loans to women in rural Bangladesh. *World Development*, 29(1), 63–84. DOI: 10.1016/S0305-750X(00)00081-4

Kabeer, N. (2005). Is microfinance a 'magic bullet' for women's empowerment? *Economic and Political Weekly*, 40(44/45), 4709–4718.

Kabeer, N. (2005). Is microfinance a' magic bullet' for women's empowerment? Analysis of findings from South Asia. *Economic and Political Weekly*, •••, 4709–4718.

Kaladhar, K. (1997). Microfinance in India: Design, Structure and Governance. *Economic and Political Weekly*, 32(42), 2687–2706. https://www.jstor.org/stable/4405979

Kandpal, V., Chandra, D., Dalei, N. N., & Handoo, J. (2023). Expanding financial inclusion through Fintech and e-governance. In *Financial inclusion in circular economy: A bumpy road towards sustainable development* (pp. 103–129). Springer International Publishing. DOI: 10.1007/978-3-031-22723-3_6

Karlan, D., & Valdivia, M. (2011). Teaching entrepreneurship: Impact of business training on Microfinance clients and institutions. *The Review of Economics and Statistics*, 93(2), 510–527. DOI: 10.1162/REST_a_00074

Karlan, D., & Zinman, J. (2011). Microcredit in theory and practice: Using randomized credit scoring for impact evaluation. *Science*, 332(6035), 1278–1284. DOI: 10.1126/science.1200138 PMID: 21659596

Karmakar, G. K., Banerjee, D. G., & Monapatra, P. N. (2011). *Towards financial inclusion in India* (1st ed.). Sage Publication.

Kaulihowa, T., & Adjasi, C. (2018). FDI and income inequality in Africa. *Oxford Development Studies*, 46(2), 250–265. DOI: 10.1080/13600818.2017.1381233

Kayongo, S., & Mathiassen, L. 2020, September. Dynamic capabilities in microfinance innovation: A case study of the Grameen Foundation. In *The Tenth International Conference on Engaged Management Scholarship*. DOI: 10.2139/ssrn.3687792

Khalidin, B., Musa, A., & Kiawan, A. (2023). MURABAHA FINANCING OF THE INDONESIAN ISLAMIC BANKS UNDER AN ISLAMIC ECONOMIC LAW AND THE FATWA DSN MUI. *Petita: Jurnal Kajian Ilmu Hukum Dan Syariah*, 8(2), 203–218. DOI: 10.22373/petita.v8i2.238

Khan, A., Mubarik, M. S., & Naghavi, N. (2023). What matters for financial inclusions? Evidence from emerging economy. *International Journal of Finance & Economics*, 28(1), 821–838. DOI: 10.1002/ijfe.2451

Khandker, S. R., & Samad, H. A. (2013). Are Microcredit participants in Bangladesh trapped in poverty and debt? *Policy Research Working Papers*. https://doi.org/DOI: 10.1596/1813-9450-6404

Khandker, S. R. (2005). Microfinance and poverty: Evidence using panel data from Bangladesh. *The World Bank Economic Review*, 19(2), 263–286. DOI: 10.1093/wber/lhi008

Khan, M. A., Iqbal, N., & Ashraf, M. (2018). Green Technology and sustainable development: A review of microfinance and renewable energy. *Sustainable Development*, 26(4), 289–298. DOI: 10.1002/sd.1692

Khan, T. (2019). Reforming Islamic finance for achieving sustainable development goals. *Journal of King Abdulaziz University. Islamic Economics*, 32(1), 3–21. DOI: 10.4197/Islec.32-1.1

Khan, T., & Badjie, F. (2022). Islamic blended finance for circular economy impactful smes to achieve sdgs. *The Singapore Economic Review*, 67(1), 219–244. DOI: 10.1142/S0217590820420060

Kim, H., & De Moor, L. (2017). The case of crowdfunding in financial inclusion: A survey. *Strategic Change*, 26(2), 193–212. DOI: 10.1002/jsc.2120

Kim, J.-H. (2016). A Study on the Effect of Financial Inclusion on the Relationship Between Income Inequality and Economic Growth. *Emerging Markets Finance & Trade*, 52(2), 498–512. DOI: 10.1080/1540496X.2016.1110467

Kismawadi, E. R., Irfan, M., Al Muddatstsir, U. D., & Abdulkarim, F. M. (2023). Fintech innovations: Risk mitigation strategies in Islamic finance. In *Fintech Applications in Islamic Finance* (pp. 35–58). AI, Machine Learning, and Blockchain Techniques., DOI: 10.4018/979-8-3693-1038-0.ch003

Kismawadi, E. R., Irfan, M., Haron, R., & Masitah, M. (2024). Bridging Finance and Sustainability: Islamic Financial Institutions' Contributions to the Transition to Sustainable Energy. In Irfan, M., Hussainey, K., Bukhari, S. A. C., & Nam, Y. (Eds.), *Issues of Sustainability in AI and New-Age Thematic Investing* (pp. 138–161). IGI Global., DOI: 10.4018/979-8-3693-3282-5.ch009

Kobugabe, C., & Rwakihembo, J. (2022). Financial Literacy and Financial Inclusion: A positivist view of Proprietors of Small and Medium Enterprises in Fort Portal City, Western Uganda. *American Journal of Finance*, 7(2), 1–12. DOI: 10.47672/ajf.1014

Kofman, P., & Payne, C. 2021. Digital financial inclusion of women: An ethical appraisal. *Handbook on ethics in finance*, pp.133-157.

Kouladoum, J. C., Wirajing, M. A. K., & Nchofoung, T. N. (2022). Digital technologies and financial inclusion in Sub-Saharan Africa. *Telecommunications Policy*, 46(9), 102387. DOI: 10.1016/j.telpol.2022.102387

Kshetri, N. (2023). *Blockchain in the Global South*. Springer Books. DOI: 10.1007/978-3-031-33944-8

Kshetri, N. (2023). Blockchain in the Global South: Key Issues and Current Status. In *Blockchain in the Global South: Opportunities and Challenges for Businesses and Societies* (pp. 1–28). Springer Nature Switzerland. DOI: 10.1007/978-3-031-33944-8_1

Kulkarni, L., & Ghosh, A. (2021). Gender disparity in the digitalization of financial services: Challenges and promises for women's financial inclusion in India. *Gender, Technology and Development*, 25(2), 233–250. DOI: 10.1080/09718524.2021.1911022

Kumar, A., Sharma, S., & Mahdavi, M. (2021). Machine learning (Ml) technologies for digital credit scoring in rural finance: A literature review. *Risks*, 9(11), 192. DOI: 10.3390/risks9110192

Kumar, P. (2022). An Analysis of Some Poverty Alleviation and Employment Generation Programmes in India. *Ideal Research Review, 72*(1). DOI: 10.1080/00036846.2017.1368990

Kumar, R., & Pathak, D. C. (2022). Financial awareness: a bridge to financial inclusion. Development in Practice, 32(7), 968-980.Milana, C., & Ashta, A. (2020). Microfinance and financial inclusion: Challenges and opportunities. *Strategic Change*, 29(3), 257–266.

Kumar, S., & Subedi, S. (2023). Microfinance Schemes for Women Entrepreneurship in India: A Case Study of Sikkim State. In Alhassan, Y., & Nwagbara, U. (Eds.), *Empowering Women Through Microfinance in Developing Countries* (pp. 124–140). IGI Global., DOI: 10.4018/978-1-6684-8979-6.ch007

Kunhibava, S., Mustapha, Z., Muneeza, A., Sa'ad, A. A., & Karim, M. E. (2020). ukūk on blockchain: A legal, regulatory and Sharī'ah review. *ISRA International Journal of Islamic Finance*, 13(1), 118–135. DOI: 10.1108/IJIF-06-2020-0120

Kuzilwa, J. A. (2005). The role of credit for small business success. *The Journal of Entrepreneurship*, 14(2), 131–161. DOI: 10.1177/097135570501400204

Lacalle-Calderon, M., Larrú, J. M., Garrido, S. R., & Perez-Trujillo, M. (2019). Microfinance and income inequality: New macrolevel evidence. *Review of Development Economics*, 23(2), 860–876. https://doi.org/https://doi.org/10.1111/rode.12573. DOI: 10.1111/rode.12573

Laha, A., & Kuri, P. K. (2014). Measuring the impact of Microfinance on women empowerment: A cross country analysis with special reference to India. *International Journal of Public Administration*, 37(7), 397–408. DOI: 10.1080/01900692.2013.858354

Lassoued, M. (2021). Control of corruption, microfinance, and income inequality in MENA countries: Evidence from panel data. *SN Business & Economics*, 1(7), 96. DOI: 10.1007/s43546-021-00099-w

Lechheb, H., Ouakil, H., & Jouilil, Y. (2019). Economic Growth, Poverty, and Income Inequality. *Journal of Private Equity*, 23(1), 137–145. DOI: 10.3905/jpe.2019.1.097

Ledgerwood, J. (1999). *Microfinance handbook: An institutional and financial perspective*. World Bank Publications.

Ledgerwood, J. (1999). *Microfinance Handbook: An Institutional and Financial Perspective*. World Bank Publications.

Ledhem, M. A., & Mekidiche, M. (2022). Islamic finance and economic growth: The Turkish experiment. *ISRA International Journal of Islamic Finance*, 14(1), 4–19. DOI: 10.1108/IJIF-12-2020-0255

Lee, J., & Kim, J. (2020). Exploring the factors influencing consumer adoption of digital payment systems: A comparative analysis pre and post COVID-19. *Journal of Retailing and Consumer Services*, 61, 102542. DOI: 10.1016/j.jretconser.2020.102542

Leng, J., Ruan, G., Jiang, P., Xu, K., Liu, Q., Zhou, X., & Liu, C. (2020). Blockchain-empowered sustainable manufacturing and product lifecycle management in industry 4.0: A survey. *Renewable & Sustainable Energy Reviews*, 132, 110112. Advance online publication. DOI: 10.1016/j.rser.2020.110112

Liao, S. H., Fei, W. C., & Chen, C. C. (2007). Knowledge sharing, absorptive capacity, and innovation capability: An empirical study of Taiwan's knowledge-intensive industries. *Journal of Information Science*, 33(3), 340–359. DOI: 10.1177/0165551506070739

Lieberman, I. W. 2020. The growth and commercial evolution of microfinance. *The future of microfinance*, pp.9-35.

Liew, V. K. S., Tan, W. Y., & Ho, L. S. (2016). The relationship between exchange rate and trade balance in ASEAN countries: Evidence from time series data. *Asian Economic Policy Review*, 11(2), 234–250. DOI: 10.1111/aepr.12157

Lioudis, N. (2023, August 22). *How the Balance of Trade Affects Currency Exchange Rates*. Investopedia. https://www.investopedia.com/ask/answers/041515/how-does-balance-trade-impact-currency-exchange-rates.asp

Liu, F., & Lyons, A. C. 2024. Use Cases in Fintech. In *The Emerald Handbook of Fintech: Reshaping Finance* (pp. 43-64). Emerald Publishing Limited. DOI: 10.1108/978-1-83753-608-520241005

Llanto, G. M. (2007). Overcoming obstacles to agricultural microfinance: Looking at broader issues. *Asian Journal of Agriculture and Development*, 4(2), 23–40. DOI: 10.37801/ajad2007.4.2.2

Lowe, 2023. *Mobile money in Tanzania: Unveiling the vision of Tigo Pesa.* [Online] Available at https://www.gsma.com/solutions-and-impact/connectivity-for-good/mobile-for-development/blog/mobile-money-in-tanzania-unveiling-the-vision-of-tigo-pesa/ [Accessed 28 September 2024].

Luarn, P., & Lin, H. H. (2005). Toward an understanding of the behavioral intention to use mobile banking. *Computers in Human Behavior*, 21(6), 873–891. DOI: 10.1016/j.chb.2004.03.003

Lucarelli, B. (2005). Microcredit: A cautionary tale. *Journal of Contemporary Asia*, 35(1), 78–86. DOI: 10.1080/00472330580000051

Luo, X., Ge, L., & Wang, C. A. (2022). Crowdfunding for microfinance institutions: The new hope? *Management Information Systems Quarterly*, 46(1), 373–400. DOI: 10.25300/MISQ/2022/15406

Lyon, D. (2012). *Surveillance after snowden.* John Wiley & Sons.

Macchiavello, E. (2017). *Microfinance and financial inclusion: The challenge of regulating alternative forms of finance.* Routledge. DOI: 10.4324/9781315623962

Maclean, K. 2017. Microfinance and the "woman" question. *Seduced and Betrayed: Exposing the Contemporary Microfinance Phenomenon; Bateman, M., Maclean, K., Galbraith, JK, Eds*, pp.251-264.

Mader, P. (2014). Financialisation through Microfinance: Civil Society and Market-Building in India. *Asian Studies Review*, 38(4), 601–619. DOI: 10.1080/10357823.2014.963507

Mader, P. (2015). *The political economy of microfinance : financialising poverty.* DOI: 10.1057/9781137364210

Mader, P. (2018). Contesting financial inclusion. *Development and Change*, 49(2), 461–483. DOI: 10.1111/dech.12368

Mago, S. (2013). Microfinance in Zimbabwe: A historical overview. *Mediterranean Journal of Social Sciences*, 4(14), 599–608.

Mahmoud Ali, I. A., & Ghoneim, H. (2019). The effect of microfinance on income inequality: Perspective of developing countries. *Journal of Economics and Management*, 35(1), 40–62. DOI: 10.22367/jem.2019.35.03

Maity, S. (2024). Rawls' difference principle, self-help group, financial inclusion and social cohesion—Lore or actuality? Experience of Central Assam. *Humanities & Social Sciences Communications*, 11(1), 1–13. DOI: 10.1057/s41599-024-02708-z

Maity, S., & Sarania, R. (2017). Does microfinance alleviate poverty and inequality? Studying self-help groups in Bodoland, Assam. *Development in Practice*, 27(7), 1006–1019. DOI: 10.1080/09614524.2017.1355353

Mandrawal, M. S. (2022). A Theoretical Evaluation of the Microfinance and its impact on Living Standards and Poverty Reduction in India. *International Journal for Global Academic & Scientific Research*, 1(3), 11–19. DOI: 10.55938/ijgasr.v1i3.21

Mani, M. (2016). Financial inclusion in South Asia—Relative standing, challenges and initiatives. *South Asian Survey*, 23(2), 158–179. DOI: 10.1177/0971523118783353

Manta, O. (2018). Financial Technologies (FinTech), Instruments, mechanisms and financial products. *Internal Auditing & Risk Management*, 52(4), 78–102.

Martinčević, I., Črnjević, S., & Klopotan, I. (2020). FinTech revolution in the financial industry. *ENTRENOVA-ENTerprise REsearch InNOVAtion*, 6(1), 563–571.

Matsuo, M. (2022). Reflection on success in promoting authenticity and proactive behavior: A two-wave study. *Current Psychology (New Brunswick, N.J.)*, 41(12), 8793–8801. DOI: 10.1007/s12144-021-01352-z

Mayoux, L. (2001). Tackling the down side: Social capital, women's empowerment and micro-finance in Cameroon. *Development and Change*, 32(3), 435–464. DOI: 10.1111/1467-7660.00212

McKinsey & Company. (2020). COVID-19: Implications for business. Retrieved from https://www.mckinsey.com/business-functions/risk/our-insights/covid-19-implications-for-business

McLaughlin, E. J. 2009. *Microfinance institutions in nineteenth century Ireland* (Doctoral dissertation, National University of Ireland Maynooth).

Mehta, A., & Bhattacharya, J. (2017). Channels of financial sector development and rural-urban consumption inequality in India. *International Journal of Social Economics*, 44(12), 1973–1987. DOI: 10.1108/IJSE-05-2015-0117

Memdani, L. (2020). Demonetisation: A move towards cashless economy in India. *International Journal of Electronic Banking*, 2(3), 205–211. DOI: 10.1504/IJEBANK.2020.111428

Metre, K. (2013). [) in Indonesia: Opportunities and Challenges.]. *Information and Communication Technologies for Development*, IC, T4D.

Meyer, J. 2002. "Track record of financial institutions assessing the poor in Asia," ADB research institute paper, N. 49 [Online}. http://www.esocialsciences.com/articles (30 September 2011) MicroEnergy International (MEI) (n.d.) Clean Energy Promotion through Microfinance in Ethiopia. https://www. climate-change.org/en/best-practices/clean-energy-promotion-through-microfinance-in-ethiopia/

Meyerowitz, J. (2021). *A War on Global Poverty: the lost promise of redistribution and the rise of microcredit*. Princeton University Press.

Mhlanga, D. (2024). *FinTech, Financial Inclusion, and Sustainable Development: Disruption, Innovation, and Growth*. Taylor & Francis. DOI: 10.4324/9781032657981

Mia, M. A. (2022). Microfinance and microfinance institutions: History, concept and purpose. In *Social Purpose, Commercialization, and Innovations in Microfinance: A Global Perspective* (pp. 17–45). Springer Singapore. DOI: 10.1007/978-981-19-0217-8_2

Milana, C., & Ashta, A. (2020). Microfinance and financial inclusion: Challenges and opportunities. *Strategic Change*, 29(3), 257–266. DOI: 10.1002/jsc.2339

Miled, K. B. H., Younsi, M., & Landolsi, M. (2022). Does microfinance program innovation reduce income inequality? Cross-country and panel data analysis. *Journal of Innovation and Entrepreneurship*, 11(1), 7. DOI: 10.1186/s13731-022-00195-7

Mishkin, F. S. (2007, January 1). *The Economics of Money, Banking, and Financial Markets*. Pearson Education. http://books.google.ie/books?id=ni8yiX9JsAsC&printsec=frontcover&dq=10:+0-13-473382-7&hl=&cd=1&source=gbs_api

Mitchell, C. (2023, September 7). *Floating Exchange Rate: What It Is, How It Works, History*. Investopedia. https://www.investopedia.com/terms/f/floatingexchangerate.asp

Mjuza, N., & Ntsalaze, L. (2019). Over-indebtedness of microfinance borrowers in South Africa. *African Review of Economics and Finance*, 11(2), 98–128.

M-KOPA. (2020). *Impact Report 2020*. https://www.M-KOPA.com

M-KOPA. (2024)."Leading Fintech African M-KOPA Reaches 5 Million Customers, Unlocking $1.5bn in Credit Across 5 Markets." *Impact Report 2024*. https://s24.q4cdn.com/538403808/files/doc_news/Leading-Fintech-African-M-KOPA-Reaches-5-Million-Customers-Unlocking-1.5bn-in-Credit-Across-5-Markets-2024.pdf

Mohammed, M. M., Tok, M. E., & Ali, S. N. (2020). The potential of islamic finance in reinforcing and regaining economic stability in qatar. *Journal of Economic Cooperation and Development*, 41(4), 191–217. https://www.scopus.com/inward/record.uri?eid=2-s2.0-85108997153&partnerID=40&md5=b6f650421b41a515a9cc8ac6bda4f18c

Mohanasundaram, T., Sathyanarayana, S., & Rizwana, M. 2021. Disruptions on India's FinTech landscape: The 5G wave. In *ITM Web of Conferences* (Vol. 37, p. 01008). EDP Sciences.

Mohd Daud, M. A., Rosly, S. A., & Muhamad Sori, Z. (2021). Structuring fund for affordable housing investment in Malaysia: An exploratory research. *International Journal of Housing Markets and Analysis*, 14(2), 260–271. DOI: 10.1108/IJHMA-03-2020-0024

Mohd Noh, M. S., Nor Azelan, S. H., & Zulkepli, M. I. S. (2024). A review on Gharar dimension in modern Islamic finance transactions. *Journal of Islamic Accounting and Business Research.* Advance online publication. DOI: 10.1108/JIABR-01-2023-0006

Molenaar, K., & Lehmann, J. M. (2016). *Microfinance, what is it all about?* The Hague University of Applied Sciences. [online]

Morduch, J. (1999). The microfinance promise. *Journal of Economic Literature*, 37(4), 1569–1614. DOI: 10.1257/jel.37.4.1569

Morgan, P. J. (2022). Fintech and financial inclusion in Southeast Asia and India. *Asian Economic Policy Review*, 17(2), 183–208. DOI: 10.1111/aepr.12379

Morgan, P. J., & Long, T. Q. (2020). Financial literacy, financial inclusion, and savings behavior in Laos. *Journal of Asian Economics*, 68, 101197. DOI: 10.1016/j.asieco.2020.101197

Mosley, P. (2009). *Assessing the success of microinsurance programmes in meeting the insurance needs of the poor*. Financing for Overcoming Economic Insecurity.

Mouka, Marina. (2024, 15 July). Top 10 fintech innovations transforming the financial sector. *bobsguide*. bobsguide.com/top-10-fintech-innovations-transforming-the-financial-sector/

Mukhlisin, M., al-Falih, A. A., Azid, T., & Shirazi, N. S. (2023). The Indonesian Islamic capital market and achievement of Maqasad Al-sHari'ah: Success or failure. In *Islamic Economic Institutions In Indonesia* (pp. 209–226). Are They Successful In Achieving The Maqasad-al-shari'ah., DOI: 10.1142/9789811272691_0012

Mukhopadhyay, J. P. (2016). Financial inclusion in India: A demand-side approach. *Economic and Political Weekly*, •••, 46–54.

Mukhopadhyay, J. P. (2016). Microfinance and consumption inequality: Evidence from a randomized controlled trial in Andhra Pradesh, India. *Journal of Developing Areas*, 50(2), 269–291. DOI: 10.1353/jda.2016.0088

Mulbah, F. F., Olumeh, D. E., Mantey, V., & Ipara, B. O. (2022). Impact of financial inclusion on household welfare in Liberia: A gendered perspective. *Review of Development Economics*.

Mulili, B. M. (2022). Digital Financial Inclusion: M-PESA in Kenya. In *Digital Business in Africa: Social Media and Related Technologies* (pp. 171–191). Springer International Publishing. DOI: 10.1007/978-3-030-93499-6_8

Muneer Babu, M.Muneer Babu M. (2016). Macroeconomic determinants of technological change in Indian Microfinance institutions. *Global Business Review*, 17(5), 1179–1195. DOI: 10.1177/0972150916656685

Mushtaq, R., & Bruneau, C. (2019). Microfinance, financial inclusion and ICT: Implications for poverty and inequality. *Technology in Society*, 59, 101154. https://doi.org/https://doi.org/10.1016/j.techsoc.2019.101154. DOI: 10.1016/j.techsoc.2019.101154

Mutamimah, M., & Indriastuti, M. (2023). Fintech, financial literacy, and financial inclusion in Indonesian SMEs. *International Journal of Entrepreneurship and Innovation Management*, 27(1-2), 137–150. DOI: 10.1504/IJEIM.2023.129331

Mutuma, K. G. 2020. *Microfinance services and financial performance of Small and Medium Enterprises in Meru Town, Kenya* (Doctoral dissertation, KENYATTA UNIVERSITY).

NABARD. (2023). *Status of Microfinance in India 2022-23*. 1–272. www.nabard.org

NABARD. (2023). *Status of Microfinance in India 2022-23*. National Bank for Agriculture and Rural Development.

Naguib, C. (2015). *The relationship between inequality and GDP growth: An empirical approach*. LIS Working Paper Series.

Nandera, S. (2016). Building women's economic empowerment. *International Trade Forum*, 2016(1), 20–21. DOI: 10.18356/ce9df046-en

Nawaz, A. (2018). Challenges faced by women entrepreneurs in Pakistan: A qualitative study. *Management and Organizational Studies*, 5(2), 13. DOI: 10.5430/mos.v5n2p13

Nazeri, A. N. N., Nor, S. M., Abdul-Rahman, A., Abdul-Majid, M., & Hamid, S. N. A. (2023). EXPLORATION OF A NEW ZAKAT MANAGEMENT SYSTEM EMPOWERED BY BLOCKCHAIN TECHNOLOGY IN MALAYSIA. *ISRA International Journal of Islamic Finance*, 15(4), 127–147. DOI: 10.55188/ijif.v15i4.568

Naz, S. A., & Gulzar, S. (2023). Islamic financial development & economic growth: The emergence of Islamic financial market in Pakistan. *Journal of Islamic Accounting and Business Research*, 14(6), 989–1012. DOI: 10.1108/JIABR-09-2022-0222

Neuhuber, T., & Schneider, A. E. (2024). The role of public social expenditure for mitigating local income inequality: An investigation across spatial scales in Austria. *Journal of Regional Science*, 64(5), 1647–1679. DOI: 10.1111/jors.12722

Ng, E., & Pan, S. L. (2024). Competitive strategies for ensuring Fintech platform performance: Evidence from multiple case studies. *Information Systems Journal*, 34(3), 616–641. DOI: 10.1111/isj.12406

Nilakantan, R. A. H. U. L., Datta, S. C., Sinha, P., & Datta, S. K. (2013). The impact of microfinance on women empowerment: Evidence from Eastern India. *International Journal of Development and Conflict*, 3(1), 27–40.

Nolan, B., Richiardi, M. G., & Valenzuela, L. (2019). THE DRIVERS OF INCOME INEQUALITY IN RICH COUNTRIES. *Journal of Economic Surveys*, 33(4), 1285–1324. https://doi.org/https://doi.org/10.1111/joes.12328. DOI: 10.1111/joes.12328

Noordin, N. H., Haron, S. N., Hasan, A., & Hassan, R. (2018). Complying with the requirements for issuance of SRI sukuk: The case of Khazanah's Sukuk Ihsan. *Journal of Islamic Accounting and Business Research*, 9(3), 415–433. DOI: 10.1108/JIABR-02-2016-0024

Nukpezah, J. A., & Blankson, C. (2017). Microfinance intervention in poverty reduction: A study of women farmer-entrepreneurs in rural Ghana. *Journal of African Business*, 18(4), 457–475. DOI: 10.1080/15228916.2017.1336915

Nwankwo, C., Kanyangale, M., Anoke, A. F., & Eze, S. U. (2023). Effect of Cyber Security on Business Sustainability of Listed Microfinance Banks in Nigeria. *The Arab Journal of the Social Sciences*, 22(1), 79–106. DOI: 10.29138/ijebd.v6i5.2279

Ojera, P. (2018). Indigenous financial management practices in Africa: A guide for educators and practitioners. In *Indigenous Management Practices in Africa: A Guide for Educators and Practitioners* (pp. 71–96). Emerald Publishing Limited. DOI: 10.1108/S1877-636120180000020005

Okeke, C. T., Ifebi, O. E., & Ekesiobi, C. S. (2023). Financial Inclusion and Unemployment in Nigeria. *Journal of Advanced Research in Economics and Administrative Sciences*, 4(4), 28–47. DOI: 10.47631/jareas.v4i4.639

Oluyemi, O., & Isaac, E. D. (2017). The effect of exchange rate on imports and exports in Nigeria from January 1996 to June 2015. International journal of economics and business management, 3(2), 66-77.

Omar, M. A., & Inaba, K. (2020). Does financial inclusion reduce poverty and income inequality in developing countries? A panel data analysis. *Journal of Economic Structures*, 9(1), 37. DOI: 10.1186/s40008-020-00214-4

Oppong, E. O., Yu, B., & Mazonga Mfoutou, B. O. (2024). The effect of microinsurance on the financial resilience of low-income households in Ghana: Evidence from a propensity score matching analysis. *The Geneva Papers on Risk and Insurance. Issues and Practice*, 49(3), 1–27. DOI: 10.1057/s41288-024-00325-0

Organizations. (2022). (pp. 417–423). Routledge.

Our philosophy | Bandhan bank. (n.d.). Bandhan Bank |. https://bandhanbank.com/our-philosophy

Oyovwi, O. D. (2012). Exchange rate volatility and imports in Nigeria. *Academic Journal of Interdisciplinary Studies*, 1(2), 103–114.

Ozili, P. K. (2020). Theories of financial inclusion. In *Uncertainty and challenges in contemporary economic behaviour* (pp. 89–115). Emerald Publishing Limited. DOI: 10.1108/978-1-80043-095-220201008

Ozili, P. K. (2021). Financial inclusion research around the world: A review. *The Forum for Social Economics*, 50(4), 457–479. DOI: 10.1080/07360932.2020.1715238

Pal, A., Dey, S., Nandy, A., Shahin, S., & Singh, P. K. (2023). Digital Transformation in Microfinance as a Driver for Sustainable Development. In *Handbook of Sustainability Science in the Future: Policies, Technologies and Education by 2050* (pp. 251–271). Springer International Publishing. DOI: 10.1007/978-3-031-04560-8_74

Pal, M., Gupta, H., & Joshi, Y. C. (2022). Social and economic empowerment of women through financial inclusion: Empirical evidence from India. *Equality, Diversity and Inclusion*, 41(2), 294–305. DOI: 10.1108/EDI-04-2021-0113

Pang, L., Zhu, M. N., & Yu, H. (2022). Is green finance really a blessing for green technology and carbon efficiency? *Energy Economics*, 114, 106272. Advance online publication. DOI: 10.1016/j.eneco.2022.106272

Parveen, S. (2009). An empirical analysis of the relationship between rural women's participation in microfinance and their empowerment: The case of rural Pakistan. *Pakistan Journal of Social Sciences*, 29(1), 189–204.

Parwez, S., & Patel, R. (2022). Augmenting women empowerment: A systematic literature review on microfinance-led developmental interventions. *Journal of Global Responsibility*, 13(3), 338–360. DOI: 10.1108/JGR-01-2021-0005

Pazarbasioglu, C., Mora, A. G., Uttamchandani, M., Natarajan, H., Feyen, E., & Saal, M. (2020). Digital financial services. *World Bank, 54*, 1-54.

Pe'er, G., Bonn, A., Bruelheide, H., Dieker, P., Eisenhauer, N., Feindt, P. H., Hagedorn, G., Hansjürgens, B., Herzon, I., Lomba, Â., Marquard, E., Moreira, F., Nitsch, H., Oppermann, R., Perino, A., Röder, N., Schleyer, C., Schindler, S., Wolf, C., & Lakner, S. (2020). Action needed for the EU Common Agricultural Policy to address sustainability challenges. *People and Nature*, 2(2), 305–316. DOI: 10.1002/pan3.10080 PMID: 32626843

Pitt, M. M., & Khandker, S. R. (1998). The impact of group-based credit programs on poor households in Bangladesh: Does the gender of participants matter? *Journal of Political Economy*, 106(5), 958–996. DOI: 10.1086/250037

Planning Commission. (2009). *Annual Report*. Government of India.

Poddar, K. K. (2015). Microfinance and self help groups. *Anusandhanika*, 7(1), 174.

Polacko, M. (2021). *Causes and Consequences of Income Inequality – An Overview. 12*(2), 341–357. https://doi.org/doi:10.1515/spp-2021-0017

Purba, B., Masbar, R., Maipita, I., & Jamal, A. (2019). The Effect of Capital Expenditure and Gross Fixed Capital Formation on Income Disparity in West Coast Region of North Sumatera. *IOP Conference Series. Earth and Environmental Science*, 260(1), 12022. DOI: 10.1088/1755-1315/260/1/012022

Putriana, V. T. (2024). Examining a distinctive loan contract "Pagang Gadai" practiced in a Muslim society: An Islamic finance perspective. *Journal of Islamic Accounting and Business Research*. Advance online publication. DOI: 10.1108/JIABR-10-2023-0341

Pytkowska, J., & Korynski, P. (2017). *Digitalizing microfinance in Europe*. Microfinance Centre.

Qanas, J., & Sawyer, M. (2022). Financialisation in the Gulf States. *Review of Political Economy*. Advance online publication. DOI: 10.1080/09538259.2022.2099669

Quartey, J. A., & Kotey, B. (2019). The effect of regulations on ability of MFIs to provide sustained financial services to small business. *Small Enterprise Research*, 26(3), 235–252. DOI: 10.1080/13215906.2019.1670236

Quinones, B., & Remenyi, J. (2014). *Microfinance and poverty alleviation: Case studies from Asia and the Pacific*. Routledge. DOI: 10.4324/9781315800455

Quirk, T. (2023). Interest Rate Caps, Segmented Markets, and Microfinance: A Cautionary Tale from Zambia. *Segmented Markets, and Microfinance: A Cautionary Tale from Zambia (April 15, 2023)*. DOI: 10.1108/JES-03-2019-0109

Rabbani, M. R., Bashar, A., Nawaz, N., Karim, S., Ali, M. A. M., Rahiman, H. U., & Alam, M. S. (2021). Exploring the role of islamic fintech in combating the aftershocks of covid-19: The open social innovation of the islamic financial system. *Journal of Open Innovation*, 7(2), 136. Advance online publication. DOI: 10.3390/joitmc7020136

Rahman, A. (1999). Micro-credit initiatives for equitable and sustainable development: Who pays? *World Development*, 27(1), 67–82. DOI: 10.1016/S0305-750X(98)00105-3

Rahman, M. O. (2023). The Impact of Microfinance on Poverty Alleviation and Employment Creation. *International Research Journal of Management and Social Sciences*, 4(3), 509–527.

Rahman, N. A. A., Hassan, S., & Said, J. (2015). Promoting Sustainability of Microfinance via Innovation Risks, Best Practices and Management Accounting Practices. *Procedia Economics and Finance*, 31, 470–484. https://www.sciencedirect.com/science/article/pii/S2212567115011806. DOI: 10.1016/S2212-5671(15)01180-6

Rahman, W. A. A. (2010). An overview of microfinance: History and evolution, definition and practice. *The Ahfad Journal*, 27(2), 3–21.

Raina, N. (2014). Financial literacy and credit counselling a demand-side solution to financial inclusion (A study of initiatives by select scheduled commercial banks in India). *Journal of Commerce and Management Thought*, 5(4), 659–675. DOI: 10.5958/0976-478X.2014.00013.5

Ramakrishnan, D. (2011). Financial literacy-the demand side of financial inclusion. *Available atSSRN* 1958417.

Ramji, M. (2009). Financial inclusion in Gulbarga: Finding usage in access. *Center for micro finance working paper, 26.*

Ranabahu, N., & Tanima, F. A. (2022). Empowering vulnerable microfinance women through entrepreneurship: Opportunities, challenges and the way forward. *International Journal of Gender and Entrepreneurship*, 14(2), 145–166. DOI: 10.1108/IJGE-01-2021-0020

Rangarajan, C. (2008). Report of the committee on financial inclusion. *Ministry of Finance, Government of India*, 155-167.

Ravallion, M. (2014). Income inequality in the developing world. *Science*, 344(6186), 851–855. DOI: 10.1126/science.1251875 PMID: 24855260

RBI. (2022). *Report on Trends and Progress of Banking in India 2021-22*. Reserve Bank of India.

Rehman, H., Moazzam, D. A., & Ansari, N. (2020). Role of microfinance institutions in women empowerment: A case study of Akhuwat, Pakistan. *South Asian Studies*, 30(1).

Reserve Bank of India. (2020). Digital payments in India: Trends, issues, and challenges. Retrieved from https://www.rbi.org.in/Scripts/PublicationReportDetails.aspx?UrlPage=&ID=996

Reserve Bank of India. (July 27, 2022). Number of microfinance non-banking financial companies (NBFC-MFI) in India as of January 2022, by city [Graph]. In Statista. Retrieved June 21, 2024, from https://www.statista.com/statistics/1244619/india-number-of-microfinance-institutions-by-city/

Rhyne, E. (2001). *Mainstreaming microfinance: How lending to the poor began, grew, and came of age in Bolivia*. Kumarian Press.

Rhyne, E. (2009). *Filling the Financial Services Gap: A Guide for Funders and Investors in Microfinance*. The Microfinance Gateway.

Ridho Kismawadi, E., Irfan, M., & Shah, S. M. A. R. (2023). Revolutionizing islamic finance: Artificial intelligence's role in the future of industry. In *The Impact of AI Innovation on Financial Sectors in the Era of Industry 5.0* (pp. 184–207). DOI: 10.4018/979-8-3693-0082-4.ch011

Rippey, P. 2007. Princes, peasants and pretenders: the past and future of African microfinance. *What's wrong with microfinance*, pp.109-20.

Robinson, M. S. (2001). *The microfinance revolution: Lessons from Indonesia* (Vol. 2). World Bank Publications. DOI: 10.1596/0-8213-4524-9

Roodman, D. (2012). *Due diligence: An impertinent inquiry into microfinance*. CGD Books.

Rubbab, U.-E., Irshad, M., Abid, S., Ejaz, S., Ejaz, F., & Hossain, M. B. (2024). Examining the impact of Islamic work ethics on employee voice behavior: Mediating effect of felt obligation for constructive change and moderating role of sanctification of work. *Cogent Psychology*, 11(1), 2348860. Advance online publication. DOI: 10.1080/23311908.2024.2348860

Sadik-Zada, E. R., Gatto, A., & Blick, N. (2022). Rural Electrification and Transition to Clean Cooking. The Case Study of Kanyegaramire and Kyamugarura Solar Mini-Grid Energy Cooperatives in the Kyenjojo District of Uganda. In: Leal Filho, W. Vidal, D.G. Dinis, M,A.P., Dias, R.C, (eds) *Sustainably Policies and Practices in Energy, Environment and Health, World Sustainability Series.* Springer, Cham. DOI: 10.1007/978-3-030-86304-3_32

Sadr, S. K. (2017). The optimum size of rotating qar asan savings and credit associations. *ISRA International Journal of Islamic Finance*, 9(1), 15–26. DOI: 10.1108/IJIF-07-2017-003

Sahabuddin, M., Sakib, M. N., Rahman, M. M., Jibir, A., Fahlevi, M., Aljuaid, M., & Grabowska, S. (2023). The evolution of FinTech in scientific research: A bibliometric analysis. *Sustainability (Basel)*, 15(9), 7176. DOI: 10.3390/su15097176

Saiti, B., & Abdullah, A. (2015). Sale of goods and sale of debts: A comparative analysis. *Al-Shajarah, 20*(Specialissue), 249–272. https://www.scopus.com/inward/record.uri?eid=2-s2.0-85028459958&partnerID=40&md5=62ee30fdd6ddfcb45946a772fe68324f

Salgotra, A. K., Kandari, P., & Bahuguna, U. (2021). Does access to finance eradicate poverty? A case study of Mudra beneficiaries. *The Journal of Asian Finance, Economics and Business*, 8(1), 637–646.

Sane, R., & Thomas, S. (2020). The Way Forward for Microfinance Institutions in India. *Economic and Political Weekly*, 55(36), 40–48.

Sanyal, P. (2009). From credit to collective action: The role of microfinance in promoting women's social capital and normative influence. *American Sociological Review*, 74(4), 529–550. DOI: 10.1177/000312240907400402

Sanyal, P. (2015). Group-based microcredit & emergent inequality in social capital: Why socio-religious composition matters. *Qualitative Sociology*, 38(2), 103–137. DOI: 10.1007/s11133-015-9301-8

Sarkar, S. S., & Phatowali, A. (2012). Urban Financial Inclusion: An Analysis Of Bankers' Perception-An Empirical Study In Assam. *SS International Journal of Business and Management Research*, 2(5), 91–104.

Sarma, M. (2010). *Index of financial inclusion* (CITD Discussion Paper No. 10-05). New Delhi: CITD, JNU.

Sarma, M., & Pais, J. (2011). Financial inclusion and development. *Journal of International Development*, 23(5), 613–628. DOI: 10.1002/jid.1698

Sarumathi, S., & Mohan, K. (2011). Role of Micro Finance in Women's Empowerment (An Empirical study in Pondicherry region rural SHG's). *Journal of Management and Science*, 1(1), 1–8.

Satar, N., & Kassim, S., 2020. Issues and challenges in financing the poor: Lessons learned from Islamic microfinance institutions. *European Journal of Islamic Finance*, (15).

Sawadogo, R., & Semedo, G. (2021). Financial inclusion, income inequality, and institutions in sub-Saharan Africa: Identifying cross-country inequality regimes. *International Economics, 167*, 15–28. https://doi.org/https://doi.org/10.1016/j.inteco.2021.05.002

Schmidt, R. H. (2018). Microfinance–once and today. *Credit and Capital Markets–Kredit und Kapital*, 51(2), 183–203. DOI: 10.3790/ccm.51.2.183

Segal, T. (2021, June 4). *Currency Fluctuations: How they Affect the Economy.* Investopedia. https://www.investopedia.com/articles/forex/080613/effects-currency-fluctuations-economy.asp

Seibel, H. D. 2005. *Does history matter? The old and the new world of microfinance in Europe and Asia* (No. 2005, 10). Working paper.

Seibel, H. D. (2013). 3 Old and new worlds of microfinance in Europe and Asia. In *Southeast Asia's Credit Revolution* (pp. 40–57). Routledge.

Seifert, A., Cotten, S. R., & Xie, B. (2021). A double burden of exclusion? Digital and social exclusion of older adults in times of COVID-19. *The Journals of Gerontology. Series B, Psychological Sciences and Social Sciences*, 76(3), e99–e103. DOI: 10.1093/geronb/gbaa098 PMID: 32672332

Sengupta, R., & Aubuchon, C. P. (2008, January/February). The microfinance revolution: An overview. *Review - Federal Reserve Bank of St. Louis*, •••, 90.

Senou, M. M., Ouattara, W., & Acclassato Houensou, D. (2019). Financial inclusion dynamics in WAEMU: Was digital technology the missing piece? *Cogent Economics & Finance*, 7(1), 1665432. DOI: 10.1080/23322039.2019.1665432

Shaikh, A. A., Glavee-Geo, R., Karjaluoto, H., & Hinson, R. E. (2023). Mobile money as a driver of digital financial inclusion. *Technological Forecasting and Social Change*, 186, 122158. DOI: 10.1016/j.techfore.2022.122158

Shaikh, S. A. (2021). Using Fintech in scaling up Islamic microfinance. *Journal of Islamic Accounting and Business Research*, 12(2), 186–203. DOI: 10.1108/JIABR-10-2019-0198

Sharma, A., Sharma, M., Awasthi, M. G., & Poojari, M. L. (2023). Role of microfinance institutions in financial inclusion in India. *Journal of Contemporary Issues in Business and Government*, 29(1), 662–669.

Sharma, R., & Dhir, A. (2020). The rise of digital payment methods amid COVID-19 pandemic: A consumer perspective. *Journal of Public Affairs*, 20(4), e2161. DOI: 10.1002/pa.2161

Shen, Y., Hueng, C. J., & Hu, W. (2020). Using digital technology to improve financial inclusion in China. *Applied Economics Letters*, 27(1), 30–34. DOI: 10.1080/13504851.2019.1606401

Shkodra, J., Ymeri, P., & Ibishi, L. (2021). Role of microfinance institutions for developing women entrepreneurship – the case study of Kosovo. *Economics & Sociology (Ternopil)*, 14(1), 120–129. DOI: 10.14254/2071-789X.2021/14-1/8

Shone, S. J. (2010). *Lysander Spooner: American Anarchist*. Lexington Books.

Shuaibu, M., & Isah, A. (2020). Exchange Rate Dynamics and Trade Balance in Selected African Countries. *Journal of African Trade*, 7(1–2), 69. DOI: 10.2991/jat.k.201218.001

Siano, A., Raimi, L., Palazzo, M., & Panait, M. C. (2020). Mobile banking: An innovative solution for increasing financial inclusion in Sub-Saharan African Countries: Evidence from Nigeria. *Sustainability (Basel)*, 12(23), 10130. DOI: 10.3390/su122310130

SIDBI. (March 22, 2024). Market share of credit lenders for microfinance industry in India from December 2020 to September 2023, by lender type [Graph]. In *Statista*. Retrieved June 21, 2024, from https://www.statista.com/statistics/1243029/india-market-share-of-lenders-for-msme/

Simatele, M., & Dlamini, P. (2020). Finance and the social mission: A quest for sustainability and inclusion. *Qualitative Research in Financial Markets*, 12(2), 225–242. DOI: 10.1108/QRFM-02-2019-0024

Sindhav, K. 2017. *Women Empowerment Through Microfinance (A Study of Need, Practices and Future Trends)* (Doctoral dissertation, Maharaja Sayajirao University of Baroda (India)).

Singh, A. (2021). Exploring demand-side barriers to credit uptake and financial inclusion. *International Journal of Social Economics*, 48(6), 898–913. DOI: 10.1108/IJSE-04-2020-0234

Singhal, N., Goyal, S., & Singhal, T. (2024). Decentralized Insurance Platforms: Innovation and Technology for Trust and Efficiency. In *Potential, Risks, and Ethical Implications of Decentralized Insurance* (pp. 95–163). Springer Nature Singapore. DOI: 10.1007/978-981-97-5894-4_3

Singh, J., & Yadav, P. (2012). Micro finance as a tool for financial inclusion & reduction of poverty. *Journal of Business Management & Social Sciences Research (JBM&SSR), 1*(1), 1-12. DOI: 10.1080/23311975.2017.1374921

Singh, M. K., & Lee, J. (2020). Social inequality and access to social capital in microfinance interventions. *The International Journal of Sociology and Social Policy*, 40(7/8), 575–588. DOI: 10.1108/IJSSP-01-2020-0024

Sinha, A., Parida, P. C., & Baurah, P. (2012). The impact of NABARD's Self Help Group-Bank Linkage Programme on poverty and empowerment in India. *Contemporary South Asia*, 20(4), 487–510. DOI: 10.1080/09584935.2012.737306

Sinha, M., Mahapatra, S. S., Dutta, A., & Sengupta, P. P. (2023). Microfinance and women empowerment: An empirical analysis. In *Research anthology on microfinance services and roles in social progress* (pp. 1–13). IGI Global.

Sinha, S. (2020). Study of the Functionally Effective Credit Lending Models of Microfinance. *International Journal of Business Insights & Transformation*, 13(2).

Sinha, S., & Ghosh, K. (2022). Organizational sustainability and performance improvement in microfinance institutions (MFIs): Managerial insights of what, why and how. *Social Responsibility Journal*, 18(2), 240–265.

Siwale, J., & Godfroid, C. (2022). Digitising microfinance: On the route to losing the traditional 'human face'of microfinance institutions. *Oxford Development Studies*, 50(2), 177–191. DOI: 10.1080/13600818.2021.1998409

Statista. (2020). COVID-19 impact on digital payments worldwide. Retrieved from https://www.statista.com/statistics/1105552/covid-19-impact-on-digital-payments-worldwide/

Subramaniam, Y., Masron, T. A., Wahab, M. A., & Mia, M. A. (2021). The impact of microfinance on poverty and income inequality in developing countries. *Asian-Pacific Economic Literature*, 35(1), 36–48. https://doi.org/https://doi.org/10.1111/apel.12326. DOI: 10.1111/apel.12326

Sulemana, M., Fuseini, M. N., & Abdulai, I. A. (2023). Effects of microfinance and small loans centre on poverty reduction in Wa West District, Ghana. *Heliyon*, 9(12), e22685. DOI: 10.1016/j.heliyon.2023.e22685 PMID: 38107329

Suneetha, V., & Ramanamma, M. V. (2018). A study on the Role of Self Help Groups in Economic Empowerment of Women. *International Journal of Research in Social Sciences*, 8(9), 270–283.

Surmanidze, N., Beridze, M., Amashukeli, M., & Tskhadadze, K. (2023). Empowering small businesses in Georgia: Access to finance, economic resilience, and sustainable growth. *Agora International Journal of Economical Sciences*, 17(2), 158–169. DOI: 10.15837/aijes.v17i2.6453

Svoboda, F. (2015). The other banking charitable loans in pre-modern era. *European Journal of Science and Theology*, 11(5), 9–22.

Swain, R. B., & Wallentin, F. Y. (2009). Does microfinance empower women? Evidence from self-help groups in India. *International Review of Applied Economics*, 23(5), 541–556. DOI: 10.1080/02692170903007540

Syed Nazim Ali, S. N. A.AliE-mail. (2020). Big Data, Islamic Finance, and Sustainable Development Goals. *Journal of King Abdulaziz University. Islamic Economics*, 33(1), 83–90. DOI: 10.4197/Islec.33-1.6

Tabash, M. I., Elsantil, Y., Hamadi, A., & Drachal, K. (2024). Globalization and Income Inequality in Developing Economies: A Comprehensive Analysis. In *Economies* (Vol. 12, Issue 1). DOI: 10.3390/economies12010023

Tafotie, R. (2020). Fostering Digital Financial Services in Africa: a case of embracing innovation for business and inclusion. *University of Luxembourg Law Working Paper*, (2020-005).

Taherdoost, H. 2023. Fintech: Emerging trends and the future of finance. *Financial technologies and DeFi: a revisit to the digital finance revolution*, pp.29-39.

Taiwo, J.N., & Benson, K.N., 2016. The role of microfinance institutions in financing small businesses. *JIBC, 21*(1).

Tariq, S., & Sangmi, M. (2019). Impact of Microfinance on women entrepreneurship. *Oman Chapter of Arabian Journal of Business and Management Review*, 8(1), 7–16. DOI: 10.12816/0052847

Taylor, M. (2011). 'Freedom from Poverty is Not for Free': Rural Development and the Microfinance Crisis in Andhra Pradesh, India. *Journal of Agrarian Change*, 11(4), 484–504. https://doi.org/https://doi.org/10.1111/j.1471-0366.2011.00330.x. DOI: 10.1111/j.1471-0366.2011.00330.x

Thahara, A. F., Rinosha, K. F., & Shifaniya, A. J. F. (2021). The relationship between exchange rate and trade balance: Empirical evidence from Sri Lanka.

Thaher, L. M., & Radieah, N. M., & WAN NORHANIZA, W. H. (2021). The effect of microfinance services on women entrepreneurship: A case study in Jordan. *The Journal of Asian Finance, Economics and Business*, 8(5), 807–815.

Thakur, S. (2016). Microfinance through self helps groups (SHGs): A key driver for sustainable growth in India. *IOSR Journal of Business and Management*, 18(2), 1–6.

Thalib, P., Hajati, S., Kurniawan, F., & Aldiansyah, K. (2021). The urgence regulation of business activities on Islamic microfinance institution according law no. 1 year 2013 of microfinance institutions. *Arena Hukum*, 14(2), 207–221. DOI: 10.21776/ub.arenahukum.2021.01402.1

Thomas, H., & Hedrick-Wong, Y. 2019. How digital finance and fintech can improve financial inclusion. In *Inclusive Growth: The Global Challenges of Social Inequality and Financial Inclusion* (pp. 27-41). Emerald Publishing Limited. DOI: 10.1108/978-1-78973-779-020191004

Thomas, K. P. 2021, October. Use of Digital Channels by Micro Loan Customers in India. In *The 2018 International Conference on Digital Science* (pp. 342-357). Cham: Springer International Publishing.

Thulani, M., Chitakunye, P., & Chummun, B. Z. (2014). Mobile money as a strategy for financial inclusion in rural communities. *Mediterranean Journal of Social Sciences*, 5(25), 216–224.

Tripathi, V., & Tripathi, V. (2014). Recent development of Microfinance in India. SSRN *Electronic Journal*. https://doi.org/DOI: 10.2139/ssrn.2462251

Trodos Investment Management. 2019. *Capital Float: revolutionising the loan market in India.* [Online] Available at: https://www.triodos-im.com/articles/2019/case-study-capital-float-revolutionising-the-loan-market-in-india [Accessed 28 September 2024].

Ucal, M., Haug, A. A., & Bilgin, M. H. (2016). Income inequality and FDI: Evidence with Turkish data. *Applied Economics*, 48(11), 1030–1045. DOI: 10.1080/00036846.2015.1093081

Ullah, I., & Khan, M. (2017). Microfinance as a tool for developing resilience in vulnerable communities. *Journal of Enterprising Communities: People and Places in the Global Economy*, 11(2), 237–257. DOI: 10.1108/JEC-06-2015-0033

van der Hoeven, R. (2019). In Nissanke, M., & Ocampo, J. A. (Eds.), *Income Inequality in Developing Countries, Past and Present BT - The Palgrave Handbook of Development Economics: Critical Reflections on Globalisation and Development* (pp. 335–376). Springer International Publishing., DOI: 10.1007/978-3-030-14000-7_10

Van Leeuwen, M. H., & van Leeuwen, M. H. 2016. The Age of the Friendly Societies: Mutual Insurance in the Nineteenth Century. *Mutual Insurance 1550-2015: From Guild Welfare and Friendly Societies to Contemporary Micro-Insurers*, pp.83-165.

Velnamby, T., & Ajanthan, A. (2021). Efficiency and financial sustainability of microfinance institutions: A study of Jaffna district. *ACADEMICIA: An International Multidisciplinary Research Journal*, 11(4), 545–561. DOI: 10.5958/2249-7137.2021.01053.3

Venkatesh, V., Morris, M. G., Davis, G. B., & Davis, F. D. (2003). User acceptance of information technology: Toward a unified view. *Management Information Systems Quarterly*, 27(3), 425–478. DOI: 10.2307/30036540

Verma, R., & Mishra, P. (2020). Understanding the impact of COVID-19 on digital payments in India. *Journal of Public Affairs*, 20(4), e2175. DOI: 10.1002/pa.2175

Visconti, R. M. (2016). Microfinance vs. traditional banking in developing countries. *International Journal of Financial Innovation in Banking*, 1(1-2), 43–61. DOI: 10.1504/IJFIB.2016.076613

Visconti, R. M. 2019. Microfintech: Outreaching financial inclusion with cost-cutting innovation. *Available atSSRN* 3533873. DOI: 10.2139/ssrn.3533873

Vossenberg, S. (2013). Women Entrepreneurship Promotion in Developing Countries: What explains the gender gap in entrepreneurship and how to close it. *Maastricht School of Management Working Paper Series, 8*(1), 1-27.

Walton, J. K. (2015). Revisiting the Rochdale pioneers. *Labour History Review*, 80(3), 215–248. DOI: 10.3828/lhr.2015.10

Walujadi, D., Indupurnahayu, I., & Endri, E. (2022). Determinants of income inequality among provinces: Panel data evidence from Indonesia. *Calitatea*, 23(190), 243–250.

Wang, F., & De Filippi, P. (2020). Self-sovereign identity in a globalized world: Credentials-based identity systems as a driver for economic inclusion. *Frontiers in Blockchain*, 2, 28. DOI: 10.3389/fbloc.2019.00028

Wang, L., Wang, Y., Sun, Y., Han, K., & Chen, Y. (2022). Financial inclusion and green economic efficiency: Evidence from China. *Journal of Environmental Planning and Management*, 65(2), 240–271. DOI: 10.1080/09640568.2021.1881459

Wanke, P., Hassan, M. K., Azad, M. A. K., Rahman, M. A., & Akther, N. (2022). Application of a distributed verification in Islamic microfinance institutions: A sustainable model. *Financial Innovation*, 8(1), 80. Advance online publication. DOI: 10.1186/s40854-022-00384-z

Wilson, J. F., Webster, A., & Vorberg-Rugh, R. (2013). *Building co-operation: a business history of the co-operative group, 1863-2013*. Oxford University Press.

Women, U. N. (2018). Turning promises into action: Gender equality in the 2030 Agenda for Sustainable Development. https://www.unwomen,org.

Wondirad, H. A. (2022). Interest rates in microfinance: What is a fair interest rate when we lend to the poor? *Quality & Quantity*, 56(6), 4537–4548. DOI: 10.1007/s11135-022-01320-0

World Bank. (2015) Global Financial Inclusion Database. https://www.worldbank.org

World Bank. (2017). Financial Inclusion: The Global Findex Database 2017. https://www.worldbank.org

World Bank. (2020). Digital payments and the COVID-19 pandemic: A cross-country analysis. Retrieved from https://www.worldbank.org/en/topic/digitalpayments/brief/digital-payments-and-the-covid-19-pandemic-a-cross-country-analysis

World Economic Forum. (2020). Advancing digital payment systems in the post-COVID era. Retrieved from https://www.weforum.org/reports/advancing-digital-payment-systems-in-the-post-covid-era

World Economic Forum. 10 January 2024. How innovative financial solutions can build climate resilience. https://www.weforum.org/agenda/2024/01/innovative-financial-solutions-climate-resilience/

Yadav, G., Luthra, S., Jakhar, S. K., Mangla, S. K., & Rai, D. P. (2020). A framework to overcome sustainable supply chain challenges through solution measures of industry 4.0 and circular economy: An automotive case. *Journal of Cleaner Production*, 254, 120112. Advance online publication. DOI: 10.1016/j.jclepro.2020.120112

Yadav, P., Lohani, V. J., Sharma, S., & Choudhary, S. (2024). Transforming Transactions: The Evolution of Fintech in Indian Banking Sector. [IRJAEM]. *International Research Journal on Advanced Engineering and Management*, 2(07), 2179–2194.

Yangdol, R., & Sarma, M. (2019). Demand-side factors for financial inclusion: A cross-country empirical analysis. *International Studies*, 56(2-3), 163–185. DOI: 10.1177/0020881719849246

Yesuf, A. J., & Aassouli, D. (2020). Exploring synergies and performance evaluation between Islamic funds and socially responsible investment (SRIs) in light of the Sustainable Development Goals (SDGs). *Heliyon*, 6(8), e04562. Advance online publication. DOI: 10.1016/j.heliyon.2020.e04562 PMID: 32904259

Yousfani, K., Aslam, Y., Mahar, Q., & Kazi, H. (2019). The impact of microfinance on growth of women entrepreneurship in Pakistan. *Journal of Entrepreneurship. Business Economics (Cleveland, Ohio)*, 7(1), 133–152.

Zain, N. S., & Muhamad Sori, Z. (2020). An exploratory study on Musharakah SRI Sukuk for the development of Waqf properties/assets in Malaysia. *Qualitative Research in Financial Markets*, 12(3), 301–314. DOI: 10.1108/QRFM-09-2018-0099

Zainuddin, M., & Yasin, I. M. (2020). Resurgence of an ancient idea? A study on the history of microfinance. *FIIB Business Review*, 9(2), 78–84. DOI: 10.1177/2319714520925933

Zanke, P. (2021). Enhancing Claims Processing Efficiency Through Data Analytics in Property & Casualty Insurance. *Journal of Science and Technology*, 2(3), 69–92.

Zawya, 2024. *GCash loans surpass $2.7bln mark in Philippines*. [Online] Available at https://www.zawya.com/en/markets/bonds-and-loans/gcash-loans-surpass-27bln-mark-in-philippines-xu55cxbm [Accessed 28 September 2024].

Zeb, N., Jalal, R. N. U. D., Fayyaz, U. E., & Zaheer, M. A. (2021). Micro finance and economic development: The role of microfinance institutions outreach in Pakistan. *The Journal of Asian Finance, Economics and Business*, 8(5), 117–126.

Zhao, M., & Han, J. (2020). Tensions and risks of social enterprises' scaling strategies: The case of microfinance institutions in China. *Journal of Social Entrepreneurship*, 11(2), 134–154. DOI: 10.1080/19420676.2019.1604404

Zimnoch, B. M. K. (2017). *The cooperative paradigm of development-towards values*. Central and Eastern Europe in the Changing Business Environment.

Zulfiqar, G. M. (2013). *Microfinance: A tool for financial access, poverty alleviation or gender empowerment?–Empirical findings from Pakistan*. University of Massachusetts Boston.

About the Contributors

Yahaya Alhassan is a Principal Lecturer in Finance and Strategic Management at the University of Sunderland in London. He is also the Head of Academic Operations responsible for quality assurance and new programme development. Dr Alhassan holds PhD in Business Management from Anglia Ruskin University, as well as an MBA in Finance from the University of Sunderland. He is also a Senior Fellow of the Higher Education Academy (HEA). He has over 20 years of teaching and management experience developed during roles in the higher education sector and the consultancy industry. Dr Alhassan is a researcher, author, finance and strategic management lecturer, and consultant, and has published over seventeen publications including books, book reviews, journal articles, and book chapters. He has served as a reviewer for highly ranked academic journals, conferences, and edited books for Springer and IGI Publishing. Some of Dr Alhassan's publications have appeared in the UK ABS 3*** rated Journals. Dr Alhassan regularly presents papers at conferences and has presented over ten papers at various conferences since 2019. His main research interests are development finance, microfinance, entrepreneurial finance, ethnic minority entrepreneurship, and microbusiness development. His current research interests focus on the nexus between financial technology and sustainable entrepreneurship, investment in artificial intelligence, and firm growth. He has also provided consultancy services to organisations nationally and internationally that positively influenced policies, and practices, and reached audiences beyond academia.

Lawrence Bellamy is the Academic Dean for the Faculty of Business, Law and Tourism at the University of Sunderland. Professor Lawrence Bellamy holds a PhD in Business and Management (strategy process) from Leeds Metropolitan University. Professor Bellamy also holds MBA from University of Leeds, as well as Master of Science in Manufacturing Systems from Leeds Metropolitan University. He is a chartered Engineer, Fellow of the Chartered Management Institute and Fellow of the Advance HE. His research interests lie in the area of Strategy, Enterprise, Small Business, International Management and work-based learning. He is a long-standing examiner for the Chartered Institute of Procurement and Supply (CIPS) and have taught and been involved with partnership development in countries including Malaysia, Hong Kong, China, Norway, Singapore, Finland, Turkey, Malta, Brunei, and various parts of Europe. Professor Bellamy has a range of experience as a Company Director, University Governor and Journalist as well as being a reviewer for several international journals.

Uzoechi Nwagbara is a professor of management at ICT University. He has BA and MA in English as well as MSc and PhD in Human Resource Management and Management respectively from University of Wales, and MEd in Higher Education as well as PG Cert in Academic Practice from University of Sunderland, UK. He is a Fellow of the Higher Education Academy (FHEA); Member Chartered Management Institute (MCMI); Member Institute of Leadership & Management (MInstLM); and Member Community Development Exchange (MCDE); and also affiliated with British Academy of Management (BAM), European Association for the Study of Literature, Culture and the Environment (EASLCE), Postcolonial Studies Association (PSA) and Royal African Society (RAS). Dr Nwagbara has over 35 years of teaching experience and has taught in higher education for upwards of 25 years. He is external examiner for University of Cumbria and University of Bolton. He has supervised over a dozen doctoral students to completion and published well over 100 publications in high impact journals in management, leadership, CSR, sustainability, employment relations and human resource management. Dr Nwagbara has examined PhD students internally and exterannly in various universities including University of Bedfordshire, Cardiff Metropolitan University, and University of the West of Scotland amongst others. He holds Visiting Teaching Positions at University of Sunderland in London, Coventry University London, London School of Commerce, University of the West of Scotland, The University of Law UK, University of Worcester, University of Wales Trinity Saint David, and University of Plymouth as well as Visiting Professorship (management) Coal City University. He is on the editorial boads of many peer-reviwed, international journals including Economic Insights – Trends & Challenges, Journal of Pan African Studies and Journal of Sustainable Development in Africa.

John Kwaku Mensah Mawutor is an astute professional Accounting and Finance practitioner with over eighteen (18) years of experience in higher education and the financial sector. Professor John Kwaku Mensah Mawutor is currently the Pro-Vice-Chancellor of the University of Professional Studies, Accra (UPSA). As an Associate Professor of Accounting, his experience spans public and private governance, Accountancy, and Finance. He has also served on several university statutory committees. Professor Mawutor's research area focuses on capital flight in Ghana and Sub-Saharan African countries. He is also a passionate anti-corruption crusader. He is an Associate member of the Institute of Fraud Examiners (USA), a member of the Institute of Chartered Accountants Ghana (ICAG) and has been a member of the University's (University of Professional Studies) Academic Board as well as a member of the Executive Committee. Professor Mawutor has served on several committees and facilitated the development of policies such as accounting and finance policies, internal control policies, remuneration policies and strategic plans/policies. As a researcher and an academic with a penchant for practically oriented research, Professor John Kwaku Mensah Mawutor has published in several indexed and ranked journals. His publications have been accepted and published by Journals ranked by Australian Business Deans Council (ABDC) and Scopus. He has also presented several papers at several conferences and seminars. He is a regular writer in Ghana's premier newspaper publishing firm (Daily Graphic) on finance and accounting-related issues. Professor Mawutor has also authored one (1) Book. Currently, Professor Mawutor's research area focuses on capital flight in Ghana and Sub-Sahara African countries. He served as UPSA Alumni President for eight years. He is also a regular Television panelist on Ghana Broadcasting Corporation, Media General, Kesben TV, Pentecost TV, TV3, GHONE TV and a host of other TV and radio programmes.

***

Maybel Fernandez-Vallado is an alumna of the University of the Philippines (Diliman), College of Mass Communication. She was a former Senior Lecturer and faculty member of the College of Arts and Sciences, University of the Philippines Visayas. She currently resides in Dubai, United Arab Emirates, with her husband Emmanuel. She is a lifelong learner and a follower of Jesus. She does consultancy work, writes and edits articles for online church publications, and is also an English Language tutor.

Mohammad Irfan is presently working as an Associate Professor at School of Business and Management, Christ University, Bengaluru, India. Dr. Irfan has done his Ph.D. from the Central University of Haryana. He is MBA (Finance), M.Com (Account and Law), and MA (Economics). He has qualified UGC-JRF/ SRF/NET in Management and Commerce. Dr. Irfan certified NSEs (NCFM) and BSEs certification. He has experience of more than sixteen years in the area of SAPM, Artificial Intelligence, Machine Learning, Blockchain, Cryptocurrency, Financial Engineering, Fintech, Green Finance, and Alternative Finance. He has to his credit more than 63+ Scopus Indexed articles, includes The Journal of Economic Cooperation and Development (Q2), International Journal of Business Excellence (IJBEX), International Journal of Economics and Management (IJEM), Montenegrin Journal of Economics (Q2), Cogent Business & Management (Taylor & Francis) (Q2), Indian Journal of Finance (IJF) and Journal of Islamic Monetary Economics and Finance (JIMF). His citations reached 494+ along with 13 H-index. Dr. Irfan has published 10 books in Springer, IGI Global Publication (Scopus indexed).

Early Ridho Kismawadi, S.E.I, MA is a lecturer at the Department of Islamic Banking, Faculty of Islamic Economics and Business IAIN Langsa, Aceh, Indonesia, he has been a lecturer since 2013, he has completed a doctoral program in 2018 majoring in Sharia economics at the State Islamic University of North Sumatra. He was appointed head of the Islamic economics Law study program (2023) Islamic banking study program (2020) and Islamic financial management study program (2019) at Langsa State Islamic Institute (IAIN Langsa), Aceh, Indonesia. His research interests include financial economics, applied econometrics, Islamic economics, banking, and finance. He has published articles in national and international journals. In addition, he is also a reviewer of several reputable international journals such as Finance Research Letters, Financial Innovation, Cogent Business &; Management, Journal of Islamic Accounting and Business Research. He has also presented his papers at various local and international seminars. Dr. Early Ridho Kismawadi, S.E.I, MA, can be contacted at kismawadi@iainlangsa.ac.id.

Sunil Kumar, currently an Associate Professor at Faculty of Management Sciences, Shoolini University, possesses extensive academic and research experience. With a background in Business Administration, Sunil's research endeavors span multiple domains, including human resource management, e-training, and the application of artificial intelligence in business. His prolific contributions are evidenced by numerous research papers, book chapters, copyrights, and patents. Dr. Kumar has a knack for teaching with expertise in subjects like HR Analytics, Talent Management, Industrial Psychology, and more. He has also successfully guided PhD students and actively contributes to various academic administrative roles. Dr. Kumar's vast research landscape includes topics like AI-based chatbots in recruitment, e-training impact, and more. His papers have been published in esteemed journals like Journal of Workplace Learning and International Journal of Law and Management. Moreover, he has authored books and edited volumes touching upon themes related to the contemporary business environment. Dr. Sunil has been a dynamic participant in numerous workshops, ranging from data analysis to stress

Vijay Kumar is working as Assistant Professor of Finance and Accounting in Shoolini University. He is working in Shoolini University from last seven years. He has a total experience of 25 years of teaching in various Universities and Institutions. He is M.Com., MBA and Doctorate from Shoolini University.

Joy Meme is a lecturer in strategic Management and finance and is also a PhD researcher at the University of Sunderland in London. She holds an MBA in Finance and an MA in Education. She is a Senior Fellow of the Higher Education Academy (SFHEA).

Pranjit Kr Paul is one of the youngest researchers in the Department of Economics, Vidyasagar University, West Bengal, India. His research focused on Health Economics, Educational Research, Entrepreneurship Development and Rural Development.

Index

G

I

M

O

P

S

T

U

W

www.ingramcontent.com/pod-product-compliance
Lightning Source LLC
LaVergne TN
LVHW080339011026
849161LV00009B/2123
* 9 7 9 8 3 6 9 3 6 6 2 2 6 *